Leading and Managing Nonprofit Organizations

Edited by
RICHARD L. EDWARDS and PAUL A. KURZMAN

NASW PRESS

National Association of Social Workers
Washington, DC

Mildred C. Joyner, DPS, LCSW, *President*
Angelo McClain, PhD, LICSW, *Chief Executive Officer*

Cheryl Y. Bradley, *Publisher*
Rachel Meyers, *Acquisitions Editor*
Julie Gutin, *Managing Editor*
Sarah Lowman, *Project Manager*
Kathleen P. Baker, *Copyeditor*
Juanita Doswell, *Proofreader*
Matthew White, *Indexer*

Cover by Diane Guy, Blue Azure Design
Interior design, composition, and eBook conversions by Rick Soldin
Printed and bound by Books International

First impression: September 2021

© 2021 by the NASW Press

All rights reserved. No part of this book may be reproduced or transmitted in any form or by any means, electronic or mechanical, including photocopying, recording, or by any information storage and retrieval system, without permission in writing from the publisher.

Library of Congress Cataloging-in-Publication Data

Names: Edwards, Richard L., editor. | Kurzman, Paul A., editor.
Title: Leading and managing nonprofit organizations / edited by Richard L. Edwards and Paul A. Kurzman.
Description: Washington : NASW Press, 2021. | Includes bibliographical references and index. | Summary: "This book is intended to be a primer on leadership and management for nonprofit managers and students who are interested in becoming executives of nonprofit organizations. The content of the book provides a comprehensive current overview of nonprofit leadership and management issues, including leading innovation, developing a sustainable fundraising program, promoting positive media relationships and marketing, providing public policy advocacy and government relations, managing human resources and a diverse workforce, ensuring sound financial management, overseeing liability and risk management, strengthening board performance, managing strategically, and leading in an era of financial uncertainty"— Provided by publisher.
Identifiers: LCCN 2021001825 (print) | LCCN 2021001826 (ebook) | ISBN 9780871015686 (paperback) | ISBN 9780871015693 (ebook)
Subjects: LCSH: Nonprofit organizations—Management. | Nonprofit Organizations—Finance. | Strategic planning.
Classification: LCC HD62.6 .L423 2021 (print) | LCC HD62.6 (ebook) | DDC 658/.048—dc23
LC record available at https://lccn.loc.gov/2021001825
LC ebook record available at https://lccn.loc.gov/2021001826

Printed in the United States of America

I dedicate my contribution to this book to my family: my wife, Carol Friedman; my children, Jeffrey Edwards, Julia Lakota, and Jenifer Flatt; and my grandchildren, Tyler Edwards, Drew and Mattox Flatt, and Joshua, Matthew, and Alex Lakota, whose love and support are greatly appreciated.

R.L.E.

I dedicate my contribution to this book to my family: Margaret Kurzman, Katherine Kluefer, David Kurzman, Harold Kurzman, Jacob Belabed, Jenna Belabed, Peter Kluefer, and Erin Kelly, who bring so much joy to my life.

P.A.K.

Contents

Acknowledgments vii

Introduction ix

Part 1: Organizing Framework 1

1 Leading and Managing Effectively in an Environment of Competing Values *Richard L. Edwards* 3

Part 2: Boundary-Spanning Skills 29

2 Successfully Promoting Nonprofits to the Media and the Public: A Practical Guide *Gregory Trevor* 31

3 Bringing about Social Change by Managing Public Policy Advocacy and Government Relations *Peter J. McDonough* 49

4 Securing Resources for Nonprofits: Developing a Successful Fundraising Program *Richard L. Edwards* 69

Part 3: Human Relations Skills 99

5 Managing Human Resources and Personnel Practices in Nonprofit Organizations *Kimberly Strom* 101

6 Cultivating a Culture of Diversity, Equity, and Inclusion *Alena C. Hampton, Amy J. Armstrong, and Susan L. Parish* 140

7 Managing Meetings to Produce High-Quality Group Decisions *John E. Tropman* 163

Part 4: Coordinating Skills 195

8 Managing the Finances of Nonprofit Organizations *Marci S. Thomas* 197

9 Program Evaluation in Nonprofits: Necessary Evil or
   Tool for Organizational Learning? *Mathieu Despard* 222

10 Managing Liability, Exposure, and Risk in Nonprofit
   Settings *Paul A. Kurzman* 249

11 Information and Communications Technology in
   Nonprofit Management and Leadership *Frederic G. Reamer* . . . 267

PART 5: Directing Skills 295

12 Achieving an Effective, High-Performing Board *Thomas P.
   Holland and Myra Blackmon* 297

13 Managing and Planning Strategically *Allison Zippay* 330

14 Social Innovation: Entrepreneurship, Intrapreneurship,
   and Enterprise *Stephanie Cosner* 349

PART 6: Leading Nonprofits in Uncertain Times 365

15 Ethical Issues in Nonprofit Leadership *Melinda Manning
   and Kimberly Strom* 367

16 Managing Financial Uncertainty *Daniel A. Lebold and
   Richard L. Edwards* 387

Appendix *Renette Bayne Issaka* 419

Index 425

About the Editors 437

About the Contributors 438

Acknowledgments

The efforts of many individuals are required to complete any book project. This is especially true in the case of an edited volume. We first want to thank the authors of each of the chapters, whose efforts were critical in completing this project. We particularly want to recognize the contribution of our colleague Thomas P. Holland, lead author of chapter 12, who passed away just before this book was published. We also want to express our appreciation to the individuals at NASW Press who provided technical support throughout the process of producing this book. In particular, we thank Cheryl Y. Bradley, publisher, Julie Gutin, managing editor, and production editors, Sarah Lowman and Crystal Maitland. We are especially grateful for the support and assistance provided by Rachel Meyers, acquisitions editor, whose expert counsel, editing skills, and encouragement throughout the process were invaluable to us. Without her efforts over many months, this book might not have been completed. We also thank Kathleen P. Baker for her expert copyediting services.

Others who deserve our special thanks include Professors Robert Quinn and John Rohrbaugh, who originally conceptualized the competing values approach to organizational and managerial leadership effectiveness that serves as the organizing framework for this book. Moreover, we thank several individuals at our respective universities who provided help when we needed it: Mary Cavanaugh, Ruth Flaherty, Anu Gupta, Joann Segarra, Jeff Wang, and Jessica Zura.

We thank and acknowledge the contributions of many people who helped us to become better leaders and managers. There are too many to list here, but we do particularly want to mention Mark Battle, Ronald Green, Stuart Kirk, Leonard Stern, Karen Stubaus, William Waldman, Barbara White, and John Yankey. Others who helped us throughout our careers include many mentors, nonprofit and business executives and board members, colleagues, and students in our classes and workshops. These folks, in a variety of ways, taught us valuable lessons about leading and managing. We truly believe that no one becomes successful without the pushes and pulls from many people throughout their lives. To all of those who pushed and pulled us throughout our careers, we are immensely grateful. For our managerial strengths and successes, we give them full credit; for our shortcomings, we take full responsibility.

Leading and Managing Nonprofit Organizations

Last, but certainly not least, we thank our wives, Carol Friedman and Margaret Kurzman. Their ongoing support and encouragement makes a project such as this book possible.

R.L.E. and P.A.K.

Introduction

The competing values framework, a metatheoretical model of organizational and managerial effectiveness, serves as the organizing framework for this book (Edwards, 1987, 1990; Edwards, Faerman, & McGrath, 1986; Edwards & Yankey, 2006; Faerman, Quinn, & Thompson, 1987; Quinn, 1984, 1988; Quinn, Faerman, Thompson, McGrath, & Bright, 2015; Quinn & Rohrbaugh, 1981, 1983). This model, described more fully in chapter 1, integrates four contrasting sets of management skills: boundary spanning, human relations, coordinating, and directing. Each set has two inherent roles that managers must perform to be successful in that sphere of organizational activity. The resulting eight roles are those of broker, innovator, mentor, facilitator, monitor, coordinator, producer, and director.

The competing values framework posits that managers must function in a world of competing values in which their daily activities do not usually represent a choice between something good and something bad. Rather, most choices that managers must make are between two or more goods, or values. As used in this book, the competing values framework helps nonprofit leaders and managers consider the complexity and multiplicity of their roles within their organizations and stresses that the performance of any of these management roles is rarely an either–or situation.

The first section of the book provides an overview of the competing values framework. The remaining chapters are organized into five additional sections. The first four of these additional sections relate to the four major sets of skills and eight managerial roles identified in the competing values framework. The final section deals with the issue of the leadership skills needed to manage in turbulent times, under conditions of financial uncertainty and changing organizational missions. Also included is an Appendix that lists organizational Web sites and periodicals that nonprofit managers may find useful.

The validity and importance of the eight roles identified in the competing values framework have been demonstrated in several empirical studies. One study of more than 700 managers revealed that measures of the eight roles met standard validity tests and that the roles appear in the four indicated quadrants (Quinn, Denison, & Hooijberg, 1989). Another study involving more than 900 managers also found support for the eight roles and indicated that, of 36 possible roles, these eight were considered the most important ones performed by managers (Pauchant, Nilles, Sawy, & Mohrman, 1989). Further research has found that managers who do not perform these eight roles well are considered ineffective, whereas those who do perform these roles well are considered very effective (Quinn, 1988).

Learning Approach

This book is designed to be used in a variety of ways. It can be used as an individualized learning tool, as a primary text for management training programs and academic courses, or as a supplement to other texts. The chapters are organized in a way that facilitates the development of competencies needed to perform the various managerial roles identified in the book. The structure of the chapters represents a variation of a learning model developed by Whetten and Cameron (1984) that involves assessment, learning, analysis, practice, and application. The first chapter includes an assessment instrument that enables readers to gain insight into their relative strengths and weaknesses in relation to the eight management roles. Each chapter contains a narrative section that provides information about particular topics and one or more skills application exercises that provide opportunities to apply the material to realistic job situations.

This text is a revision and expansion of an earlier one, *Effectively Managing Nonprofit Organizations* (Edwards & Yankey, 2006). The topics addressed in both the earlier edition and the current book were identified as a result of the editors' experiences as hands-on managers, consultants, trainers, and educators. The array of topics covers many competencies that are not typically found in a single management book but that are vitally important in the real world of nonprofit management. The authors are a diverse group in terms of gender, race, and ethnicity, and they have a wealth of real-world management experience.

References

Edwards, R. L. (1987). The competing values approach as an integrating framework for the management curriculum. *Administration in Social Work, 11*(1), 1–13.

Edwards, R. L. (1990). Organizational effectiveness. In L. Ginsberg (Ed.-in-Chief), *Encyclopedia of social work* (18th ed., 1990 Suppl., pp. 244–255). Silver Spring, MD: National Association of Social Workers.

Edwards, R. L., Faerman, S. K., & McGrath, M. K. (1986). The competing values approach to organizational effectiveness: A tool for agency administrators. *Administration in Social Work, 10*(4), 1–14.

Edwards, R. L., & Yankey, J. A. (Eds.). (2006). *Effectively managing nonprofit organizations.* Washington, DC: NASW Press.

Faerman, S. K., Quinn, K. E., & Thompson, M. P. (1987). Bridging management practice and theory. *Public Administration Review, 47*, 311–319.

Pauchant, T. C., Nilles, J., Sawy, O. E., & Mohrman, A. M. (1989). *Toward a paradoxical theory of organizational effectiveness: An empirical study of the competing values model* (Working Paper). Quebec City, Quebec, Canada: Laval University, Department of Administrative Sciences.

Quinn, R. E. (1984). Applying the competing values approach to leadership: Toward an integrative framework. In J. C. Hunt, D. Hosking, C. Schriescheim, & K. Stewart (Eds.), *Leaders and managers: International perspectives on managerial behavior and leadership* (pp. 10–27). Elmsford, NY: Pergamon Press.

Quinn, R. E. (1988). *Beyond rational management: Mastering the paradoxes and competing demands of high performance.* San Francisco: Jossey-Bass.

Quinn, R. E., Denison, D., & Hooijberg, R. (1989). *An empirical assessment of the competing values leadership instrument* (Working Paper). Ann Arbor: University of Michigan, School of Business.

Quinn, R. E., Faerman, S. K., Thompson, M. P., McGrath, M. K., & Bright, D. S. (2015). *Becoming a master manager: A competing values approach.* Hoboken, NJ: Wiley.

Quinn, R. E., & Rohrbaugh, J. A. (1981). A competing values approach to organizational effectiveness. *Public Productivity Review, 5*, 122–140.

Quinn, R. E., & Rohrbaugh, J. A. (1983). A spatial model of effectiveness criteria: Toward a competing values approach to organizational analysis. *Management Science, 29*, 363–377.

Whetten, D. A., & Cameron, K. S. (1984). *Developing management skills.* Glenview, IL: Scott, Foresman.

PART ONE

Organizing Framework

As noted in the Introduction, the organizing theme for this book is an approach to organizational and leadership effectiveness called the competing values framework. In the book's opening chapter, "Leading and Managing Effectively in an Environment of Competing Values," Richard L. Edwards discusses characteristics of effective leaders and considers the similarities and differences between management and leadership. Edwards then identifies three broad types of skills needed by managers, suggesting that the desired mix of these skills varies depending on the level the manager occupies in the organizational hierarchy. Next, he discusses the competing values framework, which organizes the roles managers must play within four distinct sets of skills and eight specific roles. The chapter concludes with a self-assessment instrument that provides a graphic profile of an individual's relative strengths and weaknesses in relation to each of the eight managerial roles. The graphic profile can help managers identify areas of content throughout this book that may help them to enhance their skills in areas that may need strengthening.

PART ONE

Organizing Framework

1
Leading and Managing Effectively in an Environment of Competing Values

Richard L. Edwards

We live in a time in which organizational life is increasingly characterized by shifting priorities, changing patterns in the allocation of resources, and competing demands. Nonprofit managers often have to lead and manage in an environment of heightened demands for their organization's services, higher expectations for accountability, and increased competition for funding, all while they and the organizations they lead are being buffeted by change. Indeed, it seems that the only constant in management today is change. "Rapid changes in our society call for the need to cope and deal with grand challenges" (Araque & Weiss, 2019, p. 5). The kinds of challenges confronting nonprofit leaders and managers may stem from a variety of things, some under their control, but many outside their control. Nonprofits may face any number of crises, and their leaders will be called on to respond. These crises may stem from hurricanes, tornadoes, wildfires, terrorist attacks, protest marches, pandemics, legislative actions, rising unemployment rates, and other events. These events, or myriad other conditions, can seriously affect nonprofit organizations and require them to engage in crisis management, institute budget cutbacks, or, in some cases, manage growth as a result of new funding opportunities.

Characteristics of Effective Leaders

Some suggest that leaders are born, not made, implying that one either does or does not have leadership abilities. I do not agree with that notion. I believe, as do many others, that leadership can be learned. As Sinek (2011) pointed out, although some

> "natural-born leaders" may have come into the world with a predisposition to inspire, the ability is not reserved for them exclusively. We can all learn this pattern. With a little discipline, any leader or organization can inspire others, both inside and outside their organization, to help advance their ideas and their vision. We can all learn to lead. (p. 1)

However, a key element in learning to lead "is about taking people to places they wouldn't otherwise have gone, and along the way, to help each person achieve the success they deserve" (Baron, 2018, p. 9). As Baron (2018) pointed out,

> You can only achieve authentic leadership when you secure absolute trust. The only way you gain confidence from your team is if you are real . . . people must know that you've got their backs, and they must know you're willing to have daring discussions when needed. . . . If your employees know you're going to help them move mountains by removing obstacles out of their way so they can do their jobs, they'll work incredibly hard for you. . . . If they don't trust you because they think you're doing it for your own benefit, and not everyone's, you'll never secure the trust you need to lead effectively. (pp. 18–19)

Management versus Leadership

There is often some confusion about the concepts of leadership and management. Some wonder whether a person can be an effective manager without also being a competent leader. It is my belief that effective managers are individuals who also exhibit leadership qualities. One can certainly exhibit leadership without being in a management position. However, I believe that one cannot be a successful nonprofit manager without being a good leader.

Bennis (1999) suggested that managers are people who do things right, whereas leaders are people who do the right thing. Bennis suggested that successful leaders demonstrate the following characteristics:

- technical competence: business literacy and a grasp of one's field
- conceptual skill: a facility for abstract or strategic thinking
- track record: a history of achieving results
- people skills: an ability to communicate, motivate, and delegate

- taste: an ability to identify and cultivate talent
- judgment: the ability to make difficult decisions in a short time frame with imperfect data
- character: the qualities that define who one is

The importance of character as a quality of leadership cannot be overstated (Araque & Weiss, 2019; Brown, 2018). Nonprofit managers have a responsibility to lead by example. They must be highly ethical individuals who follow their profession's code of ethics and ensure that their employees follow suit. "Research at Harvard University indicates that 85 percent of a leader's performance depends on personal character. Likewise, the work of Daniel Goleman makes clear that leadership success or failure is usually due to 'qualities of the heart'" (Bennis, 1999, p. 20).

Leadership is the process of influencing people to meet organizational goals and objectives. Chapman (2020) suggested that leadership is first about behavior and second about skills. He indicated that good leaders are followed chiefly because people trust and respect them, rather than because of the skills they possess. To Chapman, leadership differs from management in the sense that the latter "is mostly about processes," while "leadership instead primarily depends on **the ways** in which the leader uses management methods and processes" (pp. 1–2). Management places more reliance on planning, organizational, and communications skills. Chapman acknowledged that while leadership also relies on management skills, it relies more on qualities such as integrity, honesty, humility, courage, commitment, sincerity, passion, confidence, positivity, wisdom, determination, compassion, and sensitivity (p. 2).

Fundamental Leadership Principles

Jack Welch, a business leader and writer, proposed several fundamental leadership principles (as cited in Chapman, 2020):

- There is only one way—the straight way; it sets the tone of the organization.
- Be open to the best of what everyone, everywhere, has to offer; transfer learning across the organization.
- Get the right people in the right jobs; this is more important than developing a strategy.
- An informal atmosphere is a competitive advantage.

- Make sure that everybody counts and that everyone knows that they count.
- Legitimate self-confidence is a winner; the true test of self-confidence is the courage to be open.
- Business has to be fun; celebrations energize an organization.
- Never underestimate the other guy.
- Understand where real value is added and put your best people there.
- Know when to meddle and when to let go; this is pure instinct.

A leader's main priority is to get the job done, whatever the job is. To this end, leaders create effective, productive teams and encourage and enable them to be successful. To accomplish this, leaders need to

- Be clear about their objectives and have a plan for how to achieve them.
- Work at building a team committed to achieving these objectives.
- Invest in helping all team members give their best effort.

Leaders must know themselves; that is, they need to know their own strengths and weaknesses so they can build the best team around them. They need to be able to organize their staff around a purpose, be able to prioritize, and keep in mind the mission or primary purpose of their organizations. Moreover, leaders must hold people accountable, be accountable themselves, and, to be successful, surround themselves with great people.

Human Relations Skills

Because a key element of leadership is being able to influence others, human relations skills are critical to success as a leader. Covey (1990) identified what he called the "seven habits of highly effective people." In my view, managers who want to be effective leaders would do well to read Covey's (1990, 2004) books and should give serious consideration to learning and practicing the following habits identified by Covey, as summarized in Chapman (2020):

- Habit 1: Be proactive. Control your own environment; do not let it control you.
- Habit 2: Begin with the end in mind. Figure out where you want to be, clarifying your personal vision and mission.
- Habit 3: Put first things first. Organize and implement tasks and activities in such a way that your actions will actually lead to where you want to be.

- Habit 4: Think win–win. Remember that any achievements of organizations—and individuals—will largely depend on the cooperative efforts of many. Thus, leaders must adopt the attitude of finding solutions that enable all parties to win rather than have some folks in the organization come out winners while others come out losers.
- Habit 5: Seek first to understand and then to be understood. Be concerned about communication, but, in particular, become skilled at listening that enables leaders to diagnose before they prescribe.
- Habit 6: Synergize. Attempt to see the potential value in everyone's contributions, remembering the principle that the whole is greater than the sum of its parts.
- Habit 7: Sharpen the saw. Develop the habit of self-renewal; to be a successful leader and manager, one must be constantly concerned about taking care of one's spiritual, mental, physical, social, and emotional needs.

Leadership Mentality

In their research on leaders, which extended over more than 30 years, Kouzes and Posner (2017) identified five practices of exemplary leadership. These best practices, which bring together many of the leadership characteristics and practices identified by Bennis (1999), Chapman (2020), Covey (1990), and Welch and Byrne (2002), include the following:

- Model the way: You must believe in something, stand up for your beliefs, express your personal values, and set an example (pp. 13–14).
- Inspire a shared vision: You must envision the future, have a desire to make things happen, and want to create something better (pp. 14–16).
- Challenge the process: You must search for opportunities to innovate, grow, improve, and encourage people to experiment and take risks, and create a climate in which people learn from mistakes and failures as well as successes (pp. 16–17).
- Enable others to act: You must foster collaboration, build trust, and strengthen others by giving away some of your power through trusting others and giving them more discretion and authority (pp. 17–18).
- Encourage the heart: You must encourage your people to carry on, finding genuine ways to uplift their spirits, recognizing their contributions, and celebrating individual and team values and victories to create a spirit of community (pp. 19–20).

In addition to having leadership qualities, contemporary managers must be equipped with a broad range of knowledge, skills, and abilities to be able to perform in a competent, effective manner. Beginning with a comparison of the executive management role in for-profit, public-sector, and nonprofit organizational contexts, I next provide an overview of how managers can be effective in an ever-changing environment of competing demands and values. Then, in the remainder of the chapter, I provide an overview of the managerial skills needed at different levels of the organizational hierarchy, describe a multidimensional model of organizational and management performance, and consider the nature of managerial decision making.

Executive Management Role

In nonprofit (or not-for-profit) organizations, top-level managers, who are often called executive directors or chief executive officers (CEOs), must perform roles similar to and yet distinct from those performed by their counterparts in for-profit and public organizations (Austin, 1989). In the for-profit corporate sector, the simplest version of the role of CEO combines policy making and implementation. The CEO serves both as a member of the corporation's board of directors and as its senior administrator. The ultimate measure of the effectiveness of the executive's performance is the level of financial return to the shareholders. In the public administration model, the traditional role of the CEO has been to implement policy, not to formulate it. Elected legislative bodies make policy for public-sector managers to carry out. Several measures can demonstrate effectiveness, including the consistency of implementation with legislative intent, continuity of the government organization, and break-even financial management—in other words, operating within the limits of the available financial resources (Austin, 1989).

In the nonprofit sector, the top manager has traditionally been called the executive director, although many nonprofits now use titles that are more characteristic of the for-profit sector, such as CEO or president. Regardless of the title, the nonprofit manager's role is shaped, in part, by organizational characteristics that nonprofit organizations share with other types of formal organizations. Nonprofit managers, like their counterparts in the for-profit world, are becoming active participants in both the formulation and the implementation of policy. It is often the top-level manager, or CEO, who brings most policy issues and recommendations to the nonprofit organization's policy board, which may be called the board of trustees or board of directors.

Like their counterparts in the world of public administration, nonprofit managers are concerned with such issues as the extent to which implementation efforts are congruent with policy, the ongoing health of their organizations, and break-even fiscal performance. Also like their public administration counterparts, nonprofit managers have no direct personal economic stake in their organization's financial performance. Their salaries do not increase in proportion to the size of their organization's budgets, nor do they receive year-end bonuses that are based on financial performance. Moreover, like their for-profit and public organization counterparts, nonprofit managers need to be concerned about managing change and "keeping the organization responsive and vibrant" (Lewis, Packard, & Lewis, 2012, p. 16).

Despite these similarities, the role of the nonprofit manager differs from the role of the for-profit corporate executive and the traditional public administrator, and in many ways it is more complex. Perhaps the most significant difference is the criteria used to determine success. In the nonprofit sector, the most important measure for judging a manager's performance is the quality of the services provided by the organization (Patti, 1987).

Managerial and Leadership Skills in the Organizational Hierarchy and Life Cycle

Successful nonprofit managers must be prepared to be interactive, adaptive, and able to formulate contingency plans that take into account the operational characteristics of the particular organization and its environmental context. Managers must be proactive. However, the typical nonprofit manager is invariably confronted by a series of competing values or demands that are likely to pull them in many directions at once. This situation was captured in part by Perlmutter (1990), who pointed out that "not only is it necessary to keep the shop running smoothly and efficiently today to meet current needs, but it is also necessary to have a vision of and anticipate what is possible and necessary for tomorrow" (p. 5). Thus, successful nonprofit managers must be skilled at both tactical and strategic management and at "identifying and securing necessary resources" and have the "necessary leadership skills to inspire individuals and achieve the intended goals" (Araque & Weiss, 2019, p. 2). Moreover, the changing dynamics and complexity of issues confronting nonprofit organizations "also require new assessment lenses and newer intervention approaches" (Nandan, Bent-Goodley, & Mandayam, 2019, p. 6).

Managerial performance in any type of organization occurs in the context of organizational change (Araque & Weiss, 2019; Cooke, Reid, & Edwards, 1997; Edwards, Cooke, & Reid, 1996). Like human beings, organizations are not static; rather, they go through a variety of phases and life cycles. Hence, different stages in the organizational life cycle may require a manager to use different types of skills (Quinn & Cameron, 1983; Quinn, Faerman, Thompson, McGrath, & Bright, 2016). Likewise, organizations that perform similar work but exist in a different type of environment may require a different mix of managerial skills. For example, arts organizations may target different client groups and compete for different resources than do human services or grassroots advocacy organizations; these differences affect which management styles and skills are needed. Individuals may also shape the specific elements of their managerial positions in different ways on the basis of their personalities, training, and experience, as well as their perceptions of the organization's needs at a given point in time. As traditional funding sources dry up, many nonprofits "are being forced or encouraged to adapt their governance and management to emphasize performance, innovation, and flexibility" (Nandan et al., 2019, p. 6).

Moreover, the management position's level within the organizational hierarchy often shapes the skills that are needed (see Figure 1.1). According to Katz (1974), management skills may be categorized broadly as (1) technical, (2) interpersonal and human relations, and (3) decision making and conceptual.

In entry-level managerial positions, technical skills tend to be very important. However, the relative importance of technical skills tends to diminish as managers move up the organizational structure. On one hand, at upper-management levels, the need for decision-making and conceptual skills increases in importance. Conceptual skills are essential for top-level managers, but the nature of their jobs does not require the use of technical skills to the same extent as do lower-level managerial positions. On the other hand, interpersonal and human relations skills are equally important for managers at all levels of the organizational hierarchy (Katz, 1974; Quinn et al., 2016; Whetten & Cameron, 1984).

In nonprofit organizations, individuals who are competent direct-service practitioners in human services or health organizations are sometimes promoted to supervisory or entry-level managerial positions. They may perform effectively in their new roles because their positions require good technical and interpersonal skills. As these individuals gradually move up the managerial hierarchy into positions that require greater conceptual skills, they may continue to be successful. However, they may also begin to display deficiencies and become unsuccessful and ineffective, thereby fulfilling the so-called "Peter Principle" of being promoted to a position that is beyond their level of competence (Peter & Hull, 1969). Thus, as individuals move up the organizational management hierarchy, they must attain the

Figure 1.1 Management Skills Required at Different Levels

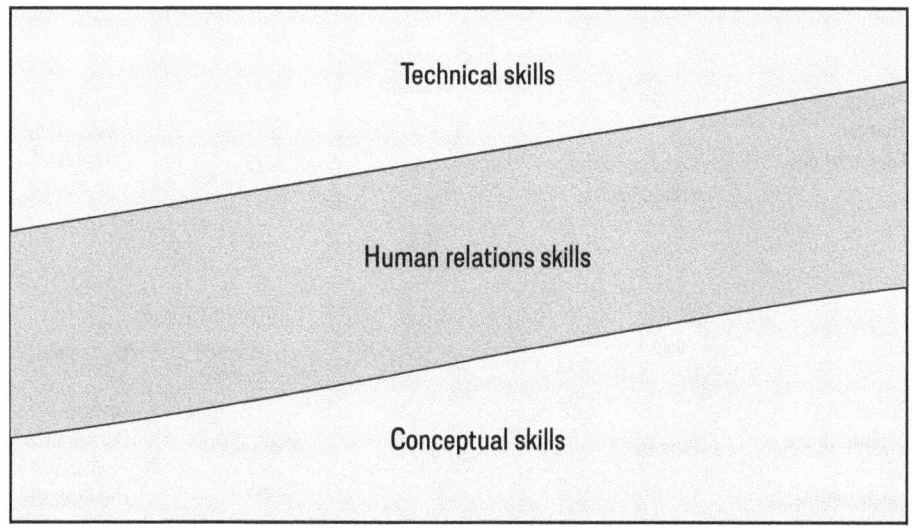

Source: Reprinted from *Developing Management Skills* (3rd ed.), *Instructor's Manual & Transparency Masters* (Transparency No. 8), by D. Whetten, K. Cameron, A. Shriberg, & C. Lloyd, 1995, New York: Addison Wesley Longman. Copyright © 1995 Addison Wesley Longman. Reprinted with permission.

additional competencies necessary to be effective. Success at one level in an organization will not necessarily guarantee success at a higher level.

Competing Values Framework

Although there is no one best style of management performance, there is an inclusive, multidimensional model of organizational and management performance. The competing values approach (Quinn, 1984, 1988; Quinn et al., 2016) can help one understand the criteria that are used to judge the effectiveness of organizations and the various roles that managers perform (Edwards, Faerman, & McGrath, 1986).

The competing values model is an analytic framework built around two dimensions representing competing orientations, or values, in the organizational context: (1) flexibility versus control and (2) internal versus external (see Figure 1.2). The combination of these two dimensions distinguishes four sectors of organizational activity, each of which embodies distinctive criteria of organizational effectiveness (Edwards, 1987, 1990; Quinn & Rohrbaugh, 1981, 1983). In combination, the four sectors identified in the model deal with two major criteria of organizational outcome: (1) the quality of services provided and (2) the continuity of the organization (Austin, 1989).

Leading and Managing Nonprofit Organizations

Figure 1.2 Competing Values Framework: Effectiveness

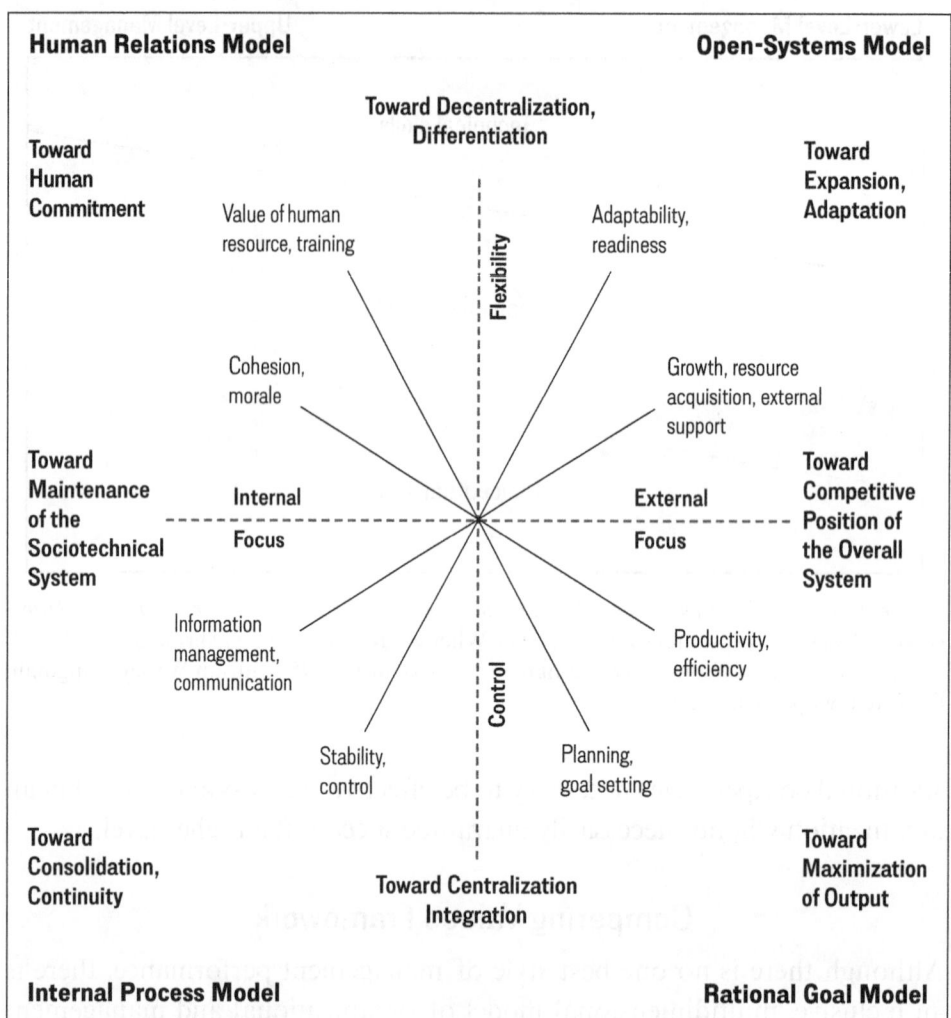

Source: Reprinted from *Beyond Rational Management: Mastering the Paradoxes and Competing Demands of High Performance* (p. 48), by R. E. Quinn, 1988, San Francisco: Jossey-Bass. Copyright © 1988 by Jossey-Bass, Inc. All rights reserved. Reprinted with permission.

For an organization to perform well with respect to the various criteria of effectiveness, managers must, to one degree or another and at various times, use these different and sometimes conflicting sets of skills:

- boundary-spanning skills
- human relations skills
- coordinating skills
- directing skills

Leading and Managing Effectively in an Environment of Competing Values

Figure 1.3 Competing Values Framework: Leadership Roles

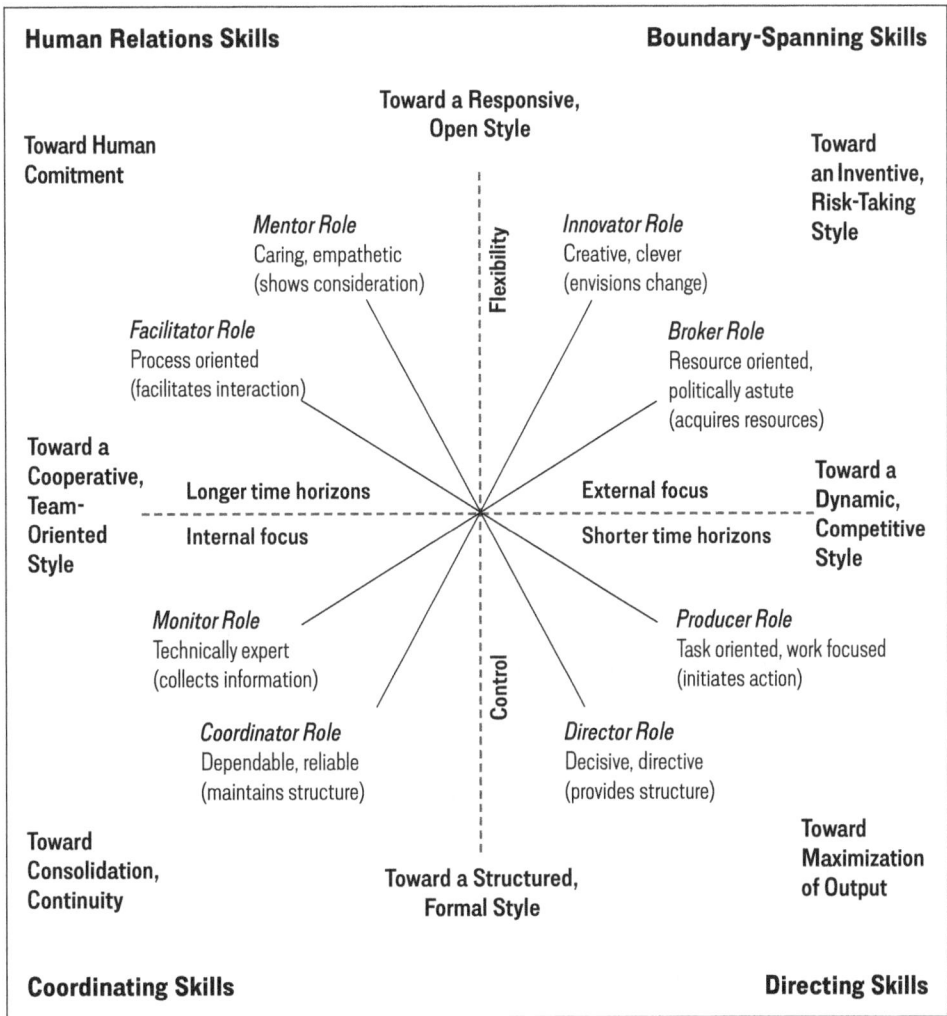

Source: Reprinted, from *Beyond Rational Management: Mastering the Paradoxes and Competing Demands of High Performance* (p. 48), by R. E. Quinn, 1988, San Francisco: Jossey-Bass. Copyright © 1988 by Jossey-Bass, Inc. All rights reserved. Reprinted with permission.

Of course, no single managerial position involves an equal emphasis on all four of these sectors. In any given organization, the top-level manager may be involved primarily in activities that require the use of certain types of skills, whereas other people who are part of the executive component, or management team, may carry major responsibilities for activities in sectors that require other types of skills. Yet, the CEO or top-level manager bears the ultimate responsibility for the effectiveness of the organization's performance in all four sectors. Some of the key concepts associated with each sector of organizational performance and the relevant managerial roles are summarized in Figure 1.3.

Boundary-Spanning Skills

Each quadrant depicted in Figure 1.3 relates to a different set of skills, and each set of skills includes the managerial traits, behaviors, and patterns of influence inherent within it. To perform roles depicted in the upper right quadrant, managers will be called on to use boundary-spanning skills. Because nonprofit organizations are highly dependent on their environment, a manager will constantly be involved in activities that cross the formal boundaries of the organization. These activities include obtaining financial resources, establishing and maintaining the organization's legitimacy, adapting organizational programs in response to environmental changes, managing external requirements for reporting and accountability, negotiating formal and informal interorganizational agreements, participating in action coalitions, lobbying, dealing with public relations and media issues, and positioning the organization to take advantage of new opportunities or withstand external threats.

In the competing values model, the boundary-spanning skills sector is defined by flexibility and external dimensions. That is, managers performing the roles in this sector will need to be adaptable and flexible because they will be participating in activities that involve dealing with individuals and organizations that are not under their direct control and that are external to the formal boundaries of the organization.

Quinn (1984, 1988) identified two managerial roles that are relevant to this sector: (1) the innovator and (2) the broker. To effectively perform the role of innovator, managers need to be creative and clever; they need to be what some have called "social architects" (Araque & Weiss, 2019; Bolman & Deal, 2008). These roles require having good conceptual skills and constantly being on the lookout for unusual opportunities. The behavior associated with the performance of the innovator role is directed toward envisioning and facilitating change. Hence, to perform this role well, the manager must be the type of individual who seeks new opportunities, encourages and considers new ideas, and is tolerant of ambiguity and risk.

To perform the role of broker effectively, managers must be resource oriented and politically astute. These roles require being aware of and sensitive to external conditions, especially those related to the organization's legitimacy, influence, and acquisition of resources. The behavior associated with the performance of the broker role is directed toward acquiring resources, so managers must be skilled in developing interpersonal contacts, monitoring the organization's environment, amassing power and influence, maintaining the organization's external image, and obtaining resources

(Quinn, 1984, 1988). Nonprofit managers must also be skilled in fundraising (DeWitt, 2011; Edwards, 2020; Heyman, 2016) and adept at navigating the political arena (Colby, 2018; Gummer & Edwards, 1995).

The boundary-spanning skills sector involves the political or open system dimension of organizational performance that is least subject to technical skills and computerization. A manager functioning in this sector will need political or negotiating skills and an understanding of the nature of power relationships in the task environment in which those management skills are practiced. Boundary-spanning skills may also require a manager to perform short-term contingency decision making, in contrast to the systematic and long-term participatory internal decision-making processes that may be important in the mobilization and motivation of human resources. This sector of activity is perhaps the least likely to be fully delegated to other members of the executive management team. However, it may also be the sector that policymakers, such as volunteers who serve on the organization's board, define as their particular area of activity and in which explicit limits may be placed on the scope of the manager's activities.

The effectiveness of the process of contingency decision making, or strategic adaptation, whether carried out by policymakers, the manager, or both, may be severely constrained by considerations involving other sectors in which policymakers and managers perform. For example, successful opportunity-seizing initiatives involving responses to short-term funding opportunities, such as responding to various requests for funding proposals, may be inconsistent with the organization's overall goals, may require substantial expenditures for the development of new technical production procedures, and may disrupt the cohesiveness and morale of the staff.

Human Relations Skills

The second major sector of executive responsibility, shown in the upper left quadrant of Figure 1.3, involves the use of human relations skills. In performing the roles in this sector, managers are responsible for ensuring that the organization has a competent workforce. Because many of the services provided by nonprofit organizations are produced and delivered through person-to-person interactions, these organizations are generally what are called "labor-intensive organizations." As a consequence, human relations activities constitute a particularly important component in the life of such organizations.

In the competing values model, the human relations skills sector is defined by the internal and flexibility dimensions. Managers deal with individuals and groups who are internal to the organization and who, as autonomous individuals or groups with the skills required to produce services, represent decentralized centers of authority and influence that managers often cannot directly control. Quinn (1984, 1988) identified two specific managerial roles in this sector: (1) the mentor and (2) the group facilitator.

In the role of mentor, managers need to be caring and empathetic. Those who possess these traits tend to view organizational members as valued resources and are alert to members' individual problems and needs. They operate in a manner that is perceived as fair and objective. Managers must also be skilled listeners and try to facilitate the development of individuals (Quinn, 1984, 1988). Behavior is directed toward showing concern about and support for staff members.

To be effective group facilitators, managers need to be process oriented, diplomatic, and tactful. They must have excellent interpersonal skills and be good at facilitating interaction among individuals and groups in the workplace. Managers should also be adept at fostering cohesion, building consensus, and bringing about compromises. The ultimate aim is to foster a cooperative, team-oriented style that permeates the organization.

The human resources—the people who make up the organization—should have the knowledge, skills, and abilities to perform their jobs effectively. In performing the roles of mentor and group facilitator, the manager's goal is to secure, retain, and motivate a qualified, competent, and committed workforce. Achieving that goal, however, is not easy. Staff often include members of one or more professions and a variety of volunteers who are involved in both the delivery of services and policymaking. In addition to having broad skill sets, the workforce is often diverse, including people from various gender, age, racial, and ethnic groups. Managing and leading a diverse and inclusive workforce comes with its own set of challenges.

Moreover, service users may be a critical element in mobilizing and motivating staff. Because of the composition and the competing needs and interests of the human resources component of the organization, managers must be concerned with the organizational culture, including symbols and traditions, and the definition of organizational values, which together may be significantly related to staff motivation (Austin, 1989). Managers also need to be skilled at team building, at bringing people together "to accomplish common goals, usually by exercising concerted efforts, applying interdependent collaboration, and sharing decision-making opportunities" (Araque & Weiss, 2019, p. 90). Successfully leading an organization also requires that managers be good listeners and exhibit care for the people they lead (Brown, 2018).

Coordinating Skills

The lower left quadrant of Figure 1.3 identifies the coordinating skills sector, which is defined by the internal and control dimensions. Quinn (1984, 1988) identified the roles in this section as the monitor and the coordinator. The activities related to this sector are focused primarily on matters that are internal to the organization and that are involved in maintaining the organizational structure. The technical areas in this sector include budgeting and fiscal controls, scheduling procedures, information and communications systems, personnel administration systems, technical training programs, reporting systems, evaluation and quality control measures, and management of technical equipment and physical facilities (Austin, 1989).

To perform the role of monitor effectively, managers must be technically competent. This suggests that the manager needs to be well informed and knowledgeable about the work of the people in the organization and have a high degree of technical expertise. The manager's role is directed toward collecting and distributing information that is necessary for the smooth functioning of the organization as well as for the orderly flow of work. To perform well in the role of coordinator, the manager must be dependable and reliable. Those who have such traits are likely to be consistent, predictable people who seek continuity and equilibrium in their work units (Quinn, 1984, 1988). The focus should be on maintaining structure, organizational stability, and workflow and using managerial skills in scheduling, coordinating, problem solving, and ensuring that rules and standards are understood and met. This is also the sector of organizational life in which systematic and rational procedures often have their widest application (Austin, 1989).

Because nonprofit organizations are typically labor intensive, the systematic organization of personnel activities and monitoring of service production activities assume great importance and become major elements in the managerial or executive position. In a small organization, it may be possible for the manager to carry out many of these tasks directly. However, in larger organizations, these types of managerial tasks, especially personnel administration, financial management, and maintenance of computer systems, most likely involve technical staff specialists and sometimes entire staffing units.

Virtually all nonprofit organizations make extensive use of computers, information management systems, and, increasingly, social networking applications. It is in the coordinating skills sector that computers are particularly valuable because the activities involved often represent structured decision-making choices among known alternatives. For example, issues such as the impact of different combinations of direct salary and fringe benefits on staff compensation; the effects of different combinations of staff work schedules; the patterns of service use by clients; procedures for handling organizational funds; and the tracking of clients or patrons have all been facilitated by the use of computers. These activities and others like them are areas in which consistent, centrally controlled decisions seem to be highly correlated with efficiency and effectiveness.

Directing Skills

The lower right quadrant of Figure 1.3 identifies directing skills. This sector is defined by the external and control dimensions. Thus, the focus in this sector tends to be on activities that are external to the organization and that are relatively structured and formalized. In the management roles in this sector, managers will be dealing with the interface between the products or output of the organization and its external environment. The technical activities involved include both tactical and strategic planning, goal setting, and activity monitoring. In this sector, Quinn (1984, 1988) identified the roles of the producer and the director, meaning that the manager must be someone who is productive and able accomplish multiple things in the workplace while at the same time being focused on providing direction and goal clarity to others in the workplace.

The point of managerial activity in this sector is the goal-oriented process, which is aimed at improving the organization's efficiency and effectiveness as well as enhancing its relative position within its environment. This sector involves activities in which the manager plays a pivotal role, such as the improvement of productivity and goal setting (Austin, 1989).

To effectively perform the role of director, managers must be decisive and comfortable in guiding the work of others. Those who have these traits tend to be conclusive individuals who can plan work appropriately and provide direction. Activities include setting goals and objectives, clarifying roles, monitoring progress, providing feedback, and establishing clear expectations (Quinn, 1984, 1988). In using directing skills, managers need to know how to stimulate individual and collective achievement. Thus, they must be comfortable with the use of authority and skilled at delegation, planning, and goal-setting technologies (Faerman, Quinn, & Thompson, 1987).

To perform the role of producer well, managers must be task oriented and work focused. Those who exhibit these traits tend to be action-oriented individuals who are highly generative. An effective manager must be the kind of individual who is willing to invest a large amount of energy and who derives a great deal of satisfaction from productive work. Efforts will be directed at stimulating the performance of staff members.

Because nonprofit organizations are established to accomplish particular societal objectives, the process of defining goals is essential. To a great extent, nonprofit organizations are dependent on their external environments. Thus, nonprofit managers must be cognizant of environmental developments and trends, including those that affect the organization's users or clients, financial and personnel resources, technology, and, ultimately, legitimacy in political terms. Moreover, organizational continuity assumes relatively great importance for nonprofit organizations because the costs involved in setting up such an organization and the goodwill represented in its legitimation by the community cannot be turned into financial resources that can be used for other purposes (Austin, 1989).

When confronted by the often difficult choices that are inherent in the competing values environment of nonprofit management, managers can use the organization's mission as a kind of litmus test for decisions. That is, they can consider how a particular decision will help or hinder the organization in achieving its mission. Thus, managers should view the organization's mission as a kind of North Star that can guide them through the wilderness of competing values and demands.

To be effective, those who occupy managerial positions must possess and use many types of skills and must perform many roles. The demands of these roles may shift over time as the organization moves through different phases in its life cycle. In small organizations, the top-level manager role may encompass many skills and roles, whereas in larger organizations, the top-level manager may delegate certain roles to others on the management team.

Nature of Managerial Decision Making

Because organizational life is characterized by an environment of competing values, managerial decision-making requirements are complex. The choices that confront managers daily are rarely choices between something that is good and something that is bad. If this were the case, the job of manager would be relatively easy. Instead, management most often involves choosing between two or more things that are valued and have positive and negative attributes. This type of choice makes the job much more difficult. For example, a manager may be confronted with shrinking resources and thus not be able to hire additional staff or provide opportunities for staff development. At the same time, the manager may be confronted with a growing demand for services from clients. Because of limited resources, the size of the workforce cannot be enlarged and the increased demand for services may cause the manager to take steps to increase the workload of the existing staff. Such an approach may result in greater efficiency; that is, more clients seen without an increase in staff. However, it may also have a negative impact on staff morale, which could lead to increased stress, burnout, and turnover. Thus, the organization may lose some of its experienced staff, which in turn can result in added expenses for recruiting, hiring, and orienting new staff. There is also likely to be some loss related to what is called the learning curve; that is, the time it takes new staff to become fully productive.

Understanding that managers are likely to experience pulls from many directions may help to identify the possible consequences of decisions and enable managers to take appropriate steps to minimize negative consequences. Viewing organizations from the competing values perspective can help managers assess particular areas of strength. Of course, no one individual is likely to be equally adept at performing all of the roles identified in Figure 1.3. However, managers who are secure about their own strengths, abilities, and areas in which they are relatively less strong are likely to surround themselves with subordinates whose strengths complement their own. In contrast, managers who are less secure tend to surround themselves with individuals whose strengths mirror their own (but who may not be as strong, so they are less threatening). This latter situation often results in the organization's needs being inadequately addressed.

A nonprofit manager must possess a range of knowledge, skills, and abilities and must perform many roles, more or less simultaneously. The particular balance of technical, interpersonal, human relations, and conceptual and decision-making skills required will vary depending on a manager's position within the managerial structure and the organization's needs at any given point in time. Each category of skills involves the performance of different managerial roles, which are related to different criteria of organizational effectiveness and which create an environment of competing values. In this environment, managerial choices most often represent a trade-off between two or more values, or "goods," rather than a choice between something that is good versus something that is bad. By understanding the job's multiple role demands and competing values, managers may be better able to guide the organization toward effective performance.

Given the challenges of competing values, the need to perform different roles, and the varied skills required, managing an organization can be difficult. However, the experience can also be extremely gratifying when one remembers that organizations are made up of individuals who, if treated with respect and dignity, can produce great things even when resources are limited.

Skills Assessment Exercise

The following instrument will enable managers to develop a profile of how they rate on each of the managerial roles identified in the competing values framework.

First, please complete the Competing Values Management Practices Survey, and then transfer your ratings to the Computational Worksheet for Self-Assessment. Place the score or rating you give each item on the survey next to the number of that item on the worksheet. Note that where "(R)" appears on the worksheet, you should reverse your score. In other words, if you rated the item 1, you should reverse your score and record it as 7; 2 thus is recorded as 6 and 3 as 5. If your rating was 4, then place 4 on the worksheet.

Next, total your scores for each category, and then divide the total by the number of items in that category. This sum will give you a score to enter on the Competing Values Skills Assessment Leadership Role Profile. When transferring your scores to the role profile, place a dot at the point on the spoke that reflects your score for that role, keeping in mind that the center of the figure is 0, and the hash mark farthest from the center is 7. When you have entered your scores on all eight spokes of the diagram, draw lines to connect them. The result will be a profile that will help you identify your areas of relative strength as well as those in which you may not be as strong. This information may be useful to you as you review other chapters in this book.

Competing Values Management Practices Survey

Listed below are some statements that describe managerial practices. Indicate how often you engage in the behaviors, using the scale below to respond to each statement. Please place a number from 1 to 7 in the space beside each question.

Almost Never   1   2   3   4   5   6   7   Almost Always

As a manager, how often do you
1. Come up with inventive ideas.
2. Exert upward influence in the organization.
3. Ignore the need to achieve unit goals.
4. Continually clarify the unit's purpose.
5. Search for innovations and potential improvements.
6. Make the unit's role very clear.
7. Maintain tight logistical control.
8. Keep track of what goes on inside the unit.
9. Develop consensual resolution of openly expressed differences.

Leading and Managing Nonprofit Organizations

____ 10. Listen to the personal problems of subordinates.
____ 11. Maintain a highly coordinated, well-organized unit.
____ 12. Hold open discussions of conflicting opinions in groups.
____ 13. Push the unit to meet objectives.
____ 14. Surface key differences among group members, then work participatively to resolve them.
____ 15. Monitor compliance with the rules.
____ 16. Treat each individual in a sensitive, caring way.
____ 17. Experiment with new concepts and procedures.
____ 18. Show empathy and concern when dealing with subordinates.
____ 19. Seek to improve the work group's technical capacity.
____ 20. Get access to people at higher levels.
____ 21. Encourage participative decision making in the group.
____ 22. Compare records, reports, and so on to detect discrepancies.
____ 23. Solve scheduling problems in the unit.
____ 24. Get the unit to meet expected goals.
____ 25. Do problem solving in creative, clear ways.
____ 26. Anticipate workflow problems; avoid crises.
____ 27. Check for errors and mistakes.
____ 28. Persuasively sell new ideas to higher-ups.
____ 29. See that the unit delivers on stated goals.
____ 30. Facilitate consensus building in the unit.
____ 31. Clarify the unit's priorities and direction.
____ 32. Show concern for the needs of subordinates.
____ 33. Maintain a "results" orientation in the unit.
____ 34. Influence decisions made at higher levels.
____ 35. Regularly clarify the objectives of the unit.
____ 36. Bring a sense of order and coordination to the unit.

Copyright © Robert E. Quinn. Reprinted with permission.

Leading and Managing Effectively in an Environment of Competing Values

Computational Worksheet for Self-Assessment

Facilitator	Mentor
9 ____	10 ____
12 ____	16 ____
14 ____	18 ____
21 ____	32 ____
30 ____	Total ____ ÷ 4 = ____
Total ____ ÷ 5 = ____	

Innovator	Broker
1 ____	2 ____
5 ____	20 ____
17 ____	28 ____
25 ____	34 ____
Total ____ ÷ 4 = ____	Total ____ ÷ 4 = ____

Producer	Director
3 ____ (R)	4 ____
13 ____	6 ____
19 ____	24 ____
29 ____	31 ____
33 ____	35 ____
Total ____ ÷ 5 = ____	Total ____ ÷ 5 = ____

Coordinator	Monitor
7 ____	8 ____
11 ____	15 ____
23 ____	22 ____
26 ____	27 ____
36 ____	
Total ____ ÷ 5 = ____	Total ____ ÷ 4 = ____

Copyright © Robert E. Quinn. Reprinted with permission.

Leading and Managing Nonprofit Organizations

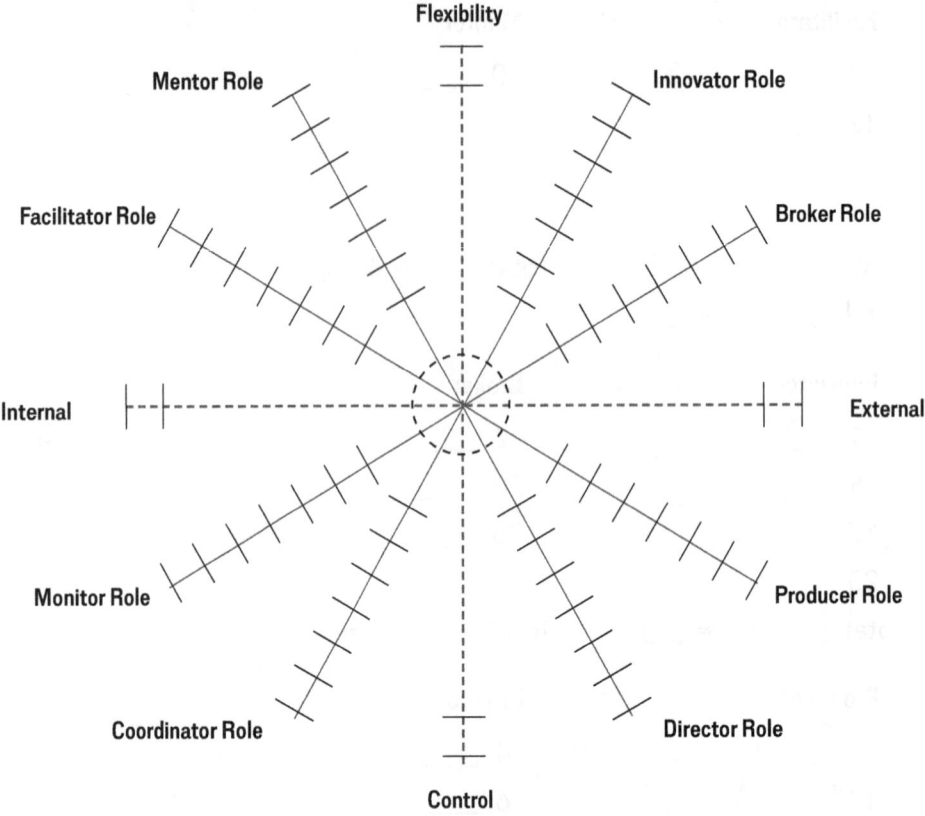

Discussion Questions

The following questions may assist you in developing managerial skills:

1. What is your reaction to the personal skills profile revealed on the role profile diagram? Do the results meet your expectations? Were there any surprises?
2. On the basis of your profile, what areas of managerial skills appear to be the highest priority for further development? What strategies can you use to assist you in developing your skills?

References

Araque, J. A., & Weiss, E. L. (2019). *Leadership with impact.* New York: Oxford University Press.

Austin, D. M. (1989). The human service executive. *Administration in Social Work, 13*(3–4), 13–36.

Baron, C. (2018). *The fearless leader: A sensible guide to practicing authentic leadership.* Middletown, DE: Impact.

Bennis, W. (1999). The leadership advantage. *Leader to Leader, 1999*(12), 18–23.

Bolman, L. G., & Deal. T. E. (2008). *Reframing organizations: Artistry, choice, and leadership.* San Francisco: Wiley.

Brown, B. (2018). *Dare to lead.* New York: Random House.

Chapman, A. (2020, September 3). *Leadership development methods and tips.* Retrieved from https://www.businessballs.com/leadership-styles/leadership-tips/

Colby, I. C. (2018). *The handbook of policy practice.* New York: Oxford University Press.

Cooke, P. W., Reid, P. N., & Edwards, R. L. (1997). Management: New developments and directions. In R. L. Edwards (Ed.-in-Chief), *Encyclopedia of social work* (19th ed., 1997 Suppl., pp. 229–242). Washington, DC: NASW Press.

Covey, S. R. (1990). *The 7 habits of highly effective people: Powerful lessons in personal change.* New York: Free Press.

Covey, S. R. (2004). *The 8th habit: From effectiveness to greatness.* New York: Free Press.

DeWitt, B. M. (2011). *The nonprofit development corporation.* Hoboken, NJ: Wiley.

Edwards, R. L. (1987). The competing values approach as an integrating framework for the management curriculum. *Administration in Social Work, 11*(1), 1–13.

Edwards, R. L. (1990). Organizational effectiveness. In L. Ginsberg (Ed.-in Chief), *Encyclopedia of social work* (18th ed., 1990 Suppl., pp. 244–255). Silver Spring, MD: National Association of Social Workers.

Edwards, R. L. (2020). *Building a strong foundation: Fundraising for nonprofits.* Washington, DC: NASW Press.

Edwards, R. L., Cooke, P. W., & Reid, P. N. (1996). Social work management in an era of diminishing federal responsibility. *Social Work, 41*, 46–79.

Edwards, R. L., Faerman, S. R., & McGrath, M. R. (1986). The competing values approach to organizational effectiveness: A tool for agency administrators. *Administration in Social Work, 10*(4), 1–14.

Faerman, S. R., Quinn, R. E., & Thompson, M. P. (1987). Bridging management practice and theory: New York State's public service training program. *Public Administration Review, 47*, 311–319.

Gummer, B., & Edwards, R. L. (1995). The politics of human services administration. In L. Ginsberg & P. R. Keys (Eds.), *New management in human services* (pp. 57–71). Washington, DC: NASW Press.

Heyman, D. R. (2016). *Nonprofit fundraising 101.* Hoboken, NJ: Wiley.

Katz, R. L. (1974). Skills of an effective administrator. *Harvard Business Review, 51*, 90–102.

Kouzes, J. M., & Posner, B. Z. (2017). *The leadership challenge: How to make extraordinary thing happen in organizations* (6th ed.). Hoboken, NJ: Wiley.

Lewis, J. A., Packard, T. R., & Lewis, M. D. (2012). *Management of human service programs.* Belmont, CA: Brooks/Cole.

Nandan, M., Bent-Goodley, T. B., & Mandayam, G. (Eds.). (2019). *Social entrepreneurship, intrapreneurship, and value creation.* Washington, DC: NASW Press.

Patti, R. J. (1987). Managing for service effectiveness in social welfare: Toward a performance model. *Administration in Social Work, 11*(3–4), 25–37.

Perlmutter, F. D. (1990). *Changing hats: From social work practice to administration.* Silver Spring, MD: National Association of Social Workers.

Peter, L., & Hull, R. (1969). *The Peter Principle: Why things go wrong.* New York: William Morrow.

Quinn, R. E. (1984). Applying the competing values approach to leadership: Toward an integrative framework. In J. G. Hunt, D. Hosking, C. Schreisheim, & R. Stewart (Eds.), *Leaders and managers: International perspectives on managerial behavior and leadership* (pp. 10–27). Elmsford, NY: Pergamon Press.

Quinn, R. E. (1988). *Beyond rational management: Mastering the paradoxes and competing demands of high performance.* San Francisco: Jossey-Bass.

Quinn, R. E., & Cameron, K. S. (1983). Organizational life cycles and shifting criteria of effectiveness: Some preliminary evidence. *Management Science, 29*(1), 33–51.

Quinn, R. E., Faerman, S. R., Thompson, M. P., McGrath, M. R., & Bright, D. S. (2016). *Becoming a master manager—A competing values approach.* Hoboken, NJ: Wiley.

Quinn, R. E., & Rohrbaugh, J. A. (1981). A competing values approach to organizational effectiveness. *Public Productivity Review, 5*, 122–140.

Quinn, R. E., & Rohrbaugh, J. A. (1983). A spatial model of effectiveness criteria: Toward a competing values approach to organizational analysis. *Management Science, 29*, 363–377.

Sinek, S. (2011). *Start with why: How great leaders inspire everyone to take action.* New York: Penguin Group.

Welch, J., & Byrne, J. A. (2002). *Jack: Straight from the gut.* New York: Warner Books.

Whetten, D. A., & Cameron, K. S. (1984). *Developing management skills.* Glenview, IL: Scott, Foresman.

Whetten, D., Cameron, K., Shriberg, A., & Lloyd, C. (1995). *Developing management skills* (3rd ed.), *Instructor's manual & transparency masters* (Transparency No. 8). New York: Addison Wesley Longman.

PART TWO

Boundary-Spanning Skills

THE TWO MAJOR ROLES MANAGERS NEED TO PERFORM IN THE AREA OF boundary-spanning skills are those of innovator and broker. The competencies involved in the innovator role include creative thinking and living with and managing change. Competencies involved in the broker role include building and maintaining a power base, negotiating agreement and commitment, and presenting ideas. The chapters in this section relate to these roles and competencies in terms of the challenges confronting nonprofit managers.

In chapter 2, Gregory Trevor provides a practical guide to gaining public awareness and support by successfully promoting nonprofits to the media and the public. Given the challenges nonprofits face in developing positive media relationships and gaining coverage, he suggests that nonprofit leaders and managers develop a media strategy and offers guidance on how they can do so. Trevor provides helpful suggestions for getting your nonprofit's story in the media and on the air.

In chapter 3, Peter J. McDonough offers suggestions for dealing with the legislative and executive branches of government to enhance the organization's chances of securing resources and favorable policy decisions. He discusses the importance of clearly understanding the organization's legislative or policy goals, forming relationships with legislators and key executive branch officials, and being involved in coalitions. McDonough stresses the importance of nonprofit leaders and managers being able to clearly articulate and present ideas, negotiate agreements, and develop creative and collaborative approaches to solving problems. Moreover, he provides guidance on developing action plans.

In chapter 4, Richard L. Edwards recognizes that nonprofit managers must spend a large amount of time confronting issues related to securing resources for their organizations. He discusses trends in fundraising for nonprofits and considers a range of issues affecting fundraising, including shifting demographics and cause-related marketing, and he urges nonprofit managers to develop multilayered strategies that place long-term benefit over short-term gain, suggesting that a successful fundraising strategy is one that generates significant revenues for the nonprofit while also increasing its visibility and credibility, thus helping to gain broad-based community support. Also discussed are major gift cultivation, prospect research, launching capital campaigns, and the role of the nonprofit board in fundraising. Finally, Edwards underscores the importance of stewardship—that is, the importance of thanking and recognizing donors.

2

Successfully Promoting Nonprofits to the Media and the Public: A Practical Guide

Gregory Trevor

Reputation, reputation, reputation!
O, I have lost my reputation!
I have lost the immortal part of myself, and what remains is bestial.
My reputation, Iago, my reputation!

—*Othello,* Act 2, Scene 3

One of the most heated public policy debates of the early 21st century in the United States was over the claim that virtually all organizations are most effective if they are managed "like a business." The business model is fundamentally transactional, driven by a profit motive in a continuous competition for market share with economic rivals. To stay afloat, for-profit businesses must convince consumers that they will directly benefit from purchasing the organization's goods and services. A business's reputation is secondary to its ability to succeed in the marketplace.

By definition, nonprofit (or not-for-profit) organizations have different priorities. The mission of most nonprofits is to support individuals, families, and communities with goods and services that they cannot immediately or completely afford and are not expected to fully reimburse—whether it be disaster relief or tax-supported services such as public education, police protection, or the arts. Note that in this chapter, I use the definition of *nonprofit* broadly and inclusively.

To finance their initiatives, nonprofits must rely on the goodwill of donors, volunteers, taxpayers, and others who will not benefit directly from the organization's generosity. To successfully cultivate this goodwill, nonprofits must build and maintain a positive reputation among the communities they serve and the supporters they solicit. Much as they rely on voluntary support from donors and volunteers, nonprofits also depend on the credibility that comes from attention they receive from independent print, online, broadcast, and social media. This attention greatly enhances the ability of these organizations to effectively communicate the importance of their missions to their key constituencies. Most nonprofits have little or no funding for marketing and advertising. Positive public relations—particularly the third-party validation that results from successful engagement with external news media—is essential for long-term success.

Scandals involving the Red Cross, the United Way, and the Susan G. Komen Foundation have shown that even wealthy organizations can suffer serious damage to their reputations from negative media coverage, no matter how hard they try to buy back goodwill through expensive marketing and advertising campaigns. As countless public figures can attest, a poor decision captured on video can quickly go viral, severely damaging an otherwise unblemished reputation that could take years to restore.

This chapter provides a practical guide for nonprofits to engage most effectively with their key constituencies directly through their own channels and indirectly through independent or "earned" media. The chapter includes

- an analysis of the evolving media landscape
- the growing importance of do-it-yourself content
- tips to successfully pitch media organizations
- crisis communications management
- best ways to measure success

The hope is that leaders and managers of nonprofit organizations will find the information contained in this chapter useful to them as they carry out their mission.

Changing Media Landscape

The press is sometimes called the fourth branch of government, but in the U.S., it's also very much a business—one whose ability to serve the public is dependent on its ability to attract eyeballs and dollars.

—Pew Research Center (2019, p. 1)

The increasing corporate consolidation of the media industry, coupled with the rising dominance of the Internet and the resulting communications technologies, including social media platforms, has been both a curse and a blessing for traditional news organizations and for nonprofits trying to work successfully with these organizations.

First, the bad news. The audience reach of traditional print and broadcast news media has been in decline for years. According to the Pew Research Center (2019), the total circulation of U.S. daily newspapers is lower today than in 1940, even though the nation's total population today is nearly two and a half times larger than it was 80 years ago. One of the most troubling factors contributing to this trend is the widespread death of daily and weekly newspapers, particularly in lower-income communities that tend to be more dependent on support from nonprofits. According to Penelope Muse Abernathy (2018), the Knight Chair in Journalism and Digital Media Economics at the University of North Carolina at Chapel Hill,

> For residents in thousands of communities across the country . . . local newspapers have been the prime, if not sole, source of credible and comprehensive news and information that can affect the quality of their everyday lives. Yet, in the past decade and a half, nearly one in five newspapers has disappeared, and countless others have become shells—or "ghosts"—of themselves. (p. 1)

Abernathy (2018) wrote, "Our research found a net loss since 2004 of almost 1,800 local newspapers. . . . The people with the least access to local news are often the most vulnerable—the poorest, least educated and most isolated" (pp. 1–2).

The ongoing consolidation of corporate ownership of media organizations across the nation, which has contributed to layoffs of print, online, and broadcast journalists, has exacerbated this retrenchment. In 1983, according to *Business Insider,* 90 percent of U.S. media were controlled by 50 companies; by 2011, the number was down to six (Lutz, 2012).

Another well-documented factor is the rise of social media platforms that provide readers and viewers with access to information without having to buy a subscription or be inundated with paid advertising. In a section of the Pew Center's (2019) report titled "Americans Are Wary of the Role Social Media Sites Play in Delivering the News," the center said,

> Almost all Americans—about nine-in-ten (88%)—recognize that social media companies have at least some control over the mix of news people see. And most Americans feel this is a problem: About six-in-ten

(62%) say social media companies have too much control. . . . While social media companies say these efforts are meant to make the news experience on their sites better for everyone, most Americans think they just make things worse. (Pew Center, 2019, p. 2)

Specifically, Americans are most concerned that news appearing on social media is biased and inaccurate, the report concluded.

According to a 2018 analysis by Philip Napoli, a professor at Duke University's Sanford School of Public Policy, "in the last two decades, technological and economic changes have undermined legitimate news production and enhanced fake news. Despite the flood of available news online, the actual proportion of original reporting is declining" (Duke University, Sanford School of Public Policy, 2018).

There is some hope, however. Creative entrepreneurs are carving out new financial models, particularly at the local level, to deliver the news. Many of these organizations rely solely on the Internet to deliver news, bypassing the expense of ink, paper, and printing presses (Hart, Greenfield, & Johnston, 2005).

One of the most intriguing examples of this new approach is TAPinto, a network of more than 80 independently owned and operated local news sites with more than 10 million annual readers across New Jersey, New York, Texas, and Florida. Unlike other hyperlocal news sites, TAPinto follows a franchise model, similar to a chain restaurant. The local news site franchisees pay an annual fee and provide a percentage of ad revenue to TAPinto. In return, TAPinto provides the technological infrastructure that supports the franchisees while encouraging journalistic consistency and quality control. If a handful of these franchisees struggle financially, their failure will not drag down the entire institution.

In a 2016 interview in the *Columbia Journalism Review*, TAPinto founder Michael Shapiro said that these news sites also have a section for news releases, "created to promote local nonprofits and other organizations without endorsing a specific cause." Shapiro explained, "A lot of these nonprofits don't have a marketing budget. We provide them with a platform to get their word out" (Xie, 2016).

The Internet also provides nonprofits with another new opportunity: to communicate directly with key constituencies, and reach new audiences, through their own online platforms. However, this new opportunity comes with a challenge: How should nonprofits create their own compelling and credible content to effectively engage these audiences—and cut through the competing clutter of often unreliable information across the Internet (Cohen, 2006)?

Be Your Own Publisher: A Do-It-Yourself Approach

Content is king.
—Bill Gates (as cited in Evans, 2017)

In the modern media environment, great coverage starts with great content. Gone are the days when a nonprofit organization could write a standard news release and expect media organizations to respond by assigning their staff to produce their own print and broadcast stories. Although it is still valuable to cultivate relationships with individual members of the media, most journalists are pulled in so many different directions that they barely have time to share a cup of coffee with a public relations representative, much less write or broadcast a series of news stories about a nonprofit.

One solution is growing in popularity: Be one's own publisher. Thanks to new technologies—such as digital publishing software, lightweight cameras that can shoot still photos and video, organizations' own social media platforms, and other Internet-based distribution services—it has become easier than ever for organizations with limited budgets to produce, publish, and distribute their own feature packages. These packages may include

- a written narrative outlining the goals of a nonprofit's initiative
- an "explainer" video showing how the initiative will benefit the public
- a photo montage of the nonprofit's volunteers carrying out the initiative
- audio testimonials of some of the beneficiaries of the initiative

When presented effectively, compelling and credible packages have the potential to connect the nonprofit to new audiences. In some cases, nonprofits have convinced news organizations to run their content verbatim, creating an informal partnership between the nonprofit and the news organization that benefits both institutions.

Unfortunately, no magic formula or algorithm for media packages guarantees success, but here are some questions to ask yourself and guidelines to consider in determining the news value of a nonprofit's content.

What Are the Goals?

First, develop a communications plan that reflects the organization's mission and priorities and includes both short-term and long-term communications goals.

- Short-term goals might include a list of the specific initiatives that the nonprofit wants to promote over the next three months, along with the number of news stories that each initiative should generate.
- Long-term goals might include year-to-year growth in the number of visitors to the organization's Web site or a campaign to secure media coverage in new markets.

What Are the Significance, Relevance, and Benefit of the Nonprofit's Initiatives?

Next, consider three terms in evaluating the value of the work that the nonprofit is attempting to promote: "significance," "relevance," and "benefit."

- *Significance:* How much of an impact will the work of the nonprofit have on the community?
- *Relevance:* How will this work affect the typical person in the community?
- *Benefit:* How will the nonprofit make things better?

The stronger the answers to these questions are, the greater the likelihood that the organization will be able to interest the news media and the public.

What Are the Takeaway Messages?

Takeaway messages are those that the organization wants the media and the public to remember about its work. To increase their potential to be memorable, pick the two or three most important messages, then craft them into short, active sentences. The consideration of potential takeaway messages leads to another helpful question: What verbs should be used? The active voice is almost always better than the passive voice. The stronger the verbs, the stronger the content—and the likelihood that the communications will connect with a broad audience. Strong verbs include

- launch
- solve
- cure
- prove

Weaker verbs include

- gather
- contemplate
- ponder
- discuss

Personal Is Better than Abstract

Put the nonprofit's work in human terms. Even better, identify individuals who are willing to discuss how they benefit directly.

At a university, for example, students might manufacture plastic shields and other protective gear to donate to doctors, nurses, and other medical professionals who are experiencing equipment shortages at local hospitals during a medical crisis. If the university decides to promote this work, it should include comments from representatives of these hospitals explaining how the donated equipment is helping them to treat patients.

Invest in Photo, Graphic, and Video Assets

Virtually all news organizations manage their own Web sites. Engaging photos, graphics, and video that effectively illustrate the nonprofit's work can make the content more appealing.

Do Not Overpromise or Make Unsubstantiated Claims

The credibility of content is vital. Nothing will damage an organization's reputation with the media and its key constituencies more than making promises or assertions it cannot substantiate.

Avoid Jargon, Unnecessary Language, and Other Marketing Speak

Empty phrases and other flowery language might dazzle bosses and colleagues, but it can disrupt the strongest elements of a narrative and turn off potential readers and viewers of the nonprofit's content.

Make sure to include the basic elements of any news story: who, what, where, when, why, and how. Specifically,

- Who: the individuals who are leading or carrying out the nonprofit's work
- What: the details of the initiative being promoted
- Where: the location or locations where the initiative is taking place
- When: the initiative's time frame
- Why: the nonprofit's motivation for launching the initiative
- How: the ways in which the initiative will benefit society

Clearly and concisely explain what the organization is doing and why it is important. This approach will entice and draw in the audience rather than talking down to them. News organizations have a simple phrase to describe this approach: "Show, don't tell."

Make Media Pitches Count

Content is king, but distribution is queen.
—Jonathan Perelman (Himler, 2013)

Creating compelling, credible content is only half of the equation to successfully communicate the nonprofit's work. The other half is effectively pitching that content to media organizations, reaching large audiences by convincing members of the media to publish or broadcast stories about the nonprofit's work (Hoefer & Watson, 2020). Of course, just because you reach out to the media does not mean they will cover the story. To increase the likelihood of success, here are some questions to ask in advance, before pitching the media.

Should You Reach Out to the Media at All?

Put more simply, is there a realistic probability that the news media will cover the announcement? This question is particularly important in the modern media environment, where news organizations have limited staff.

Every time you try—and fail—to pitch a story to the media, it will be that much harder to convince the media the next time that the next pitch is worth their attention. Concentrate resources on promoting the strongest work.

What Are the Target Audiences?

The answer to this question will influence the media organizations to which you pitch. For example, a story about a new initiative to solicit donations from professional engineers might be pitched primarily to engineering trade publications.

What Are the Key Takeaway Messages for Target Audiences to Remember?

Determining these key messages will inform which information to include in the media pitch. For example, a research lab working on a vaccine to combat influenza might underscore the importance of its work by emphasizing to the media and the public that, in a bad year, more people die from the flu in the United States than die in traffic accidents. A charitable organization promoting its fundraising efforts could include a call to action to explain to donors how their financial support will serve people in need.

What Types of Media Are Being Pitched?

The type of media can affect the timing of and approach to the pitch. Radio reporters, for example, tend to work early in the day and need audio sound bites to enhance their work. Print and online reporters tend to work later in the day, so members of the organization might need to be available after normal business hours to give interviews, answer follow-up questions, or provide additional information. If you are trying to secure a supportive editorial in a daily newspaper, for example, do yourself a favor and do not try to pitch them on a Friday. That's when most editorial page editors are trying to finish their Saturday, Sunday, and Monday editorial pages. Meanwhile, social media platforms usually respond to stripped-down pitches containing only the most essential language.

No matter which media are being pitched, the goal should be to drive all of them to the same key takeaway messages that advance the mission of the organization.

What Media Markets Are You Pitching?

Every media market has its own unique rhythm. In New York City, for example, there is often one story of the day that most media organizations will pursue at the same time. (Most of the time, that story is bad news for an organization, not good.)

Who Are the Primary Media Contacts? What Are Their Interests?

Some members of the media will be attracted to so-called "human interest" stories that focus on the individuals who benefit from the nonprofit's work. Others will prefer to write or broadcast about the public policy implications. Do your homework before connecting with them. Play to their strengths and make it as easy as possible for them to do their jobs.

What if the Media Want to Interview Someone from the Nonprofit?

Media interviews can be an effective part of the organization's communications strategy—if the subject of the interview is prepared properly. Here are some helpful interview tips.

- Anticipate the most important questions that the media might ask and suggest potential answers for the interview subject to review in advance. This will help the subject be more self-confident.
- Offer to accompany the subject to the interview. This will enable you to observe the interview and make sure the subject is treated respectfully.
- Help the subject relax before the interview begins. If you know the journalist conducting the interview, you might want to engage in some light banter. If the interview subject is particularly nervous, encourage the subject to try some deep breathing or engage in a quick relaxation exercise.

These tips can be especially beneficial to a subject who is interviewed during a crisis that threatens the success of the organization.

Crisis Communications: Hope for The Best, Plan for the Worst

In preparing for battle I have always found that plans are useless, but planning is indispensable.

—Dwight D. Eisenhower (as cited in Nixon, 1962)

As the examples cited in the beginning of this chapter illustrate, one poorly managed issue or incident can quickly and thoroughly destroy a nonprofit's reputation, severely hampering that organization's ability to carry out its ongoing mission.

Many organizations do not allocate the necessary time and resources to anticipate and plan for existential crises and other emergencies before they occur, hoping instead that they will somehow be fortunate enough to escape the inevitable. Unlike major corporations, most nonprofits cannot afford an outside consultant to assist them after the fact (Andreasen & Kotler, 2020).

There are, however, steps that any organization can take on its own to be better prepared. Below are six practical rules to prepare for and manage crises and emergencies.

Rule 1: Build Your Team before You Need It

One of the best practices is to create a "three-deep" structure, in which at least three individuals within an organization are trained and assigned to perform each key set of tasks during an emergency or crisis, including such specialized communications tasks as interacting with earned media, videography, and responding to inquiries via social media. That way, an organization can ensure that at least one staff member is always available to perform those tasks, even if someone is on vacation or otherwise unavailable.

Once these "three-deeps" are assigned, an organization should conduct regular training exercises to ensure that staff members know their responsibilities and are ready for a crisis or emergency. There is no such thing as too much preparation.

Rule 2: Before a Crisis or Emergency Becomes Public, Do a 360-Degree Download

At the very beginning of a crisis—hopefully before it goes public—the leadership of an organization should gather, preferably in person, to review important information without fear of judgment or reprisal for any decisions that have been made to that point.

It is vital for an organization's top communicators to be part of these discussions. Too often during a crisis, an organization will feed its communicators a few talking points to deliver to the media and the public without any background information or context. The advice of experienced communicators is as important as the input of an organization's legal and risk management experts.

Rule 3: Get Information Out Quickly, Thoroughly, and Accurately

Experience shows that at the beginning of a crisis, a significant portion of the initial information is unverified and can be inaccurate. Although it is always important to provide information quickly, it is even more important to take a few minutes to verify that information and make sure it is correct. Anything that damages an organization's credibility will make it harder to maintain the trust of the media and the public going forward.

There is no shame in admitting that the organization is still gathering key information. If possible, provide an approximate time when the organization will be able to distribute that information publicly—then do everything within your power to stick to that deadline.

Rule 4: Staff Appropriately and Humanely

This staffing rule is especially important during a protracted crisis that extends over multiple days. As an incident unfolds, every member of an organization has a natural tendency to want to be part of the initial response. Do not allow that to happen. If everyone responds at the beginning, after 12–16 hours the entire organization will be exhausted—and individuals will start making mistakes. Throughout a crisis, an organization's leaders must remain attentive to the physical, mental, and emotional stresses on their staff and provide judgment-free opportunities for them to rest and recharge.

Rule 5: Stay Calm—Even When You Do Not Feel Calm

This rule can be classified under the category "easier said than done." Beware managers who respond to a crisis by working themselves into a frenzy. They tend to infect their colleagues with that frenzy, significantly hampering others' ability to carry out their duties effectively. Resisting this temptation—and encouraging others to do the same—will reduce stress and increase the likelihood that the organization will manage the crisis effectively.

Rule 6: Every Situation Is an Opportunity to Learn

For more than 30 years, I have witnessed the response to dozens of crises and training exercises—everything from pathogens to terrorist attacks. I have never seen a single incident managed perfectly. As flawed human beings, people always make mistakes. It is important to acknowledge these mistakes, learn from them, and not repeat them.

A Final Note on Crisis Communications

An outside consultant, conference presenter, or other expert might advise an organization to draft a series of prewritten statements attempting to anticipate every possible negative scenario the organization might face. This can waste precious time that can be better spent focusing on how the organization can respond to a crisis. An easily understood analogy is the theory of the MacGuffin—a term usually attributed to screenwriter Angus MacPhail and popularized by his most famous colleague, film director Alfred Hitchcock ("MacGuffin," n.d.)

A *MacGuffin* is defined as a plot device—often of little or no importance in the overall context of the narrative—that nevertheless serves as the film's catalyst. (Hitchcock's quintessential MacGuffin might be the secret microfilm—the contents of which are never revealed—that sparks a cross-country adventure of mistaken identity and double-crossing in the classic 1959 film *North by Northwest*.) Hitchcock's most suspenseful films focused attention on how his characters reacted to the events in his films, rather than on the events themselves.

Each organization has a finite number of ways in which it can realistically react to a crisis. Concentrating communications efforts on those finite responses will enable an organization to allocate its resources far more efficiently and intelligently and better prepare it to face any crisis it might encounter.

Lies, Damn Lies, and Metrics

The first step is to measure whatever can be easily measured. This is OK as far as it goes. The second step is to disregard that which can't be easily measured or to give it an arbitrary quantitative value. This is artificial and misleading. The third step is to presume that what can't be measured easily really isn't important. This is blindness. The fourth step is to say that what can't be easily measured really doesn't exist. This is suicide.

—Daniel Yankelovich (as cited in Davis, 2018, para. 1)

At the dawn of the 1960s, one of the most respected business executives in the United States was Robert McNamara, the president of Ford Motor Company. By the end of the decade, McNamara was considered a disgrace by many—and a war criminal by some—for the nation's disastrous involvement in Vietnam.

One of the root causes of this failure is what is now called the "McNamara fallacy"—that is, relying solely on quantitative observations to make decisions, outlined by social scientist Daniel Yankelovich in his blunt 1972 assessment. For example, one of the primary ways the U.S. military gauged success in the war was by measuring enemy body counts—real and imagined. As author Jonathan Salem Baskin wrote,

> When the last helicopter rose above the American embassy in Saigon on April 29, 1975, the U.S. had been winning the Vietnam War for over a decade. The data said so. . . . No data model can completely or accurately model reality (that's why they're called *models*). (Baskin, 2014)

Do not fall prey to this fallacy as you analyze the success or failure of your attempts to promote your organization's work to key constituencies, either directly through the organization's own online platforms or indirectly through outside media. Carefully choose the metrics that you will rely on to measure that success.

Always remember: Not everything that is measurable is meaningful. This is particularly true when evaluating data in the ever-expanding world of social media. It can be hard for people who are unfamiliar with statistics to understand that 1,000 impressions on a social media platform do not carry the same intrinsic weight as 1,000 unique page views of a piece of content on a Web site—or 1,000 people watching a news story that is broadcast on a television station. One factor contributing to this confusion is that a significant chunk of data—such as the number of readers on a media organization's Web site—is proprietary. Nonprofits often contract with tracking services that provide audience estimates, many of them inflated. Much of this information can be unreliable when attempting to evaluate the relative success of one's promotional efforts across multiple media platforms (Rofuth & Piepenbring, 2019).

Moreover, some audience numbers are simply unavailable to these tracking services, such as the listenership of specific news stories broadcast by radio stations. If one applied the McNamara fallacy to this situation, one would conclude that radio listenership is not important. However, as crisis communications veterans can attest, traditional radio may be the only way to convey essential information to key constituencies during a power blackout or natural disaster.

So how can a nonprofit effectively measure media success? A good approach is to set consistent minimum standards to evaluate audience reach. For example, a nonprofit that serves a mid-sized metropolitan area might set the following benchmarks to measure the reach of the organization's content:

- 500 unique page views of the content on the nonprofit's Web site
- two pickups of the content by external media organizations
- 50 retweets of the content posted on the organization's Twitter feed

An organization can determine the relative success of pieces of content on the basis of whether they meet or exceed some or all of these benchmarks. This approach enables the nonprofit to evaluate its promotional campaigns relative to one another, informing the organization's leaders' decisions about

- how best to commit resources to future engagement efforts
- how to drill down and determine which content or campaigns and specific platforms appeal to specific audiences

For example, a university trying to build its national reputation might adjust the regional focus of its student, faculty, or donor recruitment in part on the basis of the geographic breakdown of readership on its news site. Plenty of meaningful information is available if one knows where and how to look.

Conclusion

Just Do It

—Popular Nike slogan

Charitable organizations, educational institutions, and other nonprofits have a long history—dating back centuries—of working to create a better society.

- Do not wait for others to brag about your nonprofit's important work. Do it yourself.
- Take advantage of the latest technologies to reach the organization's key audiences with compelling written, photographic, audio, and video content.
- Highlight the volunteers and financial supporters who make the organization's work possible—and the individuals and groups that benefit from that work.
- Measure the success—and failure—of promotional efforts to inform future decisions.

In this increasingly transactional world, your nonprofit has a powerful story. Do not be afraid to tell it.

Skills Application Exercise

You are the executive director of a foundation with holdings that include a major metropolitan art museum. A prominent family of long-time donors is giving the foundation several paintings, along with additional funding to build a new museum wing to store and display the art. The total donation is valued at more than $5 million. You have scheduled a news conference and groundbreaking to announce the donation and the museum expansion. On hand will be the donor family, along with other dignitaries, including civic leaders, local government officials, and a representative of the governor of your state. Two days before the event, you are informed by a local law firm that an individual is claiming ownership of two pieces of art that the family previously donated to the foundation. This individual says the artwork was looted during World War II and was obtained illegally by the donor family. The individual is threatening to stage a protest during the event. The donor family insists it has no knowledge of the looting. The family also demands that the event occur as scheduled, or they will withdraw their donation. You are concerned about whether and how the media will cover the event.

1. Write a media plan for the event. Explain

   - how to deal with reporters in advance of the event
   - how to focus your news release announcing the event
   - how to focus your news release to be distributed at the event
   - how to respond to reporters if protesters are present
   - how to respond to any negative external media coverage stemming from the event
   - how to respond to any negative social media posts about the event

2. Write the following key communications documents:

   - news release announcing the event
   - news release to be handed out at the event
   - message points for foundation staff to respond to external media, social media, and event attendees
   - an opinion column for after the event that focuses on the importance of the museum's expansion, the beneficence of the donor family, and the steps the foundation will take to work with all sides to resolve the potential legal conflict

References

Abernathy, P. M. (2018). *The expanding news desert.* Chapel Hill: University of North Carolina, Hussman School of Journalism and Media.

Andreasen, A. R., & Kotler, P. (2020). *Strategic marketing for nonprofit organizations* (7th ed.). Upper Saddle River, NJ: Prentice Hall.

Baskin, J. S. (2014, July 25). According to U.S. Big Data, we won the Vietnam War. *Forbes.* Retrieved from https://www.forbes.com/sites/jonathansalembaskin/2014/07/25/according-to-big-data-we-won-the-vietnam-war/#453de0cb3f21

Cohen, T. (2006). Cultivating effective media relationships and marketing. In R. L. Edwards & J. A. Yankey (Eds.), *Effectively managing nonprofit organizations* (pp. 83–100). Washington, DC: NASW Press.

Davis, B. (2018). 1960s: *Days of rage: McNamara fallacy.* Retrieved from https://1960sdaysofrage.wordpress.com/2018/05/15/mcnamara-fallacy/

Duke University, Sanford School of Public Policy. (2018, April 20). *Fake news, the First Amendment and failure in the marketplace of ideas.* Retrieved from https://sanford.duke.edu/articles/fake-news-first-amendment-and-failure-marketplace-ideas

Evans, H. (2017). *"Content is king"—Essay by Bill Gates 1996.* Retrieved from https://medium.com/@HeathEvans/content-is-king-essay-by-bill-gates-1996-df74552f80d9

Hart, T., Greenfield, J. M., & Johnston, M. (2005). *Nonprofit Internet strategies: Best practices for marketing, communications and fundraising success.* Hoboken, NJ: Wiley.

Himler, P. (2013, July 9). *Content is king, distribution is queen.* Retrieved from https://www.forbes.com/sites/peterhimler/2013/07/09/content-is-king-distribution-is-queen/#2c89f6af174d

Hoefer, R., & Watson, L. D. (2020). *Essentials of social work management and leadership.* San Diego: Cognella Academic Publishing.

Lutz, A. (2012, June 14). These 6 corporations control 90% of the media in America. *Business Insider.* Retrieved from https://www.businessinsider.com/these-6-corporations-control-90-of-the-media-in-america-2012-6

MacGuffin. (n.d.). Retrieved from https://the.hitchcock.zone/wiki/MacGuffin

Nixon, R. M. (1962). *Six crises.* New York: Simon & Schuster.

Pew Research Center. (2019). *State of the news media.* Washington, DC: Author.

Rofuth, T. W., & Piepenbring, J. M. (2019). *Management and leadership in social work: A competency-based approach.* New York: Springer.

Yankelovich, D. (1972). *Corporate priorities: A continuing study of the new demands on business.* Stamford, CT: Author.

Xie, S. (2016, Mar 25). New Jersey sites tap into local news. *Columbia Journalism Review.* Retrieved from https://www.cjr.org/united_states_project/new_jersey_sites_tap_into_local_news.php

3

Bringing about Social Change by Managing Public Policy Advocacy and Government Relations

Peter J. McDonough

Positive social change is at the heart of what all nonprofit organizations try to do. Some organizations, such as international nongovernmental organizations, aim for broad change, whereas others, such as statewide and local service providers, seek social improvements on a much smaller but no less important scale. They all want a better world; they just have different approaches to achieving that goal.

The same holds true for most elected officials. They are trying to bring about positive social change, although they sometimes differ on what that better world looks like. Although disheartening headlines in recent years speak to a dysfunctional relationship between Capitol Hill and the White House and of the partisan centrifuge that has spun the country into warring camps, the good news is that most of the important public policy advocacy and critical government actions occur at the state and local levels, where partisanship is less pronounced, where processes are more streamlined, and where progress can be swift.

State and local decisions often deal with more practical than philosophical issues and are often operational in nature. These decisions might deal with workplace conduct, reporting requirements, or social behaviors that are important to nonprofits. State and local policies may set broad new policy goals that can best be met by the nonprofit sector.

State appropriations and local grants are quite often the largest sources of funding for nonprofit organizations and service providers. In fact, studies published by the Urban Institute have found that nearly one-third of the revenue for nonprofit public charities comes from government through contracts (23.9 percent) or grants (8.3 percent; Blackwood, Roeger, & Pettijohn, 2012).

Similar studies found a significant expansion in the 1960s of the government's reliance on the nonprofit sector to provide services, a reliance that continues to increase (Smith & Lipsky, 1993). This dependency has led to nonprofits broadening their missions and becoming even more critical to helping the government meeting its responsibilities.

Government reliance on nonprofits is bipartisan and not likely to change. Leaders of both political parties have championed the use of nonprofits to provide public services, ranging from operating animal shelters to running charter schools and from operating municipal recycling centers to providing food, shelter, and counseling for one's neediest neighbors.

President Ronald Reagan embraced a privatization-based agenda and a "new federalism" that sought to shift federal responsibilities to state and local governments. Against an antitax backdrop, this shift of responsibility led to an expanded reliance on nonprofit providers for many services.

President Bill Clinton wholeheartedly supported the ideas promoted in *Reinventing Government* (Osborne & Gaebler, 1992). He established the National Performance Review, which was led by Vice President Al Gore. The National Performance Review developed hundreds of recommendations intended to make government operate more efficiently and effectively. Many of the recommendations addressed bureaucracy and red tape; another recommendation was the creation of performance-based partnership grants, many of which would ultimately be directed to the nonprofit sector for the provision of services formerly delivered by government.

The expanding dependence on nonprofits and growing use of taxpayer dollars by nonprofits have increased the accountability required of nonprofit organizations and have rightly given government a deeper authority over and oversight of how efficiently that money is spent and how effectively responsibilities are met. Nonprofits today are at the heart of the efficient and effective delivery of public services. The types of services become more varied with every passing year, and how those services are delivered continues to grow in complexity.

Notwithstanding the recognized interdependence between government and nonprofits, nonprofits are often reluctant to lobby for themselves or for their issues. For some nonprofits, "lobbying" is a dirty word. A study published in the *Journal of Sociology and Social Welfare* looked at the semantics and the use of the word "lobbying." The following passage sums up a typical view:

> Lobbying was not defined for the participants. Focus group members and interviewees were asked to define lobbying in their own terms. Most of the respondents had an understanding of lobbying and what it could accomplish. Pragmatically, they were not averse to engaging in lobbying activities and expressed the value of lobbying. Participants further understood that they engaged in the activity, though they were resistant to call it lobbying. Lobbying had a clear, negative connotation in the minds of many nonprofit participants, who often used less emotionally charged and value-laden terms such as *education* or *awareness* to describe behavior that could be defined as lobbying. One example was seen through a human services administrator from Raleigh who insisted that he did not lobby but went on to describe his organizations' activities using the following terms:
>
> I have spoken to all the school board members, one-on-one, about that, so I've presented that. I've spoken to a couple of city council members; I've spoken to a couple of county commissioners; I've spoken to the mayor of [town name].
>
> When probed about the context of the activities, he acknowledged that they were done in his role as executive on behalf of the organization. So, while he was adamant about not calling his actions *lobbying*, by most definitions, they would be classified as such. (Taliaferro & Ruggiano, 2013, p. 158)

Studies have found that there are some structural reasons why nonprofits decide not to engage in the public or government arenas. The skills needed to be an effective advocate often differ from those required to deliver community services. Advocacy activities—like so many political activities—are time consuming and take place during nontypical work hours, placing a burden on nonprofit leaders (Chaskin, Brown, Venkatesh, & Vidal, 2001).

When nonprofits do make the decision to engage, their leaders often make a strategic goal of creating relationships to embed their organizations in government and political processes. They aim to build trust with policymakers by understanding the needs of government, building the capacity to meet those needs within their organizations, and delivering on those needs. In short, nonprofit leaders think less about the tactics of advocacy than of ways to insinuate themselves into government (Berry & Arons, 2005).

Leading and Managing Nonprofit Organizations

Understanding Your Government Partner

Government today is more than just your funder; government is your partner, and all productive partnerships are built on familiarity and understanding. Who are these officeholders who are your partners, and what makes them get up in the morning?

To start with, they are your neighbors. They are everyday people who find themselves holding one of the more than a half-million elected positions in the United States, ranging from dog catcher to school board member to mayor, state legislator, member of Congress, or president of the United States (Lawless, 2012).

There are nearly 87,000 elected governing bodies at the municipal and county levels in the United States; virtually all are made up of part-time officeholders. Even state legislatures, where some of the most dramatic and sweeping policy changes and major funding decisions are made, are predominantly made up of members who have other jobs.

Indeed, according to the National Conference of State Legislatures (NCSL; Kurtz, 2015), only four states—California, Michigan, New York, and Pennsylvania—have full-time legislatures with large full-time staffs. NCSL research has shown that although 7,383 people were elected to state legislatures, only 886 (12 percent) of them were full-time legislators. Most state legislators are "citizen legislators." Other jobs that legislators hold are shown in Table 3.1.

PA is 1 of 4 full-time legislatures

Table 3.1 Legislator Jobs

Occupation	%
Business	30
Attorney	14
Retired	8
Consultant	8
Educator	6
Agriculture	5

Legislators do not get paid a lot of money for their service, especially when one considers the off-hours work, the demands to attend civic and political activities, the rigors of campaigning and fundraising, and everything else that is required to be a responsive elected official. The nation's highest paid full-time legislators in California and New York earned $110,000 per year in 2019. At the other extreme, New Hampshire paid the members of its legislature $200 for a two-year session, and other states offer only per-diem reimbursements. The average salary across all elected state legislators in 2019 was $32,602.

An additional challenge is that there is no job security. At best, a state legislator gets a four-year term; most are only elected to two-year terms. Think of it as a high-risk contract: They get a two- or four-year term, have to beg the management (voters) to renew the contract, and if they lose and the contract is not renewed, they have from mid-November to early January to empty out their offices. So, if they do not do it for the money, lifestyle, or job security, why do they do it? Although there are countless academic studies on the psychology of voters and what motivates them, there is precious little research on why people actually run for office.

It Is All about Helping People

Ask an officeholder and you are likely to find that, like people who work in the nonprofit sector, they want to make a difference in people's lives. A case in point is former Congressman Dean Gallo of New Jersey. Gallo entered politics in the late 1960s as a very young man who thought there should be better recreational facilities—actually just a few more ballfields—in his hometown. Eight years later, he had become a member of the N.J. General Assembly, and in 1984, he was elected to the first of five terms in the U.S. House of Representatives.

Upon his arrival in Congress, he set out to build a staff that had providing constituent services as its absolute top priority. Although he had become a member of the most important legislative body in the United States and was ultimately a ranking member on the powerful House of Representatives Committee on Appropriations, he still said, "If I can get constituent services right, everything else will take care of itself." Whether it was improving baseball fields as a member of the town council or solving problems as a part of the federal government, it was all about helping people. And he was not the exception (personal communication with D. A. Gallo, Trenton, New Jersey, 1980).

Officeholders, at every level, are people people. They like people, and they like to be liked by people. To be successful, they have to like people—of all stripes. "The candidate who says, 'I don't suffer fools gladly,' is he himself a fool," observed Paul Begala and James Carville (2002, p. 34) in their book *Buck Up, Suck Up and Come Back When You Foul Up.*

The art of successful campaigning—getting that contract renewal—is additive. It is all about building a bigger and better voter base than the opposition. It is about making friends and motivating them, about meeting community needs, doing a good job, and getting reelected. Like their politician counterparts, nonprofit managers should not miss the opportunity to make friends.

be a people person!

Getting It Done

The rules that follow come from lessons learned over 40 years of lobbying and being lobbied, of being an officeholder, and of helping others successfully become officeholders. (Note that the terms "officeholder," "policymaker," "legislator," and "representative" are all used interchangeably in this chapter.) These rules are mostly common sense, and they are not absolute, but they have worked for public affairs professionals from city hall to the state house and all the way to the halls of Congress and the White House.

Understand Your Policy Priorities

Clearly understanding what your legislative or policy goals are is essential. Writing them down and making sure that the leadership of the organization shares an understanding of them will help focus your efforts, guide the allocation of resources, and determine the level of commitment of time, personnel, and money that will be required of the organization.

More important, setting and understanding priorities will provide discipline—the discipline to focus like a laser on the things you want to get done and the restraint to not get distracted by every good cause that comes across your desk.

Know strengths and weaknesses

Understand Yourself

Know the nonprofit organization's strengths and weaknesses. You have a board of directors. How engaged are they with elected officials? You have clients. Can they be mobilized in appropriate ways to help achieve your goals? You have donors or contributors. How willing would they be to speak up on your behalf or, to turn an adage on its head, to put their mouths where their money is?

The answers to these questions can only come from asking. Many of the answers are not obvious. Your board members are, by definition, already involved in the community and are thus likely to already know officeholders. They give their time and money to the nonprofit organization; they have probably done the same for elected officials. The only way you will know is if you ask. You may be surprised at the result.

Know Your Legislator

Understand the connections your legislator has with the nonprofit organization. Do they have a family member or close associate who uses its services? Have they ever been invited to see how the organization functions, how it serves people, and how it makes lives better? Know your policymaker's history with your organization.

Do not let the first time you meet your legislator be the time when you need their help. Invest the time early on, and it will pay dividends for years.

Know the Bureaucracy

Elected officials set broad policy direction, but it is the bureaucracy that executes them. Getting to know career government administrators is fundamental to a successful public affairs program. The practical decisions about how and where to direct funds are almost always made by staff, not by officeholders. Rules and regulations to implement policy initiatives are always prepared by the executive branch and its bureaucrats. Like officeholders, bureaucrats are often overworked, underresourced, and underappreciated. Nonprofits can be the go-to resource to help them meet their need for information and guidance as rules and regulations are drafted and discussed.

One final point to keep in mind about the bureaucracy: Whereas officeholders tend to come and go, to move to other offices or leave public service after a few terms, bureaucrats and bureaucratic hierarchies stay in place for decades. Spending the time and effort to get to know the bureaucrats who deal with important areas is an investment that is worth making and that can last for years.

Know the System

David Gergen, a top advisor to a bipartisan group of U.S. presidents—Nixon, Ford, Reagan, and Clinton—listed seven key rules of leadership in his book *Eyewitness to Power* (Gergen, 2001). One of these rules is "understand the system." His essential observation is that one cannot succeed unless one is willing to take the time to thoroughly learn the system within which one's policies will be crafted and implemented. Gergen's admonishment is directed at officeholders, but the advice is just as important for advocates.

The processes of various governmental bodies differ. Those bodies have different cultures, different histories, and different practices. They have sets of formal and informal rules, and one must learn them all. Learning the system comes from understanding the written rules of the process and, more important, from watching it. The most fundamental rules are found in state constitutions or in municipal or county charters. More granular processes are usually described in the operating rules adopted by the governing body or in ordinances establishing the required course of events, including the introduction of bills, required public hearings, and executive actions.

The informal rules, and the traditions and culture that inform them, can only be fully understood and appreciated through deep immersion in the process. This immersion comes from being present and by finding experienced guides or mentors who will help you navigate the sometimes obscure government process. A lot can be learned, too, by just showing up.

Show Up

"Showing up is not all of life, but it counts for a lot," Hillary Clinton famously said (Kessler, 2009). Those are words for advocates to live by. Being present, even when you do not have to be, signals that you care about the process, civic discourse, and your and your community's quality of life. It is also a way to pay respect to the officeholders and staff that make the system operate.

Being a constant presence at the city hall, county administration building, or state capitol will make you or your organization the go-to source for quick information. You will be the first source policymakers think of when they want to know something about your group, your agenda, or related issues. It will establish you as a credible and reliable resource.

Be a Resource

Officeholders are experts at lots of things, but probably not at what you do. Their staff are often not full-time employees and lack subject area expertise at a granular level. Your organization can provide that information and be that resource, but it takes work.

For starters, you need to be responsive. If a policymaker has a question, get the answer, get it right, and get it as quickly as you can. Try to develop a reputation for providing meaningful answers in a timely fashion.

And make no mistake, if you get the reputation for not being forthcoming and not telling the truth, you will lose your seat at the table. Do not fake it, do not obfuscate, do not try to outsmart them, and do not ever lie.

Understand the Other Side

Understanding the other side of a policy debate is important. Appreciating your opponents' views and objectives will prepare you to address the objections they will raise with policymakers. A comprehensive and compassionate understanding of the other side's views, goals, and objectives can provide important insights into how to forge a compromise that meets the needs of both sides.

Do Not Demonize

Just as there are two sides to every story, there are always multiple sides to public issues. Recognize that people of goodwill may simply disagree. That does not make them bad, evil, or despicable. It just means that, on this one issue, you disagree and may need to find a compromise. There is no "getting to yes" with a policymaker you have demonized.

The same holds true for other organizations or interests that hold views on a particular issue that oppose yours. Do not look at them as your enemies. The organization that opposes you today could be an important ally in a future effort or endeavor.

Build Coalitions: You Do Not Have to Do It Alone

Most of the issues that are important to one nonprofit are also important to other organizations, businesses, or individuals. Coalitions can provide strength and can focus and leverage resources. They can also provide an opportunity for organizations to take a position on an issue without being front and center. More important, participating in coalitions is often reciprocal and can be a productive way to recruit other organizations into coalitions on important issues in the future.

There are countless examples of policy initiatives that could only have been enacted through the strength of a coalition. A good recent example is the success of the bail reform movement. Previous attempts at bail reform, such as ending cash bail and basing continued confinement of persons awaiting trial solely on their perceived flight risk and potential harm to the community, were largely unsuccessful when they were being promoted only by persons perceived to be soft on crime and supportive of prisoners.

Leading and Managing Nonprofit Organizations

However, success was broadly achieved in jurisdictions throughout the nation when a coalition that included prisoners' rights advocates and fiscal conservatives was developed. Together, they presented a unified argument that it was inappropriate to hold alleged criminals for months on end before a trial and, at the same time, that the overcrowded and inefficient corrections system was an unproductive drain on limited tax dollars.

Do Not Personalize

Regardless of how strongly advocates feel about an issue, they have to understand that rejection or advancement of an initiative is not personal. Many factors are at play. Governing bodies do not have an unlimited capacity for considering issues. Matters that are seen as most urgent can easily move another matter off the policy agenda. Remember that it was not about you, and keep working your agenda.

Build Bridges

The surest way to build bridges is by being responsive, truthful, and trustworthy. The fastest way to burn bridges is to not tell the truth or not keep your word. Bridges are built on a foundation of trust. To paraphrase former Wyoming Senator Alan Simpson, it is all about trust. If you have trust, nothing else matters. If you do not have trust, nothing else matters.

Outreach Programs

Few things are as powerful and compelling to elected officials than meeting with actual constituents. Putting a local face on an issue is essential. Hosting office visits between your organization's clients or members and their elected officials can be a great way for representatives to get to know your issues and associate them with their own voters.

When meeting with your officeholder,

- Make an appointment and be on time.
- Make sure the officeholder knows where the constituents are from.
- Train yourself and the others who are joining you by preparing talking points and making sure they have familiarized themselves with these talking points before the meeting.
- Do not be argumentative, and do not make assumptions.

- Be pleasant and professional, but get to the point. Your officeholder and their staff members have limited time, and they will appreciate it if you get to the point quickly.
- Prepare "leave-behinds." It is important to provide your representative or their staff with white papers, graphics, and other reports. They are great reminders of the points you want to make, and they can be a useful reference for the officeholder and their staff.
- Take careful notes regarding any follow-up that comes from the meeting. Following up is a good way to stay on the officeholder's radar, and it shows that you care and are serious.

Never Assume

Although your issue may be the most important thing for you or your organization, it is probably not something your elected official knows a lot about.

Figure out how to express your issue in simple terms. Avoid jargon, do not use acronyms, and give yourself the grandparent test: If your grandfather or grandmother would not understand your explanation, you are probably not going to be understood. The balance is to find ways to simplify your explanation without appearing condescending. One way to do that is to make sure you are talking in terms of values; talk about why the change you are seeking is important to people and how it will affect their daily lives.

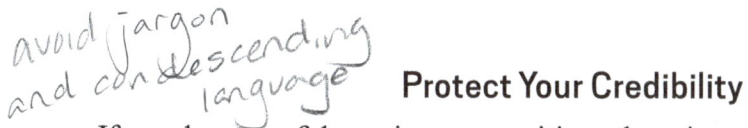

Protect Your Credibility

If you have confidence in your position, there is no reason not to be forthcoming and present the other side of the argument. If there are political or policy risks that could manifest themselves to a policymaker who has supported your position, it is always better to let the policymaker know. The policymaker is going to find out anyway, so they should hear it from you. If you provide your legislators with knowledge of the potential risks, they will be prepared for it, and it will not seem nearly as significant. Being forthcoming is key to building credibility.

Do Not Be Put Off by the Staff

Never underestimate the power of the staff. Although meetings with staff can sometimes feel like a brush-off, the fact is that it is the staff who prepares the briefings and provides the recommendations.

It is also the staff who get none of the glory and who work long hours for little pay. Giving the staff the respect, credit, and thanks they deserve creates immeasurable goodwill.

Say Thank You

Your mother was right: Wash your hands, you only get one chance to make a first impression, and remember to say please and thank you. It seems obvious, but there are far too many people in the policy arena who forget to say thank you. If an elected leader does something that you wanted done, no matter how trivial, say thank you. Send the officeholder a note. Even better, add to the thanks by informing your community—your clients, your board members, and your contributors—that the officeholder did something to support your goals and that you would like to publicly acknowledge them.

It is lonely being a politician; people love to hate them. A simple thanks can go a long way.

Keep Them Informed

Providing officeholders with regular updates about projects in which they have shown an interest or updates on the way in which your organization is serving the community or using a taxpayer-funded grant is important. These updates show respect for and recognition of the officeholder, and they provide an opportunity to reinforce the message about the good work that your nonprofit is doing. They help to build the goodwill that will serve as a bulwark against any criticism that may come from time to time.

Follow the Law

It should go without saying, but nonprofits, like all other advocates, must know and follow all the laws specific to lobbying and political engagement. Failure to follow them can result in fines, jail time, and enormous negative publicity.

There is no cause so noble that its advocates are exempt from following the law. Cutting corners or putting off compliance with requirements for registering as a lobbyist or advocate, not making timely disclosures or reports, or getting involved in partisan political efforts is never worth the negative publicity.

Each jurisdiction is likely to have its own rules about lobbying that typically require that the official representative of an organization intending to influence public policy register with a regulatory body (typically with the presenting officers of a legislative body, or perhaps the state attorney general).

Have a Plan: What, Why, How, and When

Advocacy campaigns, like political campaigns, are all about getting the right information to the right people at the right time. They are about using limited resources in efficient ways. Winning the hearts and minds of policymakers requires a plan that includes strategy and objectives, tactics and messages, and a timeline (Pelton & Baznik, 2006).

Objectives need to be clear, and they must be understood by everyone involved in the campaign. It is not enough for just the people at the top to know what a campaign is trying to accomplish—everyone, from the executive director down to the intern answering the phone, needs to know what the campaign is trying to do and why it is important. Strategy is the plan for achieving the objective, and tactics are used to execute the strategy and achieve the objective. Strategy and objectives are easily confused with tactics. Think of it this way: Strategy and objectives are the "what and why"; tactics are the "how."

Timelines, the when, are critical. Advocacy campaigns require an effective sequencing of tactics so that they work in concert and can have the most impact. A timeline must have milestones and benchmarks so that you can assess your progress and make mid-course corrections. Nothing ever goes as well as planned, and you must always be nimble.

Following is a sample action plan for an arts organization that is facing a financial crisis caused by a local elected official who wants to eliminate arts funding. The objective of the organization is to preserve the public funding; the strategy is to achieve that goal by convincing a majority of the voting members of the governing body to vote to increase the funding. Their tactics include research, outreach, and education.

Sample Action Plan

Background Situation

A nonprofit community theater that receives a major share of its funding from the local county government finds its financial future in question when a new member of the county board of supervisors introduces a measure that would eliminate all arts funding. The county charter requires a public hearing within 30 days and a vote on the measure no sooner than two weeks after the public hearing.

The new member of the board of supervisors has a background in engineering, has two children in middle school, and introduced the measure in an effort to fill a county budget gap without reducing funding for the county public school system. He has never visited the theater.

Strategy and Objectives

Preserve funding for the theater by demonstrating that there are better, more effective cost reductions that can be made to the county budget.

Tactics

- Educate the supervisors about the important educational role the theater plays:
  o Invite them to the theater.
  o Coordinate the meeting with a school visit to show outreach in action.
- Educate the supervisors about how important the theater is to their constituents:
  o Launch a letter-writing campaign by season ticketholders and subscribers.
  o Coordinate phone calls from season ticketholders and donors who are also donors to the various supervisors' campaigns.
- Educate the supervisors about the theater's importance to the community:
  o Place an op-ed in local newspaper.
  o Participate in an editorial board meeting with the local newspaper to garner editorial support for preserving theater funding.
- Build a coalition of other arts organizations that would be affected:
  o Organize weekly meetings with similarly situated organizations to coordinate activities.
  o Participate in the public hearing.

Personnel

- Overall management: The executive director of the theater company is the primary campaign manager, including coalition building and outreach.
- Figurehead leader: The board chair is the figurehead leader; he or she is the signer of the op-ed, leader of discussions at meetings, and so forth.

- Spokesperson: The executive director of the theater organization is the authoritative voice on operational aspects of the theater, attends all meetings, and speaks to the media.
- Public relations specialist: The public relations specialist writes all news releases, prepares the op-ed, prepares a template for the letter-writing campaign, and prepares talking points.
- Researcher: The researcher identifies all important connections, such as the names of the teachers who have brought their classes to the theater, and compares the names of season ticketholders with the database of contributors to the supervisors' campaigns.

Timeline

- Week 1—research, planning, and outreach: Identify the process for consideration of the measure, identify allies for coalition, collect and match contributor data with internal constituencies and supporters, request supervisor meetings at the theater, and schedule school visits to coincide.
- Week 2—preparation, planning, and outreach: Prepare talking points about the theater's cultural and educational value to the community, meet at the theater (in conjunction with a visit from a school class) with the sponsor of the measure, the chair of the board of supervisors, and any subcommittee chair. Prepare an op-ed based on talking points for the local newspaper, and prepare a series of weekly letters to the editor for the theater group and each ally. Schedule an editorial board meeting for the following week. Send communication via normal channels to identify connected supporters and contributors, outlining the value of the theater and suggesting alternative budget adjustments. Hold a weekly coordinating meeting with allies to assess their progress.
- Week 3—execution and follow-up: Participate in the editorial board meeting, submit letters to the editor, send thank-you notes to all supervisors with whom meetings were held that reinforce the talking points, and ask whether additional information is needed. Publish a supportive op-ed in the local newspaper. Prepare and practice the presentation for the public hearing. Hold a weekly coordinating meeting with allies to assess their progress.
- Week 4—execution: Have significant political contributors place phone calls to all supervisors, reinforcing the talking points. Circulate

the positive editorial to all supervisors. Organize theater board members and constituents to attend the board of supervisors' public meeting, and prepare testimony and a leave-behind package for the public meeting. Testify, along with supporters, at the public hearing. Submit a letter or letters to the editor. Hold weekly coordinating meetings with allies to assess their progress.

- Week 5—execution: Send personal notes to all supervisors thanking them for the opportunity to testify and asking whether more information is needed. Organize more phone calls from contributors. Check in with the sponsor of the measure to determine whether they have had a change of heart since the public hearing, and ask whether there are any alternatives (giving them a graceful retreat). Touch base with all supervisors to tally votes. Hold a weekly coordinating meeting with allies to assess their progress.

- Week 6—execution: Continue phone calls from political supporters. Have the board chair make a personal appeal to each supervisor. If the vote to cut is clearly opposed, thank the supervisors, and suggest to the chair of the board of supervisors that the measure be held. If the vote is close or appears to be a potential loss, propose an alternative to sponsor and chairperson. Ask for a delay for a specific period to work out a compromise.

- Week 7—wrap-up: Send thank-you notes to everyone who worked on the effort, including the letter writers, volunteers, and members of the board of supervisors. Conduct an assessment of what worked and what did not.

Closing Thoughts

Government affairs is a critical responsibility of nonprofit leaders and managers, but it can, and should, be fun. Two important thoughts to keep in mind are as follows:

- Treat the government the way you would treat your biggest single donor—because it probably is.
- Check your cynicism at the door. Successful government affairs are built on trust and a shared understanding that all are working for the greater good. Cynicism is a luxury that advocates simply cannot afford.

Resources

Table 3.2 provides online resources for anyone interested in federal or state-level advocacy. The top section includes government-sponsored resources, and the second section contains nonideological and ideological resources for advocates.

Table 3.2 Resources

Name of Resource	Web Site Address	Information Available
Government		
Library of Congress	https://www.congress.gov	All official documents, schedules, and records for Congress, including bill text and committee and floor activities
U.S. Senate and U.S. House of Representatives	https://www.senate.gov https://www.house.gov	Legislative information for each house of Congress, member biographies, leadership and committee chairs, links to members' Web sites and important information regarding public disclosure and lobbying information
U.S. states	https://www.[state name].gov	Information about all three branches of each state government, with useful links to executive departments, legislative records, schedules and other actions.
Federal Election Commission	https://www.fec.gov	Detailed federal political campaign contribution database
Internal Revenue Service	https://www.irs.gov	Detailed information regarding Internal Revenue Service regulations and nonprofits
Nongovernmental Organizations		
National Conference of State Legislatures	https://www.ncsl.org	A comprehensive Web site with information about the legislatures of all 50 states, as well as valuable information regarding emerging policy matters. The site contains an outline of the lobbyist registration and reporting requirements for each state.
Council of State Governments	www.csg.org	Guide to evolving state policy issues, mostly legislative in nature, but includes some executive branch resources
American Legislative Exchange Council	https://www.alec.org	Conservative-leaning think tank that develops model legislation and support materials

Name of Resource	Web Site Address	Information Available
State Innovation Exchange	stateinnovation.org	Progressive-leaning think tank that develops model legislation and support materials
Brookings Institution	https://www.brookings.org	Progressive think tank that provides policy research
Heritage Foundation	https://www.heritage.org	Conservative think tank that provides policy research

Skills Application Exercises

1. Understand yourself, your goals, and your opposition.

    - What are the three most important policy goals for your organization or for an organization you would like to lead? Remember that "to receive more government funding" is not a goal. Money is a tactic that one uses to achieve a goal. What are the three most important things you want to achieve? What goal would you accomplish if you had more funding?
    - Why are those goals important to multiple audiences? Why are they important to the public at large? Why are they important to elected officials?
    - Who would oppose your goals, and why? With an objective eye, defend your opponents' view. Discuss why, in their hearts, they would argue against you in the most compelling and understanding way.
    - If your opponents made unfair or untrue criticisms of your organization, what would you do?

2. Understand the system.

    - Identify the sources of government or public funding for your organization. Who are the leaders of the top two funding sources? If they are elected, of what body are they members? Where and when do they meet?

- What connections does your organization have to those funders? Do your board members or clients have connections to them? How would you find out?

3. Know your elected officials.

- If you had a 15-minute meeting with your local mayor or state representative, what would you tell them? What would be the three most important things—only three—that you would tell them? What are their names and email addresses? Take the three points, use their email addresses, and request a meeting.
- What are you going to bring with you to the meeting? What are you going to leave behind? Learn more about the official from their biography.
- Build coalitions.
- Think about the three most important goals of your organization: Who are the first-level, most obvious allies who might join you in a coalition?
- What are some second-level organizations that might join in your fight, and why would they join you?

References

Begala, P., & Carville, J. (2002). *Buck up, suck up and come back when you foul up*. New York: Simon & Schuster.

Berry, J., & Arons, D., (2005). *A voice for nonprofits*. Washington, DC: Brookings Institution.

Blackwood, A. S., Roeger, K. L., & Pettijohn, S. L. (2012). *The nonprofit sector in brief: Public charities, giving and volunteering, 2012*. Washington, DC: Urban Institute.

Chaskin, R., Brown, P., Venkatesh, S., & Vidal, A. (2001). *Building community capacity*. New York: Aldine De Gruyter.

Gergen, D. (2001). *Eyewitness to power*. New York: Simon & Schuster.

Kessler, G. (2009, February 20). "On Asia trip, Clinton shows how she'll try to repair the U.S. image around the world" *Washington Post*. Retrieved from https://www.washingtonpost.com/wp-dyn/content/article/2009/02/19/AR2009021903471.html

Kurtz, K. (2015). *Who we elect*. Denver: National Conference of State Legislatures.

Lawless, J. L. (2012). *Becoming a candidate: Political ambition and the decision to run for office.* New York: Cambridge University Press.

Osborne, D., & Gaebler, T. (1992). *Reinventing government.* Boston: Addison-Wesley.

Pelton, E. D., & Baznik, R. E. (2006). Managing public policy and government relations. In R. L. Edwards & J. A. Yankey (Eds.), *Effectively managing nonprofit organizations* (pp. 101–137). Washington, DC: NASW Press.

Smith, S. R., & Lipsky, M. (1993). *Nonprofits for hire: The welfare state in the age of contracting.* Cambridge, MA: Harvard University Press.

Taliaferro, J. D., & Ruggiano, N. (2013). The "L" word: Nonprofits, language, and lobbying. *Journal of Sociology & Social Welfare, 40*(2), Article 9.

4

Securing Resources for Nonprofits: Developing a Successful Fundraising Program

Richard L. Edwards

These days, nonprofit organizations exist in a rapidly changing world that often threatens their financial stability (Edwards, 2020). One of the most important functions of nonprofit leaders and managers, particularly those who occupy chief executive officer (CEO) positions, is ensuring that their organization has adequate resources to enable them to accomplish their mission. Consequently, nonprofit leaders and managers need to be prepared to spend a significant portion of their time fundraising. The higher the manager's position in the managerial hierarchy, the more time they will need to devote to the process of raising money.

Trends in Fundraising

Currently, the nonprofit sector in the United States is made up of approximately 1.33 million charitable organizations registered by the Internal Revenue Service (IRS) under section 501(c)(3) of the Internal Revenue Code (Giving USA, 2020, p. 57). In recent years, nonprofits have faced major challenges that have threatened their financial stability and security. Various disasters, such as hurricanes, floods, droughts, fires, armed conflicts, and pandemics, have resulted in financial stress for some nonprofits and for influxes of donations for others. Most recently, the coronavirus disease 2019 (COVID-19) pandemic has had a significant impact on nonprofits' fundraising efforts. Moreover, major changes in federal tax laws enacted in 2017 have had a negative impact on some giving to nonprofits.

Because nonprofit organizations rely so heavily on fundraising to meet their budgetary demands, it is important for nonprofit leaders to understand the primary sources of contributions to nonprofits. Although the exact portions of the nonprofit contributions pie change slightly from year to year, and the dollar amounts change somewhat, the giving data from 2019 provide a picture that is essentially what has been true for many years, with only slight variations in percentages. The largest source of contributions to nonprofits, year after year, is giving by individuals, which in 2019 amounted to 69 percent ($309.66 billion). The next largest source of contributions, 17 percent ($75.69 billion), was from foundations. This was followed by 10 percent ($43.21 billion) from bequests, and 5 percent ($21.09 billion) from corporations (Giving USA, 2020, p. 22).

Given that bequests are really gifts from individuals that come as a result of will commitments and are realized after an individual's death, from a fundraising perspective it is important to combine contributions from individuals and bequests. When taken together, in 2019, 79 percent of all contributions to nonprofits essentially came from individuals. What should that tell us as we think about fundraising for nonprofits? I believe it tells us that the bulk of a nonprofit's fundraising efforts should focus on raising money from individuals.

> Because individuals provide such a high percentage of contributions to nonprofits, you would be wise to devote significant attention to developing effective strategies to attract and retain individual donors. At the same time, you should not ignore foundations and corporations. Although foundations and corporations provide a relatively small percentage of the overall support to nonprofits, they are nonetheless extremely important sources of revenue. (Edwards, 2020, p. 3)

Although contributions from individuals can take many forms—from small annual gifts to funds raised through special events, to major gifts, to bequests—these funds are often less restricted than funding from foundations and corporations, which typically provide more restricted kinds of gifts. Foundations and corporations generally earmark their funding for specific programs and activities; they less often give unrestricted funds or funds for endowments.

Over the past several decades, significant growth has occurred in the number and assets of foundations. This is a trend that began in the 1980s, when more than 3,000 foundations were created, each with assets of $1 million or more or annual grant budgets that exceeded $100,000. The total number of foundations has continued to increase in recent decades, from 66,398 in 2003 to 86,203 by 2016 (Statista, 2019a). As the number of foundations has increased, so too have their assets. The total assets of U.S. foundations increased from $467.34 billion in 2001 to $859.96 billion in 2015 (Statista, 2019b). By 2019, the total assets of foundations in the United States increased to more than $1 trillion, although the COVID-19 pandemic and the concomitant dramatic increase in the unemployment rate and decrease in the value of many stock portfolios will likely result in a slump in the growth of foundation assets for some period of time (DiMento, 2019). The previous increase in foundations' assets is the result of the combined effect of both more foundations being created and the rise in the value of their assets owing to increases in the value of stocks that make up their endowments.

Government support for many kinds of nonprofit activities continues a decline that began in the late 1990s as the federal government has sought to shift more responsibilities to the states. Now, both the federal government and the states are being confronted with major budget deficits that may well result in reductions in government-provided services at all levels. This trend is likely to result in increased demands for services from many nonprofits, particularly in the health and human services. There are also political pressures to reduce government support for many other kinds of nonprofits, from public radio and television to the arts.

Among other things, this combination of increasing demands for many services, coupled with decreasing support for government agencies to provide many of these services, has resulted in increasing use of purchase-of-service contracts between government agencies and nonprofits for the provision of various types of services the government is required to provide. However, whereas these purchase-of-service arrangements were once almost exclusively the province of nonprofit organizations, recent years have seen the government sometimes allowing for-profit organizations to compete for some grants and contracts. In addition, in recent years there has been an increase in government agencies outsourcing to for-profit entities to run prisons, homeless shelters, drug treatment programs, and so forth. This has put increased pressure on the budgets of some nonprofits. Because of the changing nature of government funding initiatives, many nonprofit organizations have learned that it can be a risky business to become too dependent on public funding. Thus, it is prudent for nonprofit organizations to give significant attention to generating financial support from private, nongovernmental sources.

To thrive in this changing environment, nonprofit organizations and their leaders and managers must take bold and creative steps to ensure that their planning, management, and fundraising activities are keeping in step with the times. Nonprofit organizations can no longer rely on one or two funding sources for their operational needs. The key to long-term financial stability is development of a sustaining and diverse funding base that includes individual, foundation, corporate, and, in some cases, government funders. Moreover, fundraising programs should be multifaceted and include an annual fund campaign, special events, and major gift solicitations based on sound prospect research, planned giving activities, and a strong marketing and public relations component. In the years ahead, the most successful nonprofits will be those that are best able to adjust to a global philanthropic environment that is increasingly made up of expanding opportunities and players and driven by new technologies.

For a nonprofit to be effective at fundraising, it cannot rely solely on donors' goodwill. In today's changing and competitive environment, nonprofits must earn the support of donors by clearly and assertively demonstrating the value of their products or services. To do so, nonprofits need to create ample giving opportunities that take advantage of new global thinking and technologies. This requires leadership to ensure that a nonprofit approaches fundraising in a strategic way that uses the management techniques of analysis, planning, and execution.

Nonprofit leaders need not be discouraged or fearful about the challenges of becoming successful fundraisers. Giving patterns over several decades show that philanthropy is alive and well. In 2019, private-sector giving to nonprofits reached $449.64 billion (Giving USA, 2020, p. 22). As this chapter was being written, however, the United States was grappling with the effects of the COVID-19 pandemic and its impact on the economy. In the winter and early spring of 2020, as the pandemic spread throughout the United States, the stock market plummeted and was characterized by significant volatility, and the unemployment rate skyrocketed. Both of these trends unquestionably had an impact on fundraising for nonprofits, as the value of individuals' and foundations' stock portfolios declined, and the disposable incomes of many Americans decreased. Yet, it is important to keep in mind that, in current dollars, total giving to nonprofits in the United States has increased every year since 1977, with the exception of 1987, 2008, and 2009. "The Great Recession ended in 2009. For the years 2009 to 2018, the growth in inflation-adjusted total giving is 33.0 percent" (Giving USA, 2019, p. 49).

It remains to be seen the extent to which, and for how long, the economic downturn and concomitant decline in the stock market in response to the COVID-19 pandemic will continue to affect giving to nonprofits. However, history suggests that as the economy recovers, giving to nonprofits will increase. There is no question that economic downturns and recessions have a negative impact on philanthropic giving to nonprofits for some period. This puts more financial pressure on nonprofits, which need to give even greater attention to developing multifaceted approaches to fundraising.

Shifting Demographics

Shifting demographics are affecting giving patterns. As Baby Boomers age into retirement, an enormous transfer of generational wealth is taking place. It is predicted that "due to the estimated $59 trillion transfer of wealth from older generations expected to take place in the coming years, members of Generation X and Millennials will be among the most significant philanthropists in history" (Giving USA, 2019, p. 92). Women; members of racial and ethnic minority groups; and the lesbian, gay, bisexual, transgender, and queer (LGBTQ) community are also increasingly involved in charitable giving (Giving USA, 2019, pp. 89–95).

An analysis of recent giving trends points to the need to focus greater attention in fundraising efforts on the cultivation of individuals while not neglecting attention to corporate or foundation donors. Therefore, to maximize the chances of success, nonprofits should pursue fundraising strategies that emphasize the cultivation of individual donors and pay particular attention to the needs and interests of nontraditional donors, such as women, members of various racial and ethnic groups, and LBGTQ persons. This approach will enhance a nonprofit's chances for success and place it ahead of many of its peer organizations.

E-Philanthropy

Suffice it to say, the years ahead promise challenges as well as opportunities for nonprofit leaders and their organizations. Perhaps as in no other time in history, the landscape of philanthropy is changing. Many new trends and forces are requiring nonprofits to consider different and creative ways to raise funds. One of the most significant is that new technologies are enabling new ways to give. An enormous surge in e-philanthropy activities and online giving began in the early 2000s, and from that point on, many Americans have changed how they engage in giving to nonprofits. According to *The Chronicle of Philanthropy's* sixth annual survey of online fundraising activity (Wallace, 2005), online donations soared in 2004, with many nonprofits receiving twice as much in donations as they did in 2003. In 2004, more than 174 organizations received $163.3 million in electronic gifts (Wallace, 2005). In 2019, the 13th annual Benchmarks Study, "which examine[d] donor engagement and giving patterns among a sample of 135 nonprofits for the year 2018 in comparison with 2017," found that in 2018, "there were more than 7 million online gifts totaling more than $376 million" (*Benchmarks,* 2019).

Clearly, Americans are increasingly comfortable with going to their computers and cell phones for information about and access to charitable opportunities. Consequently, to be successful in fundraising, nonprofits must increasingly be comfortable with and skilled in using online approaches. More and more nonprofits are using social media to reach, cultivate, and retain donors. In 2018, "for every 1000 email subscribers, nonprofits averaged 806 Facebook followers, 286 Twitter followers, and 101 Instagram followers" (Giving USA, 2019, p. 84).

Strategic Giving and Cause-Related Marketing

Other trends and social forces are also affecting the way in which nonprofits seek charitable dollars. The blurring of the traditional public versus private sectors is creating new partnership opportunities to link the missions of nonprofit organizations and profitmaking companies. A buzzword that emerged in the 1980s, "corporate social responsibility," is again on the rise, although in new forms, pushed forward by the success and progressive thinking of such models and product lines as Ben & Jerry's, Warby Parker, Bombas, Coca-Cola, Pepsi, Avon, IBM, and Johnson & Johnson (Edwards, 2020). For-profit companies increasingly give serious consideration to public perceptions of their charitable cultures and activities, an approach sometimes called "strategic giving." In fact, U.S. companies have been giving at historic levels in response to recent domestic and global disasters, including hurricanes, fires, earthquakes, epidemics, and pandemics, among other occurrences.

For-profit companies are more and more using what is known as cause-related marketing as a key component of their overall plan for strategic giving. *Cause-related marketing* is a form of partnership between for-profit companies and nonprofit organizations, "most often defined as the action through which a company and a nonprofit organization (or educational institution or similar entity) markets an image, a product, a service, or a message for the mutual benefit of both parties" (Hartnett & Matan, 2016). These partnership arrangements are also frequently referred to as "cause marketing," "social responsibility marketing," "joint promotional marketing," "joint venture marketing," or "public purpose marketing."

Although various definitions of *cause-related marketing* have been offered since American Express registered the term in the early 1980s, all definitions emphasize the establishment of relationships between corporations and nonprofits in which the former pursue marketing and promotional objectives and the latter pursue fundraising and public relations objectives (Edwards, 2020). Daw (2006) defined *cause marketing* as

> a corporate-nonprofit partnership that aligns the power of a company's brand, marketing and people with a cause's brand and assets to create shareholder and social value and to publicly communicate values. It is a mutually beneficial relationship where the sum of the two parts can be greater than the individual ones alone; where self-interest can be combined with altruism, marketing with philanthropy, awareness with fundraising, mission achievement with business objectives, cash support with in-kind leverage contributions—all in an effort to achieve mutual benefit. Above all, cause marketing is where purpose, passion, and profits meet in a productive, strategically aligned partnership. (p. xxvii)

At its core, cause-related marketing represents a mutually beneficial business and nonprofit partnership in which a for-profit company puts the power of its brand behind the cause to generate benefits, or profits, for both. In cause-related marketing, the company uses the cause as the focus of its marketing tactics (Waters, 2011). Many for-profit companies now partner with nonprofits in cause-related marketing ventures. The Starbucks *Fuel Our Diversity* and the Pepsi *One World Together* ventures are a couple of examples (O'Neill, 2020).

Fundraising and Taxes

Many people assume that all nonprofits operate in a federal tax-free environment, but that is not always the case. Some nonprofits also engage in a variety of income-generating activities as part of their overall fundraising efforts, such as selling various kinds of items or renting space to outside organizations. If these activities are not "inherently related to the causes they support . . . nonprofits can run into the often-misunderstood unrelated business income tax (UBIT)" (Provenza Law, 2018). Although the money a nonprofit raises to support its activities is generally not subject to federal income tax if it is a 501(c)(3) organization, there may be a tax liability "when a tax-exempt organization conducts an income generation activity that is not primarily related to their tax-exempt purpose. That revenue is called unrelated business income, and it is often subject to the business income tax" (Provenza Law, 2018). The IRS considers several factors in determining what part of a nonprofit's revenue may be subject to taxation, but a critical element for a nonprofit is that the activity is not substantially related to the organization's tax-exempt purpose. Whether something falls under the

UBIT can be complex and nuanced. For instance, "an art museum that sells prints of the artwork they display may find that those sales are not subject to the UBIT, but the gift shop sales of sweatshirts with the museum logo are" (Provenza Law, 2018). Because this issue is critical to a nonprofit's maintaining its 501(c)(3) status, it is important that it obtain good legal and accounting advice.

For those who have little experience in fundraising, it is helpful to keep in mind that fundraising is largely an art rather than a science. Although no specific formula will work for all nonprofits, this chapter addresses some time-tested strategies and tools that can help one get started. In addition, the chapter considers the multiple components and strategies that make up a good fundraising program, including prospect research and tracking, annual fund activities, and major gift cultivation. Issues to consider when launching a major campaign, such as internal and external readiness, are also discussed.

Fundraising Fundamentals

Nonprofit organizations sometimes lack the experience, expertise, and resources to build or fund an effective and comprehensive fundraising program. Some lack the financial capital needed to launch new or sustain tried-and-true efforts. Consequently, uninformed or piecemeal efforts to raise funds too often occur, and the result is poor financial returns. At worst, such efforts can cause loss of both revenue and organizational credibility. Failed fundraising attempts can be devastating to organizational morale and may sometimes cause nearly irreversible damage.

Therefore, to maximize chances for success, nonprofits should approach fundraising in a planned, strategic manner that places long-term benefit over short-term gain. Fundraising is best viewed as a multifaceted process that should result in a solid and lasting foundation for the organization. Not only will a successful fundraising program generate significant revenues, it will also increase the nonprofit's visibility and credibility and enhance broad-based community support for the programs and causes the organization espouses.

Multilayered Strategies

Unfortunately, some nonprofits still seek to meet their funding needs by using a single fundraising strategy. This often takes the shape of a direct-mail appeal, a membership drive, or an annual special event, such as a black-tie gala, golf outing, or benefit concert. Nonprofits often believe that simply doing more of the same—for example, sending mail appeals to more prospects or bolstering the invitation list to an annual event—will result in increased revenues. It is true that success breeds success, and the establishment of regular and predictable giving opportunities will likely produce an increase in donors and funds over time. However, it is highly unlikely that a single fundraising strategy will enable a nonprofit organization to make significant progress in generating support over time.

Worse, relying on a single strategy may place a nonprofit in an extremely vulnerable financial position. Media attention to various scandals involving such nonprofits as United Way of America (Dundjerski, 1995), the Wounded Warrior Project (Cahn, 2016), Oxfam Great Britain (Gayle, 2018), and the World Wildlife Foundation (McVeigh, 2019) led to significant declines in funding for those organizations and also had negative spillover effects for other nonprofits (Edwards, 2020). These and other similar instances demonstrate that public sentiment and support for an organization or cause can literally change overnight. Also, many unforeseen events can cause major problems if a nonprofit relies too heavily on a single approach to fundraising. For example, an adverse weather event can wipe out an evening gala or a golf outing after months of work. An economic downturn can dramatically affect a year-end funding appeal. Or, as many nonprofits experienced, occurrences such as the September 11, 2001, terrorist attacks; the Indian Ocean earthquake and tsunami; Hurricane Katrina; Superstorm Sandy; massive wildfires in California and Texas; or the economic fallout from the COVID-19 pandemic can result in funds that a nonprofit organization was counting on suddenly being diverted to another cause or drying up completely (Edwards, 2020, p. 136).

A multifaceted approach is critical to avoiding these vulnerabilities. A key goal of any good fundraising program is to identify and cultivate a diverse network of individual, foundation, and corporate donors, as well as to secure government grants and contracts when possible. Successful fundraising requires that multiple activities take place within each 12-month period, ideally including both annual giving activities and major gift work. While actively identifying, recruiting, and retaining a base of donors who make annual gifts, nonprofits also need to be engaged in the cultivation of major gifts, with approaches tailored to the unique characteristics of diverse donor groups.

Moreover, nonprofits must recognize the important role that a strong public relations program can play in enhancing fundraising success (O'Donnell, 2019). A focused, strategic, and multifaceted approach to spreading the word about the importance and success of a nonprofit's services or products can dramatically enhance its fundraising activities. A good fundraising program is one that maintains a strong base of annual donors through timely and frequent asks, steadily increases the giving level of annual donors, regularly brings in new donors from diverse donor groups, supports active and highly personal cultivation of major gift donors, and promotes a positive public image of the nonprofit organization.

Fundraising Staffing

Success in fundraising requires time, persistence, and the capacity to juggle both internal and external demands. It also requires that a nonprofit make a tangible and multiyear commitment of staff and funding resources to adequately support fundraising activities. Balancing the needs and interests of donors with those of a nonprofit is not easy and requires the involvement of top staff and volunteer leadership. Every organization is unique in the amount of time and resources that it can allocate to raise funds. Figure 4.1 captures, in a simple way, the essence of fundraising. Nonprofits must identify prospective donors who have the capacity to give, find ways to motivate them to give to the nonprofit organization or cause, and then provide them with opportunities to give. In other words, nonprofits need to identify individuals who have resources, find ways to involve them in the organization, and then ask them to contribute to the nonprofit in an appropriate manner and at an appropriate time.

Figure 4.1 Donor Giving Triangle

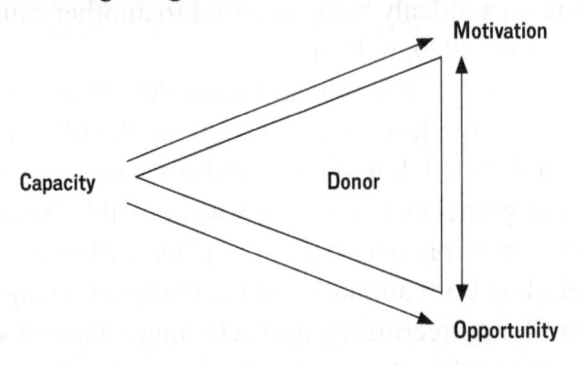

Because some nonprofits, particularly smaller or newer ones, may not have the resources to hire a professional fundraiser, the CEO, other senior managers, and key board members must often assume the fundraising role in addition to their other responsibilities. Although this arrangement may work well for some nonprofits, for others it creates an environment of competing values, roles, tasks, and time demands in which fundraising efforts may take a back seat to the other things that need to be done, with the result that little money is actually raised.

Whether a nonprofit allocates a percentage of a staff person's time to raising money or hires a full- or part-time development professional or group of professionals, a key to successful fundraising is that a clear commitment of resources be made. Although fundraising activities may depend heavily on volunteers, it is essential that staff time be clearly allocated for this purpose. Volunteers, particularly board members, are often eager to help with fundraising but may understandably lack important knowledge and skills. It is critical, therefore, for a nonprofit to designate or appoint a person who always has the big picture in mind, can readily respond to volunteers' concerns and questions, and can promptly provide material and other types of support.

Professional Standards

Fundraising success requires a commitment to the highest level of integrity and professionalism. The Association of Fundraising Professionals has established the AFP Code of Ethical Principles and, in conjunction with several other organizations, the Donor Bill of Rights (https://afpglobal.org/). Everyone in the nonprofit who will be involved with fundraising, including board members, should be familiar with these documents. The Association of Fundraising Professionals also offers valuable guidelines to nonprofit organizations on everything from IRS requirements for appropriate gift acknowledgments to the ethical rights of donors, to tips to prospective donors about issues to consider as they contemplate making a gift.

"One of the most important factors when potential donors make decisions to support your nonprofit organization is their sense of *trust* in the organization" (Edwards, 2020, p. 22). Give.org, which is a component of the Better Business Bureau, pointed out that "higher trust in charities translates to higher public engagement and confidence in giving" (Give.org, 2019, p. 3). To that end, Give.org publishes periodic assessments of charitable organizations that are based on 20 standards. Nonprofits may find these standards to be a useful template for judging how well they are structured for fundraising efforts. Accreditation by Give.org can also be explored; some research has suggested that nonprofits that meet all 20 standards have experienced an increase in their fundraising revenue, presumably at least in part because donors may have more confidence about giving to a nonprofit with such accreditation (Give.org, 2019, p. 3).

Strategies for Success

As previously mentioned, it is imperative to think of fundraising as a multifaceted process that involves engaging in numerous activities simultaneously. These activities minimally include annual fund appeals, major gift cultivation, and planned giving efforts. Planned giving strategies (i.e., securing commitments from donors to name the nonprofit in their wills or other estate plans), although not addressed in detail in this chapter, are increasingly important to nonprofits' long-term fundraising success. Fundraising efforts will succeed only if a nonprofit simultaneously engages in all three efforts.

Thorough and detailed prospect research and efficient tracking of prospect activities are essential to successful fundraising. The functions of prospect research and tracking should undergird all other activities. Without these functions, nonprofits will lack essential donor information to make thoughtful asks at the donor's giving capacity level, and they will have no system to record important steps (thus leaving no legacy for future efforts), which will diminish their overall fundraising potential.

Fundraising success requires the skills of a master juggler. The practice has little room for shortcuts. Every thoughtful and patient step taken in planning and execution enables a nonprofit to build a strong and lasting foundation of support.

Annual Fund Appeals and Creating a Culture of Giving

Annual fund activities are the bread and butter of a nonprofit organization's fundraising strategy. Most often taking the form of direct-mail appeals, annual events, telethons, or membership drives, annual appeals should

- establish a donor base that produces predictable annual income
- provide unrestricted cash support
- regularly generate new donors
- encourage the development of a culture of giving

Annual gifts typically result from a single ask. They are generally relatively small gifts, often ranging between $5 and $50 or $100, although sometimes higher, and they are usually given as cash. Direct-mail campaigns are by far the most common annual fund appeal method used by nonprofits.

Klein (2016) suggested that "direct mail remains the least expensive way an organization can reach the most people with a message they can hold in their hands and examine at their leisure" (p. 129). Traditionally, the term "direct mail" generally refers to what is sometimes called "snail mail," that is, letters sent through the U.S. Postal Service. Response rates and giving levels will vary on the basis of the strength of the association and donors' involvement with the nonprofit.

Unless a nonprofit has substantial money to invest in acquiring lists, mailing to a substantial number of people and cold prospects (i.e., individuals who have not previously been involved with the nonprofit) will likely have a very low rate of success. These kinds of mailings, often called "acquisition mailings," typically have response rates of 0.25 to 2 percent (Heyman & Brenner, 2016, p. 100). However, "mailings to past donors and individuals closely associated with your nonprofit, such as board members and volunteers, will typically produce much higher response rates than mailings to lapsed donors or 'cold' prospects" (Edwards, 2020, p. 43). These days, annual fund solicitations may take the form of email communications, the use of social network platforms, or a combination of the two. Moreover, annual fund solicitations are sometimes done via telephone calls or text messages. Any use of telephone calls, texts, emails, or other social networks is most effective when aimed at current or past donors, board members, volunteers, individuals who have previously attended one or more special fundraising events, or those who already have some connection to a nonprofit.

Annual fund success will be enhanced by efforts to personalize methods. For example, telethons will typically produce much higher participation and giving rates than will direct mail, and highly personalized appeals targeting an organization's board or key volunteers will likely show an even greater return. These days, most households are barraged daily or weekly by direct-mail requests and telephone solicitations. Therefore, creativity and thoughtfulness in approaching donors even for smaller gifts will be appreciated. Above all, personalize the approach as much as possible, carefully assessing donors' needs and interests, and express genuine appreciation for giving at all levels.

Culture of Giving

Success in annual fund efforts will be greatly enhanced if a nonprofit establishes a tangible culture of giving. Churches, synagogues, and other religious institutions are particularly adept at creating such a culture (Klein, 2016). Many factors come into play, but most important, religious organizations ask, and they do so regularly and frequently. Individuals are often brought up "passing the plate," a ritual that instills at a very young age the importance of giving. Giving is expected, participation or membership usually goes hand in hand with a financial pledge, and it is highly valued. Churches, synagogues, and other religious institutions have long known that good stewardship and accountability for expenditure of charitable dollars are critical to their fundraising success. It should come as no surprise that approximately 30 percent of all charitable dollars are given to religious organizations (Giving USA, 2020, p. 23).

A nonprofit can create a culture of giving by taking note of what works for religious entities. Ask, ask regularly, and provide feedback to donors about the impact of their gifts. Donors will tend to give, and give more generously, if they feel part of a culture in which giving is expressly valued, is an important expectation, and is rewarded with assurances of worth and accountability. Giving will be encouraged by an organization's credibility and success: Donors want to feel that their giving is a sound investment.

Motivation to Give

Gone are the days when giving was thought to be motivated solely by goodwill or charitable intent. Donors typically want to support a credible organization. At the same time, high-level donors claim that they most often give to express a belief in a specific cause or organizational mission. These donors clearly express interest in supporting organizations that are financially stable, value strong staff and board leadership, and are concerned with issues of community respect and organizational credibility.

Bray (2019) pointed out that donors

> give when they feel they will get something in return—in most cases, something that satisfies them on a deeply personal level. Although the giveaway baseball cap or coffee mug might tip the balance for a few, most are looking for something loftier, but no less tangible. (p. 74)

They want to feel good about themselves, they want to feel they are helping to solve a social, environmental, political, or medical problem they view as personally important to them or that has affected their family or friends, and they want to send a message about their beliefs.

Nonprofit fundraisers need to get to know their prospective donors, understand why they give, and recognize the complexity of reasons and motivations they may have for supporting various causes. Knowledge of one's prospective donors will enhance fundraising efforts, which can be more targeted, and success is more likely than with a scattershot or impersonal approach.

A successful annual fund program will not only ensure that a nonprofit has a strong base of operational support, it will also be the foundation on which to build major gift support for capital and other needs. Annual appeals will help a nonprofit identify potential major donors and pave the way for more intensive involvement between donors and the nonprofit. One major challenge nonprofits face is keeping annual fund support strong while at the same time garnering major gift support.

Cultivation of Major Gifts

Much has been written about cultivating major gifts and the importance of focusing energy and resources on donors with high giving potential and probability or a high motivation to give to a particular organization or cause (Edwards, 2020; Heyman, 2016; Klein, 2016; Shimer, 2017). Even if a nonprofit is not involved in a major or capital campaign, securing major gifts is a critical, ongoing component of all good fundraising programs. Although the amount that constitutes a major gift will vary from one organization to another and from one point in time to another, "the amount can depend on a number of factors: the size of your organization, the nature of the mission, the demographics of your donor population, and the variation of your funding sources" (Donor Perfect, 2019). Some nonprofits may consider $10,000 a major gift, whereas for others $100,000 or even more might be considered the threshold. Data from a recent study on major gift fundraising "revealed that while major gifts are a small percentage of the overall number of gifts a nonprofit received in a year, they add up to more than half of its annual revenue" (Donor Perfect, 2019).

Prospect Research

Major gift cultivation is best viewed as a series of thoughtful steps that begins with the identification of a potential donor and verification of that donor's giving capacity. This process applies to individual as well as foundation and corporate prospects. To ensure that time and energy are well spent on prospects who have clear giving capacity, fundraising programs must include a strong prospect research component (Edwards, 2020; Heyman, 2016; Klein, 2016). Prospect research can be as simple as seeking direct input from volunteers and board members about the giving habits of their neighbors and peers to using highly sophisticated data software designed to paint a picture of a person's wealth status.

Numerous print and online resources can be helpful, such as *Prospect Research for Fundraisers: The Essential Handbook* (Filla & Brown, 2013) and the *Who's Who* series by Marquis (https://www.marquiswhoswho.com). In addition, publications such as *The Chronicle of Philanthropy* can be useful. More useful resources with extensive information about foundation and corporate prospects are available through Candid (formed by a merger of The Foundation Center and GuideStar) (https://candid.org).

Extensive information can be obtained from company and foundation Web sites, as well as from a range of other entities that can be useful resources for nonprofits. Companies electronically file annual reports and other financial, employee, and trustee information (Edwards, 2020; Heyman, 2016). Quick access to this information via the Internet can translate into an enormous time savings for nonprofits.

Managers need not be intimidated by the continuous advancements in prospect research practice and technology. Although commonplace for most higher education fundraising units, sophisticated prospect research practices have not traditionally been part of the culture of many nonprofits. However, nonprofits can begin to gain valuable prospect information by closely following local and state charitable news and major business transactions and happenings. Many major newspapers now include regular columns devoted exclusively to local philanthropic activity, and many consulting firms publish state and local giving directories. Many states have resource organizations to assist nonprofits, and there are statewide publications that focus on philanthropy. Local foundations may also offer resource libraries to help nonprofits in their fundraising efforts. Most important, knowledge about income and asset wealth can often best be gathered through direct contact and involvement with the prospective donor. No generic publication can match the knowledge that can be gained from personal contacts.

The relatively simple process of identifying and qualifying wealthy people in the community will not bring about fundraising success. Once the giving capacity of potential donors is established, a nonprofit must do the hard work of determining whether a potential interest exists and whether this interest can be turned into tangible support. The process of turning suspects into viable prospects can in part be accomplished through good prospect research and major gift cultivation. When fundraisers have a reasonable estimate of an individual's wealth, or potential giving capacity, they should ask themselves why that individual or family unit would be interested in donating to the organization and what might help bring the individual or family closer to it. The cultivation strategy should match the potential donor's interests and passions. For example, does the nonprofit deal with issues such as child abuse or domestic violence, animal welfare, or visual arts or theater? Is there a record of the potential donor's interest in the nonprofit's area? Connect what the nonprofit does with the potential donor's interests and seek ways to get the potential donor increasingly involved with the organization.

Personal Contact

Successful major gift work requires intensive and highly personal contacts with potential donors over a long time, often over many years. In contrast to unrestricted annual giving, high-level or major giving is usually designated to support a particular need or program and often represents a commitment of assets rather than income. At the center of successful major gift work is a well-nurtured relationship that is beneficial to both the donor and the recipient organization. The key to such meaningful relationships is developing and implementing highly personalized cultivation plans. Such plans should include frequent, meaningful opportunities for the prospect to learn about the nonprofit and for you and others in the organization to learn about the potential donor. Find out about hobbies and talents, arrange for fun and educational exchanges, and seek advice on their areas of expertise. In major gift cultivation, it is important to consider each meeting with a prospect an opportunity for meaningful cultivation and acknowledgment. As part of a cultivation plan, fundraisers might consider doing the following (Edwards, 2020):

- Arrange a personal visit from the executive director or board president.
- Send a stewardship report on the impact of past giving.
- Seek advice from the prospect on their area of expertise.
- Involve the prospect in cultivating others.
- Honor the prospect with awards and special recognition.
- Send personal congratulations on birthdays, anniversaries, and promotions.
- Seek input on developing the organization's case for support.
- Recruit the prospect to serve in a key role at a special event.
- Invite the prospect to do a workshop for staff on a subject about which they have expertise.

- Invite the prospect to serve on the board of directors or trustees or an advisory board or committee.
- Communicate regularly with annual reports, brochures, and speech reprints.
- Send frequent personal notes about items and events of interest.

In fundraising parlance, steps in the process are called "cultivation moves," and these moves should be part of a clear plan that has specific goals. In fundraising, one must always have the next step in mind. Often, it is useful to discuss the organization's goal with a prospective donor in advance of a meeting or cultivation move. It is perfectly acceptable, and often helpful, to say directly that the organization will not be asking for a gift at this time but rather is seeking advice or involvement in another capacity. Donors will appreciate knowing the organization's intentions and will likely be more willing to participate in a multitude of activities. Ideally, cultivation plans will be so carefully constructed that managers and prospects will always know what comes next. Before leaving a visit with a potential donor, discuss what follow-up steps are needed and agree on a clear timeline. Then, as important to the nonprofit organization as the cultivation move itself, all donor activities and progress should be documented. This step should be part of a consistent and detailed system of prospect tracking.

Documentation

It is essential that the nonprofit establish clear procedures to document all prospect-related activities and contacts. Failure to keep adequate records can result not only in a poor transfer of knowledge but also in a loss of funds or possibly negative audit reports. Although many software programs exist to manage donor information, and information about them is widely available online, some new or small nonprofits can initially get by with a paper or computerized system that uses two simple forms and a good tickler file.

First, use a form that enables the nonprofit to maintain a continually updated record of basic biographical information on each prospect, including such categories as home and work addresses, telephone numbers, email addresses, family composition, religious affiliation, hobbies and special interests, and community service activities. The form should also include information on the nature of the prospect's association with the nonprofit, information on past giving to the nonprofit and others (if known), estimated income level and known assets, anticipated giving level, preferences on how and when to contact, and important peer relationships.

Second, use a form to document actual contacts. The type of contact, who made the contact, what was discussed, the outcome of the contact, and next steps to be taken should all be carefully recorded.

Finally, institute a tickler file system for donors' and prospects' birthdays, special occasions, and other significant dates. Of course, also maintain files of all original correspondence received as well as copies of everything sent to prospects or donors.

Keeping track of all aspects of fundraising efforts and contacts with prospects and donors is critical.

> Failure to keep adequate records that document the events and milestones in the life of an organization is a common problem for nonprofits. With respect to donor relations, adequate, comprehensive record keeping is essential. Failure to do so can result in lack of service continuity, poor transfer of knowledge, public relations nightmares, and loss of potential financial support. (Edwards, 2020, p. 101)

Nonprofits typically find that it is important to invest in a comprehensive donor management software package. Many commercially available packages are very user friendly and will enable users to document all prospect-related information, activities, and contacts. A web search for "nonprofit donor management systems" will yield many examples one can investigate.

Remember that it takes time for a nonprofit to become an important giving priority for a prospect. It is often a good strategy to ask potential donors directly what it would take for the nonprofit to become their top charitable priority. Take cues from donors. Like most relationships, much of major gift cultivation is intuitive, and success is ultimately based on the quality of the relationships one builds with donors over time. "Donors who are engaged and treated well can become life-long supporters. They also can be great sources of new donors by connecting you to others" (Heyman, 2016, p. 88).

Making the Ask

If an organization's cultivation plans are effective, making the major gift ask can be the easy part. It is usually important to ask for a specific amount for a specific program or need. It may be useful to start with a gift range and a couple of program options. However, if donor capacity, giving intent, and interest in the organization is well established, it is often better to ask for a specific amount. The major gift ask is typically done by the staff member or volunteer with the closest relationship to the donor. Often, however, involvement by a peer or high-level staff or board member is essential. With individual prospects, the solicitation is almost always done face to face, with a supplementary written proposal available. Corporate and foundation solicitations will vary widely according to proposal guidelines but more often require written requests or proposals.

Because major gifts often come in the form of a pledge that is paid out over a period of years, it is a good idea to prepare a simple pledge letter or letter of intent with a blank space for a signature, gift amount, and payout wishes. If possible, attempt to close the gift during a face-to-face meeting; that is, get the commitment in writing on the day of the solicitation. If this is not possible, a pledge letter sent immediately after the visit may suffice.

What should one do when a prospect says no? The best way to handle an objection or an unwillingness to make a commitment is to determine the nature of the problem. Has an appropriate ask level been determined? Is the timing right? Has an appropriate environment in which to make the ask been arranged, or are there distractions? Is the nature of the objection a result of a simple misunderstanding? Attempt to get to the root of the objection and address any issues or problems directly and honestly. The objection may be easily resolved, or the manager may need follow-up steps. The organization may also need to settle for a gift amount that is less than what was hoped. In any case, remember that all gifts at all levels are important, that all prospects and donors should be valued and respected, and that everything an organization does lays the groundwork for the next potential gift.

Two schools of thought exist about closing a gift that is believed to be less than what the donor can give. The first is that it is important to take small steps, to close gifts early in the cultivation process, and to settle for gift levels that are less than a prospect's capacity. The theory behind this approach is that giving encourages more giving, and as a result, the prospect will develop a stronger connection with the organization and continue to give and do so at higher levels as the prospect's involvement increases. The second school of thought is based on the notion that one cannot leap a canyon by taking baby steps. That is, one should cultivate, cultivate, cultivate until the prospect is motivated and likely to give at their capacity level. This theory is based on the notion that getting a donor to give at their capacity level requires patience and operates on the belief that smaller-level gifts solicited during the cultivation process may discourage the prospect from ultimately making a much larger one.

A good fundraiser is keenly aware of both scenarios and will tailor solicitation decisions on the basis of each potential donor's individual characteristics. It is often important to solicit early and lower-level gifts from major prospects to create momentum, encourage others, and cement interest. Giving begets giving, and one will rarely, if ever, diminish the organization's overall fundraising potential by making multiple asks. However, it is important to always maintain a focus on capacity giving and work to raise prospects' giving sights by making it clear that the organization is counting on them to be leaders. Strategic and goal-oriented cultivation is essential to instill such a level of commitment and participation.

Good major gift work requires taking appropriate steps to identify potential donors, gathering useful information about giving capacity, establishing that a viable interest in the organization exists, and engaging the prospect in meaningful involvement over time. The process then requires thoughtful and timely solicitation with the goal of long-term potential benefits. This process is the central component of any good and comprehensive fundraising program.

In today's environment, the most successful nonprofit leaders are those who are willing to take risks or think outside the box. Leaders should keep in mind that people do not give to them, they give through them. Nonprofits should think of themselves as an investment vehicle through which donors can help solve problems and community challenges and enrich life experiences (Heyman, 2016, p. 80).

Major gift work can be as tiring as it is exhilarating and as frustrating as it is rewarding. The dynamic and personal nature of major gift cultivation makes it challenging for even seasoned fundraising professionals to set aside personal feelings. For example, it is difficult not to feel personally rejected when a request is declined or not to feel personally responsible for unhappiness expressed by a donor with whom one has had a long-term relationship. However, because of the intensely personal nature of the donor relationship, sincere and lasting relationships often result. For a fundraiser who has adhered without fail to the highest standards of integrity and professional behavior, this can be major gift work's greatest reward.

Launching a Capital Campaign

One of the most important decisions a nonprofit organization will make is whether to embark on a major fundraising campaign, often called a "capital campaign." It seems today that almost every nonprofit is in the business of planning, executing, or closing a major campaign effort. Successful major campaigns can generate significant resources and, in some cases, produce the added benefit of bringing unprecedented attention to an issue or cause. However, do not be fooled by the perception that everyone is doing it and doing it well. Nonprofits often embark on campaigns with little planning or with no hands-on experience or expertise. They may fail to recognize the importance of considering many readiness factors that are both internal and external to the organization. Poorly conceived and organized campaign efforts can be devastating to staff and board morale. Worse, they can cause loss of organizational stability and credibility. Campaign planning and execution is tough work and requires special skills and knowledge.

A major or capital campaign is most often undertaken to raise a substantial amount of funding for a particular purpose or set of purposes. This might be raising funds for construction or renovation of a facility or summer camp, for scholarships, or for the purchase of major pieces of art by a gallery, but it is not for raising money for the nonprofit's general operating budget. Most often, a major campaign will extend over a period of many months; frequently, it will extend over several years.

Board Roles and Responsibilities

As a first step, consider the extent to which the nonprofit is internally prepared to launch a campaign. Is the current membership of the board of directors, or trustees, adequate to support a significant campaign effort? Ideally, the board should include members who represent the three Ws: wisdom, wealth, and workers. In other words, the board needs wise people, those with some financial resources, and those who are willing to pitch in and do the hard work necessary for successful governance and effective fundraising. A nonprofit is fortunate if it has individuals who embody all three Ws; realistically, individual board and volunteer leaders will more often embody one or two of these characteristics. Keep in mind the following primary responsibilities of board members (DeWitt, 2011, pp. 139–140):

- Policymaker: They must ensure that plans and programs are within the scope of the nonprofit's mission.
- Steward: They must ensure that the nonprofit exhibits sound business management principles and that the fiscal management is sound.
- Ambassador: They play key roles in interpreting the nonprofit and its programs to the larger community and to prospective donors.
- Builder: They are responsible for building and sustaining the nonprofit's fundraising program, ensuring its long-term ability to have resources to fund its programs and fulfill its mission.

To increase the chances for success, consider the following steps in advance of a major campaign (Edwards, 2020):

- Recruit at least one attorney and one accountant to the board to provide guidance on charitable tax law issues, deferred giving, and the appropriate handling of gifts other than cash, such as securities and property.
- Be sure that the board includes at least one representative from the local business community.
- If possible, recruit at least one highly recognizable and widely esteemed individual to the board (that is, someone such as a top-level business executive, local television or radio personality, well-known athlete, or the spouse of such a prominent person).
- Be certain that the board includes several "worker bees"—individuals who are willing to do the hard and sometimes not-so-glamorous work of fundraising, such as making telephone calls and visits, hosting gatherings, and stuffing envelopes.
- If possible, recruit at least a few individuals to the board who have wealth, can identify a peer group of other wealthy individuals whom they would be willing to contact, and who would be willing to go public with their giving.
- Include on the board someone connected to the print or broadcast media, such as an editor, news reporter or features writer, television reporter or anchor, or someone strong in public relations.
- Make sure that the composition of the board reflects the community served in terms of gender, race, ethnicity, and socioeconomic status.

Leadership Structure and Strategies

A second important step in preparing a nonprofit for a major campaign is to create a leadership structure that extends beyond its staff and board members. Many nonprofits form a time-limited fundraising advisory or steering committee. Others organize the board and other volunteer leaders into committees or task forces around specific campaign objectives. For example, one group may be responsible for cultivating and closing leadership gifts and another for the continuing success of annual fund activities. Another may address the publications, public relations, and media needs of the nonprofit during the campaign period. The key to success in developing new leadership structures is recruiting individuals who are knowledgeable about fundraising, are highly committed to the organization and cause, and are willing to work. Also key is establishing clear and highly specific objectives for volunteers. It is important to set volunteers up for success.

A major campaign effort can be strengthened by the short-term involvement of individuals who are considered high-level business and community leaders and are peers to major gift prospects and donors. Do not ask these individuals to be your worker bees. Rather, ask for their guidance and participation in learning about and contacting major gift prospects. Very busy individuals may agree to serve in name only to enhance the nonprofit's credibility and visibility; others may be willing to chair a special event, accompany staff on prospect calls, or sign a solicitation letter. Provide a specific timeline to achieve campaign objectives, and stick to it. Respecting the multitude of demands on such individuals will have enormous payoff. A creative option to involve individuals who want to support the campaign but who cannot commit their time is to formulate a document of endorsement and secure their signatures. This document can be an invaluable addition to a case statement or funding proposal.

Prelaunch Readiness

Before launching a major campaign, it is essential that leadership staff, volunteers, board members, and other constituents agree about funding needs and strategies. Nothing is more deadly to a campaign than disparate goals and solicitation attempts. Good campaign planning requires that an organization review its mission, take stock of personnel strengths and weaknesses (both staff and volunteer), and clearly determine the community impact of a campaign in terms of service and possible detriments.

Major campaigns, like fundraising activities in general, are very labor intensive and can lead to staff and volunteer burnout. However, they can invigorate an organization and dramatically increase community awareness and support. A nonprofit will be well positioned to succeed if it begins a fundraising campaign with a healthy internal environment—that is, an environment marked by staff and board cohesion, fundraising knowledge, a deep understanding of mission and goals, a clear division of labor, and enthusiasm.

In determining a nonprofit's readiness to launch a campaign, it is also advisable to assess whether the external environment is likely to be conducive. In examining the external environment, consider the following questions:

- What is the current climate of giving in the community and state?

- What other similar organizations are embarking on major campaigns, and with what success?
- Does the nonprofit represent a hot or cold issue?
- Will the current political and economic environment support or hinder the campaign?
- What is the nonprofit's public image?
- Has an adequate prospect base been identified and determined to have a sufficient interest level?
- What are the consequences, both internally and externally, if the nonprofit undertakes a fundraising campaign and fails to meet its goals?

Assessing the external environment for successful fundraising can sometimes be difficult, particularly if a nonprofit has little or no campaign experience. That is why experts suggest that a strong marketing and public relations program accompany fundraising efforts.

> There is an old saying in development that you can have a marketing program without fundraising, but you cannot have a fundraising program without marketing. . . . You must tell your organization's story to those who should care about your program and services to gain their understanding, acceptance, appreciation—and support—of your work. (DeWitt, 2011, p. 33)

Research has shown that people respond to issues, not organizations, and that issue-oriented public relations will strengthen fundraising potential. According to Harrison (1991), "Positioning an organization as an authority on an issue, and as an important part of the solution to the problem, can build tremendous credibility for the organization" (p. 22). Increasing a nonprofit's public visibility, its success in attracting positive media coverage, and its capacity to position itself as part of the solution are essential elements in enhancing fundraising success and preparing for a campaign.

Goal Setting and the Campaign Process

Setting an ambitious yet realistic goal for a major campaign is an important task. A nonprofit will be much better positioned to determine such a goal if the top-level management and board leadership have completed a comprehensive planning process that considers issues of internal and external readiness and establishes clear procedures and personnel structures to cover campaign duties.

Determining a major campaign goal requires some homework. Take a close look at past and current donors, particularly major gift donors, and assess the level of support the organization is likely to secure from this group of known supporters. Begin to develop expanded prospect lists using good prospect research strategies, keeping in mind that this list should include a broad base of individual and corporate, government, and foundation prospects. It may be helpful to establish a simple rating system that considers both giving capacity and the level of giving that will likely be secured.

Perhaps the most useful tool in determining a feasible goal is the widely accepted gift pyramid. Based on fundraising's rule of thirds, the gift pyramid suggests that at least one-third of the goal, and often significantly more, will come from an organization's top 10 to 15 gifts; another one-third of the goal will come from the next 25 or so gifts; and the remaining one-third will come from all other gifts. Using the rule of thirds, a gift pyramid with a goal of $100,000 might look something like Table 4.1.

Table 4.1 Gift Pyramid for $100,000 Goal

Gift Level	Gifts Needed	Prospects Needed	Total ($)
Top Third			
10,000	2	6–8	20,000
5,000	5	15–20	25,000
			45,000
Middle Third			
1,000	12	36–48	12,000
500	15	45–60	7,500
			19,500
Bottom Third			
200	75	225–300	15,000
<200	Numerous	Numerous	20,500
			35,500
Grand total			100,000

It has repeatedly been shown that simple average-numbers reasoning—that is, "if we can just get 100 people to give us $1,000 each"—does not work. Such reasoning actually depresses overall giving by flattening giving levels, and it falsely assumes that a single strategy or ask level will appeal to all donors. Moreover, this approach will, in some instances—perhaps many—result in getting lower-level gifts from donors who have the capacity to give more and might be convinced to do so. The gift pyramid is a reminder of the critical importance of directing time and energy at securing leadership gifts. Success in securing the top 10–15 gifts will likely determine the overall success of a campaign. However, nonprofits must understand that for each gift they are able to close, they will likely need three to four qualified prospects; that is, individuals who are believed to have the capacity to give at a particular level and who are likely to be motivated to give to the organization.

Gift pyramids are especially useful for organizations that have no past campaign experience. The exercise of developing a pyramid and identifying and qualifying actual prospects is extremely useful in determining the feasibility of a campaign goal. Gift pyramids are also a reminder that campaign fundraising should follow a specific sequence of activities. All thoughtfully executed campaigns will begin with a quiet phase that focuses on closing leadership gifts, those in the top third of the pyramid. This is a nonpublic phase that typically helps to validate campaign objectives and protects an organization from the embarrassment of failing to meet a publicized goal. As a general rule, it is advisable not to go public with a campaign until the nonprofit has received commitments for 50 percent or more of its goal.

The campaign process should begin with and focus on the cultivation of leadership gifts, and over time it should move toward securing lower-level gifts. Experience shows that securing leadership gifts is essential to campaign success. Do that first, and do it well. Success will also depend on the diversity and appropriateness of cultivation and solicitation strategies for all levels of donors, the effectiveness of the nonprofit's staff and volunteers, and the organization's capacity to generate strong public interest and support. Do not sacrifice annual giving activities, special events, and other types of fund solicitations during a campaign. The momentum and positive public relations that can be generated from a campaign often have a positive impact on annual giving.

Major, time-limited campaigns can significantly boost a nonprofit's resources, but it is important to keep in mind the necessity of building long-term major gift capacity. Major campaigns can be effective stepping stones to building stronger annual giving programs, and they can help nonprofits' donors develop giving habits that lead to sustained higher levels of support. Building a strong and lasting foundation of support requires nonprofit managers to place a high priority on long-term benefits that can accrue to an organization from a well-planned, multifaceted fundraising strategy.

Stewardship

Stewardship is a critical component of fundraising. In its simplest form, stewardship means saying thank you. The importance of this cannot be stressed enough. As Klein (2016) suggested, "People need to be appreciated . . . gifts should be acknowledged promptly—ideally within three days of receipt, and certainly within a week in any circumstance" (pp. 67–68). Heyman (2016) urged fundraisers to always keep in mind that

> it's much easier to keep an existing donor than bring on a new one! Donor retention is much higher among repeat donors than with first-time donors. . . . Thank your donors at least three times a year and give them at least quarterly updates on the impact their gifts are making possible. (p. 93)

A Final Thought

Nonprofits should have three goals for each of their donors (Klein, 2016). First, you want each donor to become a thoughtful donor, one who supports the nonprofit on an annual basis with the largest gift they can afford. Second, you want each donor to continue to support the nonprofit over time and make increasingly larger gifts as time goes by and their resources permit. Third, you want each donor to remember the organization in their will or make some arrangement benefiting the nonprofit from their estate. Although it is not likely each of an organization's donors will be able to do all of these things, they should be goals for each donor, and each should be treated accordingly.

Skills Application Exercises

1. Considering your organization or another nonprofit with which you are familiar, set a goal for a campaign and then create a gift pyramid related to that goal. How many upper-level donors will you need? Is that goal currently realistic for your nonprofit?
2. Analyze the culture of giving in your nonprofit. How would you create or enhance the organization's culture of giving?
3. Develop a cultivation plan for two or three major gift prospects. What are the key steps you need to take to bring those prospects closer to your nonprofit and the work it does?

References

Benchmarks. (2019, April 25). Washington, DC: M+R. Retrieved from https://www.mrbenchmarks.com

Bray, I. (2019). *Effective fundraising for nonprofits—Real-world strategies that work.* Berkeley, CA: Nolo.

Cahn, D. (2016, December 31). Wounded Warrior Project faces tough choices as it rebuilds following controversy. *Stars and Stripes.* Retrieved from https://www.stripes.com/news/wounded-warrior-project-faces-tough-choices-as-it-rebuilds-following-controversy-1.446785

Daw, J. (2006). *Cause marketing for nonprofits.* Hoboken, NJ: Wiley.

DeWitt, B. M. (2011). *The nonprofit development companion.* Hoboken, NJ: Wiley.

DiMento, M. (2019, August 19). Foundation assets top $1 billion, but signs point to slump. *Chronicle of Philanthropy.* Retrieved from https://www.philanthropy.com/article/foundation-assets-top-1-trillion-but-signs-point-to-slump/

Donor Perfect. (2019). *How to discover and engage major donors—3 ways to manage and grow major donor relationships.* Retrieved from https://www.donorperfect.com

Dundjerski, M. (1995, September 7). United Way: 1% increase in gifts. *Chronicle of Philanthropy,* pp. 27–29.

Edwards, R. L. (2020). *Building a strong foundation: Fundraising for nonprofits* (2nd ed.). Washington, DC: NASW Press.

Filla, J. J., & Brown, H. E. (2013). *Prospect research for fundraisers: The essential handbook.* Hoboken, NJ: Wiley.

Gayle, D. (2018, June 15). *Timeline: Oxfam sexual assault scandal in Haiti.* Retrieved from https://www.theguardian.com/world/2018/jun/15/timeline-oxfam-sexual-exploitation-scandal-in-haiti

Give.org. (2019). *2019 Give.org donor trust report: State of public trust in the charitable sector.* Arlington, VA: Author.

Giving USA. (2019). *Giving USA: The annual report on philanthropy for the year 2018.* Chicago: Giving USA Foundation.

Giving USA. (2020). *Giving USA: The annual report on philanthropy for the year 2019.* Chicago: Giving USA Foundation.

Harrison, T. A. (1991, March/April). Six PR trends that will shape your future. *Nonprofit World,* pp. 21–23.

Hartnett, B., & Matan, R. (2016). *Making the case for cause marketing: Impact on the for-profit and nonprofit communities.* Livingston, NJ: Sobel & Co.

Heyman, D. R., & Brenner, L. (2016). *Nonprofit fundraising 101*. Hoboken, NJ: Wiley.

Klein, K. (2016). *Fundraising for social change* (7th ed.). Hoboken, NJ: Wiley.

McVeigh, K. (2019, March 4). WWF accused of funding guards who tortured and killed scores of people. *Guardian*. Retrieved from https://www.theguardian.com/global-development/2019/mar/04/wwf-accused-of-funding-guards-who-allegedly-tortured-killed-scores-of-people

O'Donnell, K. (2019, September 26). *What donors really want: Why nonprofits should embrace a marketing mindset for fundraising*. Retrieved from https://learn.networkforgood.com/20190926-webinar-why-nonprofits-should-embrace-a-marketing-mindset.html

O'Neill, M. (2020, November 11). *Cause-related marketing: The best and worst examples we've seen*. Retrieved from https://www.brafton.com/blog/content-marketing/cause-related-marketing/

Provenza Law. (2018, January 2). *What are some examples of unrelated business income?* Retrieved from https://www.provenzalaw.com/blog/what-are-some-examples-of-unrelated-business-income

Shimer, J. (2017). *Show me the big money*. Bothell, WA: Book Publishers Network.

Statista. (2019a, June 20). *Number of foundations in the United States from 1990 to 2015*. Retrieved from https://www.statista.com/statistics/250878/number-of-foundations-in-the-united-states/

Statista. (2019b, June). *Total assets of foundations in the United States from 2001 to 2015*. Retrieved from https://www.statista.com/statistics/250883/total-assets-of-foundations-in-the-united-states/

Wallace, N. (2005, June 9). A surge in online giving. *The Chronicle of Philanthropy*, pp. 7–12.

Waters, J. (2011, April 27). *Cause marketing vs. sponsorship—What's the difference?* Retrieved from https://www.selfishgiving.com/blog/cause-marketing-101/cause-marketing-vs-sponsorship-whats-difference

PART THREE

Human Relations Skills

IN THE COMPETING VALUES FRAMEWORK, MANAGERIAL HUMAN RELATIONS skills are posited as those that encompass the roles of mentor and facilitator. Competencies related to the mentor role include an understanding of self and others, good interpersonal communications skills, and the ability to aid subordinates in their development as productive employees. Among the competencies related to the facilitator role are team building, participatory decision making, and conflict management. The chapters in this section provide guidance on developing the knowledge bases and abilities in relation to these roles and competencies to become an effective nonprofit manager.

In chapter 5, Kimberly Strom provides a comprehensive overview of issues that are critical to the effective management of the people in a nonprofit organization (that is, human relations skills). She points out that human resource (HR) management involves all of the choices and actions that take place in the life of the nonprofit organization's employees, including job design; recruitment and selection; compensation and benefits; performance appraisal; employee support and discipline; and employee separations, including terminations, downsizing, layoffs, furloughs, and retirements. Strom contends that the effective management of these matters is crucial in terms of both having a competent, motivated workforce and avoiding the serious legal ramifications that can result from ineffective management of HR concerns.

In chapter 6, Alena C. Hampton, Amy J. Armstrong, and Susan L. Parish stress the importance of having a workforce that is made up of a diverse range of people representing a variety of cultural, ethnic, linguistic, and racial backgrounds. They consider diversity in its broadest sense, indicating that diversity refers to lived experiences along dimensions including gender, age, sexual orientation, race, ethnicity, socioeconomic status, cultural background, religious beliefs, and disability identity. However, they point out that a nonprofit organization should go beyond a focus on diversity and embrace serious consideration of issues of equity and inclusion as well. They also consider implications of several major demographic changes that are well underway in the United States and will continue to shape the workforce for many decades to come, and they discuss managerial and supervisory responsibilities to foster a culture that values diversity, equity, and inclusion and the importance of communicating this commitment to the nonprofit's various stakeholders.

In chapter 7, John E. Tropman proposes ways in which nonprofit managers can improve the decisions made in their organizations by involving groups such as internal work groups and committees as well as the organization's board of directors in the process. He discusses the following components: management of the decision process, management of decision rules, and management of decision results. Tropman identifies "meeting masters": managers who are adept at structuring meetings of boards, committees, and other work groups so that time is used wisely and important decisions are made with maximum input from all concerned.

5

Managing Human Resources and Personnel Practices in Nonprofit Organizations

Kimberly Strom

Even with the ascendance of technology, most services in nonprofit settings are coordinated and delivered by human beings. In contrast to manufacturing sectors, in which equipment is a major cost of producing and delivering goods, the greatest costs for nonprofit organizations are their human resources (HR). Administering this element of the organization is complex. Nonprofit leaders and their HR managers must continually negotiate the tensions of efficiency and equity in carrying out their functions, maximizing productivity while minimizing costs, and using fair and respectful personnel procedures. Leaders in nonprofits must also be alert to the laws and regulations that govern their tasks and the vast knowledge base that accompanies various personnel processes.

HR management involves all of the choices and actions that take place in the life of an organization's employees, including job design; recruitment and selection; compensation and benefits; performance appraisal; employee support and discipline; and employee separations, including terminations, downsizing, and retirements. In large nonprofit organizations, specific units are dedicated to each function. In smaller nonprofits, generalists may be responsible for the entire scope of HR activities, calling on consultants or advisors as needed for specialized expertise. In both settings, HR personnel play a key role in creating policies and procedures to ensure that the organization is competitive with similar employers and compliant with regulations. HR managers also play an important advisory role with supervisors, particularly with respect to issues of fair employment practices, due process in disciplinary matters, and workplace safety. HR managers must have an understanding of the entire spectrum of personnel matters to ensure that personnel policies and practices are consistent with each other and responsive to the changing business environment.

This chapter describes the context in which HR leaders function and in which HR decisions are made. It then orients readers to five core areas of HR activity, the scope of activities in those areas, and the key concepts for effective practice in those areas.

Domain of Human Resources Management: A Competing-Values Perspective

Decisions about managing an organization's workforce take place in the context of organizational (or internal) factors and environmental (or external) factors. To advance the organization's mission, effective HR decisions must be congruent with one another and with other organizational units, such as operations and finance. HR professionals must be alert to changes in the service and regulatory environments so that practices comply with the law and respond to emerging societal trends. Effective leaders must stay abreast of the ways in which technological advances affect job functions, improve efficiency, increase costs, and influence all aspects of personnel management.

Internal Influences

The organization's mission and practice domain provide the starting place for HR decisions (Macaleer & Shannon, 2003). These factors shape how services are delivered and, thus, the kinds of jobs that need to be created and the types of employees needed to fill them. For example, a residential treatment program will need personnel around the clock and, for safety and client service reasons, may need at least two staff persons on site at all times. A mental health crisis unit will need to have staff available or on call who have the expertise and credentials to evaluate and respond to an array of psychiatric emergencies. A faith-based program for former prisoners re-entering the community might rely on volunteers and case managers to provide some services but also will link clients to the array of services that they will need on release. A nonprofit museum or art gallery might need a range of personnel, including security guards and docents, in addition to the typical range of management and administrative personnel needed by most other types of nonprofit.

Changes in the practice domain, such as the increase in integrated care, remote working, and online service provision, affect the types of employees needed by various types of nonprofit and the ways their jobs are configured. Emerging issues and strategic objectives will also influence HR decisions. For example, quarantine rules during the outbreak of the coronavirus disease 2019 (COVID-19) pandemic broke down physical barriers, opening the workforce to people with the proper capacities and Internet access, regardless of their geographic location. An emergent awareness of institutional biases in education and achievement has affected the way organizations think about the qualifications necessary for particular jobs. Increased workplace pressures have called attention to the need to modify or redesign jobs to reduce stress and burnout. Strategic objectives involving innovation and creativity will lead to diversification of the workforce and new reward systems, among other changes (Denhardt, Denhardt, Aristigueta, & Rawlings, 2020).

Few nonprofit managers start an organization from scratch, so they tend to view service and staffing patterns as relatively fixed. Effective HR, though, requires managers to step back from the way things are done and think about how services are provided, jobs are constructed, and tasks are assigned and the ways in which these variables might be most effectively combined (Capelli et al., 2018; Cohen, 2002). This assessment ensures that the organization has the right number of workers with the appropriate qualities and qualifications needed to carry out the agency's functions in anticipation of changing conditions in the practice environment. Two specific concepts apply here: job analysis and job design. "Job analysis" refers to a systematic process of collecting data and making judgments about the nature of a specific job (for example, a job's content, duties, tasks, behaviors, functions, and responsibilities). Job analysis provides data for job design.

"Job design" is more all-encompassing, integrating work content, qualifications, and rewards for each job in a way that meets the needs of employees and the organization (Denhardt et al., 2020). It looks at alternate ways in which the facets of jobs can be arranged. In practice, this may mean that roles that formerly encompassed a wide variety of responsibilities are restructured to be more specialized, or, in a growing nonprofit organization, it may mean that the executive director's job spins off HR or finance tasks into two new positions. Leaders with expertise in HR can help organizations and their leaders and managers think creatively about how to organize services and personnel to best meet the organization's objectives.

Another internal consideration for HR is the organization's financial well-being. This affects not only the number of employees but also the compensation, benefits, and services that will be offered. New nonprofit organizations and those with limited financial resources will have fewer staff and will need each to fulfill a variety of roles. These organizations may also have difficulty retaining employees, resulting in a revolving door of hirings and resignations. Established, complex, well-to-do organizations use staff with specialized expertise and have more complex systems for staff evaluation, skill tracking, career ladders, compensation, and benefits.

A third concept affecting HR decisions is the organization's culture. Organizations that espouse a corporate culture will look for that fit in the employees they hire and will use more formal and explicit procedures for HR functions such as staff development, promotions, and performance appraisals. Organizations with a culture of mistrust will convey that attitude in policies that are strict and thorough. Examples might include random drug testing, requiring doctors' notes for sick time, and monitoring workers' phone calls, e-mail correspondence, time on task, or location of out-of-office appointments. Organizations with a family culture will likely have broader, less-specific policies and HR actions that are highly individualized. Such an organization is likely to value a personal approach (for example, choosing to use a person for receptionist and telephone duties over an automated system or responding to employee needs individually rather than through across-the-board policies).

Nonprofit leaders must be mindful of the characteristics of the organization and ensure that HR decisions are congruent with its mission, niche, service structure, culture, and financial viability. Similarly, HR managers will need to have an eye on the environment outside the organization as well.

External Factors

The environment in which the organization is situated affects HR in several ways. Two strategies for keeping informed about the changing environment are benchmarking and environmental scanning. "Benchmarking" refers to using internal criteria, other organizations, or available data as a basis of comparison for an organization's practices. For example, if a leading nonprofit organization in the area develops a tuition payment program to encourage its employees to obtain graduate degrees, other organizations might follow suit or consider the implications for recruiting new staff when the competitor rolls out this benefit. When a state nonprofit association publishes the results of a statewide salary survey, and managers note that salaries for some categories of employees are well below the mean for organizations of their size, they may begin to restructure compensation and benefits in light of this benchmark.

"Environmental scanning" refers to the practice of regularly reviewing resources such as news items, electronic mailing list postings, association newsletters, and conference proceedings to be alert to innovations in HR management, to changes in the practice environment, and to changes in laws and regulations. It means networking and being alert to all sources of information that could influence HR policies, strategically taking into account the amount and immediacy of impact on one's setting (Cascio & Boudreau, 2012). For example, an HR director may read about a ruling from the Supreme Court on age discrimination and determine that it will have an immediate and significant impact if the agency does not change the ways in which new (younger) employees are compensated compared with senior (older) workers.

Benchmarking and environmental scanning can reveal a variety of environmental effects on an organization's HR practices. Three external factors addressed here are labor conditions, economic conditions, and legal and regulatory influences.

"Labor conditions" refer to a variety of features that affect the pool of people available for hire, the qualities of employees, and the salaries they may command. Key features include demographic characteristics of the workforce (for example, gender, age, educational preparation, race, culture, citizenship), the labor market (that is, the number of people available for employment), and the geographic characteristics. For example, a nonprofit serving Latinx clientele in a geographic area in which there are few Spanish-speaking professionals may find that there is stiff competition for certain types of bilingual employees (for example, physicians), although it may be easier to find clerical and paraprofessional staff from the surrounding community. When the economy is growing and the labor market is tight, employers of all types will experience greater competition for applicants and will have to pay more to hire them. When corporate for-profit sector hiring is robust, the nonprofit sector is particularly challenged in competing for employees (Noe, Hollenbeck, Gerhart, & Wright, 2017).

Economic conditions, of course, affect the financial health of the organization and thus the amount that the organization can pay its workers. Changes in tax laws, declines in the stock market, or spiking unemployment and other economic fallout from such things as the COVID-19 pandemic can all affect the donations on which many nonprofits depend while simultaneously increasing the number of people in need of care. Turbulent social and financial conditions can discourage hiring and lead to outsourcing, contracting, or contingent employment to avoid long-term personnel obligations. Beyond that, the sources and stability of funding can differentially affect employees—and thus HR policies. For example, consider a situation in which half of a nonprofit's direct services workforce is paid under a particular grant. This grant specifies the clients to be served and stipulates the response time required to open new cases. The grant provides a cost-of-living (COLA) increase each year and pay-for-performance incentives. This stream of funding will thus affect a variety of HR decisions in terms of staffing, job duties, merit awards, and pay increases. These changes may or may not be congruent with the HR practices for the rest of the agency's workforce. Thus, they can lead to concerns about fairness and can make the administration of HR policies more complicated.

An array of laws and regulations affect personnel decisions, from hiring to promotions, work conditions, and termination. HR managers must be conversant with them to ensure compliance with policies and organizational practices. The descriptions that follow provide a brief overview of key pieces of legislation.

Title VII of the Civil Rights Act of 1964

Title VII of the Civil Rights Act of 1964 (P.L. 88-352) prohibits discrimination on the basis of sex, race, color, religion, or national origin in any employment condition, including hiring, firing, promotion, transfer, compensation, or admission to training programs. It applies to organizations "with 15 or more employees working 20 or more weeks per year . . . as well as state and local governments, employment agencies, and labor organizations" (Noe et al., 2017, p. 107). Groups protected under Title VII include women, Black people, Hispanics, American Indians, Pacific Islanders, people older than age 40, people with disabilities, and veterans. Since 1964, courts have ruled that several behaviors by employers and unions are unlawful under Title VII. These behaviors fall into two basic categories: unequal (disparate) treatment and unequal impact. "Disparate treatment" refers to practices in which an organization covertly treats protected group members in a discriminatory fashion, either by treating them less favorably or by applying different standards to them than to other employees.

"Disparate impact" refers to practices that have a differential effect on the opportunities of members of protected groups. These practices are illegal unless they are demonstrably work related or necessary for safe and efficient operation of the business. Under disparate impact, the results of a personnel decision are important, not the intentions. Using the same standards for all groups can have differing consequences. For example, setting a mandatory retirement age differentially affects older employees, minimum height and weight requirements disadvantage women and individuals from small-statured ethnic groups, and inquiries about arrest records will disproportionately affect members of some minority groups. Employers must demonstrate that their personnel actions do not lead to a disparate impact on protected groups and that any such requirements are necessary and effective and could not be achieved in any other fashion. For example, former height and weight standards for firefighters were found to have disparate impact and were replaced with strength and speed tests that better reflect the demands of the job being filled.

Equal Employment Opportunity Act of 1972

The Equal Employment Opportunity Act of 1972 (P.L. 92-261) extended coverage of Title VII to include public and private employers with 15 or more employees, labor organizations with 15 or more members, and public and private employment agencies. In 1980, Equal Employment Opportunity Commission guidelines stated that sexual harassment is a form of sex discrimination (U.S. Equal Employment Opportunity Commission, 1990). Generally, two types of behaviors are of concern. Quid pro quo harassment occurs when an employee offers to reward another employee in return for sexual favors (or to punish the person for rejecting those advances). The second form of sexual harassment involves the creation of a hostile work environment through offensive language or sexually suggestive jokes, posters, or actions.

Equal Pay Act of 1963

The Equal Pay Act of 1963 (P.L. 88-38) mandates that employees in the same jobs be paid equally, except for allowable differences in seniority, merit, or other conditions unrelated to sex. It includes both direct and indirect compensation (for example, benefits, paid time off).

Pregnancy Discrimination Act of 1978

The Pregnancy Discrimination Act of 1978 (P.L. 95-555) states that pregnancy is a disability and qualifies a pregnant person to receive the same benefits as would those with other disabilities.

Family and Medical Leave Act of 1993

The Family and Medical Leave Act (FMLA) of 1993 (P.L. 103-3) requires that organizations with 50 or more employees grant up to 12 weeks of unpaid leave for the birth or adoption of a child, to care for a spouse or an immediate family member with a serious health condition, or when the employee is unable to work because of a serious health condition (Noe et al., 2017).

Age Discrimination in Employment Act of 1967

The Age Discrimination in Employment Act of 1967 (P.L. 90-202) protects people age 40 and older and prohibits arbitrary discrimination on the basis of age in organizations with 20 or more employees. Exceptions to mandatory retirement ended in 1994.

Americans with Disabilities Act of 1990
The Americans with Disabilities Act of 1990 (P.L. 101-33) prohibits discrimination on the basis of physical or mental disability by employers with 15 or more employees. Although it does not set numerical goals for hiring or promotion, it does require reasonable accommodations to support employees with disabilities. These accommodations may include redesigning jobs, installing ramps, purchasing facilitative equipment, changing workspace, and examining training and promotion opportunities.

Social Security Act of 1935
The Social Security Act of 1935 (P.L. 74-271) and subsequent amendments provides federal Old Age, Survivors, Disability and Health Insurance benefits to eligible individuals and established the basis for federal and state unemployment programs.

Fair Labor Standards Act of 1938
The Fair Labor Standards Act (FLSA) of 1938 set minimum wages and hours, child labor standards, and overtime pay provisions. It distinguished between exempt and nonexempt jobs or employees. Workers who are exempt from the FLSA include managers, executives, and professionals, such as a mental health agency's clinical staff. Employees who are not exempt, such as child care workers, clerical staff, and maintenance personnel, are covered by the regulations and thus must be provided overtime pay and other provisions of the act.

Balancing Conflict

Effective personnel management requires careful consideration of the conflicts inherent in balancing the organizational and environmental factors described earlier. For example, a 60-employee agency may embrace the spirit of the FMLA, but offering extended leave (even without pay) may place a terrific burden on service provision if several employees from a particular unit use the leave unexpectedly or at the same time.

An organization may value seniority in its workforce and have a retention program in place to ensure that, once hired, employees will stay. That strategy, though, may result in compensation costs that are top-heavy with senior, higher paid workers, and the low turnover may make it difficult to restructure programs to respond to changing economic conditions and encourage the innovation that new workers might bring.

Also, an organization, because of its mission and culture, may actively seek to hire workers who might otherwise have difficulty finding employment, such as people who have not completed high school, people with a criminal history, or those in recovery from drug problems. In response, the personnel department may offer flexible schedules and job tasks, educational or wellness benefits, and supportive supervision. The challenge in living its values, though, may mean that the organization has higher staff development and health insurance costs or excessive staffing demands as a result of greater vulnerability in the workforce.

Embedded in these conflicts is the continuous tension between efficiency and equity. Immediately dismissing an underperforming employee is efficient, but it is not fair or just. Hiring only healthy, able, single employees may yield a productive workforce, able to devote long hours to the job, but it is not legal or equitable.

The effective HR manager must use strategies to keep informed of changing organizational and environmental conditions, be familiar with the organization's personnel policies and practices to interpret the effects of those changes, and balance the competing values that those conditions create. Those considerations are illustrated further in this chapter in the discussion of each step in the HR process.

Recruitment and Selection

Attracting and selecting employees begins with a clear impression of what qualities the position demands. A precise and current job description is essential for making this determination (Figure 5.1). Flowing from job analysis and design, the job description should specify the reporting relationship of the position, job tasks, and qualifications and credentials needed. Job descriptions may be organized by areas of responsibility or by the knowledge, skills, and abilities needed to successfully fill the position (Noe et al., 2017).

The organization's HR department should develop procedures for filling vacancies so that the hiring process is cost efficient, fair, and legal. HR policies might specify who is involved in personnel decisions (for example, immediate supervisor, search committee, unit team) and who must sign off at various points in the process (for example, when an advertisement is posted, when finalists are selected, when an offer is made). Personnel specialists should also develop the selection process and train those involved in recruitment and selection to ensure that their practices are effective, inclusive, and ethical. The selection process should include decisions about the format in

Figure 5.1 Sample Job Description

Title: Clinician–Supervisor

Reports to: Director of Mental Health

Position is responsible for providing mental health and substance abuse treatment in person and via remote access technology. The Clinician–Supervisor is responsible for providing administrative and clinical supervision for at least three professional or paraprofessional staff.

Specific duties required for carrying out this role include but are not limited to the following:

1. Assist in the development of cooperative working relationships with referral sources and other agencies essential for case coordination.
2. Assist in the assessment of area needs for new programming and services in mental health and substance abuse.
3. Provide treatment at a level consistent with the prevailing direct service standard.
4. Provide consulting and education services to public groups and community agencies.
5. Open and maintain case records in keeping with agency policies.
6. Assist supervisees in professional development and effective agency practice.
7. Complete performance appraisals at least once annually.
8. Practice and provide supervision in an ethical manner, upholding agency policies and procedures.
9. Provide emergency and on-call coverage on a rotating basis.

Qualifications: This position requires a master's degree in social work, psychology, or a related field and clinical licensure in the respective discipline. The position further requires appropriate experience to ensure that the applicant is able to adequately perform the required duties and supervise the practice of others.

---

which applicants should express interest (for example, résumé versus standardized application form, online or on paper), the process and criteria for reviewing the documents submitted, and the steps in the application process, which could potentially include initial screening, preliminary telephone interviews, agency interviews, reference contacts, and drug tests or criminal background checks. HR can assist those responsible for hiring in structuring their interviews so that questions are consistent, legal, and relevant to the job and the qualifications sought and help them to develop evaluative criteria to weigh what they learn about a candidate in light of the expectations of the job. HR staff will also implement affirmative action strategies to attract a diverse pool of candidates and equal opportunity measures to ensure that the hiring process is free from intentional or unintentional discrimination.

Recruitment

The nature of the organization, the position, and the labor market will affect the strategies used to advertise for applicants and the information sought. Although the wide use of Web sites, social media, job apps, and recruiting software has democratized search processes, job candidates can also be identified via word of mouth from current employees, open houses, job fairs, and recruiting events at schools, colleges, and community sites. Recruiting for a clerical or entry-level direct practice position will primarily involve a local search and resources, whereas the search for a chief executive officer may be regional or national, involving advertising in national or global news outlets and perhaps the use of a search firm to ensure a strong and diverse candidate pool.

Advertisements for positions should use unbiased language, clearly state the type of job and the relevant qualifications (including years of experience, if appropriate), and provide direction about steps applicants should take (for example, "Send cover letter, résumé, and references to . . . ," "See our Web site for an online application," "Come to our open house on . . ."). Remember that the announcement must attract relevant candidates and discourage unsuitable candidates. An announcement that is too broad or poorly worded may result in a deluge of applicants who are incompatible with the position, thus prolonging and complicating the selection process. Including the salary range in the announcement may similarly help to narrow the pool of applicants, but it may also prematurely discourage desirable candidates, allowing salary to overshadow other benefits associated with the position.

Screening

The first step in the selection process is to screen résumés or applications to ensure that they meet the criteria advertised. Software can help to filter, track, and organize candidates and screen out people who do not meet minimum, required qualifications, such as experience, education, or credentials. Alternatively, matrices or spreadsheets help in tracking applicants and evaluating résumés or applications against the qualifications of the position by capturing in one document the relative qualifications of a large pool of candidates. The required and preferred qualifications would be listed across the top of the matrix, and the applicants would be listed down the left-hand side. This process helps differentiate the strongest candidates from the pool of applicants who meet the established criteria. On the basis of the data collected in the matrix, the organization can prioritize those it will pursue through the rest of the process.

Although not common in the nonprofit sector, some large organizations use employment tests and work samples to further narrow the field of candidates. Tests may include those that determine how well a person can learn or acquire skills (aptitude tests), their level of knowledge (achievement tests), personality type, physical abilities, and word processing and other clerical skills (Noe et al., 2017). These testing programs all share similar challenges: their validity relative to the job's requirements and the possibility that they unfairly disadvantage populations of prospective employees. A more common strategy in the nonprofit sector is to use application materials to generate a list of interviewees and conduct any necessary testing as a condition of the job offer after a finalist (or set of finalists) has been selected.

Before inviting candidates for an interview, the organization must decide who should serve as interviewers at various points in the process, whether one-on-one or group interviews will be more effective, and what types of information it is seeking from this part of the process. Ideally, interviews help reveal or bring to light information beyond that which is available in the résumé or application, and the information sought is directly relevant to the position being filled. Interviewers should be able to identify the knowledge, skills, and abilities related to the position that are tapped by each of the interview questions—in other words, what answer is the organization looking for? What will this answer tell the interviewer about this applicant's suitability for the job? The interview should also provide applicants with an accurate impression of the position and the organization so that they can evaluate its goodness of fit with their skills and interests.

Some suggestions for interviews include the following:

- Use interviewers from a variety of backgrounds who represent the diversity in the organization.
- Use the same interviewers for all candidates.
- Have interviewers review the position description, equal employment opportunity requirements, and the candidate's application materials before each session.
- Create a comfortable, private environment that is free from distractions.
- Use open-ended, nonleading questions.

- Interviewers should be aware of and regulate their vocal tones and body language to convey encouragement and engagement with the process (Hindle, 1998).
- Take notes or use an evaluation form to identify important responses by each candidate.
- Ask the same questions of each candidate, but use follow-up questions as needed for clarity or greater depth of response.
- Ask for examples that illustrate the applicant's handling of past incidents that are relevant to the position (for example, "Tell us about an experience when . . ." "you handled a conflict with a co-worker," "your experience in working with suicidal clients," "a mistake that you made and what you learned from it," "a time when you experienced an ethical dilemma," "your efforts to build a pluralistic work team") (Falcone, 2002).
- Use hypothetical situations to assess the applicant's judgment and abilities; for example, "How would you respond if . . ." "a client asks to see his record," or "a supervisee comes back from lunch with alcohol on her breath?"
- Anticipate questions that the candidate may have and allow the candidate enough time to ask them.

Table 5.1 provides specific guidelines and unlawful and lawful inquiries.

Table 5.1 Fair Inquiry Guidelines of the Equal Employment Opportunity Commission

Subject	Guidelines
Relatives, marital status	
Unlawful inquiries	Whether the applicant is married, divorced, separated, engaged, widowed, and so forth: "What is your marital status?" "What is the name of [relative, spouse, or children]?" "With whom do you reside?" "Do you live with your parents?" "How old are your children?"
Lawful inquiries	"What are the names of relatives already employed by the company or a competitor?" No other questions are lawful.
Residence	
Unlawful inquiries	Names of or relationship to people with whom applicant resides; whether the applicant owns or rents a home: "Do you live in town?"
Lawful inquiries	Inquiries about address to the extent needed to facilitate contacting the applicant (a post office box is a valid address). "Will you have problems getting to work at 9:00 a.m.?"

Subject	Guidelines
Pregnancy	
Unlawful inquiries	All questions relating to pregnancy and medical history concerning pregnancy: "Do you plan on having more children?"
Lawful inquiries	Inquiries about the duration of stay on a job or anticipated absences that are made to both men and women alike: "Do you foresee any long-term absences in the future?"
Physical health	
Unlawful inquiries	Overly general questions ("Do you have any disabilities?") that would tend to divulge disabilities or health conditions that do not relate reasonably to fitness to perform the job. "What caused your disability?" "What is the prognosis of your disability?" "Have you ever had any serious illness?" "Do you have any physical disabilities?"
Lawful inquiries	Questions must relate to the job. "Can you lift 40 pounds?" "Do you need any special accommodations to perform the job you've applied for?" "How many days did you miss from work [or school] in the past year?"
Family	
Unlawful inquiries	Questions concerning spouse or spouse's employment, spouse's salary, dependents, and child care arrangements. "How will your husband feel about the amount of time you will be traveling if you get this job?" "What kind of child care arrangements have you made?"
Lawful inquiries	Whether the applicant can meet specified work schedules or has activities or commitments that may prevent them from meeting attendance requirements. "Can you work overtime?" "Is there any reason why you can't be on the job at 7:30 a.m.?"
Name	
Unlawful inquiries	Any inquiries about name that would divulge marital status, lineage, ancestry, national origin, or descent: "If your name has been legally changed, what was your former name?"
Lawful inquiries	Whether an applicant has worked for the company or a competitor under any other name and, if so, what name. Name under which applicant is known to references if different from present name: "By what name are you known to the references you provided us?"
Sexual orientation and gender	
Unlawful inquiries	Any inquiry: "Do you wish to be addressed as Mr., Mrs., Miss, or Ms?" Any inquiry as pertains to sex, such as "Do you have the capacity to reproduce?" "What are your plans to have children in the future?"
Lawful inquiries	None
Photographs	
Unlawful inquiries	Requests that an applicant submit a photograph at any time before hiring.
Lawful inquiries	A photograph may be requested after hiring for identification purposes.
Age	
Unlawful inquiries	Any questions that tend to identify applicants ages 40 or older.
Lawful inquiries	"Are you 18 years of age?" "If hired, can you furnish proof of age?"

Subject	Guidelines
Education	
Unlawful inquiries	Any question asking specifically about nationality, racial, or religious affiliation of a school.
Lawful inquiries	All questions related to academic, vocational, or professional education of an applicant, including the names of the schools attended, degrees or diplomas received, dates of graduation, and courses of study.
Citizenship	
Unlawful inquiries	Whether an applicant is a citizen. Requiring a birth, naturalization, or baptismal certificate. Any inquiry into citizenship would tend to divulge applicant's lineage, descent, and so forth. "Are you a citizen of the United States?" "Are your parents or spouse citizens of the United States?" "On what dates did you, your parents, or your spouse acquire U.S. citizenship?" "Are you, your parents, or your spouse naturalized or native-born U.S. citizens?"
Lawful inquiries	Whether the applicant is prevented from being lawfully employed in the United States because of visa or immigration requirements. Whether applicant can provide proof of citizenship (passport), visa, or alien registration number after hiring. "If you are not a U.S. citizen, do you have the legal right to remain permanently in the United States?" "What is your visa status (if 'no' to the previous question)." "Are you able to provide proof of employment eligibility upon hire?"
National origin or ancestry	
Unlawful inquiries	Any inquiry. "What is your nationality?" "How did you acquire the ability to speak, read, or write a foreign language?" "How did you acquire familiarity with a foreign country?" "What language is spoken in your home?" "What is your mother tongue?"
Lawful inquiries	"What languages do you speak, read, or write fluently?" This is legal only when the inquiry is based on a job requirement.
Race or skin color	
Unlawful inquiries	Any question that directly or indirectly relates to a race or skin color.
Lawful inquiries	None.
Religion	
Unlawful inquiries	Any question that directly or indirectly relates to a religion. "What religious holidays do you observe?" "What is your religious affiliation?"
Lawful inquiries	None except "Can you work on Saturdays [Sundays]?" and that only if it is relevant to the job.
Organizations	
Unlawful inquiries	"To what organizations, clubs, societies, and lodges do you belong?"
Lawful inquiries	Inquiries must relate only to the applicant's professional qualifications: "To what professional organizations do you belong?" (These exclude those whose name or character indicates the race, religious creed, color, national origin, or ancestry of its members.)

Subject	Guidelines
Military	
Unlawful inquiries	Type or condition of military discharge. Applicant's experience in military other than the U.S. Armed Forces. Request for discharge papers.
Lawful inquiries	Inquiries concerning education, training, or work experience in the U.S. Armed Forces. (Note that, in many areas, veterans are a protected class.)
Height and weight	
Unlawful inquiries	Any inquiries not based on actual job requirements.
Lawful inquiries	Inquiries about the ability to perform a certain job.
Arrests and convictions	
Unlawful inquiries	All inquiries relating to arrests: "Have you ever been arrested?" (Note that arrests are not the same as convictions. An innocent person can be arrested.)
Lawful inquiries	None relating to arrests. Legal inquiries about convictions are "Have you ever been convicted of any crime? If so, when, where, and what was the disposition of case?" "Have you ever been convicted under criminal law within the past 5 years (excluding minor traffic violations)?" It is permissible to inquire about convictions for acts of dishonesty or breach of trust. These relate to fitness to perform the particular job being applied for.
Health issues	
Unlawful inquiries	Any inquiries related to prescription drugs or medications the individual may be taking or may have taken or monitoring an employee's intake of such medications. Any inquiries related to whether the individual is positive for HIV/AIDS.
Lawful inquiries	Inquiring about the individual's well-being: "How are you feeling today?"

Note: These guidelines were established by Equal Employment Opportunity Commission to provide specific protection from discrimination in hiring certain protected classes.

Selection

Interviews typically help to narrow the field of candidates or rank the preferences for hire. However, before a finalist is chosen, the organization should conduct both background and reference checks. Background checks ascertain that the information applicants provide about their education, experience, and credentials is accurate. Misrepresentation of these facts should be a significant source of concern and prompt further examination and discussion if not outright disqualification for the position. Information from references may be less helpful, in that applicants usually select references that are inclined to give favorable feedback. Other references, such as former employers, may have policies that confine the information they provide to the dates of service and whether or not the individual is eligible for rehire. Others may limit their feedback to observable, job-related behaviors (Noe et al., 2017). References and background checks may not aid in differentiating among acceptable candidates, but they may identify unacceptable ones. Even if reference checks are not always fruitful, it is incumbent on the hiring agency to thoroughly pursue them. The costs of missing potentially troubling data about an applicant are high.

If hiring is contingent on successful completion of other steps, such as drug testing or criminal background checks, those should be completed at this stage before a final offer is made.

When the candidate has been selected, the job offer should explicitly state the job responsibilities, pay, benefits, schedule and starting date, and the date by which the candidate should accept or reject the offer (Noe et al., 2017). Until the position is officially filled, other finalists should not be notified, lest the first offer fall through. However, once a candidate has accepted the job, all applicants should be contacted and thanked for their interest in the position. This information is often communicated by e-mail or letter, accompanied by a phone call to other finalists or a personal meeting with internal candidates for the position. The agency should also carefully document the pool of applicants at each stage of the process, the person selected, and the specifics of the job offer.

Internal Staffing

Internal staffing presents some special conditions for screening and selection. Successful internal candidates affect not only the position they assume but also their original or source position (Milkovich & Boudreau, 1997). Filling vacancies from within can be an effective strategy for fostering employee retention and satisfaction, but it leads to a ripple effect in creating vacant source positions that must then be filled. The aggregate result may be that the organization primarily hires only entry-level employees because senior positions are filled internally. Another outcome is the effect on the supervisors in the source positions, who may resent their investment of time and effort in what may amount to a stepping-stone for employees whose aspirations lie elsewhere in the organization.

Another challenge of internal staffing occurs when an employee is not selected for advancement. That person may be stellar in their current role but ill suited to or unprepared for the new position. Yet, unlike external applicants, this person will continue with the agency after being rejected for the new position. It is therefore essential that the notification process be handled in a tactful and timely manner. The failed application should be used as an opportunity to explore additional education or work experiences that may enhance the worker's portfolio for future promotions.

Compensation and Benefits

Compensation is typically a worker's salary or hourly wages, merit pay or incentives, and COLA adjustments. Benefits, or indirect compensation, include paid time away from work, health insurance, pension, employee services (for example, wellness center, day care, smoking cessation program), and payments on legally mandated benefits (for example, Social Security, unemployment compensation, workers' compensation, FMLA leave in organizations with more than 50 employees). Compensation decisions are shaped by other laws as well, including those setting the minimum wage and overtime rules and those forbidding discrimination on the basis of gender, race, age, and ability. Compensation decisions are also shaped by organizational goals, external competitors, and the wages paid to existing employees.

An organization's structure and strategic objectives will shape the type of compensation system it adopts (for example, flat or steep, closely guarded or transparent), its interest in using pay-for-performance incentives, and the degree to which it seeks to match or exceed the pay offered by competitors. Some organizations that embrace an egalitarian pay policy will have little differentiation among salary or wage levels. Other, often larger, organizations will use a more hierarchical system, with ranges or salary bands and explicit rules about how people move up the salary scale (that is, seniority, performance, or both).

Organizations must be alert to competitive pressures and may make a conscious decision to pay less than the going rate offered by similar agencies, making up for the deficit with more generous benefits, flexible hours, or an enjoyable working climate. Agencies must also be alert to internal pressures. Two are of particular importance. Compression occurs when new hires are brought on at higher pay than that of existing workers with similar seniority. Typically, compression results from stagnant salary increases within an organization and robust increases at other organizations in an environment. Thus, the new worker's pay has progressed further outside the organization than it has for those workers who have remained in an agency with a history of offering uncompetitive raises. Equal employment opportunity concerns also arise when pay differences among positions are unjustifiable. Differences in pay for equal work are allowed if they result from differences in seniority, in the quality of performance, and in quantity and quality of production or from other factors such as shift differentials (that is, for working an overnight shift) or hazard pay (that is, for undesirable or riskier work). Differences in race, gender, marital status, and age cannot be used to legitimize differences in pay.

Beyond base salary or hourly wages, many organizations offer merit pay, bonuses, or percentage increases on base pay offered for achieving various goals (for example, attendance, productivity, exemplary service). Bonuses differ from merit increases in that the former are one-time occurrences and do not alter the recipient's base pay. These are easier to administer, in part because they create no long-term financial obligations, but they may be less satisfying to employees who would like the promise that a permanent increase in wages affords. "Profit sharing" refers to merit awards that are given to units of employees on the basis of the organization's profitability at the close of the operating year; in gain sharing, rewards may be obtained by cost savings as well as by profits. Neither is common in the nonprofit sector, and they may have questionable capacity to motivate employees if workers have little hope that the rewards are within their control. In fact, merit pay systems can be problematic for the following reasons:

- The proportion of variable pay to base pay is so small that the merit system has little leverage.
- Some merit systems have high risk in that the probability of an increase in pay is low commensurate with the amount of additional effort needed to get it.
- The system by which merit is measured and distributed is perceived as unfair.
- The agency lacks sufficient funds for the system to have much impact on employees.
- Merit systems have unintended consequences; for example, incentives to reduce length of hospital stays lead to premature patient discharges.
- Annual rewards are not proximal to the efforts that workers must make to achieve them; thus, they lose their motivational impact.
- Measuring the qualities that nonprofits seek to reward can be difficult.
- Workers become discouraged and unmotivated when limited rewards are available and thus only go to a few top performers.
- Employees may overrate their performance or the availability of merit funds and are disappointed when merit awards do not meet their expectations.

A nonprofit must carefully review its direct compensation system to determine the legal and strategic advantages of different options. It must do the same with its indirect compensation, or benefits package. What benefits, beyond those mandated, will employees receive? Will those differ by classes of employees or seniority? What benefits can the organization afford, in terms of financial obligations and staffing? How much choice will workers have in selecting the benefits that best suit them? It is appealing to offer a "cafeteria plan," by which employees can select the array of benefits that best meet their individual needs. However, such programs can be expensive to design and complex to administer, rendering them unfeasible for small organizations.

Staff Orientation and Staff Development

In most organizations, the HR director or department is responsible for creating and administering the onboarding and staff development programs. The overall goal of staff development activities is to improve employees' current and future performance. Staff development generally encompasses those programs designed to meet the employees' needs and those designed to meet the organization's needs, although effective training is generally of benefit to both parties. Staff development on behalf of employees may include providing or funding clinical supervision or continuing education to help workers meet their license requirements. It may also involve financial support, schedule adjustments, or time off so that employees can pursue education to fulfill their personal interests. For example, a bachelor's degree may not be a requirement for an administrative support position, but the organization may support workers in that role who want to pursue a degree for their personal development.

Staff development for an organization's benefit typically includes mandatory training needed for accreditation or regulatory purposes, such as CPR certification, compliance with universal health precautions, and procedures for safe client restraint. Organizations may also promote training that helps advance their strategic objectives (for example, training on antiracism and implicit bias to improve organizational culture or education in a particular therapeutic technique to respond to new service demands).

Orientation (or onboarding) is a particular form of staff development designed to acquaint new workers with the organization's formal and informal rules and expectations. It has several purposes, including helping workers learn job procedures; begin to establish relationships with colleagues, subordinates, and administrators; and become familiar with the ways their role fits into the larger organizational structure and mission (Abramson, 1993). Orientation should be more than a tour of the building and a long afternoon spent reading the policy and procedures manual. It should be an ongoing process designed to provide workers with the information that they need at the points at which they need it.

Those responsible for planning staff development must decide

- how to assess job, organizational, and individual needs
- what kinds of skills and knowledge should be targeted (for example, communication, technical skills, diversity and inclusion, broad knowledge on particular topics)
- who should participate in what kind of training
- who should provide the training
- under what auspices the training should be offered
- how training transfer (use of new information on the job) will be ensured (Kraiger & Aguinis, 2001)

Although organizations can have highly sophisticated methods for identifying employees' existing abilities and aspirations for career and personal development, in most small- to medium-sized organizations, supervisors are key to uncovering and tracking this information. HR personnel may encourage supervisors to be attuned to this information in supervisory conferences with workers and, at the very least, during the annual performance review and planning process. Employee communication vehicles (for example, newsletters, e-mail, staff meetings) can also be used to solicit ideas for continuing education and encourage individual employees to identify training needs.

At least one person in the organization will need to keep track, through environmental scanning and coordination with administrators and personnel records managers, the training topics that are required by contracts, licenses, and regulations; the necessary frequency; and the requisite certification of competence or completion. Once a schedule of compulsory training has been created, administrators should consider the resources available for other forms of staff development and the strategies that the agency might use to deliver it.

Each of the many types of training delivery methods has particular strengths and disadvantages. They involve different costs to the organization in terms of travel, instructional expenses, and time away from the workplace. Various methods are suited for different learning objectives; Table 5.2 captures some of these distinctions (Asamoah, 1995; Beckett & Dungee-Anderson, 1996; Griffin, 1995; Johnson, 2001; Mathis, Jackson, Valentine, & Meglich, 2017; Weinbach, 1998).

Organizations can meet multiple objectives through an effective staff development program. They can ensure various forms of regulatory or legal compliance and improve workforce relations by helping employees meet their needs for growth and mandatory continuing education hours without

Table 5.2 Staff Development Models

Type of Staff Development	Common Uses	Considerations
On-the-job training; supervision	Orientation; improving performance; safety training; student internships	Relevant to job; trainer can evaluate comprehension or mastery and provide immediate correction; some elements of job may be hard to observe or replicate; costs include supervisor's or trainer's work time and development of curriculum or ancillary materials
Mentoring	Orientation; preparing for promotion	Highly individualized; linked to personal development and career planning; content typically relevant to job; helps with employee retention; can be difficult to find suitable mentor; can be part of diversity and inclusion efforts
Coaching	Orientation; adjusting to promotion; addressing performance problems	Highly individualized; linked to personal development and career planning; content typically relevant to job; can be costly if coach is not in house; not cost efficient for large numbers of employees; may be useful for senior leadership or people moving from direct service to administration
Videos/webinars	Skills training; ethics; risk assessments; new research or interventions	Low interaction; less transferability of content to job; cost effective; timing (can be viewed at employees' convenience); better for knowledge acquisition than skill development
Teleconferences	New knowledge; emerging issues	Timing generally fixed; may conflict with employee schedules; may introduce coverage or scheduling problems if several employees want to attend; can be passive; few opportunities for informal networking
Workshops (in house; using internal or external educator)	Mandatory training; commonly needed training (for example ethics hours for licensure, CPR); multicultural practice	Cost effective; convenient for workers; using coworker as educator can diminish innovation and sense of legitimacy of content; need to arrange office coverage or staffing when workforce is at training
Off-site workshops and retreats	To fill continuing education hours; organizational integrity; networking; new skills and knowledge	Can expose workers to innovations; can give workers a break, sense of respite from work; may incur travel costs and additional time away from the office; may be challenging to transfer training
Conferences	Networking; opportunity to get away from the office; change of pace	Usually offer an array of topics, so attendees have high latitude in choice of content; training transfer may be limited, depending on what sessions employees select and quality and relevance of delivery
Credit-bearing coursework	To achieve a degree or additional credentials; to obtain new knowledge or abilities	Expensive; time consuming; assignments or coursework may benefit agency; may help with employee retention; worker may not stay at the agency after attaining degree, although payback provisions may be stipulated in advance

Type of Staff Development	Common Uses	Considerations
Web-based instruction	Ethics compliance; training on regulations; education on new or emerging fields (for example pandemic safety, harm reduction, or medically assisted treatment)	Can be self-paced to worker schedule; easy to update content; feedback or evaluations immediate; can be delivered to a large number of workers; may be difficult to ensure that worker thoroughly completed program

incurring a cost or losing time off. In that respect, a robust staff development system may be seen as a form of employee benefit. Last, a strategic examination of the workers' ambitions and the workplace's internal and environmental conditions will lead to staff development plans that ensure a stable pool of workers who are prepared with the skills and knowledge to meet the agency's changing needs.

Performance Appraisals

Performance appraisal is the formal, structured system of measuring, evaluating, and influencing an employee's job-related attributes, behaviors, and outcomes. Organizations use performance evaluations to accomplish a variety of objectives, including providing feedback to improve work performance, acquiring data for merit pay determinations, developing a candidate pool for internal promotions, identifying training needs and career goals, documenting and addressing poor performance, reorganizing work assignments, and preparing for long-range planning. Some authors have contended that performance assessments should be uncoupled from pay-for-performance strategies (for example, Millar, 1998; Petersen, 2019). They have argued that the developmental goals of such assessments are distorted when linked with pay and that what should be a constructive process becomes a charged and potentially punitive experience. Others have criticized performance systems for being too vague, biased, and punitive (for example, Clifford, 1999). Some have contended that the evaluative element in performance reviews undoes the developmental and supportive functions and it furthermore undermines morale and teamwork (for example, Roberts, 1998). These critiques should be taken into account when designing and implementing an effective, meaningful system of employee evaluation and feedback.

In nonprofit organizations, managers must develop, implement, and evaluate the performance appraisal or management system. The steps in doing so include determining the performance criteria (for example, what performance will be measured? What will constitute exceptional or unsatisfactory performance?), identifying and preparing the personnel who will carry out the appraisals, determining the frequency and types of evaluation instruments to be used, and linking the results to other systems in the organization (for example, compensation, staff development, discipline).

Performance criteria typically result from the aforementioned job analysis, which reflects the demands of the job and how the performance of that job affects the agency's outcomes. Examples of performance criteria (Milkovich & Boudreau, 1997, p. 104) are shown in Table 5.3.

Table 5.3 Examples of Performance Criteria

Skills, Abilities, and Traits	Behaviors	Results
Job knowledge	Performs tasks	Contacts made
Dependability	Follows rules	Caseload and clients served
Creativity	Regular attendance	Client satisfaction
Leadership	Maintains records	Initiated new project

These criteria should then be reflected in the evaluation instrument and in the data sources (or evaluators) who participate in the appraisal. In some workplaces, the evaluative instruments are highly individualized, with the elements of the worker's job description forming the basis of the appraisal. In others, a more universal form is used, reflecting broad objectives that apply to the majority of the organization's personnel. Figures 5.2 and 5.3 provide examples of each.

As indicated in Figures 5.2 and 5.3, many sources of data and multiple evaluators can be involved in a performance appraisal system. Although direct supervisors typically have primary responsibility for conducting the evaluation and discussing it with their employees, they may also seek the input of others. Sources of data include client satisfaction surveys, peer or team feedback, self-appraisal (verbally or on ratings forms), records, service statistics, and other forms of quantitative data.

Figure 5.2 Sample Position-Specific Performance Appraisal

Position: Assistant to the Director

Reports to: Executive Director (ED)

Directions: Under each principal function, list the performance expectations. Record the performance indicator(s) at the acceptable performance level and the source(s) of data used to evaluate it.

Function 1: Coordinates the center's Administrative Office. Informs ED of client or staff issues as they arise, notifies ED of approaching deadlines, aids in the anticipation of concerns, and offers assistance in troubleshooting. Maintains confidentiality regarding sensitive information as it applies to staff, clients, and regulatory bodies.

Performance Expectations

Performance Indicator(s): Exchanges timely information with the ED through written, electronic, and verbal communications. Develops systems for supplying needed information. Consults with ED regarding staff, client, or community issues; timelines; and their subsequent impact. Generates options for addressing problems. Maintains confidentiality of information exchange specific to this role.

Source(s) of Data: Self-report. Direct observation and feedback from ED, board, staff, clients, and other constituents.

Function 2: Communicates effectively with staff regarding policies, policy changes, and procedures under the auspices of the ED. Serves as information resource on established policies by directing parties to sources regarding procedures, rules, and regulations.

Performance Expectations

Performance Indicator(s): Provides timely, clear, and accurate written and verbal communication with staff regarding policies and procedures.

Source(s) of Data: Self-report. Direct observation and feedback from ED and staff.

Function 3: Provides back-up support for finance and client data managers. Is familiar with accounting and client file systems, has the ability to use them, and offers resolutions to problems associated with those systems in the absence of the assigned personnel.

Performance Expectations

Performance Indicator(s): Whenever the assigned staff are unavailable, individuals who have financial or other data inquiries are assisted promptly. Problems that arise are resolved satisfactorily and completely; accurate information is provided.

(continued)

Source(s) of Data: Self-report. Direct observation, feedback from staff and related departments such as the funding agencies and insurance companies. Review of reports generated.

Function 4: Provides coordination and editing support for the agency's publications, including brochures and reports. Coordinates the agency's online newsletter. Processes press releases and requests from the media.

Performance Expectations

Performance Indicator(s): Documents are completed in a timely manner (within the realm of the staff member's control) and are in the correct format so that deadlines are rarely missed. Information is complete and accurate so that follow-up requests are rare. Errors noted are corrected promptly and rarely require a second request for correction.

Source(s) of Data: Self-report. Number, quality, and timeliness of products produced. Review of completed documents and works in progress. Observation and feedback from collaborators and end users.

Figure 5.3 Sample General Appraisal Instrument

Rate the employee using the following scale:

1 = Seldom 2 = Occasionally 3 = Usually 4 = Frequently 5 = Always NA = Not Applicable

To what extent does this employee

___ Consistently produce an acceptable quantity of work?

___ Complete tasks in an accurate and timely manner?

___ Complete tasks with a minimum of supervision?

___ Accept responsibility for new or difficult projects?

___ Follow appropriate agency procedures?

___ Seek appropriate input from supervisor or colleagues?

___ Communicate clearly and concisely?

___ Actively advance the organization's mission and objectives?

___ Work cooperatively with staff from other units to advance the organization's goals?

___ Arrive at work and return from breaks on time?

When to Measure Performance

Performance appraisals are generally conducted annually, either on the employee's annual date of hire or during a specified period, such as the end of the fiscal year, when all workers are reviewed simultaneously. An advantage of doing all evaluations at the same time is that the performance review does not get misplaced among other projects or activities, which can happen when they are done individually throughout the year. Mass reviews can also be advantageous when an organization uses a pay-for-performance compensation system because the financial obligations for merit awards are all determined and allocated at the same time. This helps in financial planning. A disadvantage of the clustered evaluation is that employees may have different lengths of service that are not accommodated by such a system. In addition, there is always a danger that appraisals will not be sufficiently individualized or will get short shrift with the volume of evaluations to be completed in a fixed time.

Variations in the annual use of appraisals occur at the outset of employment; workers on provisional status may get evaluated at three- or six-month intervals until they have completed their probationary period. Likewise, some progressive discipline programs will require more frequent interim appraisals for employees with performance problems.

How to Measure Performance

After deciding what to measure, the sources of information used for evaluation, and the timing of appraisals, the organization must then determine its system for measuring performance. The methods described here can be used alone or in various combinations to capture the data the organization values.

A commonly used method is the graphic rating scale (Milkovich & Boudreau, 1997). It involves statements of performance criteria (for example, "Submits forms in a timely manner," "Successfully matched volunteer tutors with students") followed by a graph of three to seven boxes indicating levels of performance (for example, "outstanding, good, fair, poor," "all the time, usually, rarely, never"). Key in effectively using this method is ensuring that evaluators are properly trained with a common understanding about what each anchor or score is meant to reflect. For example, an employee may only rarely start new projects because of the nature of their job, but whenever they are supposed to start one, they always do. Which rank should that item be given? Organizations must also consider what it is they are trying to rate: the frequency with which a task occurs or the quality with which the task is done? Different priorities or objectives will lead to different ranking schemas.

Two other techniques provide nice complements to the graphic rating scale. Essays are open-ended narratives about the worker's strengths and weaknesses (or any aspect of performance) during the evaluation period. Critical incidents are statements describing very effective and ineffective behaviors critical to job tasks. Both strategies help illuminate numerical scores and thus are more useful when combined with quantitative methods.

A management-by-objective (MBO) performance review system is highly individualized. For each evaluation period (for example, six months, one year), the worker and supervisor set several highly specific and measurable goals that are relevant to the person's job or organizational goals. The supervisor and supervisee should set clear time lines and indicators of quality that will reflect superior, acceptable, or unacceptable performance (for example, "superior = employee will complete all charting within 48 hours of a client's session," "acceptable = employee will complete charting on at least 80 percent of assigned cases within one week of client session," "unacceptable = employee fails to update any charts within two weeks of client session"). The worker is then evaluated on whether the objectives were met in the time frame indicated. An advantage of an MBO performance review system is that the expectations placed on employees can be tailored to their interests and ambitions and to the organization's needs in a changing environment. Two disadvantages are that the system is time consuming to design and carries risks for inequity in the treatment of various employees. For example, are the goals selected by all employees of equal feasibility or difficulty? Do some supervisors set the bar for superior performance unreasonably high or unreasonably low?

Checklists and behaviorally anchored rating scales (BARS) are two evaluation systems that use different strategies to limit the potential for unfair variability in raters. Checklists involve a list of statements about characteristics of the worker (for example, "requires extensive prompting to complete paperwork on time"). The supervisor checks it if it is true of the worker and leaves it blank if it is not. This reduces the potential for differing interpretations about the frequency or quality of behaviors, as may happen with scales. Unfortunately, some important worker characteristics (for example, initiative, autonomy, communication skills) do not lend themselves to simple yes-or-no determinations, in part because of the nuances in how and where these skills are used.

BARS address the variability problem by providing examples or critical incidents to serve as anchors for each point on the scale. Table 5.4 provides an example (Milkovich & Boudreau, 1997).

Table 5.4: Behaviorally Anchored Rating Scale

Position: Home Monitor

Performance Dimension: Displays concern for nursing home residents and responds to their needs with genuine interest. A home monitor should:

Good				Poor
Recognize when a resident is depressed and has a problem they want to discuss.	Respond to residents' need for information on financial support or other resources in the community.	See a person, recognize him or her as a resident, and say "hello."	Respond to a resident's need to talk; get into a discussion but fail to follow up later on the concern with either the resident or other staff.	Criticize a resident for being unable to solve his or her own problems.

The challenge with a BARS system is that it is time consuming and complex to create an instrument that meaningfully captures unique examples of performance for the array of tasks that encompass any particular job. The system is most useful in large organizations in which multiple employees are covered by the same job description. The time invested up front in instrument development reduces the potential for evaluator error or inequity and is cost effective in the long term.

Limiting Errors and Bias in Performance Appraisals

Whatever evaluation system the agency uses, supervisors should be thoroughly trained in the instruments used and in the evaluative process. Likewise, employees must be informed about their job expectations and the ways in which those will be measured. Employees should not learn at the review session that colleagues will be consulted about their performance or that their dress will be considered as an indicator of professionalism. For example, the National Association of Social Workers (2021) *Code of Ethics* speaks to both of these issues: "Social workers who provide supervision should evaluate supervisees' performance in a manner that is fair and respectful" (p. 21) and "Social workers who have responsibility for evaluating the performance of others should fulfill such responsibility in a fair and considerate manner and on the basis of clearly stated criteria" (p. 22).

Beyond avoiding employee discomfort and ethical challenges, communications about performance expectations serve to motivate employees to live up to the expectations associated with their positions. When employees understand the supervisor's expectations, they can better prioritize tasks, seek assistance in areas in which growth is needed, and use supervisory sessions to receive periodic feedback on progress (Langdon & Osborne, 2001). The performance review is thus not an annual process but an ongoing discussion of strengths and weaknesses, culminating in a written appraisal at least once per year. It is also not a unidirectional process but rather an interchange between the worker and reviewer in which self-appraisal is combined with other sources of data to form an overall impression of how the employee is meeting the organization's expectations. Ideally, it should also be an opportunity to evaluate how the organization is meeting its workers' expectations and how a better fit between the two may be achieved. In addition to seeking staff input, all performance review systems should include a mechanism for employees to comment on their ratings and to indicate their agreement or disagreement with the appraisal.

Evaluators should be especially alert to several common errors in reviewing employees. HR managers can help educate supervisors about these mistakes and can construct systems that mitigate these problems. They include the following (Langdon & Osborne, 2001; Noe et al., 2017):

- Halo or horn error: This type of error occurs when a worker's performance on one dimension influences ratings on all dimensions. For example, all ratings may be marked down if the worker does not get to work on time or marked up because of the worker's friendly customer service.
- Leniency: This refers to giving a worker a higher rating than they deserve. It typically occurs because the rater wants to avoid conflict or does not want the worker's eligibility for a raise to be jeopardized by less-than-excellent performance.
- Strictness: This refers to giving a worker a harsher rating than their performance deserves, usually because of the rater's inexperience, prejudice, low self-confidence, or inability to take a range of variables into account. Strictness (and also leniency) can result from the absence of clear evaluative standards.
- Central tendency: This error occurs when everyone is given average ratings, regardless of differences in performance, usually to avoid complaints from or dissent among workers. It can also result from the reviewer giving insufficient time or attention to their evaluation responsibilities.
- Primacy and recency effects: These errors result when first impressions or more recent events inappropriately influence the evaluation, and the totality of performance over the entire appraisal period is

not taken into account. Those who criticize the efficacy of performance appraisals note the rise in worker productivity in the weeks immediately preceding the review, with a corresponding drop in performance after the review is complete. A good appraisal arrangement and proper training for reviewers helps ensure that the system is not skewed by such recency effects.

- Contrast effects: These errors are most likely to occur when job-based evaluation criteria are not used because employees are compared with each other (which, for example, can make an average employee appear outstanding when compared with a group of poor employees). This type of forced ranking can also present an inaccurate and unfair picture of employee performance when all employees perform above expectations but are treated differently when ranked against each other.

Evaluation Session

As noted earlier, a successful appraisal system means that employees know what is expected of them, and these criteria are evaluated throughout the year. The evaluation should thus take place in the context of a trusting relationship, built through the supervisory process, where the worker is free to share job-related successes and challenges and to seek the supervisor's guidance and support. As the date for the evaluation session approaches, the reviewer should gather the necessary data, including from the employee, and set a mutually agreeable time for the session.

The nature of the feedback will affect the way that the session is structured, although all sessions should involve an opening in which the purpose of the meeting is established, a middle section in which strengths and areas for improvement are addressed, and a closing in which follow-up steps are enumerated (Millar, 1998). When the employee's performance is exemplary, the interview will largely be an opportunity to review the ratings and share those impressions with the worker, using more time to look forward to the year ahead rather than at the year past. These sessions are a great opportunity to get feedback from the worker and to learn more about staff development needs and career aspirations as part of the goal-setting process for the years ahead.

When there are concerns about areas of the employee's performance, the supervisor should offer specific, behaviorally focused feedback and clear expectations about what would constitute improved functioning. Table 5.5 provides examples of general, ineffective feedback and descriptive, effective feedback. The reviewer should avoid tangents that are focused on assigning blame or determining why the performance was unsatisfactory and instead use the time to ensure that the employee understands the nature of the concerns and the conditions for improvement. If the detrimental review initiates a progressive discipline program, the elements of that process must be made clear to the employee. If accommodations are called for to assist in improving the employee's performance (for example, closer supervision, additional training, referral to an employee assistance program for personal difficulties), the expectations of both parties must be clearly discussed and documented.

Table 5.5: Examples of Ineffective and Effective Feedback

Ineffective	Effective
"You make the whole team look bad by never showing up on time."	"The team needs your expertise. When you were late three times last week, we couldn't proceed until you arrived. We expect all of the team members to be here at 8:00 a.m."
"You need to be more reliable."	"On at least five occasions in the past month, the intake worker was unable to reach you when you were on call. The expectation is that on-call staff will leave a number where they can be reached. If you fail to leave a number or cannot be reached at it during the next six months of on-call service, you will be placed on probation, and the progressive discipline process will be initiated."

Whether the review addressed stellar performance or poor performance, the reviewer must ensure that all documentation is properly completed and submitted. Because evaluative processes are often linked to other HR decisions (for example, promotions, bonuses, merit pay, disciplinary procedures), failures in record keeping have reverberating consequences.

Supervisors and others involved in the evaluative process should regularly evaluate their own performance and the effectiveness of the appraisal process. Areas to address might include the following: "Have I taken steps to improve my appraisal skills?" "How well did I prepare for the session?" "How much did I talk, and how well did I listen?" "Have I treated all staff equally?" (Langdon & Osborne, 2001). Honest and consistent self-appraisal helps ensure that performance assessment processes are efficient and equitable. Like performance appraisals, such self-reviews also identify areas for work and growth.

Employee Separations
In HR, the term "separation" refers to the circumstances in which the employee and the organization part company. This typically happens in four

unique circumstances: (1) when employees quit, (2) when they retire, (3) when they are dismissed, and (4) when they are laid off. Note that the first two types are typically initiated by the employee (although the agency can influence those decisions), and the last two are initiated by the employer (although the worker's position or performance may have a role in the decisions).

Separations are not necessarily negative phenomena. Terminations can be good when they involve someone who has not been a productive or constructive part of the workforce or when the loss of a worker improves morale or makes way for new organizational direction or energy. Separations are most negative when they involve unnecessary or illegal losses or when the separation process creates dissent or discouragement among continuing employees.

Terminations are linked to other HR decisions. For example, compensation policies may specify the conditions under which any benefits continue when an employee leaves. Policies on paid time off may limit the amount that an employee can accrue or carry over from year to year to control the expenses the agency may incur when an employee leaves. Managing layoffs by freezing vacant positions may differentially affect staffing in units rather than spread cuts evenly across the organization. Discharging ineffective employees can lead to a reexamination of hiring and supervisory practices to determine whether improvements might mean the avoidance of future disciplinary actions. Separations are also linked to each other. For example, a financial crisis that might ordinarily necessitate layoffs might be addressed by early retirement incentives that reduce high payroll expenses associated with long-term employees. Special considerations go with each type of separation (Milkovich & Boudreau, 1997).

Employee decisions to resign are influenced by a variety of factors, some of which may not be in the organization's control. Typically, they involve the worker balancing the satisfaction with and expectations of their current job against the satisfaction with or expectations of the alternative. When there are fewer alternatives (for example, in a tight job market), there are fewer resignations, but there may also be more withdrawal behavior, such as absenteeism, work slowdowns, and unwillingness to undertake new projects.

Too often, employers assume that workers are motivated solely by money, and they therefore resign themselves to excessive turnover and do not take steps to study and address other sources of dissatisfaction. By researching the amount and pattern of resignations and by conducting exit interviews, employers can better assess the causes of resignations and the personnel, policy, or programmatic changes that might be initiated to keep valued employees. For example, if workers under one supervisor are quitting at a higher-than-usual rate, is there something going on with that unit or that individual that might need to be addressed? If employees typically leave after a very brief period on the job, is there something that must be changed in the screening and selection process to ensure that applicants understand the nature of the work and the employer does not hire those who are ill suited to the job? Perhaps workers in single-parent households find on-call or evening hours untenable. Could another scheduling or service delivery system be developed that would be more accommodating? It is expensive to search for and hire new employees. Taking the time at the end of their service to get feedback on the organization may cut down on those costs by avoiding unnecessary losses.

Retirements differ from other resignations in that they occur at the end of a person's career, and the worker is opting for a lifestyle change rather than another work environment. Retirements may be prompted by employer incentives such as adding time to years of service for pension calculations, offering severance pay, or providing part-time employment with full-time benefits. Sometimes, however, the organization may want to institute measures to retain experienced employees who might otherwise retire, especially if there are negative implications of mass retirements, such as diminished quality of the remaining workforce, less variability in seniority, or expensive buyouts.

Discharges are also known as "fires." Employee dismissals are a complex and challenging process, regulated by laws and agency policies. They are also a significant area of organizational risk when poorly managed. A key concept to introduce at this point is the notion of employment at will. In essence, employment at will means that within state law, the employer–employee relationship at private organizations exists at the will of both parties, subject to whatever contractual obligations were arranged at the outset of employment (for example, requirement of two-week notice before termination). The implications for poor-performing workers, then, would be that the employee can be let go for any reason at any time, as long as the process and the rationale is in keeping with the organization's policies and procedures. However, as noted in the section on the regulatory influences on HR, employees are protected from wrongful discharge because of age, sex, religion, and other factors. They are also protected from termination for such actions as whistleblowing, refusing to engage in unlawful acts (such as insurance fraud), filing a worker's compensation claim, engaging in lawful union activities, and others (Falcone, 2002).

Therefore, even when an employment-at-will relationship exists, administrators should institute and use a progressive discipline system whereby performance concerns are addressed in a multistage process escalating from verbal warnings to written warnings to termination, should performance problems continue unabated. The system should spell out unacceptable behaviors and consequences. Of course, all evidence and material related to each step in the disciplinary process, including efforts to assist the employee to improve performance, and the ultimate decision to discharge must be thoroughly documented.

Employees can be terminated for many reasons, including:

- Incompetence in performance that does not respond to training or accommodation
- Gross or repeated insubordination
- Civil rights violations, such as harassment
- Too many unexcused absences or repeated lateness
- Illegal behavior, such as theft
- Drug activity or intoxication on the job
- Verbal abuse
- Physical violence
- Falsification of records
- Conflicts of interest

These behaviors vary in their severity and in the degree of risk they pose for the organization, its clients, and its workers. Therefore, organizations may differentiate, in their disciplinary policy, the ways in which each category of infraction will be handled (for example, by suspension, automatic discharge, or discipline). Organizations can establish just cause for discipline by ensuring that workers are adequately informed of the consequences of certain forms of conduct, that the agency's performance expectations are reasonable and appropriate for safe and efficient operations, that the agency engaged in a fair and objective investigation before determining that the worker was in error, that the investigation yielded support that a violation took place, that policies were applied without discrimination, and that the discipline was appropriate for the infraction (Falcone, 2002).

The discipline system should thus be characterized by clarity and fairness, not only in the way in which policies are applied but also in the way that people are treated throughout the process. The latter is referred to as "interactional justice," wherein an organization takes the employee's feelings into account in carrying out its disciplinary policies (Noe et al., 2017). Fairness is conveyed by treating the employee with respect and empathy, listening to the employee's perspective, providing opportunities for improvement, and preserving the worker's dignity, even in the face of a decision to discharge the worker. The principles of progressive discipline are sometimes summarized as the hot-stove rule because, like a hot stove, effective discipline provides fair warning, reacts at once, is consistent and objective, applies equally to all, and does not apologize for what it is (Noe et al., 2017).

Once the decision has been made to terminate an employee, it should be carried out swiftly, firmly, and privately. The person conducting the dismissal meeting should begin with a clear statement of the purpose of the meeting, the basis for the decision, and the next steps in the process (Rivas, 1998), for example,

> Paul, we are meeting today to discuss your discharge from the organization. This morning you missed a case staffing despite the stipulation in your performance plan that you attend those meetings. As described in your last disciplinary warning, such an absence is cause for termination from the agency. Today will be your last day. This sheet describes your options for appealing this decision and the payment of your remaining salary, vacation days, and benefits.

These are difficult conversations, and it is often helpful to practice or role-play them with a superior before the actual meeting. It may also be helpful to have a third party attend the meeting (for example, another manager, HR professional) to ensure that the steps are carried out properly and to provide corroboration should the employee dispute the facts of the meeting at a later date. Having support at the meeting may also enhance the sense of safety if concerns exist about the employee's reaction (Falcone, 2002). Practice can help the supervisor avoid pitfalls in the dismissal meeting, including backpedaling from the decision, negotiating, and blaming others for the decision (Rivas, 1998).

When an organization determines that downsizing is necessary, the first step is diagnosis: What is the nature and extent of the budgetary shortfalls? Are they time limited? Are they due to miscalculations in income or overexpenditures? Are they centered in one department or program? This analysis should lead to tentative options, which must then be weighed in terms of their adequacy for addressing the problem and the ramifications for clients, services, personnel, and morale. Must staff be cut? (Sometimes cutting staff will also diminish the ability to generate revenue.) Should cuts be across the board, or should they eliminate an entire service line or division? What are the pros and cons of options to layoffs, such as hiring freezes, downsizing through attrition, early retirements, voluntary furloughs (unpaid days off), or mandatory across-the-board furloughs (during traditionally slow periods)? The decisions should ensure equity, taking into account the organization's objectives, the maintenance of key programs, the needs of the workers who remain, and the costs of the layoffs (for example, paying out unused vacation time or arranging job search assistance).

The downsizing process must be carefully managed, and communications should be characterized by honesty and frequency. To the extent that the agency functioned effectively before the financial crisis, the better able it will be to weather the layoffs. To the extent that it has been characterized by unhappiness, distrust, and hopelessness, the more difficult the downsizing experience will be.

Conclusion

HR management involves an array of interlocking steps and strategies that are used to help the agency achieve its goals through an effective and stable workforce. HR decisions are shaped by variables that are specific to the organization and by external factors, such as labor market characteristics, economic factors, and laws and regulations. Across the array of personnel actions, from employee selection to compensation, training, and evaluation to separations, HR managers must be mindful of the competing tensions of equity and efficiency and understand the interlocking and sometimes unintended consequences of HR actions.

Skills Application Exercises

1. Do a structured interview simulation as a class exercise or training for a work group. In small groups, develop a set of interview questions and a rating rubric for candidates for a position in a nonprofit organization. Select one group member to role-play as an applicant for the position, select another member to lead the interview, and assign other group members particular questions to ask the candidate. Then conduct a candidate interview. Each interviewer should complete the rating rubric and then compare their evaluations of the candidate. Did the interview questions capture the important qualities needed for the position? Did the rubric align with the questions and the candidate's qualifications? How did the ratings compare within the interview team? What might account for differences? What feedback does the team have for the interviewee? What suggestions does the interviewee have for the interviewers and for the process?

2. Obtain a performance evaluation instrument from a nonprofit organization, and interview individuals responsible for overseeing performance evaluation, such as the director of HR management or the chief executive officer. Assess the strengths and weaknesses of the organization's performance evaluation system.

References

Abramson, J. S. (1993). Orienting social work employees in interdisciplinary settings: Shaping professional and organizational perspectives. *Social Work, 38*, 152–157.

Age Discrimination in Employment Act of 1967, P.L. 90-202, 29 U.S.C. §§ 621 *et seq.*

Americans with Disabilities Act of 1990, P.L. 101-33, 42 U.S.C. §§ 12101 *et seq.*

Asamoah, Y. (1995). Managing the new multicultural workplace. In L. Ginsberg & P. R. Keys (Eds.), *New management in human services* (2nd ed., pp. 115–127). Washington, DC: NASW Press.

Beckett, J. O., & Dungee-Anderson, D. (1996). A framework for agency-based multicultural training and supervision. *Journal of Multicultural Social Work, 4*(4), 27–48.

Cascio, W. F., & Boudreau, J. W. (2012). *Short introduction to strategic human resource management*. Cambridge University Press.

Capelli, P., Charan, R., Carey, D., Barton, D., Burrell, L., Gherson, D., & Tavis, A. (2018). HR goes agile. *Harvard Business Review, March–April*. Retrieved from https://hbr.org/2018/03/the-new-rules-of-talent-management

Clifford, J. P. (1999). The collective wisdom of the workforce: Conversations with employees regarding performance evaluation. *Public Personnel Management, 28*, 119–150.

Cohen, B. J. (2002). Alternative organizing principles for the design of service delivery systems. *Administration in Social Work, 26*(2), 17–38.

Denhardt, R. B., Denhardt, J. V., Aristigueta, M. P., & Rawlings, K. C. (2018). *Managing human behavior in public and nonprofit organizations* (5th ed.). Washington, DC: CQ Press.

Equal Employment Opportunity Act of 1972, P.L. 92-261, 42 U.S.C. §§ 2000e.

Equal Pay Act of 1963, P.L. 88-38, 29 U.S.C. §§ 206d.

Fair Labor Standards Act of 1938, 29 U.S.C. §§ 201 *et seq.*

Falcone, P. (2002). *The hiring and firing question and answer book*. New York: Amacom.

Family and Medical Leave Act of 1993, P.L. 103-3, 29 U.S.C. §§ 2601 *et seq.*

Griffin, W. V. (1995). Social worker and agency safety. In R. L. Edwards (Ed.), *Encyclopedia of social work* (Vol. 2, 19th ed., pp. 2293–2305). Washington, DC: NASW Press.

Hindle, T. (1998). *Interviewing skills.* New York: DK Publishing.

Johnson, C. E. (2001). *Meeting the ethical challenges of leadership.* Thousand Oaks, CA: SAGE.

Kraiger, K., & Aguinis, H. (2001). Training effectiveness: Assessing training needs, motivation, and accomplishments. In M. London (Ed.), *How people evaluate others in organizations* (pp. 203–219). Mahwah, NJ: Erlbaum.

Langdon, K., & Osborne, C. (2001). *Performance reviews.* New York: DK Publishing.

Macaleer, B., & Shannon, J. (2003). Does HR planning improve business performance? *Industrial Management, 45,* 15–20.

Mathis, R. L., Jackson, J. H., Valentine, S. R., & Meglich, P. A. (2017). *Human resource management.* Boston: Cengage Learning.

Milkovich, G. T., & Boudreau, J. W. (1997). *Human resource management* (8th ed.). Homewood, IL: Irwin.

Millar, K. I. (1998). Evaluating employee performance. In R. L. Edwards, J. A. Yankey, & M. A. Altpeter (Eds.), *Skills for effective management of nonprofit organizations* (pp. 219–243). Washington, DC: NASW Press.

National Association of Social Workers. (2021). *Code of ethics.* Washington, DC: Author.

Noe, R. A., Hollenbeck, J. R., Gerhart, B., & Wright, P. M. (2017). *Fundamentals of human resource management* (10th ed.). Boston: McGraw-Hill.

Petersen, L. (2019, March 5). Advantages and disadvantages of pay-for-performance strategies. *Chron.* Retrieved from https://smallbusiness.chron.com/advantages-disadvantages-payforperformance-policies-44264.html

Pregnancy Discrimination Act of 1978, P.L. 95-555, 42 U.S.C. §§ 2000 *et seq.*

Rivas, R. F. (1998). Dismissing problem employees. In R. L. Edwards, J. A. Yankey, & M. A. Altpeter (Eds.), *Skills for effective management of nonprofit organizations* (pp. 262–278). Washington, DC: NASW Press.

Roberts, G. E. (1998). Perspectives on enduring and emerging issues in performance appraisal. *Public Personnel Management, 27,* 301–320.

Social Security Act of 1935, P.L. 74-271, 42 U.S.C. §§ 301 *et seq.*

Title VII, Civil Rights Act of 1964, P.L. 88-352, 42 U.S.C. §§ 2000e.

U.S. Equal Employment Opportunity Commission. (1990). *Policy guidance on current issues of sexual harassment.* Retrieved from https://www.eeoc.gov/laws/guidance/policy-guidance-current-issues-sexual-harassment

Weinbach, R. W. (1998). *The social worker as manager* (3rd ed.). Boston: Allyn & Bacon.

6

Cultivating a Culture of Diversity, Equity, and Inclusion

Alena C. Hampton, Amy J. Armstrong, and Susan L. Parish

Nonprofit organizations can play a vital role in building and supporting inclusive and equitable communities for historically underserved populations. Nonprofits often strive to address systemic disparities and advocate for equitable opportunities so all community members can experience an enviable quality of life. We are now at a time in our collective U.S. history when successful organizations understand the important role diversity plays in their success. For example, numerous studies have found evidence that organizations are better able to execute plans, have more productive employees, have employees with greater commitment to the organization, and are more harmonious when the workplace is diverse (Bond & Haynes, 2014; Hamilton, Nickerson, & Owan, 2003; Kapoor, 2011).

As noted in chapter 1, the competing values framework points out that among the various skills and competencies managers must exercise are the roles of mentor and facilitator. The goal in relation to fulfilling these roles is to have an organization that has a heterogeneous, diverse mix of employees that make up a productive, motivated, and committed workforce.

For organizations to truly be successful, they must move beyond diversity. Similarly, successful leaders are those who move beyond managing diversity to cultivating equity and inclusion by supporting the growth and contribution of all employees. We believe this is true for all organizations, including nonprofit organizations.

But what does diversity mean? For the purposes of this chapter, diversity underscores that everyone is unique, and these differences enrich the communities in which one works and lives. From an organizational perspective, diversity refers to the distribution of people in an organization. Specifically, diversity refers to lived experiences along dimensions that include gender, age, sexual orientation, race, ethnicity, socioeconomic status, cultural background, religious beliefs, and disability identity. Although an understanding of diversity is essential for both organizations and leaders, we assert that moving beyond diversity to understanding and cultivating equity and inclusion is a critical aspect of individual and organizational flourishing.

The Race Equity and Inclusion Action Guide by the Annie E. Casey Foundation (2015) distinguishes between diversity and inclusion by noting that inclusion speaks to a sense of belonging and an ability to participate. Although diversity refers to the representation of different types of people, inclusion refers to actions taken to ensure individuals feel welcome and be full participants in a community or organization. A distinction should also be made between equity and equality. Equality means that everyone receives the same thing, and everyone is treated the same. By contrast, in a social justice context, equity is the process of differentially giving people what they need to survive, succeed, and thrive. Taken together, it is possible to have a diverse organization that is not inclusive and similarly, an individual can feel included without experiencing equity. An organization can have a membership that represents the larger population in its diversity, but members may not feel welcome or included, despite the representational diversity present in the organization or community.

This chapter provides a framework for understanding the importance of diversity, equity, and inclusion in the workplace and the essential role leaders play in cultivating all of them. After a brief overview of the shifting demography of the United States, models of leadership and managerial and supervisory responsibilities that foster inclusion and equity are presented. We then consider the ethical and economic impact of attending to these phenomena and briefly discuss managing various stakeholders. The chapter concludes with an overview of an organizational exemplar and vignettes that reflect effective approaches to cultivating diversity, equity, and inclusion.

Changing Demography

The increasing diversity of the U.S. population is a demographic reality that organizations cannot avoid. As nonprofits seek to lead in ways that are inclusive, understanding how the nation's population is changing is warranted. We briefly note several of the major changes that have emerged over the past century and that will continue to shape the workforce for many decades to come. The major changes we describe are as follows: (1) The number of racial and ethnic minorities is increasing in comparison with the number of people who identify as non-Hispanic White, (2) immigration continues to power population growth in the country overall, (3) people with disabilities are living longer than ever and are in the workforce in the greatest numbers since data collection began, and (4) the portion of the U.S. population that is elderly (age 65 years or older) is increasing relative to other age groups.

Increasing Racial and Ethnic Diversity

The non-Hispanic White population of the United States has been projected by the U.S. Census to decline from 199 million to 179 million by 2060 (Vespa, Medina, & Armstrong, 2020). The two key drivers of the shrinkage of this subgroup are declining fertility and increased death rates because this subset of the population is older. As the population of non-Hispanic Whites gets older, the number of deaths in this group increases.

In contrast with the declining number of non-Hispanic White people, the numbers of people who are Hispanic, Asian, and multiracial are growing. The fastest increasing subgroup of the U.S. population is individuals of more than one race. Growth in the nation's population of Hispanics and multiracial individuals is occurring for the same reason: Births will exceed deaths as a result of the younger overall structure of these groups (Vespa et al., 2020). The fast growth of the Asian population in the United States is being catalyzed by the relatively high number of Asians immigrating to the United States. By contrast, the number of Black or African American babies born in the United States is projected by the Census Bureau to remain approximately constant at between 15.5 percent and 16.0 percent of all U.S.-born children (Vespa et al., 2020).

Immigration

The United States has been a nation of immigrants since its founding. The historic high occurred in 1890, when 14.8 percent of the population was deemed by the U.S. Census to have been born outside the country (Vespa et al., 2020). However, current projections indicate that this percentage will be surpassed in 2030, and the number of people living in the country but born elsewhere will continue to grow to 17 percent by 2060 (Vespa et al., 2020). Notably, enumeration of the population of enslaved people during the decennial censuses did not record names or birthplaces until after the Civil War and emancipation. The 1870 census was the first to identify African

Americans by full name and birthplace (National Archives and Records Administration, 2012) and thus more accurately reflect the true population born outside the United States.

Although immigration has always propelled population growth in the United States, the variety of "sending countries," set by U.S. policy, has and will continue to change in the coming decades. For example, a majority of newcomers to the United States between 1990 and 2000 were from Latin America. In the decade 2010–2020, a majority of immigrants came from Asia. Finally, the number of Black immigrants has increased substantially, growing by 30 percent between 2010 and 2018 to exceed 4 million annually (New American Economy Research Fund, 2020). Immigrants from different countries form a highly heterogeneous group. For example, Black immigrants are much more likely to be proficient English speakers than other immigrants (74 percent versus 51 percent, respectively) (Anderson & López, 2018), and they also have greater educational attainment than the overall U.S. population (New American Economy Research Fund, 2020). The profound heterogeneity of people living in the United States but born in other countries contributes racial, ethnic, educational, religious, cultural, and refugee status diversity to American nonprofits, in terms of both workforce and populations served.

People with Disabilities

In the United States, approximately 20 percent of the population has a disability. In the aggregate, people with disabilities form the single largest minority in the United States. However, this group is also highly heterogeneous and includes people with intellectual, psychiatric, physical, and sensory impairments. Notions of disability identity and disability culture are relatively recent phenomena, emerging late in the 19th century with the rise of American schools and institutions for the Deaf and for blind people (Braddock & Parish, 2001). The disability civil rights movement ensued in the 1970s when disabled activists emulated the activism and civil disobedience of the Black civil rights movement (Braddock & Parish, 2001).

Despite important legal and civil rights victories, particularly passage of the Americans with Disabilities Act of 1990 (P.L. 101-336), the employment rate of working-age adults with disabilities remains exceptionally low. In 2019, the unemployment rate for disabled adults was more than twice that of nondisabled adults (U.S. Bureau of Labor Statistics, 2020). Like all other employers, nonprofit organizations are prohibited from discriminating on the basis of disability, and they are required by law to offer reasonable disability accommodations in all aspects of their hiring, promotion, and evaluation practices (Heymann, Stein, & Moreno, 2014). Despite the legal mandates of the Americans with Disabilities Act, however, the unemployment and underemployment of individuals with disabilities persists as a serious problem (Heymann et al., 2014).

Aging of the U.S. Population

The so-called "graying" of the U.S. population mirrors similar trends in developed nations around the world, in which the proportion of the population that is elderly is increasing relative to other age groups. This trend in aging is driven by medical and public health advances that propel longevity, particularly of the baby boom generation born after World War II (Vespa et al., 2020). As projected by the U.S. Census Bureau, the child population will grow by 6.5 million between 2016 and 2060. By contrast, the elderly population is expected to grow by 45.4 million, or nearly seven times the growth of the child population (Vespa et al., 2020). Widespread discrimination experienced by older people and rampant ageist attitudes across society have been well documented by researchers (Gendron, Inker, & Welleford, 2018). These pervasively negative views of aging and of elderly people are directly at odds with the facts: Older adults are increasingly working well into their retirement years, and this trend will continue for decades to come (Toossi & Torpey, 2017). Older workers often contribute valuable knowledge and experience to the workforce, and as longevity continues to increase, many older people are healthy enough to work past the traditional retirement age (Toossi & Torpey, 2017).

On balance, the U.S. population is richly heterogeneous. Highly credible projections from the U.S. Census Bureau and the Pew Research Center indicate that this diversity, across all types of identity, will deepen in the decades to come.

Leadership Models that Foster Inclusive and Equitable Environments

Research has indicated that the manager or leader is the single most predictive variable of employee and organizational well-being, accounting for 70 percent of the variance in team engagement (Gallup, 2019). An engaged employee is enthusiastic and invested in the workplace and in the work they perform. Currently, only 34 percent of the U.S. workforce is considered engaged, leaving a sizable majority disengaged at work (Gallup, 2019). Effective managers possess relationship skills and engage in professional and personal conduct that facilitates a generative culture. Grounded within this research are several leadership models that promote a culture of inclusion and equity, which in turn leads to higher levels of satisfaction, engagement, and performance outcomes: relational leadership, appreciative leadership, and strengths-based leadership.

Relational Leadership

Relational leadership is the idea that leaders and colleagues exist in reciprocal relationships that build trust, mutuality, and respect (Clarke, 2018). Leadership is seen as a social process in which relationships are dynamic and evolving, and it is socially constructed because followers have a leadership relationship with leaders. This model recognizes the contribution of all members to achieving the goals and mission of an organization.

Appreciative Leadership

Appreciative leadership is the relational capacity to mobilize creative potential to make a positive difference in the world. Appreciative leadership is framed within the evidence-based practices associated with appreciative inquiry leadership, positive psychology, and the strengths movement (Whitney, Trosten-Bloom, & Rader, 2010). The strategies of appreciative leadership include inclusion, inspiration, illumination of strength, and integrity. These strategies lead to an increase in respect of differences and stronger relationships. Appreciative inquiry is a leading process for business and societal change that identifies the life-affirming force of individuals and organizations (Cooperrider & Whitney, 2005). Positive psychology is the scientific study of positive human functioning and flourishing on multiple levels, including biological, personal, relational, institutional, cultural, and global dimensions (Seligman & Csikszentmihalyi, 2014). The strengths movement focuses on the identification and utilization of an individual's talents to achieve aspirations, goals, and outcomes (Buckingham & Clifton, 2001).

Strengths-Based Leadership

Building on the strengths-based movement, Peter Drucker (as cited in Cooperrider & Whitney, 2005) defined the purpose of leadership as the ability to use strengths so that weaknesses are no longer relevant, thereby perpetuating performance, efficiency, innovation, well-being, and growth that benefits the world. Strengths-based organizations outperform competitors. Benefits include putting untapped talent to use throughout an organization, recruitment and retention of employees needed by an organization, improved individual and team performance, engagement, a positive emphasis on difference, and enhanced achievement of goals (Brun, Cooperrider, & Ejsing, 2016; Harter et al., 2020; Northouse, 2020).

These models intersect because they support the development of generative and collaborative relationships based on mutuality and trust, positive communication, and feedback. Moreover, each model promotes fostering a climate of appreciation, empathy, and gratitude and identifying individual and collective purpose to achieve the mission of the organization. Viewing diversity, equity, and inclusion through these paradigms presents an opportunity to facilitate meaningful and sustainable systemic change in which the self-efficacy and competence of all employees are acknowledged, respected, and valued.

Managerial and Supervisory Responsibilities that Foster Diversity, Equity, and Inclusion

Successful managers and supervisors not only have an understanding of leadership models that are conducive to cultivating inclusion and equity but also possess cross-cultural knowledge. This knowledge includes an awareness of their own biases and blind spots as well as strategies they can use (Russell, Brock, & Rudisill, 2019). Let's take a closer look at the impact managers and supervisors can have on the creation of an equitable and inclusive environment through (1) recruitment and hiring, (2) professional development, and (3) building team culture.

Recruitment and Hiring

Diversifying the workplace begins with recruitment and hiring. Despite the widely held belief that discrimination is declining, a recent study found no change in the extent of hiring discrimination against African Americans in the past 25 years (Quillian, Pager, Hexel, & Midtboen, 2017). Coupled with the racial unemployment gaps that have persisted since 1980, the need for managers and supervisors to be intentional about implementing recruitment and hiring strategies to combat discriminatory practices is clear. Such strategies include formal recruitment fairs (that is, career fairs), advertising postings in minority-serving publications, using images of diverse employees, and using minority recruiters (Newman & Lyon, 2009). Collectively, these strategies constitute what Newman and Lyon (2009) referred to as "targeted recruitment," which refers to practices that affect the number or types of targeted individuals interested in applying to or accepting a given position. Targeting qualified minority applicants, then, facilitates diversification of the applicant pool and helps mitigate the adverse effects of hiring discrimination.

To fully capitalize on the benefits of a qualified diverse pool of applicants, managers and supervisors must ensure that search committees are prepared to do the important work of reviewing and evaluating candidates. Diversified search committees should be trained to embrace nontraditional résumés and to understand the danger of bias in the selection process. *Implicit bias*, for example, is defined as the unconsciously held set of attitudes and associations one has about a group. This bias, which all people have, can lead to prejudicial behavior and evaluations on the basis of gender, race, ethnicity, sexual orientation, disability status, and other dimensions of diversity (Prestia, 2019). *Affinity bias* refers to people's preference for others who are like them. In a hiring context, affinity bias indicates that a White man is more likely to evaluate another White man more positively than a non-White man. The composition of the search committee, then, can have an impact on which candidates rise to the top of the pool, so it is imperative that hiring teams receive proper training about these biases and how to mitigate them so as not to impede the work of the committee (Prestia, 2019).

Implicit, affinity, and other biases are prevalent not just in hiring practices but also in promotion and career advancement. Specifically, supervisors' biases may affect the justification and rationale of employee selection for awards, projects, or expanded duties (Russell et al., 2019). As a result, underrepresented employees are not promoted and recognized at the same rate as their White counterparts (Bezrukova, Jehn, & Spell, 2012; James, 2000). Successful leaders cultivate inclusion and equity by developing an awareness of their own biases and by ensuring that awards, bonuses, promotions, and other professional development opportunities are distributed in an equitable fashion.

Professional Development

Retention strategies also facilitate an inclusive environment. These strategies include professional development, communication and feedback, and facilitation of an appreciative climate. Mentorship and employee training are two critical professional development opportunities, and, unfortunately, there is extensive evidence that minority groups have limited access to such opportunities. Mentorship has long been known as an effective strategy to diversify an organization. Specifically, the insight gleaned from a mentor and the access to their professional network can be invaluable to one's individual career trajectory. It is not surprising, then, that women and minorities are more likely to report that mentoring is extremely important to their career (Emrich, Livingston, Pruner, Oberfeld, & Page, 2017). As it relates to training, women and racial and ethnic minority groups receive less career information and fewer opportunities for training and development for additional responsibilities. As such, these populations are often not recognized for their achievements and excluded from professional networks (Siu Chow & Crawford, 2004). Organizations committed to creating an environment in which everyone can be successful are encouraged to offer mentorship and professional development opportunities with a particular emphasis on supporting minority populations.

Notably, a comprehensive professional development or training program must also include diversity training for all members of the organization. This is key to individual development, as well as to building a culture of teamwork. Many organizations, particularly nonprofits, have diversity as a central theme in their mission statements, yet their employees lack a basic understanding of diversity concepts. Such trainings can decrease discrimination and facilitate positive cross-cultural interactions (Bezrukova et al., 2012). Moreover, they can provide opportunities for employees to develop skills, explore their own areas of bias, and evaluate the role they can play in creating an inclusive and equitable environment (Bezrukova et al., 2012). Managers and supervisors can set expectations about the frequency at which employees participate in such trainings, and they can model an openness and willingness to learn and self-reflect. Reframing diversity training as an opportunity for new learning and growth can lead to a process of discovery that strengthens relationships, interpersonal congruence, and engagement. It is important to note that such training is successful only when it is coupled with other meaningful efforts designed to create an inclusive environment, such as those described in this chapter.

Providing and receiving feedback is an essential element of professional development. Leaders can provide ongoing, constructive strengths-based employee feedback in conversations throughout the year versus the traditional end-of-year performance evaluation (Rigoni & Asplund, 2016). These conversations focus on the employee's strengths and overall contribution to the organization's mission. Ongoing positive communication and feedback increases team engagement and performance and can support employee growth and learning (Asplund, Harter, Agrawal, & Plowman, 2016). For example, high-performing teams typically have a higher ratio of positive to negative communication and feedback. Conversations may also specifically focus on team behavioral attributes such as professional conduct, respectful and civil interactions, and collaboration. Managers and supervisors may need to provide developmental feedback; however, the key is to focus more on strengths than on weaknesses.

Building Team Culture

Managers and supervisors have the opportunity to have a positive impact on team culture by setting a tone of appreciation of all differences, not just those related to race, ethnicity, gender, sexual orientation, age, and disability. For example, managers and supervisors should recognize various learning styles represented on their team and provide information in ways consistent with those styles. In recognition of heterogeneous communication styles, supervisors should ensure that team members can, for example, provide feedback verbally, in writing, at the time of the solicitation, or at a later time. This includes the opportunity to provide feedback on leadership as well.

Research has suggested that leaders can use a range of strategies to foster a culture of inclusion and appreciation. Clifton and Harter (2019) offered three requirements for leaders related to diversity and inclusion: (1) treating employees with respect, (2) valuing employees for their strengths, and (3) leading with integrity—doing the right thing. Leaders can establish such a culture of inclusion and appreciation by focusing on strengths and ensuring respect and civility for all. This includes fostering an environment of innovation and creativity in which all voices are heard, providing growth opportunities, and engaging in radical collaborations (Tamm & Luyet, 2019). In addition, facilitating employee well-being, helping employees connect their work to meaning through a shared vision and mission that is based on shared core values, and recognizing and celebrating successes contribute to an appreciative culture (Dutton & Spreitzer, 2014; Porath, 2016; Whitney et al., 2010). A leader who exhibits positive energy and embodies a culture of integrity increases an employee's productivity, facilitating not only personal well-being but also job satisfaction, job performance, and engagement with the organization (Cameron, 2012; Dutton & Spreitzer, 2014; Whitney et al., 2010).

Finally, managers and supervisors should ensure that they are monitoring and working to improve the organizational culture through climate assessments. With an understanding of diversity, inclusion, and equity comes a realization that an organization may fall short of its aspirations in terms of its culture and practices. Periodic climate assessment gives all members of the community the opportunity to share their experiences and feedback anonymously, giving the supervisor valuable information about problem areas and issues that need to be addressed, as well as elucidating what is working well in an organization and should be scaled up and sustained. Tracking (identifying) and fanning (growing) such practices can have a profound and positive impact on the culture. Intentional and proactive management of such assessment is necessary to understanding where change should be implemented to improve the climate (Levin, 2000), and it ensures that all voices can be heard. Leadership must also have the courage to address attitudes and practices that undermine diversity and inclusion.

Ethical and Moral Imperative for Cultivating Diversity, Inclusion, and Equity

Nonprofit organizations and leaders must heed the ethical and moral imperative to cultivate diversity, equity, and inclusion. In fact, codes of ethics promulgated by various professional organizations typically have a built-in notion of treating others with respect. The National Association of Social Workers' (2017) *Code of Ethics,* for example, sets an expectation that "social workers challenge social injustice" and that they treat everyone in a "caring and respectful fashion, mindful of individual differences and cultural and ethnic diversity." Similarly, "respect for people's rights and dignity" is one of the guiding principles of the Academy of Management's (AOM, n.d.) *Code of Ethics.* AOM members are expected to "respect cultural, individual, and role differences" and to "eliminate the effect on their work of biases."

Beyond the ethical principles promulgated by associations, there is ample evidence of the collective moral call for change in the United States related to how marginalized populations are treated. This evidence includes the increased attention on implicit bias after its mention in a presidential debate, the fight for marriage equality, the protection of voting rights, and the focus on health care and health disparities. Social activism has been affecting how people see themselves as a country and how they see themselves as individuals. This was highlighted in Spring 2020, which brought a social justice awakening across the United States, and to some extent the world, borne out of another murder of a Black man in police custody. The death of George Floyd in Minneapolis, Minnesota, prompted weeks of protest against police brutality. More than that, these protests reignited the existing Black Lives Matter movement, whose mission is combating White supremacy in all its forms, including police reform, education, justice reform, and immigration.

As noted earlier, although many organizations have mission and vision statements that reflect a commitment to diversity, in practice, diversity and inclusion are often a supplement to rather than an integrated, central component of the organization. Truly inclusive cultures, which discourage bias and discrimination and work toward true systemic transformation, develop shared values that are integrated and permeate vision statements, missions, and strategic plans. From these organizational artifacts, practices, policies, and procedures emerge to foster an inclusive culture.

We emphasize that it is imperative for organizations to operationalize their mission with action. The National Council of Nonprofits (2020) noted recently on its Web site that it is not enough for organizations to have such statements or to issue statements decrying discrimination. They have a responsibility to take intentional steps to understand how they have contributed to systemic oppression and to put an end to practices that perpetuate it. It is critical for organizations to examine their practices and culture and to explore how they treat their employees and customers, as well as how their values and mission reflect inclusion and equity.

Economic Impact of Cultivating Diversity, Equity, and Inclusion

Beyond organizational well-being and ethical and moral considerations, attending to diversity, inclusion, and equity will have a notable impact on the economics and image of an organization. In terms of retention, more than one in three employees voluntarily left their jobs in 2018 as competition for workers increased. Voluntary turnover costs are in excess of $600 billion nationally (Work Institute, 2020). Workplace discrimination based on race, gender, or sexual orientation alone results in turnover that costs businesses an estimated $64 billion annually (Burns, 2012). Turnover can also lead to lost productivity and knowledge and lower employee morale that subsequently affects culture, as well as the organization's public image. Jones and Harter (2005) found that when managers and employees of different races are highly engaged, employees' intent to remain with the organization is greater. Burns (2012) identified that businesses who place an emphasis on demographic characteristics versus competence and qualifications to perform the tasks associated with a position place themselves at a competitive disadvantage. Beyond workplace turnover, disengaged employees may also cost an organization in terms of absences, lower quality or less productivity, and a negative impact on the work culture (Sorenson, 2013).

Diversity, inclusion, and equity lead to cognitive diversity in decision making and problem solving, which in turn leads to creativity, innovation, and productivity (International Labour Organization, 2019; Lorenzo et al., 2017). Equity leads to the bridging of skills gaps and development of strengths. Diverse organizations are also more adept at attracting and retaining talented employees. Diversity and inclusion are increasingly attractive features for those considering employment with a particular employer (Weber-Shandwick Inc., 2016). That is, many job seekers consider diversity and inclusion in hiring decisions. The economic impact of cultivating diversity, inclusion, and equity is essential to performance and creates a thriving organizational culture that is publicly identified with such values.

Communicating Commitment to Diversity, Equity, and Inclusion to Stakeholders

Nonprofit organizations benefit from thinking about how they share their commitment to diversity, equity, and inclusion with their stakeholders. This includes client, patron, or customer relations; reputation management; and managing boards of directors (National Council of Nonprofits, 2020).

Typically, it is common practice to include stakeholders in strategic planning processes. This practice is imperative when developing and evaluating processes, policies, and plans relevant to diversity management, equity, and inclusion (Maj, 2015). Client, patron, or customer populations can provide valuable feedback regarding how the organization serves or may best serve its constituents. Conducting focus groups, needs assessments, surveys, and interviews with clients, patrons, or customers who are from marginalized groups fosters a deeper understanding and connection between community members and the organization. This practice communicates a strong commitment to inclusion and building a diverse workforce while having a positive impact on the organization's reputation.

Many communities are advocating for inclusive cultures within organizations and agencies. Organizations are increasingly cognizant of the benefits of sustaining a reputation for valuing diversity, equity, and inclusion (International Labour Organization, 2019). Intentionally strategizing how to incorporate an organization's mission, values, and vision into daily practice is critically important not only to the organization's functioning but to building a positive public image. Working cooperatively with other nonprofit, governmental, or for-profit organizations within a community is a networking strategy that facilitates a positive reputation and organizational well-being (Wei-Skillern & Marciano, 2008). Leaders who are working with peers from other organizations can strengthen their organization's multicultural capacities, often learning strategies that have been effective in other organizations.

The role of social media in systems advocacy has been well documented (Obar, Zube, & Lampe, 2012). The use of social media for calls for equity and inclusion is a prevalent and powerful factor that has the potential to affect an organization's economic health. A negative reputation can have a profound impact on finances and customer utilization of supports, services, and products, perhaps leading to demands for change, a call to boycott such organizations, or both. A positive reputation enhances the overall image, vitality, and well-being of an organization.

Boards of directors must reflect the diverse communities served by the organization. All too often, as with corporations, nonprofits and foundations experience a lack of diversity at all levels of leadership (Battalia Winston, 2015). Boards that are not diverse perpetuate homogeneity and will have difficulty identifying new and diverse members (National Council of Nonprofits, 2020). Organizational bylaws that require proportional representation of diverse membership that is not tokenistic yet truly values diverse demographics, experiences, perspectives, and backgrounds is a central practice.

Leaders and staff can work interchangeably with board members to develop and implement policies and procedures that prioritize diversity, equity, and inclusion. Leadership can inform board members of current workforce trends and state and federal policies to ensure compliance, as well as setting policies and procedures that may be more progressive and supportive of workers than federal standards. Organizations may consider policies that promote flextime, telework, job sharing, and paid caregiving leave to support dual roles as employees and caregivers. Such forward and equitable practices reflect a commitment to diversity and are workforce-centric.

Conclusion

Shifts in U.S. demographics, ethical and moral imperatives, and economic considerations collectively demand that leaders and organizations alike take seriously their responsibility to create an environment that cultivates diversity, inclusion, and equity. Current models of leadership, including relational leadership and positive organizational development, equip leaders to approach their supervisory duties with an intention to do just that. Leaders who are successful in this effort are those who address bias in their recruiting, hiring, and promotion practices; provide professional development opportunities that include mentorship; and adopt a practice in which they act as a coach to grow employees. Moreover, those who lead by example to create a culture that develops relationships and trust, resolve conflicts quickly, offer diversity training, and adeptly manage stakeholders can foster an equitable and inclusive environment. Finally, it is critical that organizations and leaders foster a team culture by regularly engaging in climate assessment and by creating space for all learning and communication styles, ensuring that all voices are heard. Leadership is accountable for the organization's culture and how it engages its stakeholders. We conclude this chapter with organizational exemplars and case vignettes that further illuminate these ideas.

Organizational Exemplars and Vignettes

Rush University Medical Center is part of the Rush University System for Health, an academic health system located in Chicago, Illinois. As the first medical school in the city, Rush has long been part of the fabric of Chicago. Rush University consists of colleges of health sciences, nursing, medicine, and research training. Rush Health is a network of physicians and hospitals, including a community hospital, Rush Oak Park. In 2019, these hospitals were ranked first for quality of care, they received top ratings for patient safety, and several of their specialties were rated the best in the country or in Illinois (Anderton, 2020).

Rush has demonstrated its commitment to diversity particularly as it relates to the lesbian, gay, bisexual, transgender, and queer/questioning (LGBTQ+) community. They have cultivated an inclusive culture by (1) providing LGBTQ+ health education to clinicians and staff, (2) developing nondiscrimination policies that include sexual orientation and gender identity, and (3) offering transgender health benefits for their employees and beneficiaries (Human Rights Campaign Foundation, 2020). Moreover, to combat the health care disparities faced by members of the LGBTQ+ community, Rush created a center that provides safe and accessible comprehensive care to this community. Affirm: The Rush Center for Gender, Sexuality and Reproductive Health provides training to clinicians and offers liaison services from a clinical social worker to patients, visitors, employees, and students. Finally, Rush has created an affinity group for members of the LGBTQ+ community and their allies, it has made curricular changes to ensure that it is more inclusive, and it provides a variety of resources and programming to the Chicago community. As a result of Rush's efforts, the 2019 Healthcare Equality Index designated Rush a "leader in LGBTQ+ health equality" for its treatment of its patients and employees who identify as LGBTQ+.

United Way of Greater Cincinnati (UWGC) has 140 community partners and serves the greater Cincinnati region. In 2019, UWGC wrote its first report regarding diversity, equity, and inclusion (DEI), based on data collected from community partners in 2018. UWGC's vision is to eliminate poverty in the region. They believe that intentionally focusing on DEI will improve equitable outcomes for all community members. UWGC (2019) valued the voices of all stakeholders to build an environment that truly honors and embraces differences while encouraging authentic participation. This creates trust and enhances the opportunity for all to thrive. They believe that each United Way community member, donor, volunteer, advocate, and employee must have the ability to participate in creative problem solving to address community problems, thereby creating sustainable change and true impact.

The baseline assessment identified several challenges, including staff and board diversity; serving clients with unique needs, including people with disabilities and LGBTQ+ people; and ongoing training and development, as well as cultural competency. UWGC believes not only that advancing DEI is the right thing to do but that it is a moral imperative. The report provided insights into the strengths, opportunities, and challenges related to DEI. On the basis of the data collected, UWGC has issued a call to action by identifying the following strategies: modernizing data collection, including expanding diversity fields and using inclusive language to encourage self-identification; identifying six meta-themes to engage equitable practices that advance DEI and achieve social change; diversifying funding streams as well as the donor base; investing in DEI by moving beyond trainings and conversations; and allocating funding resources to this work (UWGC, 2019). The six meta-themes for equitable social change were identified by another nonprofit organization (a social innovation firm). By using both individual and system strengths, UWGC is moving toward intentional action and positive change to cocreate an aspirational vision that will redesign the system from a DEI paradigm.

Vignette 1

A manager has an open position she would like to fill, and it is important to her that she has a diverse, qualified applicant pool from which to select a candidate. As such, she updated the job description to ensure that the language was gender neutral. Although her organization could not afford to engage a professional recruiter, she advertised the job posting on a variety of minority-serving publications, Web sites, and email distribution lists. In addition, when giving her charge to the hiring committee, she reminded them of their organization's values and mission related to diversifying their staff so that it is representative of the customers they serve. The manager also invited a community partner to the meeting to provide training on bias, its impact on hiring and selection, and how to combat it. She directed the committee to ask a standard set of questions of all applicants, including questions about their understanding of and commitment to inclusion and equity. In the end, the committee provided a list of three unranked qualified candidates. When selecting the successful candidate, the manager was intentional about staying aware of her own biases to identify the most qualified applicant who would allow her organization to reach its goals.

Vignette 2

A large nonprofit organization that serves people with disabilities has been experiencing high turnover over the past two years. Leadership has noticed that workforce diversity has been affected by this turnover, which is a stated value of the organization. The board of directors, at the urging of leadership, has charged the organization to conduct an assessment of the work culture and how it may affect staff engagement and retention.

Leadership identified a core team to conduct the assessment. The team facilitated community member and customer focus groups and interviews with current and former staff. They found that some of the concerns involved limited resources, limited professional development, high caseloads, an unclear sense of value to the organization, and a lack of opportunities to be involved in decision making. However, they also found that customers valued their relationships with the organization and were satisfied with services, that staff are committed to the mission of the organization and working with clients and customers, and that the organization has a long and positive history in the community. On the basis of this initial feedback, the team formulated a plan with the aspiration of creating an inclusive culture that values all staff members. They held a one-day advance (retreat), using a strengths-based approach to planning founded in appreciative inquiry called SOAR (strengths, opportunities, aspirations, results) (Stavros & Hinrichs, 2019). "Strengths" involved an exploration of what the organization can build on. "Opportunities" focused on what stakeholders are asking for. "Aspirations" looked at what the organization cares deeply about. "Results" addressed how the organization would know it was succeeding. During this process, the team focused on what was working well in the organization, what skills or practices could be improved, and what was important for stakeholders. They invited community members, board members, clients, staff, and leadership.

The outcome of the advance resulted in the identification of several themes and action steps. The themes were establishing practices for employee recognition and appreciation; creating a shared vision and feedback or decision-making model; expanding workforce diversity; and identifying and creating opportunities for professional development and growth. Each theme was adopted by a subcommittee that included staff and two stakeholders who were invested in the respective theme. Subcommittee members established a designated person who was accountable for action steps, benchmarks of success, and timelines. Updates were provided quarterly at staff and board of directors meetings. The plan was reassessed after one year. During this time, staff reported a higher sense of engagement, and leadership noted improved practices that had an impact on performance. Three successful hires reflecting diversity occurred, and these staff have communicated their intent to remain with the organization. These individuals have also become active in the diversity subcommittee.

Skills Application Exercises

1. Contact the director of human resources of your nonprofit organization and request an inventory of current staff by their racial, disability, gender, and ethnic group membership. Also, seek a breakdown of the diversity of the organization's management and supervisory personnel and of its board of directors. To what extent are the overall staff, managerial and supervisory staff, and members of the board of directors representative of the larger community in which the nonprofit is located? Is the current reality a potential problem for the organization? Why or why not?

2. Conduct a diversity audit of your nonprofit. Examine and evaluate all facets of the organization's practices related to recruitment and selection of personnel, professional development, employee evaluation, and teamwork enhancement. In what ways are these practices welcoming to persons from diverse backgrounds? In what ways do they promote the inclusion of a workforce that is diverse and representative of the larger community in which the nonprofit is located?

Develop a specific plan with specific tasks and strategies to improve the organization's management of diversity across population subgroups. What might stand in the way of implementing such a plan? How might you overcome roadblocks to implementation of the plan?

References

Academy of Management. (n.d.). *AOM code of ethics.* Retrieved from https://aom.org/about-aom/governance/ethics/code-of-ethics

Americans With Disabilities Act of 1990, P.L. 101-336, 42 U.S.C. §§ 12101–12213 (2000).

Anderson, M., & López, G. (2018). *Key facts about black immigrants in the U.S.* Washington, DC: Pew Research Center. Retrieved from https://www.pewresearch.org/fact-tank/2018/01/24/key-facts-about-black-immigrants-in-the-u-s/

Anderton, K. (2020). *Two Rush Hospitals earn top rating from CMS.* Retrieved from https://www.news-medical.net/news/20200130/Two-Rush-hospitals-earn-top-rating-from-CMS.aspx

Annie E. Casey Foundation. (2015). *Race equity and inclusion action guide: Embracing equity: 7 steps to advance and embed race equity and inclusion within your organization.* Retrieved from https://www.aecf.org/resources/race-equity-and-inclusion-action-guide/

Asplund, J., Harter, J. K., Agrawal, S., & Plowman, S. K. (2016). *The relationship between strength-based employee development and organizational outcomes: 2015 strengths meta-analysis.* Retrieved from https://static1.squarespace.com/static/577a17d9d482e9e2bce9bc68/t/58d4e81a20099e1b037cbced/1490348060515/2015+Relationship+between+Strengths-based+employee+development+and+organizational+outcomes+-+Gallup+StrengthsFinder+Singapore.pdf

Battalia Winston. (2015). *The state of diversity in nonprofit and foundation leadership.* Retrieved from https://www.battaliawinston.com/wp-content/uploads/2017/05/nonprofit_white_paper.pdf

Bezrukova, K., Jehn, K. A., & Spell, C. S. (2012). Reviewing diversity training: Where we have been and where we should go. *Academy of Management Learning and Education, 11*(2), 207–227. doi:10.5465/amle.2008.0090

Bond, M. A., & Haynes, M. C. (2014). Workplace diversity: A social-ecological framework and policy implications. *Social Issues and Policy Review, 8*, 167–201.

Braddock, D., & Parish, S. (2001). Disability history from antiquity to the Americans with Disabilities Act. In G. L. Albrecht, K. D. Seelman, & M.

Bury (Eds.), *Handbook of disability studies* (pp. 11–68). Thousand Oaks, CA: SAGE.

Brun, P. H., Cooperrider, D., & Ejsing, M. (2016). *Strengths-based leadership handbook.* Brunswick, OH: Crown Custom Publishing.

Buckingham, M., & Clifton, D. (2001). *Now, discover your strengths.* New York: Gallup Press.

Burns, C. (2012). *The costly business of discrimination: The economic costs of discrimination and the financial benefits of gay and transgender equality in the workplace.* Retrieved from https://www.americanprogress.org/issues/lgbtq-rights/reports/2012/03/22/11234/the-costly-business-of-discrimination/

Cameron, K. (2012). *Positive leadership: Strategies for extraordinary performance.* San Francisco: Berrett-Koehler.

Clarke, N. (2018). *Relational leadership: Theory, practice and development.* New York: Routledge.

Clifton, J., & Harter, J. (2019). *It's the manager.* New York: Gallup Press.

Cooperrider, D., & Whitney, D. (2005). *Appreciative inquiry: A positive revolution in change.* San Francisco: Berrett-Koehler.

Dutton, J., & Spreitzer, G. M. (2014). *How to be a positive leader: Insights from leading thinkers on positive organizations.* San Francisco: Berrett-Koehler.

Emrich, C., Livingston, M. H., Pruner, D., Oberfeld, L., & Page, S. (2017). *Creating a culture of mentorship.* Chicago: Heidrick & Struggles. Retrieved from https://www.heidrick.com/Knowledge-Center/Publication/Creating_a_culture_of_mentorship

Gallup. (2019). *The manager's experience: Top perks and challenges.* Washington, DC: Author. Retrieved from https://www.gallup.com/workplace/259820/manager-experience-challenges-perk-perspective-paper.aspx

Gendron, T. L., Inker, J., & Welleford, A. (2018). "How old do you feel?" The difficulties and ethics of operationalizing subjective age. *Gerontologist, 58,* 618–624.

Hamilton, B. H., Nickerson, J. A., & Owan, H. (2003). Team incentives and worker heterogeneity: An empirical analysis of the impact of teams on productivity and participation. *Journal of Political Economy, 111,* 465–497.

Harter, J. K., Schmidt, F. L., Agrawal, S., Blue, A., Plowman, S. K., Josh, P., & Asplund, J. (2020). *Q12 meta-analysis: The relationship between engagement at work and organizational outcomes* (10th ed.). Washington, DC: Gallup Press. Retrieved from https://www.gallup.com/workplace/321725/gallup-q12-meta-analysis-report.aspx

Heymann, J., Stein, M. A., & Moreno, G. (2014). *Disability and equity at work.* Oxford, England: Oxford University Press.

Human Rights Campaign Foundation. (2020). *Healthcare equality index 2020.* Retrieved from https://hrc-prod-requests.s3-us-west-2.amazonaws.com/resources/HEI-2020-FinalReport.pdf

International Labour Organization. (2019). *Women in business and management: The business case for change.* Retrieved from https://www.ilo.org/global/publications/books/WCMS_700953/lang--en/index.htm

James, E. (2000). Race-related differences in promotions and support: Underlying effects of human and social capital. *Organization Science, 11*, 493–508. Retrieved from https://www.jstor.org/stable/2640341

Jones, J. R., & Harter, J. K. (2005). Race effects on the employee engagement-turnover intention relationship. *Journal of Leadership & Organizational Studies, 11*, 78–88.

Kapoor, C. (2011). *Benefits of diversity in the workplace.* Retrieved from benefitof.net/benefits-of-diversity-in-the-workplace/

Levin, I. M. (2000). Five windows into organization culture: An assessment framework and approach. *Organization Development Journal, 18*(1), 83–94.

Lorenzo, R., Voigt, N., Schetelig, K., Zawadzki, A., Welpe, I., & Brosi, P. (2017, April 26). *The mix that matters: Innovation through diversity.* Boston: Boston Consulting Group. Retrieved from https://www.bcg.com/publications/2017/people-organization-leadership-talent-innovation-through-diversity-mix-that-matters

Maj, J. (2015). Diversity management's stakeholders and stakeholders management. *Proceedings of the International Management Conference, 9*, 780–793.

National Archives and Records Administration. (2012). *African Americans and the federal census, 1790–1930.* Retrieved from https://www.archives.gov/files/research/census/african-american/census-1790-1930.pdf

National Association of Social Workers. (2017). *Read the Code of Ethics.* Retrieved from https://www.socialworkers.org/About/Ethics/Code-of-Ethics-English

National Council of Nonprofits. (2020). *Why diversity, equity, and inclusion matter for nonprofits.* Retrieved from https://www.councilofnonprofits.org/tools-resources/why-diversity-equity-and-inclusion-matter-nonprofits

New American Economy Research Fund. (2020). *Power of the purse: The contributions of black immigrants in the United States.* Retrieved from https://research.newamericaneconomy.org/report/black-immigrants-2020/

Newman, D., & Lyon, J. (2009). Recruitment efforts to reduce adverse impact: Targeted recruiting for personality, cognitive ability, and diversity. *Journal of Applied Psychology, 94*, 298–317.

Northouse, P. G. (2020). *Introduction to leadership: Concepts and practices* (5th ed.). Thousand Oaks, CA: SAGE.

Obar, J., Zube, P., & Lampe, C. (2012). Advocacy 2.0: An analysis of how advocacy groups in the United States perceive and use social media as tools for facilitating civic engagement and collective action. *Journal of Information Policy, 2*(2012), 1–25.

Porath, C. (2016). *Mastering civility: A manifesto for the workplace.* New York: Grand Central Publishing.

Prestia, A. (2019). Sabotaging success: The role of unconscious bias. *Nurse Leader, 17*, 561–564.

Quillian, L., Pager, D., Hexel, O., & Midtboen, A. (2017). The persistence of racial discrimination in hiring. *Proceedings of the National Academy of Sciences, 114*, 10870–10875.

Rigoni, B., & Asplund, J. (2016). *Strengths-based employee development: The business results.* Retrieved from https://www.gallup.com/workplace/236297/strengths-based-employee-development-business-results.aspx

Russell, J. A., Brock, S., & Rudisill, M. E. (2019). Recognizing the impact of bias in faculty recruitment, retention, and advancement processes. *Kinesiology Review, 8*, 291–295.

Seligman, M., & Csikszentmihalyi, M. (2014). Positive psychology: An introduction. In *Flow and the foundations of positive psychology* (pp. 279–295). Dordrecht, the Netherlands: Springer. doi:10.1007/978-94-017-9088-8_18

Siu Chow, I. H., & Crawford, R. B. (2004). Gender, ethnic diversity, and career advancement in the workplace: The social identity perspective. *SAM Advanced Management Journal, 69*(3), 22–31.

Sorenson, S. (2013). *How employee engagement drives growth.* Retrieved from https://www.gallup.com/workplace/236927/employee-engagement-drives-growth.aspx

Stavros, J. M., & Hinrichs, G. (2019). *Thin book of SOAR: Creating strategy that inspires innovation and engagement* (2nd ed.). Bend, OR: Thin Book Publishing.

Tamm, J. W., & Luyet, R. J. (2019). *Radical collaboration: Five essential skills to overcome defensiveness and build successful relationships* (2nd ed.). New York: HarperCollins.

Toossi, M., & Torpey, E. (2017). *Older workers: Labor force trends and career options.* Retrieved from https://www.bls.gov/careeroutlook/2017/article/pdf/older-workers.pdf

United Way of Greater Cincinnati. (2019). *Diversity, equity and inclusion community report.* Retrieved from https://www.uwgc.org/docs/default-source/annual-report-documents/dei_communityreport2019.pdf

U.S. Bureau of Labor Statistics. (2020, February 26). *Persons with a disability: Labor force characteristics summary* [Economic News Release]. Retrieved from https://www.bls.gov/news.release/disabl.nr0.htm#:~:text=Employment%20In%202019%2C%20the%20employment,percentage%20point%20over%20the%20year

Vespa, J., Medina, L., & Armstrong, D. M. (2020). *Demographic turning points for the United States: Population projections for 2020 to 2060.* Retrieved from https://www.census.gov/content/dam/Census/library/publications/2020/demo/p25-1144.pdf

Weber-Shandwick Inc. (2016). *Millennials at work: Perspectives on diversity.* Retrieved from https://www.webershandwick.com/news/millennials-at-work-perspectives-on-diversity-inclusion/

Wei-Skillern, J., & Marciano, S. (2008). *The networked nonprofit.* Retrieved from https://ssir.org/articles/entry/the_networked_nonprofit

Whitney, D., Trosten-Bloom, A., & Radar, K. (2010). *Appreciative leadership.* New York: McGraw Hill.

Work Institute. (2020). *2019 work retention report: Trends, reasons and a call to action.* Retrieved from https://info.workinstitute.com/retentionreport2019

7

Managing Meetings to Produce High-Quality Group Decisions

John E. Tropman*

Nonprofit executive leaders and managers have many tasks. It is a constant challenge for them to lead, manage, improve, and transform their organizations. Accomplishing these tasks means working with groups to achieve high-quality decisions. Leading provides direction for the organization, and managing makes it work. Leading and managing require different competencies, but they also have the following two things in common:

- enabling the organization to run efficiently (doing things right) and effectively (doing the right thing)
- producing efficient meetings that guide the building of effective decisions

The term "executive leader" refers to two parts of the senior manager's job. The executive part is essentially tactical and involves routinizing and organizing the work of the organization and its people, and the leader part involves strategy and decision making, as well as instilling meaning and worthwhileness in the organization's mission and role.

This chapter focuses on the competencies (knowledge and skills) that produce authentic, productive meetings that result in high-quality decisions. The competencies fall into two parts: setting up the meeting and orchestrating the decision process within the meeting.

---

*The author would like to express deep appreciation to Richard Edwards and Dan Madaj for their amazing and helpful suggestions for and work on this chapter

Although there are many roles nonprofit executive leaders must play and sets of tasks they must accomplish, one primary set of tasks involves managing or running the organization. Many of these tasks concern issues of human resources, budgeting and securing funding, and the general work involved in keeping the organization running. Thus, a primary first task of nonprofit executive leaders is to keep the organization in the "on" position—to deliver high-quality products or services that produce outcomes that help clients, patrons, and consumers to achieve positive change.

A second important set of tasks is to develop a high-performance organization, which is different from actually running the organization. In this case, the executive leader is challenged not only to do the job but also to do it faster, better, and cheaper. Achieving these goals involves innovation (doing things one already does but in new ways) and invention (doing things one has not done before).

The third set of tasks involves transforming the organization. Nonprofit organizations periodically need to be reinvented, and it is the mandate of executive leaders to initiate and lead those efforts. In today's financially strapped environment, margin can replace mission. This process—sometimes called "mission creep"—occurs when the organization slips off its mission and follows the funding. That said, the mission needs to be periodically refurbished and refinished to remain current.

Success in each of these task bundles requires decisions. Executives manage the many elements of the decision process. This chapter identifies a package of crucial elements in that process, providing both analysis of the decision process and suggestions about how executives can improve their work in this area.

Important Concepts in the Decision Process

As managers think about decision making in the organization, it is important to re-emphasize decision verities and introduce some new decision concepts (Tropman, 2003). This chapter, then, examines problems in decision making and concludes with some ways to address them.

Choosing Often Means Losing

Decision making usually involves the painful necessity of choice. This observation is a well-known decision truth, but it is one that people often forget because of the pain of making a choice and because it is hard for winners and losers to work together after a choice is made. One cannot avoid choosing, as the motto "not to decide is to decide" reminds. Choosing often means losing—someone wins and someone loses. There are ways to maximize the gain of multiple stakeholders and interests; however, there will inevitably still be losses. Some sets of values will be maximized, and others will be minimized. Creative decision management is the management of competing values and interests in which losses move into the less unacceptable or more acceptable range. There are always at least two points of view, interests, ideas, or perspectives that must be blended, prioritized, selected, and organized as executives and managers go about their decision-making work. Often, there are several perspectives about which people feel strongly.

Decision Quality

Decisions are the product of a decision-building process. As such, they can be considered in terms of whether they are excellent, good, satisfactory, poor, or awful. Many people do not think of decisions as being qualitatively ranked from awful to excellent, like a restaurant meal, but that is an important perspective to adopt. A high-quality decision does not mean "I win," however satisfying that might be. Generally, an excellent decision is an "all-win" decision in which all stakeholders gain, although not necessarily equally; a good decision is one in which many stakeholders win, although a minority do not; a satisfactory decision is one in which the specific winners and losers shift around, but there is no net gain or loss; and a poor decision is one in which some win big, but a majority lose. Finally, an awful decision is one in which every stakeholder is worse off after the decision is made.[*]

Conflicting Values

One element of decision making that creates continuous issues is the problem of conflicting values. If one considers a value as an idea to which commitment is attached, then losing very easily becomes "wrong." Managing conflicting values is a key component of the job of nonprofit executives.

Decision Rules

One package of conflicting values is the set of rules (or norms) that groups use to legitimize decisions, called "decision rules." In a typical decision situation, there are no neutral decision rules; any rule (for example, one person,

---

[*]Decision evaluation is discussed in more detail later in this chapter.

one vote) conflicts with one or more others (honoring deeply felt preferences of minority groups who never win a vote). Group members often become committed to what they view as the rightness of one or another decision rule (for example, "one person, one vote" is best and right). Finding solutions (decision candidates) that fit or address several rules is a vital task of nonprofit executives.

Decision Culture

Decision culture is defined as a situation in which one package of decision rules, meeting rules, and preference schedules attains a privileged status and is routinely, almost automatically, used. At times, this can be good, because it provides structure for the meeting that can be comforting to the members. However, it can be a disadvantage if it results in too much rigidity and stifles creativity.

Decision Building and Constructing versus Decision Making

"Decision making" is a popular phrase in common parlance, but are decisions really "made"? Perhaps a better, more effective, and accurate description of decision work might be decision "constructing." Terms such as "decision construction" or "decision building" convey the step-by-step process of decision work that is obscured in the term "decision making." It is truer to say that decisions are built—piece by piece, element by element—very much like a menu for Sunday dinner might be built. One thinks about the main course; then one thinks about the vegetable, the starch, and the dessert; and then one assembles the components one by one. Once the entire range of possibilities is in place, the chef looks at the overall fit and sees whether everything harmonizes with everything else, making adjustments as necessary. One might call that "decision sculpting." My term for the skill set of helping a group through a decision-building process is "decision management."

Decision Mosaic: Some Assembly Required

The word "decision" is really a collective noun. The concept of a decision mosaic invites thinking of a decision as being made up of many smaller parts called elements. These elements are assembled together to make the whole picture, the decision. An example is when a board makes a decision to hold a black-tie dinner and auction as a major fundraising event. This decision has many components, including, for example, setting a date, securing a site, developing a realistic budget with accurate cost projections and a reasonable fundraising goal, obtaining sponsors, and so forth.

Decision Management

Decision management is the competent operation of a mindful and intelligent process of decision production. Competence involves knowledge of the decision process and skill in its application. Knowledge involves understanding the steps in the decision process (need, or problem specification; alternative, or option development; appropriate consideration of gains and losses for the options; and selection). Skill in decision management involves helping the decision community (decision builders plus stakeholders) move through the decision process in a timely and productive manner).

Decision Manager

A decision manager is the person who designs and operates the decision process and guides decisions through it. It is one of the important roles of the nonprofit executive. One might also use the term "decision guide."

High-Quality Meetings

Decision production usually involves a series of meetings in which various stakeholders are gathered. These meetings need to be effectively and efficiently structured so that the chances of securing a high-quality decision are enhanced. Think of this as similar to a road trip where you know where you are going, have a map or GPS to assist you, and have your car serviced and your gas tank full. The outcome you want is to have a good trip. Ideas for running successful meetings are described later in the chapter.

Meeting Rules

Meeting rules are norms that collectively create effective and efficient meetings. They are the best practices that, if followed, create the greatest chance of success. To use the road trip metaphor, consider the adage "if you don't know where you're going, any road will take you there." Doing so, however, may result in your not arriving where you want to be. Similarly, meeting rules provide the structure that enables participants to reach the destination they seek. Without such structure, a meeting can be a chaotic experience, one that is unsatisfying to the participants and not a productive use of their time. Meeting rules best practices are also discussed in greater detail later in this chapter.

Solo versus Ensemble Process

In the decision-building approach, it is more usual for many parties to be involved, and very frequently there are meetings, conferences, and discussions during which the decision construction and decision building occur. Hence, nonprofit managers must manage competing values in the decision-making process itself because, by implication, construction occurs over time rather than at a single moment in time.

Issues in the Decision Process: Conflicting Decision Cultures

Conflicting values and their resultant cultures have an important place in thinking about the job of the nonprofit manager. The theory of competing values (Tropman, 1989) emphasizes the diversity of values that people entertain and addresses the importance of understanding that competing values are not either–or situations but rather both–and situations. For example, one is committed not to either equality or achievement but to both equality and achievement in some mix, the proportions of which may change over time and space.

When packaged or bundled, competing or conflicting values become conflicting cultures. In thinking about decision making and its requisite skills, it is often helpful to think about organizations as being characterized by differing and competing subcultures. In the management area, Quinn (1988) has perhaps been the most articulate spokesperson on competing values. He has identified four cultures based on differing positions an organization might assume on the dimensions of flexibility and control (see Table 7.1). Each organizational subculture has dominant skills and a dominant basis around which decisions are informed and built. These decisions are built around (a) consensus, (b) information and data, (c) results, and (d) influence. As decision making progresses, certain organizational styles—decision cultures—emerge and become typical.

Each quadrant has its own cultural archetype or cultural name. The clan subculture is low on flexibility and formal control. It is a culture driven

Managing Meetings to Produce High-Quality Group Decisions

Table 7.1 Four Archetypical Agency Cultures and Agency Properties in Relationship to Level of Control and Amount of Flexibility

Level of Organizational Control	Amount of Flexibility — Low	Amount of Flexibility — High
Low	**Clan** *Skills:* Facilitating, mentoring. *Decision method:* Consensual, decision building[a] *Decision bases:* Consensus	**Adhocracy** *Skills:* Innovating, brokering *Decision method:* Political *Decision bases:* Influence
High	**Hierarchy** *Skills:* Coordinating, monitoring *Decision method:* Empirical decision building *Decision bases:* Data and information, position in the agency	**Market** *Skills:* Producing, directing. *Decision method:* Results, decision building *Decision bases:* Probability of results

Note: From "Automated Decision Conferencing: How It Works," by R. E. Quinn, J. Rohrbaugh, and M. R. McGrath, 1985, *Personnel, 62*(11). Copyright © by Williams and Wilkins. Adapted with permission. See also Quinn (1988).
[a] In the original, Quinn had *decision making*, which I have changed to *decision building* to reflect the emphasis here.

by membership, and the main reward is acceptance into membership. Key skills are facilitating and mentoring. Decisions are built around consensus.

The hierarchy subculture is low on flexibility and high on formal control. It is driven by adherence to rules and structure, and the reward is promotion. Important skills are coordinating and monitoring. Decisions are built around data.

The market subculture is juxtaposed to the clan subculture. High on flexibility and control, this subculture pays almost no attention to membership (for example, how long one has been with an organization, who one is, who one's parents are) and almost entirely stresses results. Control comes only through results. Someone who produces is in; someone who does not is out. In the market culture, the question is "What have you done for me lately?" Whereas the clan subculture is more like a country club or sorority, the market subculture is more like an investment bank—no one cares how nice their investment banker is, they just want results. Core skills are producing and directing. Decisions are built around results.

Finally, there is the adhocracy quadrant, as opposed to bureaucracy. Adhocracy is high on flexibility and low on control. Whereas bureaucracy is focused on rules and structure and the "routinization" of events, adhocracy is like a pickup baseball game or a jazz band. Whoever is around may do what needs to be done. There is an exciting openness, fluidity, and porosity to the adhocratic subculture, but it can also be chaotic and nondirectional. Central skills are innovating and brokering. Decisions are built around influence.

These organizational and decision cultures are, in some sense, present in all organizations. Everyone needs some consensus, some results-based work, some political activity and uses of influence, and some work based on data and information. The problem for executives as decision managers is to balance the competing demands and styles over the course of the day, week, and year. Different issues would arguably require a different mix—or perhaps a different sequence of skill bases and methods. In decision management and decision building, one important job of the executive is to assemble the right package of conflicting values and bases for the appropriate situation. Of course, however, they each clash with the other, so the executive is continually managing them—like prickly guests at a dinner party—so that their benefits can be enjoyed and their contentions minimized.

Issues in the Decision Process: Subculture Solidification

Each decision subculture has great strengths. One problem, however—the one just discussed—is its clash with another decision subculture. However, that is not the only potential problem. Difficulties arise when any one subculture becomes too overweening. These are well illustrated by Quinn, Rohrbaugh, and McGrath (1985), who wrote of the decision-making perspectives of each subculture. I have adapted their perspective slightly here (see Table 7.2).

Employees will frequently want one or the other perspectives to obtain. Indeed, conflict with those in the organization who want other emphases and foci is common. Here, the role of executive leaders or managers is to encourage and support all decision approaches, as appropriate, and to manage the conflict that will inevitably result.

The clan subculture uses a consensual perspective. Participation in and commitment to decisions is high. All members of the organization characterized by this subculture would typically be involved and would participate. Members of this subculture feel that if one participated in the process, one must and will support the resulting outcome. However, too

Table 7.2 Four Archetypical Agency Cultures and Agency Decision Styles in Relationship to Level of Control and Amount of Flexibility

Level of Organizational Control	Amount of Flexibility — Low	Amount of Flexibility — High
Low	Clan Consensual perspective Supportability of decision Participatory process	Adhocracy Political perspective Legitimacy of decision Adaptable process (who is in the room?)
High	Hierarchy Outputs perspective Accountability of decision Empirical or data and rules- or position-based process	Market Outcomes perspective Efficiency of decision Expertise or experience-based decision process

Note: Based on Quinn, Rohrbaugh, and McGrath (1985).

much participation leads to a poky and sometimes stalled decision process. Attending to and caring about membership involvement is, of course, important; overattention to member wishes means that one member with a different view can hold up the whole process. Nonprofit organizations are heavily represented in the clan quadrant, and delay in decision making is a common problem.

The strength of the hierarchy subculture is twofold. One strength is in its empirical perspective—doing it by the numbers. The other is in its rules and position-based processes. Decision makers use database processes and explicit decision accountability. Knowing where the buck stops is a hallmark of a hierarchical subculture's decision-making process. It is important to touch base with each of the relevant positions and follow all the appropriate rules. Going by the numbers alone, though, can lead to a decline in effective participation and empowerment. As numbers go up, people frequently go down. Database processes are fine, but qualitative perspectives are also important. Then, too, rules are fine, but they are usually formed on past experiences and not always relevant to current situations. Positional involvement is fine as well, but sometimes the person in a particular position at a particular time does not have the expertise or perspective needed for the job.

In the market subculture, goal attainment and efficiency—results, results, and more results, and fast—become crucial. Decisions are made quickly and rationally, usually by those closest to the possible result rather than by the "right" official or all of the members. Premature decisions are often characteristic of the market culture. Short-run, immediate perspectives are dominant, and a longer-run perspective is driven out by the need for "more for me, sooner."

In the adhocracy subculture, adaptable and stakeholder buy-in elements are strong. Who makes decisions often depends on who is around to do it. However, the decision making is focused less on the decision maker than on the decision supporters. In thinking politically, the decision maker is more often the decision packager, seeking views from others and putting them into an acceptable package. Hence, who makes the decision is less important than the success of the decision. Of course, getting everyone on board is important, but adhocracies can let leadership shift from the decision-making core to the periphery and suggest only what will pass, as opposed to what is right.

Cultural solidification is the problem of overemphasis on one particular decision subculture. Organizations may have a default style, but if executives operate in a way that uses a diversity of decision subcultures and manages the values and bases for the appropriate situation, then the organization can remain reasonably healthy.

The problem is that too few executives recognize the need for decision subcultural diversity, and organizations tend, rather, to follow the rule of "the more, the more." This means that the more one uses one particular style, the more one is likely to use it. That is why management is work. Nonprofit chief executives need to be the outriggers on the decision canoe—balancing with their weight the preferred approaches. Hence, if an organization is tending toward clan styles, the executive needs to ask about results; if the organization emphasizes numbers and rules, the executive needs to introduce adhocratic considerations. The executive, in short, often acts as a counterweight. If the executive supports conventional decision cultures too much or too often, the organization enters culture lock and uses that method exclusively. That is when the strength becomes fatal.

Executive overemphasis is one cause of cultural solidification. A second has to do with organizational stress. Individuals tend, under stress, to revert or default to preferred comfortable ways of acting, even if they are inappropriate for the moment at hand. Organizations are the same. Hence, organizational stress and pressure tend to encourage or force organizations to revert to a preferred decision style, even if it is absolutely the wrong approach.

Issues in the Decision Process: Subculture Culture Lock

Culture solidification is a problem, but culture lock is even worse. Solidification still allows—or can allow—for a bit of decision diversity. Culture lock not only goes for exclusivity, but, because the strengths are unchecked or unbalanced, they morph into problematic practices and become fatal flaws. The organization has then moved into the negative zone.

Quinn (1988) dealt with this idea of strengths and weaknesses in his concept of positive and negative zones (see Figure 7.1), pointing out that every strength becomes a weakness if pushed too far. On the outer circle of the figure are familiar problems of group decision making. When the strengths of a subculture are pushed too far or are overstressed, they pass

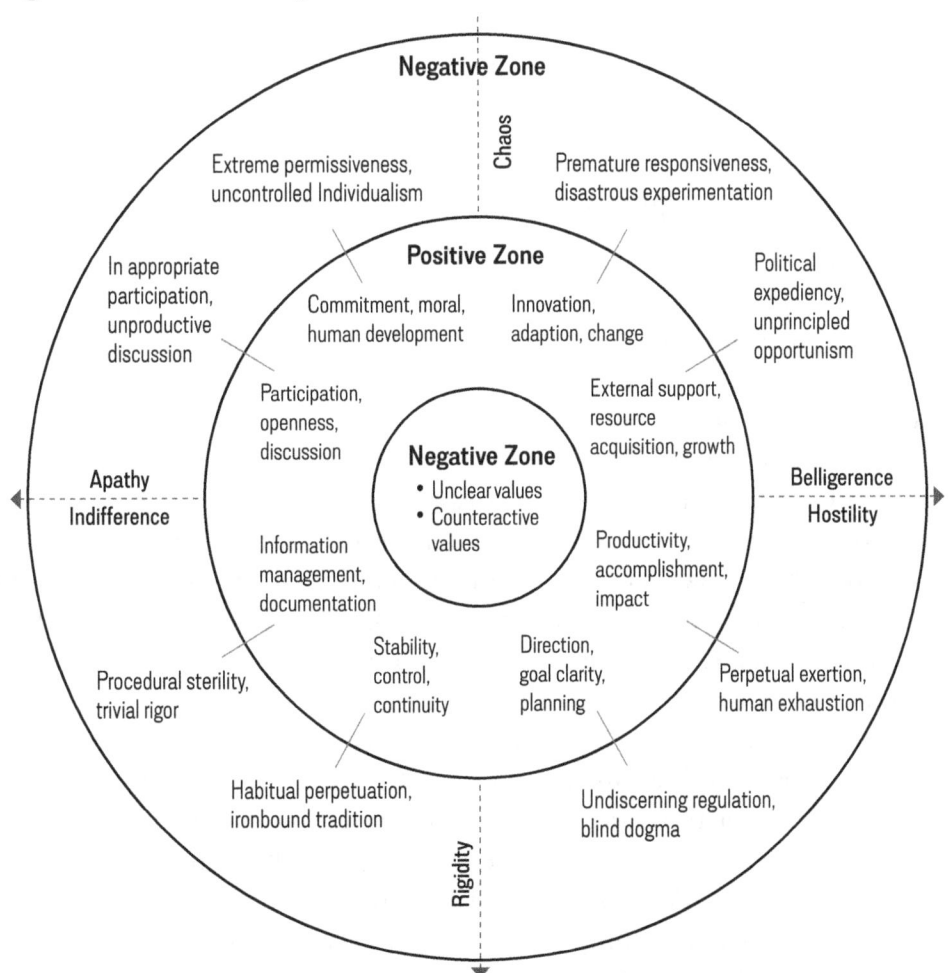

Figure 7.1 Positive and Negative Zones

Negative Zone (outer):
- Chaos (top)
- Extreme permissiveness, uncontrolled Individualism
- Premature responsiveness, disastrous experimentation
- Inappropriate participation, unproductive discussion
- Political expediency, unprincipled opportunism
- Apathy / Indifference (left)
- Belligerence / Hostility (right)
- Procedural sterility, trivial rigor
- Perpetual exertion, human exhaustion
- Habitual perpetuation, ironbound tradition
- Undiscerning regulation, blind dogma
- Rigidity (bottom)

Positive Zone (middle):
- Commitment, moral, human development
- Innovation, adaption, change
- Participation, openness, discussion
- External support, resource acquisition, growth
- Information management, documentation
- Productivity, accomplishment, impact
- Stability, control, continuity
- Direction, goal clarity, planning

Negative Zone (inner):
- Unclear values
- Counteractive values

the utility point and become overdone, leading to problems. In the clan subculture, extreme permissiveness and inappropriate participation become key, sprinkled with a good helping of unproductive discussion. In the hierarchy subculture, procedural sterility and trivial rigor become hallmarks (as in the saying, "You have erroneously initialed the attached memo; please erase your initials and initial your erasure"). Ironbound tradition is also common in the hierarchy subculture ("It's the weekly meeting; we have it every week; we always have"). In the market subculture, perpetual exertion and human exhaustion can become problems ("What results have you produced this morning?"). In the adhocratic subculture, premature responsiveness and unprincipled opportunism can become difficulties as well.

How might an executive approach managing these issues? In the next section, I discuss three managerial foci that can provide help. One involves managing meetings, where decision opportunities occur in any culture. The second involves managing decision rules, which are the cultural norms that make decisions okay. The third is managing decision results—avoiding problematic results such as groupthink (Psychology Today, n.d.) and the Abilene paradox (Blackburn, 2016).

Managing Meetings

The group context of decision making is key because one setting—meetings—is where much decision making happens. In meetings, groups are a key locus in which values are enacted and expressed, and the group decision contest is a place where executive success is seen and judged. It is the playing field of executive work.

The myth that it is lonely at the top suggests that chief executive officers (CEOs) and other managers work alone. Decision work is presented as a solo operation—an executive gets information and retreats to their office to make the decision. A common observation is "I didn't get any work done today; I spent my whole day in meetings." The perspective here is that decision building is an ensemble event, with many points and stops along the way. These stops are often called meetings.

Meetings are universally disliked, and even ridiculed. A Google search on "I hate meetings" results in more than 64 million entries. Meetings are also the subject of thousands of cartoons expressing the same negative or derisive attitudes. That view of meetings suggests that American culture assumes that real work is not done in a collective setting. It suggests that the collective setting is something of a waste of time and that real work is done alone in one's office. That idea is not only erroneous but also pernicious, because it devalues the most common setting in which a decision construction goes on: the group context or group setting. It devalues work that might be undertaken to improve one's skill as a decision manager in the group context, and it offers stereotypic and negative views of the group context.

In most nonprofit organizations today, the group context is ubiquitous. People spend a lot of time in meetings. The degree of their formality varies, and they are run using whatever technology the individual in charge has picked up in their training. Nevertheless, people's experience with meetings is often—in fact, almost regularly—negative. Jokes about meetings abound—for example, comments that a camel is a horse assembled in a staff meeting or that a nonprofit board is a group that takes minutes to waste hours. Negative and hostile humor is an attempt on the part of the culture to either control or make understandable and comprehensible the ubiquity of meetings.

Meetings can, however, be viewed more positively as an organizational process, the output of which is a decision stream. What that means for the executive leader and other management staff is that, as with other organizational processes (for example, the budget process, capital improvement process, and fundraising process), meetings must be managed carefully.

Finally, because of its ubiquity and its centrality in organizations, the effort to manage the group decision context—that is, the meeting—is where management success can be most telling. The most successful CEOs and top-level managers have the ability to manage group decision making at the board, staff, community, and other levels where they sit with colleagues, superiors, subordinates, peers, and citizens and try to create policies that will be a positive force for their communities.

What, then, might be the antidote to some of these problems that people have with meetings? A common meeting structure that allows the difficulties to be avoided and the strengths to be blended is part of the answer. Most of the material written about meetings is anecdotal and lacks evidence. The material I share here comes from the Meetings Masters Research Project at the University of Michigan (Tropman, 2018, 2020), which involved identifying people termed "meeting masters," observing them and their practices, interviewing them, and extracting the common practices they developed that became the fundamental infrastructure of great meetings. Their conceptual approaches have led to a menu of specific preparatory actions.

The meeting masters whom I have interviewed and videotaped over the years have meetings that are astonishing because they are so different from the meetings one might typically experience. These meeting masters ran terrific meetings—meaning that high-quality decisions were made and the participants enjoyed themselves.

As one of the masters observed, "Here is the deal. My groups give me their time and their effort; I give them accomplishment in the form of participation in high-quality decisions. Each of us needs to keep our end of the bargain."

What did these meeting masters do differently? First, they thought about the decision-making process differently. From their point of view, the decision-making process was like an orchestra performance or a play. It required preparation and organization. Their meetings with their boards, staff, citizen groups, and volunteer groups were at the end of a process of preparation rather than at the beginning. They never said, "Let's get together and see if there's any reason for having gotten together." They always had some sense of what needed to be done, although they never had a sense of the exact outcome. Thus, the gatherings they orchestrated were never rubber stamps; instead, they were honest, open, participatory forums, organized within decent, reasonable time frames and with decent and reasonable alternatives available to the participants. Attendees were always alerted ahead of time to the topics and the hoped-for outcomes, whether it was a decision outcome or a brainstorming outcome, so they could prepare intellectually and conceptually before they came. One of the meeting masters told me,

> You know, there are only three things done at meetings. You announce things, you decide things, and you brainstorm about things. The way I organize my meetings is that I gather all of the announcements and put them at the beginning. Then I take the decision-making items and put them in the middle. And finally, when it comes to the brainstorming items, I put those at the end. It works out very well.

This way of organizing meetings can be called the "three-characters rule."

Because the meeting masters felt that the play or drama was an apt metaphor for a meeting, they put less emphasis on the personalities of the participants and more emphasis on the scripts that they did or did not have. The meeting masters, through the agenda and other preparatory processes, spent a good deal of energy on providing scripts for the individuals coming to the meeting. This allowed individuals to come prepared, participate authentically, fully achieve decisions, and actually enjoy the meeting.

The meeting masters followed several rules to enhance members' ability to fully participate. Among the most important was the rule of halves, under which the masters simply asked the participants, whether it was a board, staff, or volunteer meeting, to hand in agenda items that they wanted considered at the next meeting at least halfway between the meeting dates. That meant that, for a typical staff meeting on Monday, the staff had to turn in items by the preceding Tuesday or Wednesday. This gave the meeting master a chance to see what was afoot, organize the material sensibly, and get the necessary information and people set up to attend the meeting. Very little is worse than getting together with colleagues, board, or staff and having an issue come up for which one could have been prepared if one had only known about it. No one likes to look foolish.

Another rule the meeting masters followed is the rule of sixths. One of the meeting masters described this rule in the following way:

> When I put my agenda together, I like to think of it this way. About a sixth of the material should be from the past. And if we have more than that, we're simply not moving quickly enough through the material that we have. About four-sixths of the material should be from the here and now, and about one-sixth—and this is the fun part for my board—is from the future. At each meeting, we take time to look ahead and to speculate about what issues are coming down the pike that might or will affect us. We share ideas and feelings, we brainstorm about them, then begin to prepare ourselves intellectually and, I might add, emotionally, for what's just ahead. This process means that my board is never surprised by issues. They've always had a chance to think them through. And I do the same thing with my staff, as well.

This manager used the rule of sixths to create a sense of anticipation, to get a feel for where her board and staff were in terms of issues of the future.

Having also talked with the board and staff, I can share their reactions. One of the board members remarked,

> This is a great system. We always go through things in about the same way. We finish some leftover matters, usually rather quickly, get to matters at hand, and then wrap up our meeting with brainstorming, anticipating the future, and getting our ideas. I have a really deep sense of participation in this board, and it's more than I can say for the other boards I'm on, let me tell you.

The meeting masters also followed the rule of three-quarters. About three-quarters of the way between meetings, whatever the schedule was, they sent out a package including the agenda, the minutes, and any reports. Although many people do this for boards of directors, it is infrequently done for staff. However, the same principle applies. Individuals need a chance to think about the material that is coming up. As one of the masters said,

It's a little bit like playing a musical instrument. If I give you a piece of music and say, "Play this on the piano," we call that sight-reading in music. And it has all the squeaks and grunts that a sight-reading rendition frequently has. And how much better we sound if we have a chance to practice a bit. Yet, in meetings, we routinely engage in sight-reading, except we don't recognize all those crazy little bits of participation as a result of the fact that individuals have just gotten the agenda and the materials, are struggling through it, are struggling to understand it, and struggling to make sense of it. It doesn't make any sense to me not to send stuff out a little bit ahead.

The meeting masters also followed the rule of the agenda bell, outlined in Figure 7.2. The agenda bell is a system for organizing the agenda itself. It contains seven categories of items. The first is the minutes of the previous meeting. If a group has minutes, they should be sent out in advance of the meeting so meeting attendees have a chance to read them and submit any corrections in advance of the meeting. Then when the meeting begins, the minutes can be approved right away. If it is a board meeting and a quorum is not present, meeting masters said, "Approve them anyway and reapprove them later. It's important to begin on time, and you don't want to wait, punishing those who have shown up on time and rewarding those who, for whatever reason, can't seem to make it."

The second category is announcements—short, factual, noncontroversial statements of things that might be of interest. Announcements are not

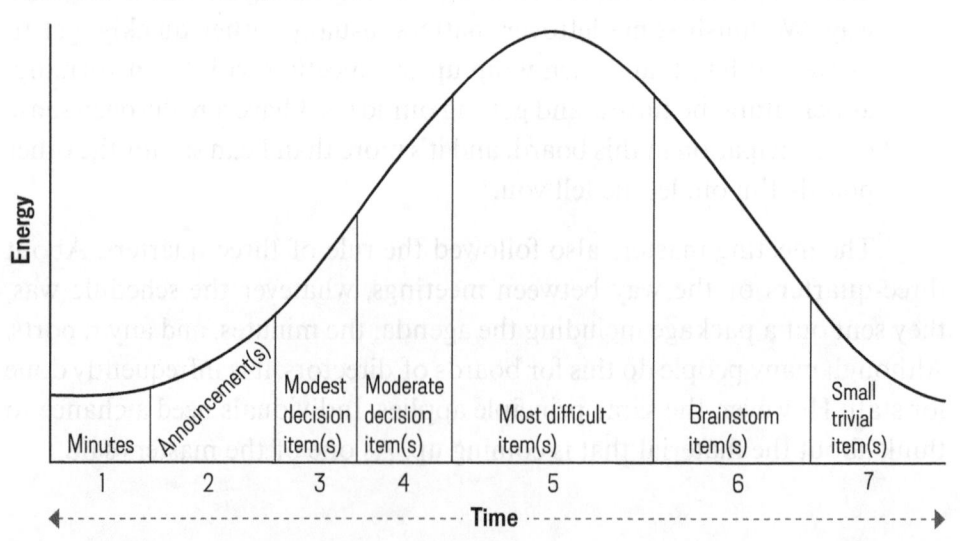

Figure 7.2 Tropman's Agenda Bell

discussed except for a quick factual question, and they should not contain matters that people would logically want to discuss.

The third, fourth, and fifth categories in the agenda bell structure are items for decision. Here, the meeting masters did an interesting thing. They divided the items for decision (and they knew which items needed a decision because they had already gotten them under the rule of halves) into three categories: easy ones (for example, items 3a, 3b, and 3c), moderately difficult ones (items 4a, 4b, and 4c), and one really tough one (item 5).

The idea behind this structure is that the group begins by acting on those items that are fairly easy to deal with but that require formal approval. There is a transition into the somewhat more difficult items, and at about the halfway point of the meeting, the group tackles the toughest item. After that item has been dealt with, the group moves to item 6, a category containing the brainstorming items. Finally, an easy item, perhaps a thank you or even a motion for adjournment, is put in as item 7. Table 7.3 provides a sample.

Table 7.3 Sample Agenda

Item No.	Item Content	Time	Notes
1	Minutes	2:00–2:05 p.m.	
2	Announcements: New desks ordered	2:05–2:10 p.m.	
3	Retreat location: Key West seems best ACTION	2:10–2:15 p.m.	
4a	Vendor selection: A new software vendor wants to make a presentation ACTION	2:15–2:25 p.m.	
4b	Medical coverage: Should we extend medical coverage to staff's gay or lesbian partners? ACTION	2:25–2:35 p.m.	
5	Dress code: Should we retain casual Friday, go casual all week, or return to professional dress all week? ACTION	2:35–3:00 p.m.	
6	Annual community appreciation event: ideas for an exciting, different way to show our stakeholders that we appreciate their support BRAINSTORMING	3:00–3:38 p.m.	
7	Adjournment	3:38–3:40 p.m.	

There are a couple things to note about this sample agenda. First, each item includes a brief description of what the item is about. Second, time frames are listed for each item, which can greatly help keep everyone on track as the meeting progresses from the beginning to the end. If one thinks of the agenda as a menu in a restaurant, having items without times attached is like having a menu without prices. One of the meeting masters explained the rationale behind this structure in the following way:

> The way I set up my meetings is a little bit like the way I exercise. There's a get-going period, a heavy work period, and a decompression period. You know, decision making tears at the fabric of the group, so I try to finish up the big decision item about two-thirds of the way through the meeting. This means that we can spend the last part of the meeting working together—because, of course, in many instances, when you're making decisions there's conflict—on items for the future. It really works well.

It also turns out that the division of decision items into an easy group, a somewhat more difficult group, and the toughest group means that individuals are more likely to be buoyed by success on some easy items as they tackle harder items and, one hopes, buoyed by success on those when they tackle the toughest item. Thus, the agenda is shaped rather than handled in a random fashion.

These basic processes—getting information ahead of time; shaping and structuring the agenda, including items from the future; sending the agenda and attendant documents out ahead of time; and structuring the actual meeting according to the agenda bell principle—prove immensely helpful in managing competing or conflicting values. Although people might have different perspectives, they will all be singing from the same music. Common structure, although it is not a total antidote to unusual issues that may arise, serves a useful function. People with various differing orientations or perspectives can be accommodated: Those with a clan orientation can have an adequate chance at appropriate participation, whereas people with a market orientation can see that there is a structure that will probably lead to action. Thus, these two kinds of commitments are balanced. The agenda itself provides the kind of structure often preferred by those with a hierarchy orientation, whereas the rule of sixths and the brainstorming and speculative material at the end of the meeting provides something that those with an adhocracy orientation value and cherish. In this sense, then, a common agenda structure is a tool for managing conflicting cultural orientations.

There were also some practices that the meeting masters avoided or changed from traditional practice. One of these was the no-new-business rule. Using the rationale of the rule of halves, participants were encouraged to present new business in agenda items they submitted before the meeting rather than at the meeting itself. As one of the meeting masters said,

> New business is the worst enemy that a meeting can have, in my opinion. People come in with half-thought-out concerns and worries, no one has had a chance to adequately prepare, and it tends to draw people away from the agenda at hand. We try to get people to think ahead about what they want to discuss at the meeting and let us know. Then we can have the information and people ready.

Another thing that the meeting masters eliminated was the traditional report. One of the masters described the no-more-reports rule:

> Many meetings are just oral newsletters. They go around the room, and people try to put the best face on whatever they're doing. It's a curious mixture of announcements, decisions, and discussions, and nobody knows really when to cut in or how. I've been able to get rid of all of that and have completely reorganized. Now, I ask people to "break up" what would have been their report into an announcement item [that] I put . . . in the announcements section . . . or a decision item . . . I can . . . then put . . . in the decision section, or a brainstorming item, which I can then put in the brainstorming section. This means that we don't have a finance committee report anymore. If the finance chairperson has a simple announcement, as I said, it goes there. If there are items from the finance committee that we need to act on from a decision point of view, they go into the middle section. If the finance committee wants us to brainstorm around some issues, I put that at the end. It works very well.

Naturally, these techniques will not completely solve the problem of managing competing or conflicting values in a group decision-making setting, but they provide a different kind of answer. Typically, when people think about managing conflicting values, they tend to think about people getting together on the values themselves. The problem is that the structures or processes that we use for these kinds of settings often exacerbate their very differences, leading to worse fissures and cleavages than there were at the beginning. Providing a common structure and an indirect way of managing conflicting values appears to be successful (see Table 7.4).

Table 7.4 Key Meeting Rules from the Meeting Masters

Rule	Procedures
Three characters or agenda bell: organizes items according to what must happen with them	Announcement items first
	Decision items second: Easy decision items, then tougher decision items, then the toughest decision items
	Brainstorming discussion items third
Rule of halves: gets people to think ahead	Get upcoming items halfway between meeting times. Then organize them and get the information and people needed.
Rule of sixths: reaches ahead for tough items and deals with them proactively	About one-sixth of the items should be for brainstorming and discussion only and should relate to the future.
Rule of three-quarters: invites people to prepare intellectually and psychologically before the meeting	Send material out about three-quarters of the way between meetings so that people can read and think about it.
No-new-business rule: creates the expectation of getting items in early and preparing for them rather than bringing them up at the last minute	New business is sent in ahead of time so it can be structured into the ongoing flow of the meeting.
No-more-reports rule: reports are gone, replaced by individual items	Individuals who might have given reports now divide up that content into three parts that appear in the appropriate place under the rule of the agenda bell

Putting in the Fix: Building High-Quality Decisions by Managing Conflicting Decision Values and Rules

Decision rules are norms that make decisions legitimate or okay; they legitimize the decision process. It is important to note, there is no decision rule that is fair or neutral. The application of any of the decision rules—and at least nine have been identified as a result of the Meeting Masters Research Project—advances some interests and retards others (Tropman, 2020). Whether consciously or unconsciously, people bring various decision rules into decision-making settings—board meetings, staff meetings, volunteer meetings, and so forth—from their wider life. In effect, decision rules represent different cultural preferences about how decisions should be made. So managing decision rules is, in effect, managing conflicting cultures. These nine decision rules are as follows:

1. Extensive rule: What do most people want? "One person, one vote" is a typical application of this rule. In this situation, everyone has a say, and everyone's say is weighted equally.
2. Equity stake rule: This rule comes from the realm of publicly traded companies, in which the number of votes individuals may have is based on the number of shares they hold or own, so one person effectively has many votes. In the nonprofit world, equity may be seen as weighting the interests of those who may have the most to gain or lose on the basis of a particular decision.
3. Intensive rule: Who feels very strongly about an issue, and how can they be accommodated? Who cares the most? Some individuals get heavily involved in particular projects and tend to think of those projects as most important. Deeply caring about an issue is seen as a kind of equity, much like shares in a for-profit company.
4. Involvement rule: Who might have to carry out a particular decision? This rule gives weight or preference to the implementers—the doers—and is typically viewed as "let the person who has to do the job have the most say about it."
5. Expert rule: What do the experts say? What does the evidence say? What do the lawyers, doctors, accountants, or the most knowledgeable people say? People who like to follow this rule want to be sure the right experts and officials sign off on any decision.
6. Power rule: This is sometimes known as the "what does the boss think?" rule. What do the most prominent people at the table want? In some nonprofit organizations, a lot of weight may be given to the wishes of prominent donors.
7. "Occam's razor" rule: Is the proposal too complicated or too costly? (Occam's razor is the principle that, of two explanations that account for all the facts, the simpler one is more likely to be correct.)
8. Optics rule: How will the decision look? Will the decision fly with multiple and important publics?
9. Stakeholders-not-in-the-room rule: Given that not everyone can be in the room when a decision is being made, are there important publics or stakeholders who need to be considered?

A key element to understand with respect to decision rules is that they are often unarticulated and that although all nine operate in almost all groups, they often conflict with each other. In this context, "conflict" means that the distribution of outcomes would be different if only one rule was followed, as opposed to a blending of some or all nine. This can lead to two kinds of problems. First, in a situation in which all or most of the nine rules are operating, the executive leader or CEO must continually manage the situation to be sure that breadth, depth, involvement, expertise, and power all have their proper place. The proposals most likely to go forward and reach a decision point in a timely fashion are those that can meet and be shown to meet the interests of most of these decision rules. Formulating and expressing options that are linked to these rules is the process of decision crystallization.

For example, a group was discussing where to have lunch. There was much talk, and among the issues that came up were what most people wanted to do (the extensive rule), what the vegetarians wanted to do (the intensive rule), who was going to drive (the involvement rule), whether they had harmful additives at the place everyone might have been thinking of (the expert rule), and what the boss would say (the power rule). A meeting master in this discussion suggested that they go to a nearby Chinese restaurant because it would satisfy most of their preferences (the extensive rule addressed). It appealed to the vegetarian colleagues because it had vegetarian dishes (the intensive rule addressed). The meeting master said that she would drive (the involvement rule addressed) and that the restaurant did not put monosodium glutamate in their food (the expert rule addressed). Last, she stated that the boss did not care where they spent their lunch money (the power rule addressed).

This was an amazing occurrence because the group understood that issues of concern to them in decision making, including breadth, depth, involvement, power, and expertise, were addressed. Everyone in the group agreed, and off they went. Although the issue was small, the performance was masterful. This example is one that nonprofit managers might want to keep in mind because in situations with potentially conflicting values or preferences, people will accept a reason for a decision as legitimate.

The second problem can occur when one value or preference is very dominant. In this type of organization (for example, clan, market, hierarchy, adhocratic), one rule tends to be dominant over all others. For instance, in the clan culture, the extensive decision rule might be given preference so that the highest number of votes wins. This means that people who feel strongly—experts, people with power, and people who might have to carry out decisions—are not given the kind of weight that a high-quality decision truly deserves. In these instances, the manager wants to be sure that the other bases of decisions are articulated and brought into play. Obviously, organizations will have their preference for decision rules, but the exclusion of appropriate alternative bases for decisions will create a weaker, poorer quality decision than might otherwise be expected.

For example, a task force from a clan-oriented organization was working on a proposal. In this group, experts were not well regarded, power was very well regarded, and involvement was not well regarded. Depth of preference was given short shrift. After a considerable amount of time, effort, and work, a proposal was voted on, to the great satisfaction of the task force, and proudly presented to upper management. The proposal was quickly rejected. The first mistake the task force made was that it had not considered the wishes of the boss. The second mistake was that it had not considered certain legalities. The third mistake was that the individuals who had to carry out the recommendation had serious questions about it. And the fourth mistake was that the people who felt deeply but differently about the proposal had not been consulted or involved. Hence, if the chairperson had articulated the alternative decision bases and pointed out that these perspectives needed to be included and addressed, it is likely that the result would have been much better.

Given that decision rules are often unarticulated, people tend to learn them informally, through a kind of cultural osmosis, without really having been taught them. Although most people know most of these rules, organizations tend to use two or three predominantly. The military, for example, does not do much voting ("All who want to attack the enemy dug in up on that hill, please raise your hands!"). It is important to figure out which decision rules are most characteristic of the organization because these rules represent its decision culture, and almost any decision will have to be aligned with them, although others will, on occasion, come into play.

Putting in the Fix: Building High-Quality Decisions by Managing Conflicting Values in Decision Results

A good deal of thought has been given to documenting awful decisions or awful types of decisions. Perhaps the most famous kind of bad decision is the groupthink decision, a concept developed by Janis (1972). In a groupthink situation, group cohesion is very high, and individual members of the group are reluctant to bring up contrary points of view because they do not want to put stress on the group's cohesion and disturb the peace. Groupthink is typically a problem of the clan organization.

A second kind of decision problem is decision randomness, exemplified by what has been called a "garbage can model of organizational choice" (Cohen, March, & Olsen, 1972, p. 1). For high-quality decisions, the following four types of people or perspectives are typically needed in the same room at the same time:

1. problem knowers (individuals who know the problems the organization faces)
2. solution providers (creative individuals who can solve problems if they know what the problems are)
3. resource controllers (individuals who sign off on the allocation of money and people and are therefore crucial to implementation)
4. decision makers looking for work (usually the top-level managers who have to bless a decision if it is to go forward)

Cohen et al. (1972) argued that most organizations assemble these individuals at random, as though tossed into a garbage can. This randomness is a feature of the adhocratic culture. A few people get together and do this, then a few more get together and do that, then others get together and do yet a third thing, and there is a huge amount of rework and very little orchestration and organization.

A third decision problem is the "do-it, fix-it method." This phrase, which has become common, is associated with Walmart's strategy for evolutionary growth. Collins and Porras (1994) shared the following from a Walmart executive: "We live by the motto 'Do It. Fix It. Try Something Else'" (p. 148), which is characteristic of a group that is so eager to act that it often takes premature action. This also could be called the "fire, ready, aim" group. Although groupthink becomes mired in process and the failure to surface authentic alternatives, the do-it, fix-it group grabs the first gold ring that seems reasonable, proceeds with it, and often winds up needing to revise and repair, sometimes very quickly.

The last decision problem is "same as last year," a decision type characteristic of hierarchical cultures. Given the rigidities and often ponderous nature of hierarchies, making decisions that are new, different, risky, or odd is very difficult. This method seems to fit with a conservative mentality. After all, hierarchies are very good at doing something on a repeated basis over time and space. In a sense, this method continues that skill or competence into the decision-making area.

Each of these bad decisions occurs because of an overemphasis on the specific strengths of a particular culture and because those strengths get carried over into the decision-making process. For example, the adhocracy structure tends toward chaos, and so it has a tendency toward randomness in its decision-making process. The clan subculture, with its skills in involving participants and processing issues and concerns, may never reach a decision or may succumb to groupthink.

The antidote to these problems is complex. First, the commonly used decision processes ensure that a certain amount of structure, openness, participation, and promptness will be present simultaneously. Thus, the potential perils of using only one cultural preference as the basis for decision making are reduced. Second, the management of decision rules goes a long way toward creating the balance culturally necessary for a high-quality decision. Third, one can do assessments of the decisions themselves. One way to assess decisions is to go back into the history of a particular group, such as a nonprofit's board. Look at the decisions the board has made and ask these questions: Are these decisions good? Why or why not? A discussion about the quality of the decisions can be useful. The announcement ahead of time that decisions will be evaluated in the future changes the nature of the process itself. People pay more attention when they know that they are going to be evaluated. If a man knows that he will be weighed at the end of the week by his physician, he will probably be careful, during that week at least, to exercise and watch his diet. Hence, what the physician sees when she looks at the man's weight is a modified weight, not a true weight. Similarly, boards, staff groups, and volunteer groups working on a decision will be more careful and articulate and will participate with more authenticity if they know that they are going to be evaluated.

In addition, a no-fault discussion of why certain decisions were good and why certain decisions were not so good helps everyone to understand their mission, task, and role as a group working together for the good of the organization.

The executive leader or manager running or chairing a meeting has three steps to consider. First, group members need to be provided with an opportunity, if they wish, to express themselves about each item on the agenda. This is often thought of as a round of discussion. Ideally, a round of discussion should be ended when everyone who wants to say something has said it. Care should be taken to ensure that everyone has had a chance to speak. At that point, there will be a brief pause in the flow of commentary. This pause offers a crucial opportunity, and the chairperson or leader of the meeting needs to act. If the leader does not, then participants will begin to reparticipate, reiterating what they have already said. The leader's role here involves tying up the previous discussion and enabling the group to move on to what is called a decision crystallization modality.

Decision crystallization is the process of moving from general discussion and observations to an action result—that is, a decision. The chairperson or meeting leader will have been participating, but more in an interrogative way, asking for clarification, calling on those who are not joining in the discussion, and asking them to do so. The chair may make supportive statements, such as "that's interesting" or "good thought," that convey support but not agreement.

In seeing how the meeting masters handled running meetings, I identified four steps that lead to decision crystallization. These may seem simple, but early in my research it was very hard to distinguish them because they were seemingly natural and unscripted. When the meeting masters were provided feedback, the most effective of them, labeled "maestros" (because they functioned much like a chef or orchestra conductor in the sense of taking many ingredients or parts and bringing them together to create a great meal or a terrific symphony), quickly recognized the following steps.

Taking advantage of the small break that occurs after the first round of discussion, the maestros engaged in summative reflection, a sort of summary of what had been said. This has been found to be very useful because too often people do not really listen to what others have been saying. However, this summative reflection was much more than just a report, hence the word "summative." The reflection was organized to underscore the areas of agreement or similarity leading to the action, which leads to the legitimization of why the suggestion (almost always made in the passive voice and without a personal pronoun) make sense. Here, the suggestion needs to be attached to the decision culture and any other appropriate decision rules. The maestros did not use the term "decision rules," of course. Rather, to go back to the earlier example of a group deciding where to have lunch, they said things such as "This restaurant seems to meet the needs of most of us [rule 1], has great vegetarian and vegan options [rule 3], has great ratings on Yelp [rule 5], and the boss doesn't care where we go for lunch [rule 6]."

At this point, there is frequently an affirmation, and the meeting chair might say something such as "Well, we have lunch nailed—let's pick a dinner spot" or, in a real meeting, "Now that we've reached agreement on this item, let's move on to consider the next agenda item." However, if a decision is not forthcoming, the meeting leader may go to a second round of discussion, with the admonition to members to please not repeat what has already been said but rather to add any new considerations.

Most meeting leaders will say, at some random point, "Well, where are we?" meaning that they do not know how to close and want someone else to do it. Over time, others can and will do it.

When the decision mosaic has been completed—the orchestra program is developed, the event is planned, or the dinner menu is finished—it is time for a final look. This step is called decision sculpting, and it is meant to ensure that the overall decision has not accidently left anything out.

Let me share an example. My grandmother was of German ancestry, and my favorite meal of hers was a pork dinner that consisted of roast pork, mashed potatoes, sauerkraut, applesauce, and mashed rutabaga. Most of the food was usually covered with a light brown gravy. My wife is of Italian background, and she feels my grandmother's meal is "lacking in presentation." She once opined that she could not tell if this meal had been eaten yet or not! I seem to recall that the phrase "pig's breakfast" was also used. To be fair, my grandmother's meal, this favorite of mine, was a fairly bland, white dinner, with the rutabagas and the gravy providing just a twinge of color. Surely, the meal's presentation could have been improved with a greater variety of colors.

So, in the groups I work with, we are always looking for the pork dinner. We ask what is missing—What or whom have we left out? Have we accidentally scheduled something on a religious holiday? And so on. Going through this kind of routine after a decision has been made is worth a few extra minutes because it will ultimately result in higher quality decisions.

Meeting and Decision Evaluations

At the conclusion of a meeting and during the course of business, it is recommended that some attention be given to the following three types of evaluation:

1. evaluation of the meeting itself
2. evaluation of the overall decisions and functioning of the decision group
3. organizational evaluation to assess lessons learned

Meeting Evaluation

A quick "keep, stop, start" approach works well for evaluating meetings. Use it every third meeting or so. Ask these questions: What is going well and what should we keep? What is not going as well, or is not needed, and what should we stop? What are we not doing now that we should start? Look for patterns.

Decision Evaluation

In evaluating the quality of decisions made at meetings, the following schema or portfolio analysis—grades A–F—works well. An A decision is an all-win decision, but all do not have to win equally. To use an analogy from the stock market, an A decision would be if all your stocks went up, although not necessarily in equal amounts. A B decision involves some losses but some major accomplishments. In this case, some of your stocks went down, but overall your portfolio is ahead. A C decision is a wash; some are winners, some are losers, but overall, your portfolio is the same. A D decision sets you further behind, such as if all of the stocks in your portfolio went down. An F decision is the nuclear situation, one in which you have lost all, such as if the stock market collapsed and your entire portfolio was lost. Obviously, you would like to be able to conclude that most of the decisions reached at your meetings fall into the A or B categories, or at worst the C category. If not, your organization is in serious trouble. This kind of decision portfolio analysis should be done at least in the beginning of the third quarter and again soon after the end of the organization's fiscal year.

Organizational Evaluation

Usually once a quarter, and sometimes more if a big event has gone on, one should use an after-action report, a procedure used in the military and other institutions.

For the quarterly version, use the first three months of the fiscal year, or some other three-month time frame, and look over the flow of events using a "things gone right–things gone wrong" (TGRTGW) analytic frame. On the basis of the TGRTGW analysis, a lessons-learned document is produced.

For the remaining quarters, the after-action report begins with the TGRTGW analysis and proceeds through the second three months. The third and fourth quarters are the same, except that the last quarter takes a look at all three TGRTGW documents and uses an annual perspective. The goal is to always be looking for continuous improvement. Correlatively, one might also use the after-action approach for major events, missions, and incidents.

Preparing for Change: The Cost of Meetings

This chapter has given meetings and decision making much more leadership attention than is typical. Although a lot of time is spent in meetings and decision making, many executive leaders and individuals who participate in meetings suggest that probably at least half of meeting time is wasted. In 2018, there were just under 15 million people in managerial occupations in the United States. They earned, on average, $75,000 per year. That totals $1.25 trillion. If the average manager spends 65 percent of their time in meetings, the dollar value of their time spent in meetings is $731.25 billion. If one estimates the time spent as 60 percent, the cost of that time is $438.25 billion. If one takes into account the variability of the nonprofit manager's schedule and includes breakfast meetings, lunch meetings, and evening and weekend meetings, that number can be rounded up to $500 billion in wasted resources.

How Can Such Appalling Waste Be Explained?

Terrible meetings and awful decisions are a result of the waste production process in organizations worldwide. I have routinely asked my management classes this question: "How much work actually goes on at work?" The answers of many years and dozens of classes is remarkably consistent: about three days worth, plus or (more often) minus. Meetings are a key component of what David Graeber calls "bullshit jobs" (Graeber, 2013, 2019). This waste production process, days of make-work, arises because a large majority of leaders and managers do not know how to manage. There are a series of commentaries on managerial incompetence. Let's start with the World War II concept of SNAFU (situation normal, all f** up) and then consider Steve Kerr's (1995) classic *On the Folly of Rewarding A, While Hoping for B*. Sometimes managers are just assholes (Sutton, 2010, 2017). One can also explore Thomas Chamarro-Primuzik's (2019) question, "Why do so many incompetent men become leaders?"

Finally, there is actual personal and organizational malevolence. There is a lot of rotten behavior in and by organizations. As Donald Palmer (2012) observed,

> Although most who write about organizational wrongdoing implicitly consider it to be an abnormal phenomenon, a growing number of scholars implicitly regard it as normal. ... The normal organizational wrongdoing perspective assumes that wrongdoers are ordinary; that is people who do not possess unusual human traits (e.g. sociopathic tendencies). (p. 8)

Bullshit jobs, messy meetings, and disgusting decisions are produced. And, oddly, folks seem to tolerate them. We could do better, but we seem to be satisfied with a low bar. My work in working toward meeting mastery and high-quality decisions has led me to this conclusion: Never underestimate people's commitment to rotten practices. Nonetheless, it is worth a try.

Change to a Better Practice: Often a Sisyphean Task

Given the direct and indirect costs of spending time in poorly designed and poorly run meetings that lead to poor decisions, one might be tempted to try to make things better using evidence-informed practices. The examples of such practices in this chapter have been very useful and, in many cases, transformative. However, one important thing to remember is my observation to never underestimate people's attachment to rotten practices. As Yul Brenner opined in *The King and I,* "It is a puzzlement" as to why people are not more interested in meeting improvement. Perhaps it is a kind of change avoidance psychosis.

Untold hours and billions of dollars are wasted annually in awful, unproductive meetings. There are precipitating and predisposing etiologies and manifest and hidden functions at play. Too often, executive leaders, managers, staff, board members, and volunteers spend time in make-work, useless meetings, all supporting the current status quo. So how do we change that? Do not think that changing meeting practices will be easy, but I hope you will try.

Conclusion

The management of group decision making, or decision building, is one of the most important tasks that nonprofit managers can undertake simply because so much of their time is spent in decision-making groups. Many CEOs and other top-level managers spend more than half of their time in meetings. Most of them express mild disbelief to vigorous dislike of this allocation of their time, and consider this time largely wasted, ceremonial, useless, and not productive. One can only imagine what it would be like if the decision-making groups in which everyone participates so frequently were to become so productive and useful that people looked forward to attending. Yet, the meeting masters created such groups and sustained enthusiasm in them over considerable periods of time. Their peers, superiors, and subordinates turned to them to undertake difficult tasks and chair difficult task forces, and they almost always did an outstanding job. Their goal was to make high-quality decisions, and the tips and suggestions presented in this chapter will help nonprofit managers move in that direction.

Skills Application Exercises

1. Thinking of the organizational subculture quadrants, rank your organization according to the dominance of the clan, hierarchy, market, and adhocracy subcultures. Consider whether your organization has the decision-making problems discussed in this chapter. Feel free to add more problems, other problems, and different problems.
2. Think specifically of the kinds of problematic decisions discussed in the chapter: that is, groupthink; garbage can or randomness; do-it, fix-it; and same as last year. Considering the past six months at your organization, count how many of these types of decisions your organization has been involved with. Think of one or two really awful decisions. Try to understand what went wrong and think about some of the ways the material in this chapter (and other chapters) could help you fix it.
3. Observe a meeting at your organization (or somewhere else) and see whether you can identify the decision rules in action (or, more likely, in nonaction). Develop a plan to practice thinking up possible solutions that meet or can be shown to meet most of these rules. It will be a little bumpy at first, but you will be surprised at how quickly you become good at it.

References

Blackburn, J. (2016, December 2). *The Abilene paradox—definition & examples.* Retrieved from https://study.com/academy/lesson/the-abilene-paradox-definition-examples.html

Chamorro-Primuzik, T. (2019). *Why do so many incompetent men become leaders?* Retrieved from https://www.youtube.com/watch?v=iSZaRoL213U

Cohen, M. D., March, J. G., & Olsen, J. P. (1972). A garbage can model of organizational choice. *Administrative Science Quarterly, 17*(1), 1–25.

Collins, J., & Porras, J. (1994). *Built to last.* New York: HarperCollins.

Graeber, D. (2013). On the phenomenon of bullshit jobs: A work rant. *Strike Magazine, 3*(Summer). Retrieved from http://www.strike.coop/bullshit-jobs/

Graeber, D. (2019). *Bullshit jobs: A theory.* New York: Simon & Schuster.

Janis, I. (1972). *Victims of groupthink.* Boston: Houghton-Mifflin.

Kerr, S. (1975). On the folly of rewarding A, while hoping for B. *Academy of Management Journal, 18,* 769–783.

Palmer, D. (2012). *Normal organizational wrongdoing: A critical analysis of theories of misconduct in and by organizations.* Oxford, England: Oxford University Press.

Psychology Today. (n.d.). *Groupthink.* Retrieved from https://www.psychologytoday.com/us/basics/groupthink

Quinn, R. E. (1988). *Beyond rational management: Mastering the paradoxes and competing demands of high performance.* San Francisco: Jossey-Bass.

Quinn, R. E., Rohrbaugh, J., & McGrath, M. R. (1985). Automated decision conferencing: How it works. *Personnel, 62*(11), 49–55.

Sutton, R. (2010). *The no asshole rule: Building a civilized workplace and surviving one that isn't.* New York: Grand Central Publishing.

Sutton, R. (2017). *The asshole survival guide.* New York: Houghton, Mifflin, Harcourt.

Tropman, J. E. (1989). *American values and social welfare: Cultural contradictions in the welfare state.* Englewood Cliffs, NJ: Prentice Hall.

Tropman, J. E. (2003). *Making meetings work* (2nd ed.). San Francisco: Jossey-Bass.

Tropman, J. (2018). *Team impact: Achieving twice as much in half the time.* San Diego: Cognella.

Tropman, J. E. (2020). *Supervision, management and leadership: An introduction to building community benefit organizations.* New York: Oxford University Press.

Additional Reading

Collins, J. (2001). *Good to great: Why some companies make the leap . . . and others don't.* New York: HarperBusiness.

Levitt, T. (1960). Marketing myopia. *Harvard Business Review, 38,* 45–56.

McCaskey, M. (1982). *The executive challenge: Managing change and ambiguity.* New York: HarperCollins College.

Quinn, R. E., Faerman, S. R., Thompson, M. P., McGrath, M. R., & Bright, D. S. (2015). *Becoming a master manager: A competing values approach* (6th ed.). Hoboken, NJ: Wiley.

Simon, H., Smithburg, D., & Thompson, V. (1991). *Public administration.* Piscataway, NJ: Transaction Books.

Tropman, J. (2014). *Effective meetings.* Thousand Oaks, CA: SAGE.

PART FOUR

Coordinating Skills

COORDINATING SKILLS INVOLVE OVERSEEING THE OPERATIONS OF AN ORGAnization. One has to respond daily to multiple internal and external inquiries and demands and balance the needs of many stakeholders and legitimate constituencies. Although this skill is often not given the recognition it deserves, the progress and stability of public and private nonprofit organizations are dependent on this role being performed consciously and well.

In chapter 8, Marci S. Thomas looks closely at one of the primary functions of a nonprofit manager—overseeing the ever-limited finances of such organizations. Many senior executives are hired (or internally promoted) to top management positions on the basis of their expertise in their profession (for example, educational administration, social work, performance arts) but do not come with an understanding of accounting or financial management and therefore will need the primer that she presents.

In chapter 9, Mathieu Despard offers a close-up look at modern program evaluation for its appropriate application to nonprofit settings. With a focus on impact and outcomes, he makes a strong case for ensuring systematic and ongoing performance assessment. Despard also stresses the need for evaluation to be attentive to ever-changing community need. Eschewing oversimplification, he looks squarely at the challenges in conducting meaningful evaluation and presents sound strategies for addressing dilemmas and overcoming them, providing a detailed discourse on the importance of both clear conceptualization and participatory implementation.

In chapter 10, Paul A. Kurzman puts forward the myriad risks and exposures confronted by nonprofits today and the liabilities they consequently face on a daily basis. With the concept of sovereign immunity no longer likely to protect service institutions under public auspices, or the doctrine of charitable immunity to shield those under a private aegis, such agencies are increasingly finding that their exposure to litigation and other adversarial actions has increased. After citing the principal risks, Kurzman then offers a prescription to help nonprofit leaders position their organizations to ensure the presence of sound risk management strategies and planful prevention.

Finally, in chapter 11, Frederic G. Reamer looks at the present and emerging information and communications technologies (ICT) on which nonprofits have become increasingly dependent. He explores the many technology options, the major functions they perform, their appropriate role when formulating a strategic plan, and the often less visible ethical issues presented by some aspects of ICT implementation. Looking closely at the laws and regulations and their prevailing application, Reamer provides a detailed road map for managers to use when navigating this new and ever-shifting terrain. He concludes with a reminder of the rapidly changing nature of the field and hence the need to be attentive to its permutations, challenges, and conundrums.

8

Managing the Finances of Nonprofit Organizations

Marci S. Thomas

Nonprofit organizations are formed to serve either a public purpose or a mutual benefit. Generally, they are distinguished from business enterprises because they

- receive significant contributions from donors who do not expect a commensurate or proportionate return
- have charitable, religious, or educational operating purposes
- are not owned by individuals

Nonprofits can have these characteristics in varying degrees, depending on the nature of their mission and operations. Examples of nonprofits include voluntary health and welfare organizations, colleges and universities, churches and synagogues, federated fundraising organizations, civic and community organizations, museums and art galleries, trade associations, and social and country clubs. Entities such as health care organizations are also formed as nonprofits but are reliant less on contributions and more on the fees charged for services.

The Internal Revenue Service (IRS) provides certain benefits to nonprofits if they meet specific criteria, the most important of which is that no part of the net earnings of the entity may benefit a private individual or shareholder of the nonprofit. In addition to exemption from federal and state income tax, other benefits of tax-exempt status include the ability to attract donations that are tax deductible to the donors and to issue debt at lower interest rates. Nonprofits are required to pay federal payroll tax and may also be required to pay real estate tax and sales or other local taxes as required by state law.

For many people, the word "nonprofit" conjures up the image of an entity created to do good works in an environment in which there is an abundance of donors. Unfortunately, this is far from the truth. Nonprofits exist in a very competitive environment. The more than 1.3 million nonprofits in the United States today compete for dollars not only in the form of donations but also in the form of grants and contracts from federal, state, and local governments; foundations; and larger nonprofits.

Donors and other funding sources are concerned about how nonprofits manage their resources. On the basis of hits on GuideStar's (https://www.guidestar.org) national database of nonprofit financial information on the Internet, it is evident that the public is scrutinizing the financial activities of nonprofits before making donations. GuideStar uses data from nonprofits' informational tax returns (Form 990) to populate its database with financial information about them. It is important to remember that nonprofits serve the community and, as such, have a responsibility to function with integrity and efficiency.

Focus on Accountability

In response to high-profile frauds and corporate failures, Rep. Michael Oxley (R-OH) and Sen. Paul Sarbanes (D-MD) authored the Sarbanes–Oxley Act (P.L. 107-204), which became law in 2002 (American Bar Association, n.d.; BoardSource, 2003). Although it applies to publicly traded entities, in the years since its passage, nonprofits and other nonpublic companies have generally used the Sarbanes–Oxley Act as best-practice standards in their operations. Sarbanes–Oxley requires, among other things, that the chief executive officer (CEO) and chief financial officer attest to the fair presentation of the entity's financial statements on a quarterly (and yearly) basis and that the entity undergo an audit of internal controls over financial reporting. In addition, some provisions govern the use of audit committees and auditor independence.

Nonprofits attest to the fair presentation of financial statements as well as their responsibility for their internal controls over financial reporting when they sign an audit representation letter. For this reason, among others, donors tend to prefer to give to nonprofits that have audited financial statements.

In these complex times, nonprofit managers need more than just a basic knowledge of financial management principles. In recent years, the overall presentation of the financial statements has changed in four major areas:

1. recognition of revenue
2. lease accounting
3. grants and contribution accounting
4. overall financial statement presentation

This chapter focuses on grants and contribution accounting and overall financial statement presentation. It also introduces the basic financial concepts that nonprofit executives and leaders need to understand to manage a nonprofit. It is important that management have sufficient knowledge to know when to call on accounting and finance professionals for assistance.

Financial Statements

Financial statements summarize the activities of the nonprofit and are used to communicate this information not only to those responsible for leading and managing the nonprofit but also to the nonprofit's board of directors and external parties such as donors and other funding sources, bond holders, and creditors. Generally accepted accounting principles require that a nonprofit present a statement of financial position, a statement of activities, a statement of changes in activities, and a statement of cash flows. The footnotes to the financial statements are an integral part of them and provide a description of the organization's accounting policies as well as the detail behind the balances. The financial statements should be read as a complete set. Each statement presents a different perspective on the nonprofit's financial condition. Relying on one statement alone can give readers a misleading picture.

The discussion that follows describes the financial statement elements that are most important for nonprofit managers to understand. It is safe to say that, depending on the size and complexity of the nonprofit, management may need assistance from outside experts to ensure that they are properly accounting for and disclosing the organization's transactions and activities.

To illustrate nonprofit financial statements, this chapter uses the statements for a hypothetical homeless shelter that is a 501(c)(3) organization. The shelter's mission is to provide assistance to homeless individuals. It also provides job placement services in the community on a sliding-scale basis. This nonprofit derives the majority of its financial support from small contributions from individual donors and government grants.

Statement of Financial Position

The statement of financial position presents the finances of an organization, or what the IRS generally refers to as an entity, at a given point in time: the end of the month, the end of a quarter, or the end of the year. The statement lists, in order of liquidity, the assets, the liabilities, and the equity of the entity. Statements of financial position can also be classified; that is, the assets and liabilities are segregated into current and noncurrent categories. Current assets and liabilities are expected to be collected or paid, respectively, within the year. Noncurrent assets and liabilities have a longer cycle. Because nonprofits almost never issue stock, the net assets are the cumulative results of operations and restricted donations of the entity since its inception.

In 2016, the Financial Accounting Standards Board (FASB; 2016b) made dramatic changes to financial statement presentation that came into effect at the end of the 2018 calendar year. When the user looks at the financial statement, the most evident change is a change in the composition of net assets.

Previously, net assets were classified according to the level of restriction specified by the donor: unrestricted, temporarily restricted (as to purpose or time), and permanently restricted. Subsequent to the issuance of the standard, entities must classify net assets as either with donor restriction or without donor restriction. This change highlights the fact that even though other entities can restrict cash or assets, only donors can restrict net assets. The disclosures were broadened to identify the different types of donor restrictions, such as purpose, time, in perpetuity, and even those net assets over which the organization has no control, such as net assets held in a perpetual trust.

The statement of financial position for Canton Cares, a homeless shelter, is shown in Figure 8.1.

Cash and Cash Equivalents
Cash can be held in checking or savings accounts or, in the case of petty cash, in a locked safe. Many nonprofits keep a supply of petty cash on hand, but this should be carefully controlled. Cash equivalents are short-term financial instruments such as certificates of deposit and money market funds with an original maturity of three months or less.

Figure 8.1 Sample Homeless Shelter Statement of Financial Positions for June 30, 2020, and June 30, 2021

	2020	2021
ASSETS		
Cash and Cash Equivalents	$18,366	$311,984
Investments	265,019	14,859
Pledges Receivable Less Allowance for Doubtful Accounts	56,933	36,059
Grants Receivable	187,507	251,089
Inventories	50,550	65,550
Prepaid Expenses	21,365	20,251
Property and Equipment:		
Land	358,092	358,092
Buildings	780,258	780,258
Equipment	475,142	335,114
Less Accumulated Depreciation	(295,847)	(256,889)
	1,917,385	1,916,367
Other Assets	55,349	57,999
TOTAL ASSETS	$1,972,734	$1,974,366
LIABILITIES		
Accounts Payable	$87,912	$71,945
Accrued Expenses	22,350	25,409
Deferred Revenue		108,529
Mortgages and Notes Payable	1,092,517	1,060,057
Other Liabilities	3,202	1,823
TOTAL LIABILITIES	$1,205,981	$1,267,763
NET ASSETS		
Net Assets Without Restrictions	$698,553	$601,603
Net Assets With Donor Restrictions	68,200	105,000
TOTAL NET ASSETS	$716,753	$656,603
Total Liabilities And Net Assets	$1,972,734	$1,974,366

Investments

Short-term investments can be in the form of debt or equity securities. Accounting literature has prescribed that, although they are initially recorded at cost or, if donated, at fair value, they are written up or down to the market value at each financial statement date. Nonprofits may also have other types of investments such as derivatives, investments in split-interest agreements, investments in other entities, and investments in real estate or other tangible property. These investments are initially recorded at fair value, but the accounting for subsequent valuation is complex.

Derivatives are investments in which the value of the investment is derived from an underlying asset. Derivatives require no initial net investment or one that is smaller than would be required for contracts that would have similar response in market factors. An example of a derivative would be an option to purchase stock. Derivatives may or may not be short-term investments. They are complex instruments and should be used only by someone with the knowledge and skills to be sure that they are used appropriately.

Nonprofits are frequently the beneficiaries of split-interest agreements. Although there are numerous types of split-interest agreements, all involve an interest going to both the nonprofit and the donor. Some agreements call for the donor to receive a periodic annuity (for example, yearly, quarterly, or monthly) for life, with the remainder of the investment going to the nonprofit at the death of the donor. Some provide the nonprofit with an annuity during the life of the donor, but the remaining assets revert to the donor's heirs at death. With today's life expectancies and lower rates, some nonprofits are having problems with these investments because the payment to the donor may be greater than the income generated by the investment. Before accepting them as donations, management should consult with professionals who have experience with this sort of investment if the requisite knowledge is not available within the nonprofit.

Nonprofits may also hold investments in for-profit entities or other nonprofits. For example, an educational institution may have created a foundation for the purpose of fundraising. The rules that govern when the entities are consolidated or whether one merely has an interest in the net assets of another are complex. Management should consult financial professionals to determine the appropriate accounting treatment for a given situation.

Pledges and Accounts Receivable

Nonprofits are required to record pledges when the pledges are made at the amount that the entity expects to collect. This is especially important in a building campaign when experience suggests that although most donors will honor their pledges, not all will. In addition, if donations are long term (more than one year before they are paid), they should be discounted to reflect the time value of money. Each period, management should evaluate the collectability of pledges and, if necessary, establish an allowance for those that may not be collectable. Pledges should be segregated by net asset class (that is, with donor restrictions or without donor restrictions).

Accounts receivable arise when the entity sells goods or services. Receivables should only be recorded when the organization has the right to bill and performance obligations have been met. "Performance obligations" is a term that describes the goods or services that have been promised to the customer. In 2014, the FASB issued a significant amendment that introduced a principles-based approach to revenue recognition and a host of new terminology. The guidance applies to transactions with commensurate benefit. Nonprofits frequently have commercial operations (such as stores) and sometimes sell services in keeping with their missions. This is especially true in the health care and educational settings. Revenue recognition guidance is complex, and a detailed discussion is beyond the scope of this chapter. Accounts receivable are amounts due the nonprofit from these transactions and should be stated at the value that the organization expects to collect. Because the revenue recognition guidance focuses on the amount that the organization expects to collect, allowances for bad debts are much less common. However, if a customer (patient, student, and so on) has a change in circumstances, such as a bankruptcy or some other issue that would prevent payment, then this would constitute a bad debt. Price concessions and similar write-offs are a reduction of previously recorded revenue. Accordingly, the nonprofit would perform an analysis of historical bad debt and record an allowance to ensure that the receivables are not overstated. The revenue recognition standard is effective for all entities by the end of 2021.

Grants Receivable

In 2018, the FASB issued an update on accounting for grants. Before this time, there was little guidance on how an organization should account for a government grant, and most entities accounted for them as though they were reciprocal transfers. The FASB's guidance contradicts this prior assumption and also provides clarity on grants and contracts no matter the source. If a resource provider provides or promises funding to an organization, management should determine whether the exchange is reciprocal. This means that there is commensurate benefit on each side. If the benefit is mainly to society rather than the funder (that is, the government), then the transaction is deemed to be a contribution.

Once a transaction is established as a contribution, then the organization must decide whether it is conditional or unconditional. Revenue cannot be recognized until conditions are substantially met. For example, Canton Cares, a homeless shelter, receives grants from the federal government. The benefit is not reciprocal, because it is the society that receives the benefit, not the government. Canton Cares considers whether it is possible to recognize revenue right away. The organization looks at two criteria:

1. Is there a barrier that has to be met according to the grant?
2. Is there a requirement in the grant that, if the funding is not spent, either it will be returned (if provided in advance) or the funding source is relieved of further funding?

If the answer to both of these questions is yes, then the organization waits to recognize revenue until the barrier is overcome. Barriers can take the form of units of service to be provided; specific criteria, such as a schedule of allowable costs that need to be met; or raising funds to receive funds, such as in a matching grant.

Once the barrier is overcome, then the contribution becomes unconditional and can be recognized as either donor restricted, for reasons of purpose or timing, or without donor restrictions, meaning it can be spent for any purpose. This change was effective for 2019 and after calendar year-ends.

Inventories

Inventories are not generally a major item on a nonprofit's statement of financial position because most nonprofits provide services as opposed to sell products. However, when a nonprofit has product inventories (such as publications), they are recorded at cost and periodically evaluated for obsolescence or any kind of damage that would cause them to lose value and trigger a write-down.

Prepaid Expenses

Nonprofits are sometimes called on to prepay certain items, such as insurance or rent. This means that the cash is paid before the item is used. The asset reflects the unused portion of the insurance, rent, or other prepaid item.

Property and Equipment

Property and equipment typically consist of land, buildings, computer and other devices, tools, and leasehold improvements. These are recorded at cost if purchased. If donated, assets are recorded at the fair value at the date of donation. Each period, a portion of the asset is recorded as expense. Accumulated depreciation represents the cumulative depreciation since the asset was placed in service. Land is the only asset in this category that is not depreciated. Property and equipment accounts are periodically evaluated for impairment. Another change that resulted from the guidance that changed financial statement presentation is that when contributed long-lived assets are placed in service, the net assets become without donor restriction. Previously, the FASB provided an option to continue to reflect donated long-lived assets as donor restricted and release them from restriction as they were depreciated.

Other Assets
Other assets is a category in which items without financial significance are aggregated. An example might be a deposit on leased space or equipment.

Accounts Payable and Accrued Expenses
Accounts payable are liabilities to vendors for goods purchased or services that have been rendered for which payment has not been made. Accrued expenses are liabilities for which there is typically no invoice. Examples might be amounts owed to employees for time worked within a period for which they have not been paid or amounts expected to be paid for worker's compensation claims.

Deferred Revenue
Deferred revenue is a liability to the party that paid the entity to perform service before the service was performed. For example, when a company has paid the nonprofit in advance to perform contract research and the service has not yet been performed, the amount of payment would be considered deferred revenue until the performance obligations are met (for example, research was performed).

Mortgages and Notes Payable
Mortgages and notes payable are debt instruments that are generally long term. In classified statements of financial position, the amounts would be separated into the amount to be paid in the coming year and the long-term portion. The notes to the financial statements would disclose the interest rate, the maturity of the debt, and any kind of debt covenants with which the entity must comply.

Nonprofits may also enter into lease agreements. The FASB (2016a) issued new guidance for leases that will be effective for all entities in 2021. The change that affects most nonprofits is that operating leases will now be reported on the balance sheet. The organization will record an asset and a liability that essentially reflects the present value of the minimum lease payments over the period of the lease. Lease accounting is very complex and beyond the scope of this chapter.

Other Liabilities

Other liabilities is a category in which items without financial significance are aggregated. For example, these could be amounts owed or health insurance payments, amounts to be paid for property taxes, or anything that is not significant in amount.

Statement of Activities

The statement of activities represents the activities of the organization over the past year (or less, in the case of interim financial statements). When nonprofits such as health care or educational organizations have commercial operations, this statement is often referred to as a statement of operations. The revenue is categorized as either without donor restriction or with donor restriction. Expenses are always categorized as without donor restriction. Health care organizations have a slightly different presentation because they are required to report a performance indicator so that they can be compared with their for-profit counterparts. The statement of activities for a hypothetical homeless shelter and a description of its elements are presented in Figure 8.2.

Figure 8.2 Example Homeless Shelter Statement of Activities and Changes in Net Assets, Years Ended June 30, 2020, and June 30, 2021

Net Assets without Donor Restrictions	2020	2021
Contributions	$971,650	$1,121,729
Government Grants	560,554	622,649
Program Revenues	1,104,816	896,857
Investment Income	3,135	3,973
Other Revenue	13,446	15,854
TOTAL REVENUES	$2,653,601	$2,661,062
Net Assets Released From Restriction		
Expiration of Time Restriction-United Way	12,800	10,000
Restrictions for Training	25,000	25,000
Total Revenues and Other Support	$2,691,401	$2,696,062
EXPENSES		
Salaries and Wages	$1,334,735	$1,247,349
Payroll Taxes	209,084	197,431
Contract Services	157,200	150,209

Net Assets without Donor Restrictions	2020	2021
Supplies	125,144	117,271
Telephone	82,306	80,489
Postage and Shipping	14,502	12,689
Occupancy	38,752	39,932
Equipment Rental and Maintenance	74,500	76,249
Printing and Publications	1,502	1,488
Travel	9,300	9,470
Drug Testing and Treatment	38,500	34,043
Relocation Assistance	18,443	19,322
Interest	88,500	90,501
Depreciation	85,550	84,000
Utilities	76,003	73,537
Food	91,020	82,916
Auto and Truck	2,200	5,997
Marketing	13,222	13,091
Professional Fees	34,262	58,885
Security	12,355	12,326
Bus Tokens	12,235	14,716
Licenses and Fees	13,133	12,422
Insurance	62,003	62,500
Total Expenses	$2,594,451	$2,496,833
Increase in Net Assets without Donor Restriction	$96,950	$199,229
Net Assets with Donor Restrictions		
Contributions Restricted for Use in Training Program	1,000	1,800
Net Assets Released From Restrictions	(37,800)	(35,000)
Decrease in Net Assets with Donor Restricted		
Net Assets	($36,800)	($33,200)
Increase in Net Assets	$60,150	$166,029
Net Assets at Beginning of Year	$656,603	$490,574
Net Assets at End of Year	$716,753	$656,603

Support and Revenue

Support and revenue includes the following components:

- **Contributions.** Contributions are unconditional voluntary gifts from a donor who does not receive equal value in exchange. Conditions were discussed earlier in this chapter as they relate to grants. Other conditions exist that cause a contribution to be disclosed and not recognized, such as amounts specified in a will. A will can be changed, hence the condition. Contributions often have restrictions, which are stipulations put on the gift by the donor that might affect the purpose for which the gift is used or the timing of when the gift is used. For example, a donor might restrict a gift of $1,000 to be spent for research or might state that it should be used for operations in a subsequent year.

    When amounts have been donor restricted and the restrictions are met, the amounts are reclassified as without donor restrictions. The statement of activities shows a line item titled "net assets released from restriction." A nonprofit may elect a policy whereby donor-restricted gifts are classified as without donor restriction when the purpose or timing is achieved in the same period as the gift was made.

    Gifts can also be restricted in perpetuity. Generally, this happens with endowed funds when the donor intends that the corpus be allowed to grow and only the return on the investments spent. The Uniform Prudent Management of Institutional Funds Act (National Conference of Commissioners on Uniform State Laws, 2007) provisions enacted at the state level determine whether the corpus can be spent and whether there are any limitations on spending. The donor may also make stipulations on how the return can be spent. The return on investment refers to the interest or dividends plus any appreciation or depreciation in the investment. However, if the donor makes no stipulations, then the investment return will be classified as without donor restriction. The changes made to the financial statement presentation require that the nonprofit present footnote disclosures that discuss endowment spending if the endowment corpus has fallen below the amount of the original gift. Investment return is reported net of investment expenses. The new financial presentation standard requires that investment expenses include direct internal and external investment expenses.

    Nonprofits may also receive contributions of goods and services. These are called "gifts-in-kind." Donated goods should be recorded at the fair value of the gift. Contributed services may be recorded only if they meet two criteria: (1) They either create or enhance a nonfinancial asset (for example, building an addition to a building) or are provided by a professional working in that capacity (for example, an attorney offering services), and (2) the nonprofit would have purchased those services if they had not been given in donation. Services of volunteers not meeting these criteria are disclosed in the notes to the financial statements.

In 2020, the FASB issued a new disclosure standard for gifts in kind. The new standard, effective after June 30, 2022, requires nonprofit organizations to present in-kind donations as a separate revenue line item within the Statement of Activities. The standard also requires additional disclosures in the footnotes regarding the amounts of in-kind donations, broken out by category of assets received. Nonprofits will disclose information on whether the not-for-profit organization used or sold in-kind donations during the reporting period and their intentions for the asset in the future as well as any donor restrictions on the item. Nonprofits will also disclose the valuation techniques used to measure the donation at fair value.

- **Government grants.** These grants are generally identified as conditional contributions and are recognized as contribution revenue when performance barriers are overcome. The FASB does not require this revenue to be reported separately from other contributions.
- **Program revenue.** This category is used for instances in which an entity has charges for goods or services associated with a program. These instances are considered exchange transactions and are recognized when performance obligations are met.
- **Investment income (or return).** This category includes dividends, interest, rents, royalties, and other types of payments. The income is recognized when it is earned. As noted earlier, investment income should be reported in the appropriate net asset class.
- **Expenses.** Expenses are recognized when they are incurred. They may be reported in the statement of activities by natural classification (for example, payroll, rent) or by functional classification (for example, program, management, and general fundraising). If the entity chooses not to present functional expenses in the body of the statement, the information must be disclosed in the notes to the financial statement. Effective with the new financial presentation standard (FASB, 2016b), all entities are required to report expenses in their natural and functional classification. Generally, this takes the form of a matrix, because the information is required to be presented for all expenses

except investment expenses, which are netted with investment return. The nonprofit is also required to disclose how expenses benefiting more than one functional category are allocated.

- **Special events.** Special events are generally fundraisers such as golf tournaments or dinners. Generally, the donor will buy tickets. The tickets may be sold at different levels and will often have an element of contribution to them. The contribution is the amount that is greater than the fair value of the benefits to the donor. Nonprofits are required to show both the revenue and the direct donor expenses related to special events. Direct donor expenses are generally the cost of the food, rental cost of the venue, and the special items given to the donor, such as golf shoes or other items of value. Direct donor expenses must be shown separately from the revenue and included in the functional expense presentation.

- **Joint costs.** Nonprofits are held by donors to a high standard when it comes to how money is spent. Donors tend to prefer their donations be spent on programs. As noted earlier, donors will look at the entity's financial statements or informational tax return Form 990 to see how much of the entity's resources are being spent on support services (for example, management, fundraising). For managers and board members to have an accurate picture of how much events actually cost, as well as to show the percentage of the budget spent on support services in a favorable light, management should consider looking for ways to move as much of those costs as possible into programs. One way to do this is by allocating joint costs. For example, a newsletter may contain a request for donations and may serve an administrative function to notify interested parties of the nonprofit's activities. If the entity inserts information in the newsletter that is program related, the portion of the costs to produce and mail the newsletter can be allocated to programs as well. Very specific accounting rules govern joint costs to prevent abuse. The activity must be relevant to a program, it must include a call to action on the part of the recipients of the newsletter (for example, a plea to stop domestic violence by reporting instances to authorities), and the distribution must be wider than just the donor base.

Statement of Cash Flows

The statement of cash flows is the financial statement that illustrates the entity's cash inflows and outflows as well as noncash activity over the reporting period. Cash inflows and outflows can be from operations, investing activities, and financing activities. Two methods are used to present the cash flow statement. Most entities prefer the indirect method because it presents the noncash items, such as depreciation and changes in the operating-related balance sheet items. It is easier to prepare. Others use the direct method, which is a combination of the indirect method that also presents the information in terms of cash payments received and cash payments made. The investing and financing sections are the same regardless of preparation methods. The new FASB (2016b) guidance allows nonprofits using the direct method to omit the reconciliation to operating activities used in the indirect method so that the organization only has to present the cash receipts and cash payments made.

Notes to the Financial Statements

The notes to the financial statements provide additional disclosures on the financial statement elements as well as other information that is important to external users. Examples of disclosures that enhance the user's ability to make decisions related to the entity are as follows:

- description of the nonprofit, including tax status (for example, 501[c][3])
- significant accounting policies
- composition of receivables, including maturity dates
- composition of investments, including unrealized and realized gains and losses
- information on liquidity management and the availability of net assets to be used to pay operating expenses within the next 12 months (this is a new requirement)
- composition of property and equipment if not shown on the face of the statements
- composition of long-term debt, including interest rates and maturities
- concentrations of risk
- contingencies
- transactions with related parties
- litigation
- commitments (for example, rental commitments)

Audits

Many nonprofits obtain audits of their financial statements. An audit may be required annually by lenders or funding sources as a condition of obtaining a loan or grant. Some nonprofits obtain audits at the request of their boards or because it is good business practice.

In 2013, the U.S. Office of Management and Budget (OMB) replaced OMB circular A-122, which had previously replaced OMB circular A-133, with the OMB Uniform Guidance (OMB, 2017). The purpose was to streamline several OMB circulars into one comprehensive set of criteria. Under the Uniform Guidance, if a nonprofit expends more than $750,000 in federal awards, it is subject to an audit under Government Auditing Standards and OMB Uniform Guidance. The OMB Uniform Guidance audit has two components: one relates to the testing of internal control over major grant programs, and the other relates to auditing the entity's compliance with requirements of Uniform Guidance with grant agreements related to those major programs (Uniform Administrative Requirements, 2013).

Tax Returns

Tax-exempt entities are required to file an informational tax return, Form 990, with the IRS (IRS, 2020). Smaller entities can file a postcard that is significantly abbreviated. A nonprofit may be required to pay income tax on earnings that are not related to its tax-exempt purpose, commonly known as unrelated business income tax.

Budget and Control Mechanisms

Budgeting is a very important exercise for a nonprofit because it provides the nonprofit with a focal point for management and board members to plan and prioritize the activities of the organization. A well-thought-out budget also provides a basis for financial analysis and monitoring of the nonprofit's activities.

The most common method of budgeting is the incremental–decremental approach. In this method, the nonprofit examines the activities from the prior year and creates a budget based on anticipated changes. No matter which method is used, budgeting should be treated as an important part of the nonprofit's planning and administrative processes.

Once the budget is constructed, a variance analysis should be performed to measure the budget against the actual results of operations. The nonprofit

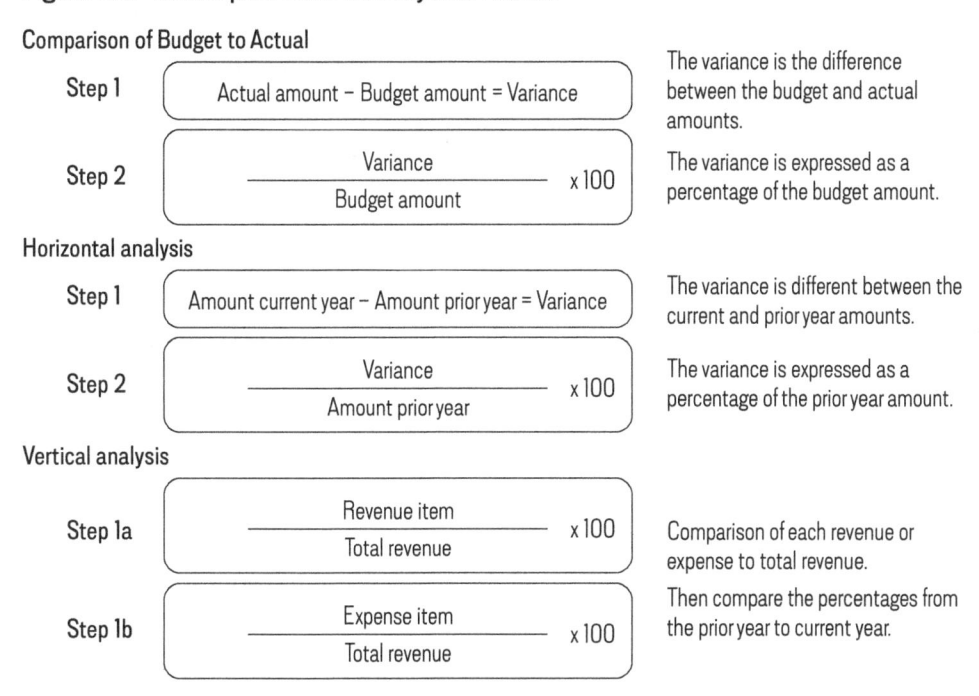

Figure 8.3 Techniques Used in Analytical Review

Comparison of Budget to Actual

Step 1: Actual amount − Budget amount = Variance
The variance is the difference between the budget and actual amounts.

Step 2: $\dfrac{\text{Variance}}{\text{Budget amount}} \times 100$
The variance is expressed as a percentage of the budget amount.

Horizontal analysis

Step 1: Amount current year − Amount prior year = Variance
The variance is different between the current and prior year amounts.

Step 2: $\dfrac{\text{Variance}}{\text{Amount prior year}} \times 100$
The variance is expressed as a percentage of the prior year amount.

Vertical analysis

Step 1a: $\dfrac{\text{Revenue item}}{\text{Total revenue}} \times 100$
Comparison of each revenue or expense to total revenue.

Step 1b: $\dfrac{\text{Expense item}}{\text{Total revenue}} \times 100$
Then compare the percentages from the prior year to current year.

---

should also consider performing a horizontal analysis, which measures the actual results of operations against the operations in the prior year. Another important form of financial analysis is vertical analysis, which attempts to factor out the growth in the entity by comparing the different sources of revenue as a percentage of total revenue and the expense line items as a percentage of revenue. These analytical techniques are illustrated in Figure 8.3.

Ratio analysis is another useful tool for analyzing operations. A *ratio* is an expression of the relationship between two numbers as a single number or a percentage. Ratios can be computed using financial information in both the numerator and the denominator. They can also be computed using both financial and nonfinancial information. They can be compared with ratios computed in the prior year or years and with published information for similar entities. Nonprofits should consider forming an expectation of what the ratios and other analytics will show, based on their knowledge of the external environment and the nonprofit's activities, rather than simply look at what has changed over the period.

Once the calculations have been completed, management should review the results with an eye toward how much they differ from expectations. For example, if the nonprofit organization hired three additional employees during the year, it is reasonable to expect that expenditures for salaries and benefits would increase. Expectations are not always easy to develop, however. For example, management may have a difficult time forecasting certain financial statement items, such as revenue from planned fundraising activities or events, because their donors are influenced by factors such as the economy; pandemics such as coronavirus; or natural disasters such as hurricanes, earthquakes, fires, or external forces that can negatively affect giving behavior. These forces tend to influence a donor's decision to give and are beyond the nonprofit's control. These and other factors, such as those listed here, should be considered when forming expectations and when determining the threshold over which the variance warrants investigation:

- personnel hired or terminated during the year
- new or terminated contracts or grant agreements
- fundraising constraints
- loan covenants
- changes in number or square footage of facilities
- changes in inflation, interest rates, or other economic factors
- changes in the level of programs and services
- changes in certain expense line items due to outside factors (for example, increase in postage or insurance rates)
- increased marketing or fundraising efforts

Nonprofits should be aware that people who embezzle through nonprofits frequently hold expense line items constant so they will not be investigated.

Internal Controls and Risk of Fraud

Those who work in nonprofits should not be misled into thinking that they are not likely to be the victims of fraud. The Association of Certified Fraud Examiners (2020) found that the most costly fraud and abuses occur in entities with fewer than 100 employees. In fact, by their very nature, nonprofit organizations are more susceptible to fraud because of the following characteristics:

- an atmosphere of trust that assumes that all employees and others who work for or with the entity are honest
- revenue sources that are difficult to estimate and control; contributions may come to the entity in the form of cash, an asset that is highly susceptible to theft

- employees who lack business experience and understanding of good internal controls
- financial constraints that keep them from being able to hire sufficient people to properly segregate duties
- use of volunteer board members who may have a personal relationship with the cause but do not have sufficient knowledge and understanding of business and financial management issues
- leaders such as an executive director or CEO who have passion for the nonprofit's mission and less respect for its business processes

All nonprofits, regardless of size, should institute as many strong internal controls as resources permit to help prevent both errors and fraud. Damage to an organization's reputation because of fraud loss is often difficult to repair.

Internal control is a process designed by the entity's executive and principal financial officers or people performing similar functions to provide reasonable assurance regarding the reliability of financial reporting. It also promotes the timely detection of unauthorized acquisition use or disposition of the entity's assets.

In 2013, the Committee of Sponsoring Organizations of the Treadway Commission published an update to an integrated framework for internal controls, which is summarized in Table 8.1. In the update, additional emphasis was placed on technology; cyberfraud; and the importance of good governance, accountability, and competence.

As presented in Table 8.1, the following five categories of internal control should be considered when designing a nonprofit's system of internal controls:

1. The control environment is the foundation for all of the other controls and provides the "tone from the top." Factors are integrity and ethical values, commitment to competence, management's consideration of the knowledge and skills necessary to accomplish an employee's responsibilities, attention and direction provided by a board of directors or audit committee, management's approach to taking business risks and emphasis on meeting financial targets, manner of assigning authority and responsibility, and human resources policies and procedures. The control environment may be the most important of all controls. Without the appropriate tone coming from top-level management and the board of directors, it is less likely that other controls will operate as designed to prevent fraud and error.

Table 8.1 Components of Internal Control

Category	Components
Control environment	• Integrity and ethical values • Commitment to competence • Management's consideration of the knowledge and skills necessary to accomplish an employee's responsibilities • Attention and direction provided by a board of directors or audit committee • Management's approach to taking business risks • Emphasis on meeting financial targets • Manner of assigning authority and responsibility • Human resources policies and procedures
Risk assessment	• Management's risk assessment process • Board-approved policies that address significant business control and risk management policies
Control activities	• Top-level reviews • Comparing budget with actual results, actual results with benchmarks or industry standards, prior year against current year • Investigating variance (also a monitoring control) • Information process controls • Segregation of duties • Controls designed to safeguard assets
Information and communication	• When appropriate, obtaining and disseminating information that is necessary to run the business • Adequate information technology
Monitoring	Management and supervisory responsibilities

2. The entity should engage in a risk assessment process. Generally, risk pertains to operations, compliance with laws and regulations, and financial reporting (including the possibility of theft of assets). The entity should perform an analysis of the likelihood that these types of issues could occur and the magnitude of the problem should they occur.

3. Control activities generally consist of an entity's having a policy as well as a procedure for implementing the policy. Examples of control activities are top-level reviews, including comparing budget with actual results, actual results with prior-period performance, or actual result with benchmarks or industry standards. The key with top-level reviews is that management investigates unusual relationships and takes corrective action. If performed by supervisory personnel reviewing the work of others, these reviews may also be monitoring

controls. Other examples are information processing controls, those designed to safeguard assets and records, and segregation of duties.

4. Information and communication relates to the identification, capture, and communication of information, both financial and nonfinancial, to parties that need it. An information system that is able to handle the number and complexity of the entity's transactions is also important.

5. Monitoring involves assessing the design and operation of controls on a timely basis and determining whether they are still relevant and effective so that corrective action can be taken when necessary. Monitoring activities can be ongoing or separate evaluations, and they include management and supervisory activities, comparisons of budget with actual results, reconciliations of account detail to the general ledger, and review of exception reports generated by the company's information system.

Segregation of Duties

As noted earlier, nonprofits are frequently under financial constraints that limit the number of administrative personnel whom they are able to keep on staff. This leads to concern with the segregation of duties. Fraud is more likely to occur when employees have duties that are incompatible and give them the opportunity to commit fraud. For example, if an employee has the ability to create a new vendor in the accounting system, approve invoices for payment, and post transactions to the general ledger, theft could occur. The employee could set up a fictitious vendor in the system, create an invoice and submit it for payment, approve the invoice, post it to the accounting system, and then wait for the check to be sent to them.

Duties can be segregated even with a limited number of people in the office. In addition, management should consider using program personnel and the executive director to help segregate duties. Figure 8.4 illustrates ways to segregate duties when there are two and three people available. Tables 8.2 and 8.3 illustrate the common fraud schemes that can be prevented by proper segregation of duties.

Figure 8.4 Segregation of Duties for Small Nonprofits

With Two People

A receptionist or administrative employee could open mail and create a deposit log for incoming checks.

Accountant and Other Financial Personnel

- Record pledges
- Mail checks
- Write checks
- Reconcile bank statement
- Record credits/debts
- Approve payroll
- Disburse petty cash
- Authorize purchase orders
- Authorize check requests
- Authorize invoices for payment

Executive Director

- Receive and open bank statements
- Sign checks
- Make deposits
- Perform interbank transfers
- Distribute pay checks
- Review petty cash
- Review bank reconciliations
- Approve vendor invoices
- Perform analytical procedures
- Sign important checks
- Make compensation adjustments
- Discuss matters with BOD and audit committee

With Three People

Accountant and Other Financial Personnel

- Approve payroll
- Process vendor invoices
- Mail checks
- Authorize invoices for payment
- Perform analytical procedures
- Dispense petty cash
- Open mail and log cash
- Receive bank statements

Accounting Staff

- Record pledges
- Write checks
- Reconcile bank statement
- Record credits/debts
- Reconcile petty cash
- Distribute payroll

Executive Director

- Make compensation adjustments
- Sign important contracts
- Discuss matters with BOD and audit committee
- Sign checks
- Complete deposit slips
- Perform interbank transfers
- Review bank reconciliations

Table 8.2 Prevention of Fraud Schemes by Segregation of Duties: Cash Disbursements

Segregation of Duties	Helps Prevent
Purchasing should be separate from requisitioning, shipping, and receiving.	Excessive purchasing
Requisitioning, purchasing, and receiving should be different from those who process invoices, accounts payable, cash receipts and disbursement, and general ledger functions.	Stealing to make personal capital improvements; fictitious or inflated invoices or altering checks
Invoice processing and accounts payable should be separate from general ledger function.	Duplicate payments
Persons who are independent of purchasing and receiving should follow up on unmatched open purchase orders, receiving reports, and invoices.	Fictitious or altered invoices

Segregation of Duties	Helps Prevent
Persons who prepare payroll should be independent of time keeping, distribution of checks, and hiring. They should not have access to other payroll data or cash.	Fictitious employees; overpayment of wages; stealing payroll checks; diverting payroll taxes; embezzling wages; keeping terminated employees on payroll or stealing checks and colluding with them.

Table 8.3 Prevention of Fraud Schemes by Segregation of Duties: Cash Receipts

Segregation of Duties	Helps Prevent
Person who opens mail and logs in cash receipts should be different from the person who functions as cashier or posts to accounts receivable. A lock box and restrictive endorsements on checks should be used.	Skimming cash
Bank reconciliations should be performed by persons independent of cash receipts (and disbursements).	Theft and alteration of checks
Periodic statements to donors or customers are mailed by a person other than the one responsible for posting to receivables.	Lapping of accounts or pledges receivable
Customer follow-up on complaints is independent of cash handling or receivables posting.	Lapping of accounts receivable
Credit memos are handled by those who handle cash or post to accounts receivables.	Cash larceny
Person who signs checks should be different from the one initiating purchases, approving purchases, shipping, receiving, cash receipts, accounts payable, and custody of cash. Check signer should be authorized by board of directors.	Kickbacks, fictitious invoices, inflating invoices
Mechanical check signers and signature plates should be under the control of management. That person should be independent from the person initiating purchases, approving purchases, shipping, receiving, cash receipts, accounts payable, and custody of cash.	Fictitious invoices, inflating invoices, stealing checks

Conclusion

Financial management of nonprofits can be complex and deserves significant attention from nonprofit managers and the board of directors. Today's economic and regulatory climate represents a particularly challenging environment for nonprofits because of the financial constraints with which nonprofit managers have to contend. Nonprofit organizations are stewards of public resources, and it is important that nonprofit managers demonstrate fiscal responsibility and accountability to their boards, donors, foundation and government grantors, and the community.

Skills Application Exercises

1. Obtain a balance sheet and operating statement from a nonprofit organization. Review them, trying to apply the definitions and concepts presented in this chapter. Classify the various accounts, identifying assets, liabilities, fund balances, revenue, and expenses.
2. Review the financial statements, assessing the financial status of the organization and identifying any concerns or issues that the statements may indicate.
3. Identify any strategies in place in the organization aimed at preventing fraud.

References

American Bar Association. (n.d.). *Nonprofits and Sarbanes-Oxley*. Retrieved from https://www.americanbar.org/groups/center-pro-bono/resources/program-management/nonprofits_sarbanes_oxley/

Association of Certified Fraud Examiners. (2020). *Report to the nations on occupational fraud and abuse.* Austin, TX: Author.

BoardSource. (2003). *The Sarbanes-Oxley Act and implications for nonprofit organizations.* Retrieved from https://trust.guidestar.org/the-sarbanes-oxley-act-and-implications-for-nonprofit-organizations

Committee of Sponsoring Organizations of the Treadway Commission. (2013). *2013 internal control–Integrated framework.* Retrieved from https://www.coso.org/Pages/default.aspx

Financial Accounting Standards Board. (2014). *Revenue recognition.* Retrieved from https://www.fasb.org/jsp/FASB/FASBContent_C/CompletedProjectPage&cid=1175805486538

Financial Accounting Standards Board. (2016a). *Leases.* Retrieved from https://www.fasb.org/leases

Financial Accounting Standards Board. (2016b). *Update 2016-14—Not-for-profit entities (topic 958): Presentation of financial statements of not-for-profit entities.* Retrieved from https://www.fasb.org/cs/ContentServer?c=Document_C&cid=1176168381847&d=&pagename=FASB%2FDocument_C%2FDocumentPage

Financial Accounting Standards Board. (2018, June). *Accounting standards update—Not-for-profit entities: Clarifying the scope and accounting guidance for contributions received and contributios made.* Retrieved from https://

www.fasb.org/cs/ContentServer?c=Document_C&cid=1176170810258&d=Touch&pagename=FASB%2FDocument_C%2FDocumentPage

Financial Accounting Standards Board. (2020, September). *Accounting standards update—Not-for-profit entities: Presentations and disclosures by not-for-profit entities for contributed/nonfinancial assets.* https://www.fasb.org/cs/ContentServer?c=Document_C&cid=1176175227486&d=&pagename=FASB%2FDocument_C%2FDocumentPage

Internal Revenue Service. (2020). *Annual electronic filing requirement for small exempt organizations—Form 990-N (e-Postcard)*. Retrieved from https://www.irs.gov/charities-non-profits/annual-electronic-filing-requirement-for-small-exempt-organizations-form-990-n-e-postcard

National Conference of Commissioners on Uniform State Laws. (2007). *Uniform Prudent Management of Institutional Funds Act*. Retrieved from https://www.uniformlaws.org/HigherLogic/System/DownloadDocumentFile.ashx?DocumentFileKey=d7b95667-ae72-0a3f-c293-cd8621ad1e44&forceDialog=0

Sarbanes–Oxley Act of 2002, P.L. 107-204, 116 Stat. 745.

Uniform administrative requirements, cost principles, and audit requirements for federal awards, 2 C.F.R. § 200. (2013).

U.S. Office of Management and Budget. (2017). *Uniform administrative requirements, cost principles, and audit requirements for federal awards*. Retrieved from https://www.govinfo.gov/app/details/CFR-2017-title2-vol1/CFR-2017-title2-vol1-part200

9

Program Evaluation in Nonprofits: Necessary Evil or Tool for Organizational Learning?

Mathieu Despard

In their seminal book on program evaluation, now in its eighth edition, Rossi, Lipsey, and Henry (2019) defined *program evaluation* as "the systematic assessment of programs designed to improve social conditions and our individual and collective well-being" (p. 1). A related practice is performance measurement, through which nonprofits use data to monitor and improve the implementation and effectiveness of programs to support performance management processes (Tatian, 2016), often as a precursor to evaluation (Lynch-Cerullo & Cooney, 2011). These practices are common among nonprofits. Among a sample of 1,125 U.S. nonprofits surveyed in 2016, 90 percent used outcome evaluation, performance measurement, or process or implementation evaluation (Innovation Network, 2016).

Although program evaluation is assumed to be completed by a third party (Lynch-Cerullo & Cooney, 2011; Tatian, 2016), only 27 percent of nonprofits have worked with an external evaluator (Innovation Network, 2016). Program evaluation, particularly outcome evaluation, is also viewed as a means of being accountable to funders—a necessary evil (Carman, 2011). Certainly, a key reason why most nonprofits use program evaluation is that they are expected by most public- and private-sector funders to demonstrate how their programs are improving the lives of the people and communities they serve (Carman, 2011; Lynch-Cerullo & Cooney, 2011; Sullivan, 2011). However, the vast majority of nonprofits identify executive staff (85 percent) and the board of directors (76 percent) as their primary audiences for evaluation (Innovation Network, 2016).

These results suggest that nonprofits are embracing program evaluation and performance measurement as tools to produce insights that can be used to better fulfill their missions and pursue their visions. Indeed, nonprofits can use program evaluation and performance measurement for a variety of reasons, including to assess

- whether a program remains aligned with community need
- the feasibility of a new program
- the degree to which a program is being implemented as intended
- whether a program is culturally relevant, anti-oppressive, or both
- factors related to participant engagement in a program

Although not an exhaustive list, these reasons illustrate that the purposes of program evaluation and performance measurement extend beyond measuring outcomes and complying with funder requirements.

Although the focus of this chapter is on nonprofit organizations that provide direct human services (for example, mental health services, youth development), program evaluation and performance measurement can also be used to assess nonprofits' progress in achieving community- or systems-level change. For example, a nonprofit that focuses on employment can use program evaluation to gauge progress in getting local employers to "ban the box" (that is, remove the checkbox on job applications concerning criminal records). Thus, program evaluation and performance measurement can be used as tools to gauge nonprofits' progress in achieving change at any level of intervention.

Performance measurement is an ongoing process of collecting and using data to improve programs, whereas program evaluation is a process of collecting and analyzing data to answer a predetermined set of questions, usually after a program has been implemented (Lynch-Cerullo & Cooney, 2011; Tatian, 2016). For brevity and because of their similarities, I use the term "program evaluation" to refer to both practices.

Despite its versatility, program evaluation is a very challenging practice for nonprofits. Staff may feel overburdened in collecting data and may lack training in evaluation methods, and the nonprofit may lack the information technology needed to effectively collect, manage, and analyze data. Compounding these capacity challenges, multiple funders may impose different reporting requirements, and it can be difficult to measure certain types of objectives.

In this chapter, I describe common challenges related to and practical steps for engaging in program evaluation among nonprofits. The strategies presented are supported with case illustrations, offer ideas for increasing evaluation rigor, and relate program evaluation to larger trends and issues such as evidence-informed practice; social innovation; and diversity, equity, and inclusion.

Program Evaluation and the Competing Values Framework

According to the competing values framework discussed in chapter 1, organizations must manage tension along two competing value dimensions: (1) an internal and external focus and (2) flexibility and control (Edwards, Faerman, & McGrath, 1986; Quinn, Faerman, Thompson, McGrath, & Bright, 2016). For many nonprofits, program evaluation is an externally oriented process—a necessary task to meet the expectations of funders and other external stakeholders (Carman, 2010). Accordingly, resource dependence theory suggests that organizations devote most of their efforts to obtaining external resources and are largely controlled by the organizations providing these resources (Pfeffer & Salancik, 1978). Indeed, 70 percent of nonprofits consider funders a primary audience for program evaluation (Innovation Network, 2016).

A resource-dependence perspective of program evaluation originated in large part with the outcome measurement initiative of the United Way of America in the mid-1990s and a similar push for results and accountability in the public sector in the early 1990s. Ushering in a new era of accountability, many local United Ways required partner agencies to measure program outcomes, not just report the number of people helped and services provided (Hendricks, Plantz, & Pritchard, 2008). Yet program evaluation can also be used to support nonprofits' internally focused improvement processes, such as

- continuous quality improvement (Giffords & Dina, 2004; Mensing, 2017)
- organizational learning (Ebrahim, 2005)
- strategic planning (Carman, 2011)
- social innovation (Berzin & Camarena, 2018; Cnaan & Vinokur-Kaplan, 2015)

For example, through organizational learning, the nonprofit uses evaluation results to inform and guide its decision making (Ebrahim, 2005) and to identify and internally disseminate best practices (Milway & Saxton, 2011). Using program evaluation in these ways may engender a culture of reflection and curiosity.

Program evaluation can also support the nonprofit's public relations, marketing, and fundraising efforts. The Web site GiveWell (https://www

.givewell.org/) purports to identify nonprofits that "save or improve lives the most per dollar," and GuideStar (https://www.guidestar.org/) includes a "programs and results" section of nonprofit profiles, anticipating donors' increased interest in the difference that nonprofits are making, not just whether nonprofits are responsible stewards of their donations.

Nonprofits' use of program evaluation also relates to the flexibility and control dimension of the competing values framework. With respect to flexibility, nonprofits can use program evaluation to test and iterate new ideas for addressing emerging needs and problems (Brown & Wyatt, 2010). Concerning control, nonprofits can use program evaluation to ensure that existing programs are implemented consistently and with fidelity or to strengthen and scale up programs (Seelos & Mair, 2013).

Program Evaluation Challenges and Strategies to Overcome Them

The capacity to use program evaluation is affected by various resources and functions of nonprofits. Topping the list of evaluation challenges among nonprofits surveyed was a lack of staff time, identified by 79 percent of nonprofits as a barrier, followed by a lack of funding (52 percent) and insufficient staff expertise (48 percent) (Innovation Network, 2016). Carman and Fredericks (2010) produced similar findings: 68 percent, 51 percent, and 50 percent of nonprofits surveyed ($N = 179$) identified lack of time, funding, and expertise, respectively, as their top challenges.

Nonprofits also need organized systems for collecting, managing, and analyzing data (Cousins, Goh, Elliott, & Bougeois, 2014), yet fewer than half of nonprofits are satisfied with their evaluation-related data systems. Carman and Fredericks (2010) noted that the information technology capacity issues that nonprofits described actually had less to do with the technology than with the lack of evaluation expertise among staff. Only 6 percent of nonprofits have dedicated evaluation staff; in most nonprofits, evaluation responsibilities fall to executive leadership and program managers (Innovation Network, 2016). Similarly, lack of staff awareness of what the organization is trying to accomplish may pose a barrier. Perez Jolles, Collins-Camargo, McBeath, Bunger, and Chuang (2017) found that fewer than half of frontline workers in nonprofit child- and family-serving agencies were aware of their organizations' performance measures.

Last, nonprofits also experience evaluation challenges related to a lack of standard outcome definitions and measures. Funders may define outcomes differently than nonprofits or each other, may hold unrealistic outcomes expectations, or may require data to be collected in a different format than that the nonprofit uses. In addition, there is wide variation across resources available to nonprofits in how outcomes are defined (Benjamin, 2013).

Certain factors are associated with overcoming evaluation challenges in nonprofits, including receiving technical assistance (Despard, 2016); executive directors and boards of directors who value evaluation; and the use of evaluation data to support other organizational functions, such as strategic planning and program development (Alaimo, 2008; Carman & Fredericks, 2010; Mitchell & Berlan, 2018). Winkler and Fyffe (2016) argued that nonprofits need to transition from a compliance culture in which evaluation data are used to meet funder requirements to a learning culture marked by curiosity, inquiry, and the use of data by all staff to guide internal decision making. To achieve this, nonprofits should

- include evaluation activities in the job descriptions of newly hired staff
- offer a combination of group training and individual technical assistance to staff to build evaluation skills as part of their professional development
- match staff with a "data mentor"
- integrate evaluation activities into regular program activities and operations
- share evaluation data and results with staff and through various communication channels (for example, newsletters, blogs, staff meetings)

Also, to help overcome resistance to evaluation among staff, Carnochan, Samples, Myers, and Austin (2014) recommended engaging staff as users of the evaluation data system to identify improvements.

The solutions to overcoming these evaluation challenges are broad. In the next section, I dive into the weeds to offer suggestions for improving program evaluation through each major step of the evaluation process.

Practical Guidance for Nonprofit Program Evaluation

In this section, I outline the major steps of the evaluation process, discuss important considerations, and offer practical recommendations for nonprofits that plan to conduct their own evaluation. For a more comprehensive and in-depth treatment of program evaluation methods, readers should consult a source such as Rossi et al. (2019) or Newcomer, Hatry, and Wholey (2015).

Step 1. Program Theory and Design—What Do We Hope to Accomplish and Why Do We Think the Program Will Work?

The first step in program evaluation is to describe the program's theory of change—a set of assumptions about the community need, opportunity, or problem the nonprofit hopes to address with the program and how the program will achieve its intended results (Rossi et al., 2019; Tatian, 2016). Theories of change are depicted graphically in logic models, which outline a program's inputs, activities, outputs, and outcomes (W. K. Kellogg Foundation, 2004). Logic models and theories of change are used by 58 percent of nonprofits (Innovation Network, 2016) and are a common part of grant proposals, yet nonprofits can use these tools to help clarify and assess not just new but existing programs.

Theories of change begin with articulating "SMART" objectives—Specific, Measurable, Action-oriented,* Realistic, and Timed (W. K. Kellogg Foundation, 2004)—that articulate the program's intended outcomes. Examples of SMART objectives are the following:

- Free clinic patients with Type II diabetes will experience a decrease in hemoglobin A1c (HbA1c) levels within 90 days of beginning a disease management program.
- Shelter residents will secure safe, affordable, and permanent housing within 90 days.

Each of these objectives is specific—the positive change for participants is clear. The free clinic could be even more specific by adding targets; for example, 80 percent of patients would experience an A1c decrease of at least 1 percentage point. However, nonprofits should specify target indicators only when they have baseline data or some other research-based reference point rather than arbitrarily choose a target.

Each objective is measurable, meaning the nonprofit can determine whether the change took place, although measurable does not only mean quantitative. Qualitative measurement methods—focus groups, interviews, and observations—are common among nonprofits (Innovation Network, 2016). Nonprofits should not exclude an outcome objective only because it may be difficult to measure quantitatively.

Each objective is action oriented and realistic because services and activities can be implemented to address these objectives, and it is reasonable to assume that a nonprofit program could influence these outcomes.

---

*The A may also stand for "attainable" or "achievable."

Conversely, nonprofits should not choose objectives that reflect longer term outcomes or community-level impacts they cannot realistically influence; for example, "Poverty in Anytown will decline by 25 percent by 2024." Too many macroeconomic, political, historic, and social factors (for example, structural racism) affect poverty and are beyond the influence of a single nonprofit.

Last, each of the objectives is timed with the point by which the outcome is expected to have occurred. Timed objectives should relate to when participants are in the program or soon after they end participation; the nonprofit should not hold itself accountable for a long-term outcome affected by factors beyond its control (unless it is participating in a longitudinal experimental study). Similarly, nonprofits should be careful not to define and hold themselves accountable for outcomes for which indicators may lag significantly. For example, a nonprofit that provides financial counseling and assesses changes in participants' credit scores might anticipate that program influences on scores may not be detectable until several months after the end of the program.

Articulating outcome objectives is challenging. Nonprofits that offer programs that are common to certain fields of practice (for example, homeless shelters, youth development) should try to identify taxonomies of outcome objectives. For example, the Outcome Indicators Project offers a set of outcome and performance indicators in 14 different program areas, such as affordable housing, adult literacy, and prisoner re-entry (Urban Institute and Center for What Works, n.d.).

Objectives related to program implementation and engagement should also be specified, especially to assess the feasibility of new programs. Examples include

- Fifty percent of free clinic patients with Type II diabetes will enroll in a disease management program.
- Shelter residents will receive a behavioral health screening within three days of admission.

These types of objectives are important because variation in implementation and engagement may relate to outcomes. For example, imagine that only 25 percent of free clinic patients with Type II diabetes enroll in the disease management program. If one measures changes in HbA1c for all patients with diabetes, the result after a six-month period may be disappointing because too few patients participated in the disease management program. Also, as a nonprofit manager at the free clinic, I would want to know why the clinic was underperforming on enrollment. Fix the enrollment issue first, then measure outcomes—that is, use performance management before conducting the evaluation.

The next step is to explain how the program's services and activities will result in the intended outcomes by revealing and testing assumptions underlying the program's theory of change, often through a series of if–then statements. The free clinic's disease management program includes four components: (1) quarterly visits with a physician who monitors and coordinates patient care, (2) receipt and use of glucose monitoring equipment, (3) self-monitored adherence to dietary guidelines, and (4) receipt and use of prescription medication. If–then statements would be as follows:

- If patients with Type II diabetes enroll in a disease management program, then they will have a better chance of reducing their HbA1c levels.
- If these patients lower their HbA1c levels, then they will be at lessened risk for complications due to diabetes, such as eye and kidney disease.

To test these assumptions, the free clinic should consider both evidence (Despard, 2016) and perspectives of diverse stakeholders (Wike et al., 2014). Indeed, research has indicated that reducing HbA1c lowers risk for complications of Type II diabetes. Ideally, one would also find evidence that disease management programs are effective in helping low-income, uninsured, and racially diverse patients living with Type II diabetes.

To find evidence, nonprofits can consult repositories of evidence-based or best practices, such as Blueprints for Healthy Youth Development (https://www.blueprintsprograms.org/) or the Evidence-based Practices Resource Center of the federal Substance Abuse and Mental Health Services Administration (https://www.samhsa.gov/ebp-resource-center). This advice comes with a few caveats. First, the availability of evidence-based practices varies considerably across nonprofit fields of practice (Despard, 2016). In behavioral health nonprofits, funding is typically tied to the use of specific evidence-based practices (Mosley, 2020). Yet in other fields such as human trafficking, there is less research about the effectiveness of interventions.

Second, even if an evidence-based model exists, it may not align with the needs, life experiences, culture, preferences, and community context of prospective participants. For example, a program from the Blueprints for Healthy Youth Development repository might not be relevant to, helpful for, or welcomed by transgender youth of color.

Third, an important part of the nonprofit's theory change may be how to advocate for community change to establish certain evidence-based practices. For example, nonprofits serving homeless people who want to implement a housing-first model—despite having evidence on their side—may have to devise a strategy for addressing "NIMBYism" ("not in my backyard"; Wellar, 2018), or resident opposition to proposed developments. Similarly, an education or youth development nonprofit may develop a theory of change for how to get local school districts to adopt evidence-based practices for improving educational outcomes of Black students (Same et al., 2018).

Evidence can come from the nonprofit itself. Using the free clinic example, what is known about patients with Type II diabetes that may indicate whether a disease management program might work? Has a disease management program been implemented before? How did it go? Institutional history is important here. One might find that, in fact, a free clinic tried to implement a similar program five years ago, with the key problems that patients enrolled but did not follow through with required self-care and that scheduling their quarterly physician visits was difficult. Thus, one may realize that additional assumptions need to be tested:

- Free clinic patients with Type II diabetes want to tackle their HbA1c, reduce their risk for medical complications, and are willing and able to participate in a disease management program.
- The free clinic is able to provide all disease management program components consistently and for free.

This is where the perspectives of diverse stakeholders come in. The free clinic ought to engage its medical director, volunteer health care workers, frontline staff, and patients themselves in offering feedback about program feasibility. Engaging patients is a great opportunity for nonprofits to apply principles of human-centered design (HCD), especially when designing a new and innovative program (Nandan, Jaskyte, & Mandayam, 2020). The basic idea with HCD—which is used widely in for-profit product development—is to learn from prospective users of a new service whether and how they might use the service. Does it meet their needs? Is the experience a pleasant one? Do they experience any barriers? Are there better ways to meet the underlying need?

Testing assumptions is an important opportunity to promote diversity, equity, and inclusion by engaging different stakeholders to ensure there are no implicit biases embedded in the theory of change. For example, a nonprofit that helps low-income families may want to offer a financial education program on the basis of the assumption that these families do not understand why it is important to save or how to save. Yet if this nonprofit talked to low-income families and to other nonprofits serving this population, they might learn that low and volatile wages, unaffordable housing, expensive child care, and other structural barriers and forms of oppression are reasons why these families do not save. It is especially important to test program assumptions to reveal blind spots, given that many nonprofits have a misalignment between the racial, ethnic, and socioeconomic makeup of boards of directors and executive staff and the individuals and communities these nonprofits serve.

The process of articulating a theory of change and testing assumptions also helps nonprofits assess the nature and complexity of the community or social problem they hope to address. Chronic homelessness is a complex and wicked problem wherein risk factors operate at all levels; for example, serious mental illness, lack of affordable housing units, and lack of mental health service access and coordination. Does the theory of change for a housing-first model hold if there is a question about the availability of housing subsidies?

Logic models and theories of change have important limitations to note. First, they do not work well with complex problems and nonlinear change processes. A better design method might be a causal loop diagram that depicts complex and dynamic relationships, particularly for systems- or community-level phenomena. Second, logic models and theories of change may be poor predictors of behavior. Third, they assume that the program will be implemented as intended. Fourth, by planning so much in advance, they may stifle creativity and innovation. As such, they are not recommended for new programs. Instead, nonprofits should consider design methods such as lean experimentation (Murray & Ma, 2015) in conjunction with formative evaluation and similar approaches, which are described next.

Step 2. Specify Research Questions—What Do We Hope to Learn about the Program?

A natural starting point is to specify questions based on the program's SMART objectives, yet it is important to expand on these objectives to generate insights that are important to the nonprofit and that support its performance measurement and organizational learning processes. This relates to the competing values framework, where the purposes of program evaluation are different in relation to internal and external audiences. Using the SMART objectives described earlier as examples, a funder may principally be interested in the free clinic's overall progress in achieving outcomes such as lowering HbA1c levels among patients with Type II diabetes. Yet the free clinic may be exploring additional, internally focused questions, such as the following:

- What proportion of patients with Type II diabetes attend physician visits on a quarterly basis?
- Are there any differences among patients who do and do not make quarterly visits?
- What are reasons why some patients do not make quarterly visits?
- What proportion of patients receive most care from the same provider?

Answering these questions will generate useful insights to help guide the free clinic's volunteer management, patient outreach and enrollment, and clinical care efforts.

Research questions may also align with or relate to organizational strategic initiatives. For example, a nonprofit trying to improve its diversity, equity, and inclusion efforts may want to know whether there are any racial or ethnic disparities concerning program enrollment, engagement, and outcomes.

Good research questions for program evaluation are

- answerable—an evaluation method can be used to answer the question
- meaningful—answering the question will reveal something important about the program
- relevant—the question is clearly related to the program
- actionable—the nonprofit can use the answer to help improve the program

Step 3. Choose the Type of Evaluation—Which Types Will Best Answer the Research Questions?

Nonprofits can choose one or more types of evaluation to answer their research questions:

1. Formative evaluation: Assessing program feasibility, implementation, and effectiveness as the program is being implemented to provide quick feedback and make modifications or determine whether the program should proceed (developmental evaluation is a very similar method)
2. Process evaluation: Assessing the degree to which a program was implemented as designed and intended after the program has concluded
3. Outcome evaluation: Assessing the degree to which the program achieved its outcome objectives among program participants

4. Impact evaluation: Assessing the causal effect of a program on outcomes among program participants or on a community- or population-level outcome

Process, outcome, and impact evaluations are all examples of summative evaluation—an evaluation that assesses whether program goals were met after the conclusion of the program. In particular, outcome evaluation is probably most familiar to nonprofits in meeting funder requirements. Yet formative evaluation is useful for identifying challenges while the program is still being implemented, which is particularly important for new programs. For example, Collier and Lawless (2016) described a formative evaluation of Circles® USA, which aims to move families out of poverty using a 16-week training program that includes topics such as financial stability and using community resources and supportive relationships with middle- and upper-income volunteer allies. Interviews with participants, allies, and staff were conducted using a critical reflexivity approach to examine training materials and participant–ally relationships as influenced by differences concerning race, income, and education. Findings included instances of class bias and privilege among allies, such as complaints about a lack of effort among low-income participants, revealing tensions concerning issues of diversity and equity related to program implementation and outcomes (Alvesson, Hardy, & Harley, 2008).

Formative evaluation is useful for creating an innovation feedback loop to support the testing of new ideas for addressing community needs (Brown & Wyatt, 2010), and it supports performance management, using data to improve program performance (Tatian, 2016). Before nonprofits commit to an outcome evaluation of a program, they should feel certain that the program is performing as intended—that participants are interested in and engaged with the program and that services and activities are being implemented as intended.

Developmental evaluation is a method similar to formative evaluation, albeit with an emphasis on flexibility and adaptation to support continuous improvement in dynamic environments (Patton, 2010). Similarly, Murray and Ma (2015) described lean experimentation, an iterative process very similar to formative evaluation in which program ideas are rapidly tested, modified, and retested to establish proof of concept—that prospective participants are interested in and willing to use the program. Seelos and Mair (2013) described a similar process in which nonprofits design, test, and refine new ideas before formalizing and expanding programs.

Process evaluation is very similar to formative evaluation, but it is conducted after the program has concluded and can answer important questions concerning engagement, including monitoring implementation of evidence-based practices. For example, Assertive Community Treatment (ACT) is an evidence-based practice for helping people living with serious mental illness and a history of psychiatric hospitalization to remain living in the community. Nonprofit mental health agencies that implement ACT must follow standards of care for interdisciplinary teams, staffing ratios, 24/7 crisis response, and more (for example, see Center for Evidence-Based Practices, n.d.).

Process evaluation is also useful for assessing engagement among participants, which may help explain program outcomes. For example, a financial counseling program may find that women and participants with income between $25,000 and $50,000 participated in more sessions than men and participants with income below $25,000. Follow-up interviews with staff might have revealed that women were more engaged because they are more likely to be the financial decision makers in their households, whereas individuals with very low incomes were struggling just to meet basic needs. These insights could help guide recruitment and marketing efforts to enroll participants who will most benefit from the program.

Outcome evaluation examines whether program participants experienced changes in knowledge, skills, behaviors, or circumstances. This is usually done descriptively, without trying to make a definitive claim that the program caused the outcomes to occur. In contrast, impact evaluation estimates a counterfactual to make a causal inference about the program, which is usually done by randomly assigning a group of people to receive the program or not. Assuming that after random assignment the two groups had very similar characteristics (for example, age, gender identity, level of need, desire to receive the program), any differences in outcomes can be attributed to the program and not to some other factor.

Impact evaluation goes a step further than outcome evaluation by implementing a research design that allows the nonprofit to make a causal inference—a claim that the program and not some other factor resulted in the observed outcomes. The classic example is a randomized evaluation in which individuals are randomly assigned to a group that receives an intervention or to a control group that does not receive the intervention. Any differences between the two groups can be attributed to the intervention. This is usually infeasible for nonprofits because they do not want to deny help to a group of individuals in need or because it would be hard to keep random assignment intact. However, I next describe certain quasi-experimental designs nonprofits can use to increase the rigor of outcome evaluations—not quite to the level of impact evaluations, but close—without denying help to anyone.

The choice of evaluation type depends on what the nonprofit wants to learn. For new programs, nonprofits should stick to formative evaluation and similar innovation-testing methods such as lean experimentation. Developmental evaluation should be considered in highly dynamic and complex situations such as systems- or community-change efforts. For example, consider how nonprofits across the country may be interested in engaging with local law enforcement agencies to reimagine ways to respond to police calls that involve unarmed citizens and minor offenses to promote de-escalation tactics in the wake of the killing of George Floyd in Minneapolis, Minnesota, in May 2020. Amid calls to defund the police and in engaging stakeholder groups with varying interests such as police unions, neighborhood organizations, and advocacy groups, such change efforts could evolve in unpredictable ways for which developmental evaluation is well suited.

Process evaluation is a good idea if proof of concept has been established, yet the nonprofit needs to further understand how the program works and how participants respond to and interact with services and activities. For example, Extraordinary Ventures is a nonprofit in Chapel Hill, North Carolina, that operates various social enterprises such as dog walking and laundry services to provide neurodiverse adults with meaningful job opportunities. Before examining participant outcomes, Extraordinary Ventures could use process evaluation to examine a host of issues related to the operation of each enterprise in the early stages of serving customers—whether participants enjoyed their work experience, had proper training and supervision, were meaningfully engaged in work tasks, and so forth.

Last, it is not just the type of evaluation nonprofits should consider but how different stakeholders will participate. The typical approach in nonprofits is for program participants to just complete surveys or interviews—to be sources for data collection. Yet through participatory evaluation, program participants and others whose lives are affected by the program participate in all steps of the evaluation process, including crafting research questions, choosing the evaluation type and design, and interpreting results. As such, nonprofit staff and evaluation consultants ensure that power is shared so key stakeholders are meaningfully engaged (Burke, 1998). For example, Quintanilla and Packard (2002) described a participatory evaluation of an inner-city science enrichment program through which students and their parents engaged in all steps in the evaluation alongside staff, board members, and consultants. A key advantage for nonprofits in using a participatory process with their evaluations is that the odds of generating important insights to improve the program are increased by engaging end users.

Outcome Evaluation Design: Strengthening Program Success Claims

In the age of accountability for outcomes, a key challenge for nonprofits is to use a feasible evaluation design that helps them strengthen claims that the program was responsible for observed outcomes. Common designs to assess outcomes are single-group posttest only and pretest–posttest (Hoefer, 2000), as reflected in the following display, where X is the program, O is the outcome, and the subscripts 1 and 2 are the time points, before and after the program:

Posttest only: —   × O_2
Pretest–posttest: O_1 × O_2

For example, with a single-group posttest-only design, a nonprofit that provides after-school tutoring and mentoring for middle-school students who are struggling academically might assess students' course grades at the end of a school year and determine an outcome such as "73 percent of students' grades were a C or higher." With a single-group pretest–posttest design, the nonprofit might find that "82 percent of students showed grade improvements in at least half of their courses" when comparing first- and fourth-quarter grades. With both of these designs, one cannot know whether these outcomes might have happened on their own, without tutoring. Yet nonprofits can seldom implement experimental designs in which some participants receive the program and others do not to make causal inferences. Some alternatives to consider follow:

- Comparison group study: The nonprofit could gather data on the grades of a similar, if not matched (that is, on age, grade level, first-quarter course grades), group of students who did not participate in the tutoring program. After verifying that the two groups are similar, the school could provide just the aggregated data for the comparison group to protect students' identities. However, there may be selection bias: The group of students who received tutoring may differ from the comparison group in important and hard-to-measure ways, such as motivation to succeed academically and willingness to work with a tutor.
- Waitlist control group: Many nonprofits are unable to serve all who seek services and have to put people on waitlists. This is a good opportunity for a control group to compare outcomes between people who did and did not participate in the program. However, to use this type

of design, the nonprofit needs to conduct posttest-only or pretest–posttest measures for both groups. This could be challenging if it is hard to remain in touch with and engage individuals on the waitlist to collect data. Yet this design has the distinct advantage of reducing, if not eliminating, selection bias. Both groups of individuals—participants and those on the waitlist—selected into getting help from the program, meaning both groups were motivated to get help.

- Interrupted time series: The idea with an interrupted time series is to use multiple measures of a behavior or condition over time; changes in the measure that occur after the introduction of the program can be considered to be associated with the program. This requires having multiple measures before the program. For example, a nonprofit that provides financial counseling services could use participants' credit histories (for example, credit scores, number of delinquent accounts) to assess change after receiving services. In Figure 9.1, the x-axis represents different time intervals, the y-axis represents the credit score, the black line indicates when the program was offered to participants, and the gray line illustrates the change in credit scores over time.

- Treatment-as-usual control group: Using this method, nonprofits can experimentally test a program enhancement, service addition, or change without denying anyone help. For example, a nonprofit mental health agency that operates a supported employment program for individuals living with serious mental illness could test an online social skills training module intended to improve participant work experiences and outcomes. One group of participants would be treatment as usual, meaning they would experience no changes. The other group would receive the online training. Positive differences in outcomes would suggest that the program enhancement produced a marginal benefit for participants. This design is good for nonprofits that want to test new ideas for strengthening their programs and outcomes.

- Dosage analysis: The idea with dosage analysis is that the nonprofit compares outcomes for participants who received different doses of a program over the same time period, such as the number of counseling or group education sessions. For example, my colleagues and I studied credit score outcomes among lower-income workers who received financial counseling from Neighborhood Trust, a national nonprofit social enterprise (Despard, Zeng, Fox-Dichter, Frank-Miller, & Grinstein-Weiss, 2021). We found that workers who received three or more counseling sessions had better credit score outcomes than workers who received just one or two sessions. The key limitation of this approach is that there may be both observed (for example, age, gender identity) and unobserved (for example, motivation, persistence) differences among groups of participants who received different doses of the program.

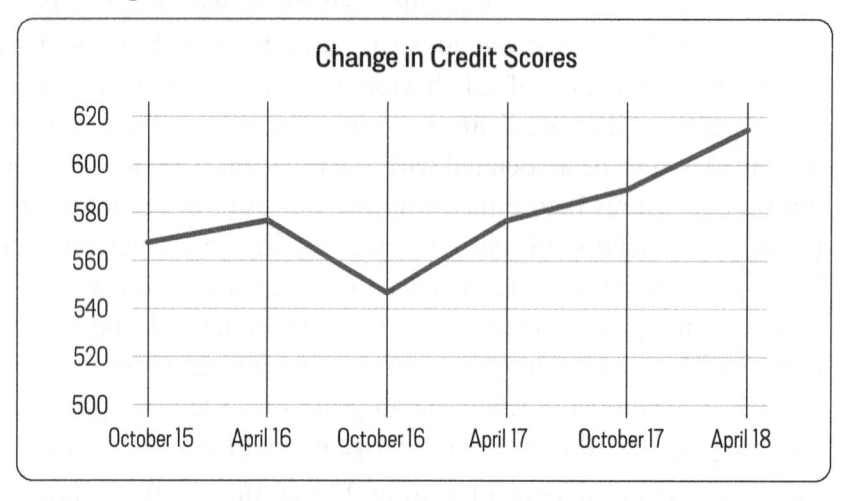

Figure 9.1 Change in Credit Scores

```
Change in Credit Scores
620
600
580
560
540
520
500
    October 15  April 16  October 16  April 17  October 17  April 18
```

With outcome evaluation, an important decision is how to identify the group of individuals whose outcomes will be measured because they were enrolled in or otherwise influenced by a program. For example, for a nonprofit that offers a drop-in center program for lesbian, gay, bisexual, transgender, and queer/questioning youths, 120 youths came to the center at least once, yet 30 of the youths did not return, and 30 returned only once over a 12-month period. One approach would be to define all 120 youths as having participated in the program and measure outcomes from a survey administered to youths at the end of the period. Another approach would be to define a program participant who came to the center on at least four occasions over a period of at least six months as having received the minimum level of program exposure and measure the outcomes of only those participants. Yet another approach would be to use a dosage analysis as outlined earlier, comparing high- and low-dose youths. The important consideration for nonprofits is to determine the intensity and duration of program engagement through which change is to occur, which could be specified with the theory of change. With the preceding example, the nonprofit would also want to conduct a process evaluation to better understand levels of engagement, interviewing youths who came only once to find out why they did not return in order to help inform outreach and marketing efforts.

Step 4. Measurement and Analysis—How Will Objectives Be Measured and Data Be Analyzed?

This step in the evaluation process is especially challenging for nonprofits for three key reasons. First, many nonprofits lack staff with formal training in measurement and statistics. Second, collecting data takes time and may feel burdensome to already busy staff. Third, nonprofits may lack the information technology needed to store, query and retrieve, and analyze data, a challenge made greater for nonprofits with multiple programs with different data needs.

Fortunately, nonprofits may already have some of the data needed to measure objectives for formative and process evaluation, including client intake, assessment, treatment plan, and participation data (for example, progress notes) and meeting minutes. In addition, managers will need to keep detailed notes about program implementation, particularly concerning barriers and challenges, and consider conducting semistructured interviews (UCLA Center for Health Policy Research, n.d.) with program participants and staff.

Assessing outcome objectives is very challenging for most nonprofits. Here are recommendations and considerations to make the process more manageable:

1. Use existing data: Nonprofits should start by considering whether the data they are already collecting about program participants may be used as outcome measures. Regarding the free clinic example presented earlier, I realized that, to assess health outcomes of patients with Type II diabetes, we had all the information we needed in their medical charts. We took a random sample of patients and recorded key indicators (for example, blood pressure, HbA1c levels) at multiple time points to assess the outcomes of the disease management program.

2. Use existing measurement tools and outcome frameworks: Nonprofits should consult resources such as the Urban Institute's Outcomes Indicators Project or Guidestar's Common Results Catalog for a list of outcome indicators for different types of programs and Candid's IssueLab (https://www.issuelab.org/) to search for evaluations across many fields of practice. Experts have developed surveys and scales to measure many types of knowledge, behavior, attitudes, and skills, and these instruments are listed in databases such as the Measurement Instrument Database for the Social Sciences (https://www.midss.org/). For nonprofit managers with formal research training,

the Inter-university Consortium for Political and Social Research (https://www.icpsr.umich.edu/web/pages/) has a searchable database to locate study variables that can be traced back to a measurement instrument. Also, nonprofits may consider using variables from different government surveys such as the Youth Risk Behavior Survey (Centers for Disease Control and Prevention, 2020). Many of these measurement tools have been tested for reliability and validity, although it is important to carefully follow instructions for administration and scoring. Outcome frameworks and measurement tools are especially important for nonprofits whose programming is challenging to evaluate. For example, most museums offer specialized out-of-school programs, outcomes for which are poorly documented. Luke, Stein, Kessler, and Dierking (2007) suggested that museums map their activities to the "six Cs" framework of positive youth development (PYD; Lerner et al., 2005) as a way to link their program to an existing outcome framework.

3. Extrapolate from existing research evidence: Sometimes it is only possible for a nonprofit to measure its outputs because measuring outcomes is infeasible. For example, an after-school youth arts program could measure its outputs in terms of the degree to which program activities reflect and achieve various aspects of a PYD framework. These outputs—measures of program quality—could then be linked to research on outcomes of PYD programs such as academic success and prosocial behavior (Catalano, Berglund, Ryan, Lonczak, & Hawkins, 2004).

4. Use survey design techniques: Many nonprofits will end up using client surveys for at least some outcomes and should follow guidelines for writing questions that will generate valid responses (Harvard University Program on Survey Research, 2007). For example, nonprofits should use nontechnical language that is free of jargon, avoid leading and double-barreled questions, and use standardized response scales.

5. Leverage free information technology: To help collect, store, and manage evaluation data, nonprofits can use free online survey tools such as SurveyMonkey (including text message surveys) and database platforms such as SalesForce, which offers the Nonprofit Success Pack. This platform is a free and open-source client relationship management system, which also allows nonprofits to track donors and volunteers.

6. Integrate measurement with service delivery: Whenever possible, nonprofits should make data collection a part of the service delivery process. For example, in a Head Start program, I worked with family support case managers to code information about family self-sufficiency outcomes from case plans and progress notes that was then aggregated at the program level.
7. Categorize case-specific data: A key challenge for nonprofits is that outcomes for certain services such as counseling are very case specific (Carnochan et al., 2014). For example, a client may recognize that a source of her anxiety is related to messages she received from her parents about being the best in whatever she did. This outcome might belong to a category called "developed clinical insight."

Analyzing data collected from evaluation activities need not be a daunting task. For quantitative data (for example, survey data), nonprofits can use descriptive (for example, frequencies, means) and inferential statistical functions (for example, t tests, chi-square tests) in programs such as Microsoft Excel or Google Sheets to analyze data concerning participant characteristics and program engagement and outcomes. Inferential statistics determine whether a difference is noteworthy or just due to chance. For example, the free clinic may find that patients with Type II diabetes are 70 percent female and 30 percent male, yet participation in the disease management program among these patients is 82 percent female and 18 percent male, a difference that is statistically significant at the $p < .05$ level, meaning that the chance that this finding is a fluke is less than 5 percent. The Web site https://www.statisticshowto.com/ is a great resource for program managers to learn basic descriptive and inferential statistics, including statistical procedures in Microsoft Excel.

In analyzing quantitative evaluation data, it is critical that nonprofits use all measures of central tendency—mean, median, and mode—and standard deviations to understand the distribution of the data. For example, in working with Neighborhood Trust to assess their financial counseling program (Despard et al., 2021), we found that the average change in credit scores over a 12-month period was an increase of 5 points. However, the standard deviation was a whopping 55 points, and score changes ranged from a 220-point decrease to a 264-point increase, meaning that there was a lot of variation in participants' success in improving their credit scores.

Disaggregating data and examining subgroup differences is another important aspect of data analysis. With the financial counseling example, we discovered that participants who had the lowest pretest credit scores experienced the greatest score increases and that participants who participated in three or more sessions experienced larger score increases. With the free clinic examples, we might learn that program participants had no changes in HbA1c level. From this main finding, we might conclude that the program made no difference. However, we might find that patients who received at least three of four program components experienced decreases compared with patients who received two or fewer.

A general rule of thumb is to look beyond the main findings for a program and look for variation in the data to understand whether the program is more or less effective for participants with different characteristics, at different dosage levels, or both. It is not just a question of "was the program effective?" but of "for whom and under what circumstances was the program more or less effective?"

For qualitative data—such as findings from interviews and focus groups—a structured analytical process is critical. Although analyzing qualitative data can be very time consuming, Watkins (2017) described the rigorous and accelerated data reduction technique, which can be used with common word processing and spreadsheet software to produce tables of data representing key themes. A similar technique is mind mapping, a type of rapid analysis in which ideas related to a central theme are visually organized and fed back to participants immediately after a focus group to correct any misinterpretations and offer modifications and additions (Burgess-Allen & Owen-Smith, 2010). The most important rule of thumb for qualitative data analysis is to make sure at least two people review and identify themes from the data and compare and reconcile findings.

Step 5. Sense-Making and Learning—What Do the Findings Tell Us about Our Program and What Are We Learning?

At this point in the chapter, I hope readers understand the different ways in which nonprofits can use evaluation results to reveal insights to help improve programs and support organizational learning, not just to submit results to a funder to assess whether a program worked. To achieve this goal, nonprofits should consider the following guidelines for interpreting and using evaluation findings:

- Engage diverse stakeholders: Use evaluation results as an opportunity to engage the board of directors, program participants, partner organizations, frontline staff, and funders in a process to make sense of the findings. This may result in some conflicting perspectives, which is fine.

The report can say something like "However, program participants viewed this result a little differently. They thought that. . . ." Engaging frontline staff is especially important. They are seldom asked for their opinion, yet they can help generate important insights based on their deep knowledge of the program and its participants. Celebrating encouraging results can boost morale and promote a deeper sense of meaning in work.

- Be circumspect: Be careful not to use findings from a descriptive evaluation design to make bold claims that the program caused certain outcomes.
- Put findings in context: Nonprofits should avoid thinking about quantitative results as though they are on an academic grading scale. If only 30 percent of participants achieved a very difficult outcome, this may be more meaningful than an easy outcome achieved by 90 percent of participants. If possible, relate current to past findings while noting any major differences in program design, implementation, and participant characteristics. Findings should also be understood in relation to important events that may have affected program implementation and participant responses, such as the coronavirus disease 2019 pandemic.
- Translate into action: Consider how findings can be used to make program improvements, yet be careful not to overreach. Your nonprofit may need to collect more data to determine whether an important program change is warranted. Engaging frontline staff to consider the feasibility of program changes is important.

Conclusion

Program evaluation is a common practice among nonprofits to meet external stakeholder expectations and to generate insights used internally to improve performance. Different types of evaluation can be used depending on the life stage of the program. A good starting point for nonprofits is to establish what they want to learn from an evaluation and to anticipate how they will use findings to improve their program. Although most nonprofits are unable or unwilling to run randomized experiments, there are ways to strengthen efforts to assess outcomes. Nonprofits can also use external resources to define and measure outcomes and common software programs to store, manage, and analyze data. Engaging diverse stakeholders in reviewing and making sense of evaluation data is an important step in the process that should not be skipped, particularly to promote participant and frontline staff empowerment.

Skills Application Exercises

Identify a program of a nonprofit organization that provides direct services. For this program, do the following:

1. Write one SMART outcome objective and determine whether it is a short-, intermediate-, or long-term outcome.
2. Identify an indicator for this outcome and how this indicator is or could be measured.
3. Identify one way in which outcome results could be analyzed to help understand variation based on participant characteristics or engagement.
4. Identify one or two key assumptions regarding the program's theory of change regarding this outcome; that is, how program services or activities will produce this outcome.
5. On a scale from one to five, with one being the lowest and five the highest, how well reasoned is this assumption?
6. How might this assumption be supported with evidence?
7. Describe a program implementation challenge that could be better understood by using process evaluation.
8. Describe an innovative program this nonprofit could consider to address community challenges in a new and creative way.
9. How could the nonprofit use lean experimentation (Murray & Ma, 2015), formative evaluation, or developmental evaluation (Patton, 2010) to help test ideas related to this innovation?
10. Identify an evaluation design strategy this nonprofit could use (for example, waitlist control group) to strengthen efforts to assess outcomes.
11. Describe two to three different ways frontline staff and program participants could be engaged in designing an evaluation, interpreting and applying results, or both.
12. Identify one program in the organization and explain why a process evaluation would be needed before an outcome evaluation.

References

Alaimo, S. P. (2008). Nonprofits and evaluation: Managing expectations from the leader's perspective. *New Directions for Evaluation, 2008*(119), 73–92.

Alvesson, M., Hardy, C., & Harley, B. (2008). Reflecting on reflexivity: Reflexive textual practices in organization and management theory. *Journal of Management Studies, 45*, 480–501.

Benjamin, L. M. (2013). The potential of outcome measurement for strengthening nonprofits' accountability to beneficiaries. *Nonprofit and Voluntary Sector Quarterly, 42*, 1224–1244.

Berzin, S. C., & Camarena, H. (2018). *Innovation from within: Redefining how nonprofits solve problems.* New York: Oxford University Press.

Brown, T., & Wyatt, J. (2010). Design thinking for social innovation. *Stanford Social Innovation Review, Winter*, 31–35. Retrieved from https://ssir.org/articles/entry/design_thinking_for_social_innovation

Burgess-Allen, J., & Owen-Smith, V. (2010). Using mind mapping techniques for rapid qualitative data analysis in public participation processes. *Health Expectations, 13*, 406–415.

Burke, B. (1998). Evaluating for a change: Reflections on participatory methodology. *New Directions for Evaluation, 1998*(80), 43–56.

Carman, J. G. (2010). The accountability movement: What is wrong with this theory of change? *Nonprofit and Voluntary Sector Quarterly, 39*, 256–274.

Carman, J. G. (2011). Understanding evaluation in nonprofit organizations. *Public Performance & Management Review, 34*, 350–377.

Carman, J. G., & Fredericks, K. A. (2010). Evaluation capacity and nonprofit organizations: Is the glass half-empty or half-full? *American Journal of Evaluation, 31*, 84–104.

Carnochan, S., Samples, M., Myers, M., & Austin, M. J. (2014). Performance measurement challenges in nonprofit human service organizations. *Nonprofit and Voluntary Sector Quarterly, 43*, 1014–1032.

Catalano, R. F., Berglund, M. L., Ryan, J. A., Lonczak, H. S., & Hawkins, J. D. (2004). Positive youth development in the United States: Research findings on evaluations of positive youth development programs. *Annals of the American Academy of Political and Social Science, 591*, 98–124.

Center for Evidence-Based Practices. (n.d.). *Assertive community treatment: The evidence-based practice.* Retrieved on June 26, 2020 from https://www.centerforebp.case.edu/client-files/pdf/actgettingstartedguide.pdf

Centers for Disease Control and Prevention. (2020). *Youth Risk Behavior Surveillance System (YRBSS).* Retrieved from https://www.cdc.gov/healthyyouth/data/yrbs/index.htm

Cnaan, R. A., & Vinokur-Kaplan, D. (Eds.) (2015). Social innovation: Definitions, clarifications, and a new model. *Cases in innovative nonprofits: Organizations that make a difference* (pp. 1–16). Los Angeles: SAGE.

Collier, M. J., & Lawless, B. (2016). Critically reflexive dialogue and praxis: Academic/practitioner reflections throughout a formative evaluation of Circles® USA. *Journal of Applied Communication Research, 44*, 156–173.

Cousins, J. B., Goh, S. C., Elliott, C. J., & Bourgeois, I. (2014). Framing the capacity to do and use evaluation. *New Directions for Evaluation, 2014*(141), 7–23.

Despard, M. R. (2016). Strengthening evaluation in nonprofit human service organizations: Results of a capacity-building experiment. *Human Service Organizations: Management, Leadership & Governance, 40*, 352–368.

Despard, M. R., Zeng, Y., Fox-Dichter, S., Frank-Miller, E., & Grinstein-Weiss, M. (2021). Can workplace financial counseling help lower-income workers improve credit outcomes? *Journal of Financial Counseling and Planning.* Advance online publication. doi:10.1891/JFCP-19-00081

Ebrahim, A. (2005). Accountability myopia: Losing sight of organizational learning. *Nonprofit and Voluntary Sector Quarterly, 34*, 56–87.

Edwards, R. L., Faerman, S. R., & McGrath, M. R. (1986). The competing values approach to organizational effectiveness: A tool for agency administrators. *Administration in Social Work, 10*(4), 1–14.

Giffords, E. D., & Dina, R. P. (2004). Strategic planning in nonprofit organizations: Continuous quality performance improvement—A case study. *International Journal of Organization Theory and Behavior, 7*(1), 66–80.

Harvard University Program on Survey Research. (2007). *Tip sheet on question wording.* Retrieved from https://psr.iq.harvard.edu/files/psr/files/PSRQuestionnaireTipSheet_0.pdf

Hendricks, M., Plantz, M. C., & Pritchard, K. J. (2008). Measuring outcomes of United Way–funded programs: Expectations and reality. *New Directions for Evaluation, 2008*(119), 13–35.

Hoefer, R. (2000). Accountability in action? Program evaluation in nonprofit human service agencies. *Nonprofit Management and Leadership, 11*, 167–177.

Innovation Network. (2016). *State of evaluation 2016: Evaluation practice and capacity in the nonprofit sector.* Retrieved from https://stateofevaluation.org/media/2016-State_of_Evaluation.pdf

Lerner, R. M., Lerner, J. V., Almerigi, J. B., Theokas, C., Phelps, E., Gestsdottir, S., & Smith, L. M. (2005). Positive youth development, participation in community youth development programs, and community contributions of fifth-grade adolescents: Findings from the first wave of the 4-H study of positive youth development. *Journal of Early Adolescence, 25*, 17–71.

Luke, J. J., Stein, J., Kessler, C., & Dierking, L. D. (2007). Making a difference in the lives of youth: Mapping success with the "Six Cs." *Curator: The Museum Journal, 50*, 417–434.

Lynch-Cerullo, K., & Cooney, K. (2011). Moving from outputs to outcomes: A review of the evolution of performance measurement in the human service nonprofit sector. *Administration in Social Work, 35*, 364–388.

Mensing, J. F. (2017). The challenges of defining and measuring outcomes in nonprofit human service organizations. *Human Service Organizations: Management, Leadership, & Governance, 41*, 207–212.

Milway, K. S., & Saxton, A. (2011). The challenge of organizational learning. *Stanford Social Innovation Review, 9*(3), 44–49.

Mitchell, G. E., & Berlan, D. (2018). Evaluation in nonprofit organizations: An empirical analysis. *Public Performance & Management Review, 41*, 415–437.

Mosley, J. E. (2020). Social service nonprofits: Navigating conflicting demands. In W. W. Powell & P. Bromley (Eds.), *The nonprofit sector: A research handbook* (3rd ed.; pp. 251–270). Palo Alto, CA: Stanford University Press.

Murray, P., & Ma, S. (2015). The promise of lean experimentation. *Stanford Social Innovation Review, Summer,* 34–39. Retrieved from https://ssir.org/articles/entry/the_promise_of_lean_experimentation#

Nandan, M., Jaskyte, K., & Mandayam, G. (2020). Human centered design as a new approach to creative problem solving: Its usefulness and applicability for social work practice. *Human Service Organizations: Management, Leadership & Governance, 44*, 310–316.

Newcomer, K. E., Hatry, H. P., & Wholey, J. S. (2015). *Handbook of practical program evaluation* (4th ed.). New York: Wiley.

Patton, M. Q. (2010). *Developmental evaluation: Applying complexity concepts to enhance innovation and use.* New York: Guilford Press.

Perez Jolles, M., Collins-Camargo, C., McBeath, B., Bunger, A. C., & Chuang, E. (2017). Managerial strategies to influence frontline worker understanding of performance measures in nonprofit child welfare agencies. *Nonprofit and Voluntary Sector Quarterly, 46*, 1166–1188.

Pfeffer, J., & Salancik, G. R. (1978). *The external control of organizations: A resource dependence perspective.* New York: Harper & Row.

Quinn, R. E., Faerman, S. R., Thompson, M. P., McGrath, M. R., & Bright, D. S. (2016). *Becoming a master manager—A competing values approach.* New York: Wiley.

Quintanilla, G., & Packard, T. (2002). A participatory evaluation of an inner-city science enrichment program. *Evaluation and Program Planning, 25*, 15–22.

Rossi, P. H., Lipsey, M. W., & Henry, G. T. (2019). *Evaluation: A systematic approach* (8th ed.). Los Angeles: SAGE.

Same, M. R., Guarino, N. I., Pardo, M., Benson, D., Fagan, K., & Lindsay, J. (2018). *Evidence-supported interventions associated with black students' educational outcomes: Findings from a systematic review of research.* Chicago: American Institutes for Research. Retrieved from https://files.eric.ed.gov/fulltext/ED581117.pdf

Seelos, C., & Mair, J. (2013). Innovate and scale: A tough balancing act. *Stanford Social Innovation Review, Summer*, 12–14.

Sullivan, C. M. (2011). Evaluating domestic violence support service programs: Waste of time, necessary evil, or opportunity for growth? *Aggression and Violent Behavior, 16*, 354–360.

Tatian, P. A. (2016). *Performance measurement to evaluation.* Washington, DC: Urban Institute.

UCLA Center for Health Policy Research. (n.d.). *Section 4: Key informant interviews.* Los Angeles: Author. Retrieved from https://healthpolicy.ucla.edu/programs/health-data/trainings/Documents/tw_cba23.pdf

Urban Institute and Center for What Works. (n.d.). *Outcome Indicators Project.* Retrieved from https://www.urban.org/policy-centers/cross-center-initiatives/performance-management-measurement/projects/nonprofit-organizations/projects-focused-nonprofit-organizations/outcome-indicators-project

Watkins, D. C. (2017). Rapid and rigorous qualitative data analysis: The "RADaR" technique for applied research. *International Journal of Qualitative Methods, 16*(1), 1–9.

Wellar, K. (2018, October 26). "Housing first" model for addressing homelessness vs. NIMBYism. *Nonprofit Quarterly.* Retrieved from https://nonprofitquarterly.org/housing-first-model-for-addressing-homelessness-vs-nimbyism/

Wike, T. L., Bledsoe, S. E., Manuel, J. I., Despard, M., Johnson, L. V., Bellamy, J. L., & Killian-Farrell, C. (2014). Evidence-based practice in social work: Challenges and opportunities for clinicians and organizations. *Clinical Social Work Journal, 42*, 161–170.

Winkler, M. K., & Fyffe, S. D. (2016). *Strategies for cultivating an organizational learning culture.* Washington, DC: Urban Institute.

W. K. Kellogg Foundation. (2004). *Logic model development guide.* Retrieved from https://www.wkkf.org/resource-directory/resources/2004/01/logic-model-development-guide

10

Managing Liability, Exposure, and Risk in Nonprofit Settings

Paul A. Kurzman

The life of the law has not been logic: it has been experience. The felt necessities of the time, the prevalent moral and political theories, intuitions of public policy, avowed or unconscious, even the prejudices which judges share with their fellow-men, have a good deal more to do than the syllogism in determining the rules by which men should be governed.

—Justice Oliver Wendell Holmes, Jr.

Few topics cause more concern for nonprofit managers than the issue of risk management. This concern is well founded, given the increase in litigation against nonprofit organizations and their boards and staff. Much of the current vulnerability has resulted from changes in the practices and funding of organizations. Human services agencies, for example, are no longer seen merely as compassionate caretakers but as professional service providers. Youth recreation programs, senior citizens' outings, crafts projects, and remedial reading programs have been supplemented (if not supplanted) by sophisticated employment, child development, group home, employee assistance, and family treatment programs. Similarly, voluntary charitable contributions to fund programs in nonprofit organizations (through theater benefits, bequests, thrift shops, community foundations, and United Way contributions) have, in many cases, given way to major contracts and fee-for-service arrangements with governmental agencies, which now provide the bulk of the income. Human services agencies are no longer playing sandlot ball; they are playing in the big leagues and have correspondingly big risks to manage (Kurzman, 1995; Tremper, 1989).

As nonprofit organizations come of age, they find that maturity involves new risks and responsibilities. This is true for such disparate entities as museums, hospitals, camps, research institutes, public television stations, zoos, libraries, orchestras, philanthropic foundations, colleges, churches, civic associations, historical societies, technology institutes, private schools, nursing homes, missionary societies, fraternal lodges, community improvement districts, literary guilds, botanical gardens, university presses, and animal welfare societies (Herman, 2005; Slater & Finck, 2012). Using social work and social agencies as a template for discussion, one may view the nature and complexity of the change for nonprofit organizations more broadly.

Legal Environment

In tandem with rapid social change has come the recognition of social work as a full-fledged mental health profession. Social workers are by far the largest professional group in the human services arena today. In 1973, only 11 states provided for the legal regulation of social work practice; now, all 50 states do. Similarly, professional social workers enjoy the status of qualified providers of mental health services under state insurance laws in most states today, whereas such vendorship status for social work did not exist in a single state in 1980 (Association of Social Work Boards, 2020). With licensure and vendorship has come the authority to be direct and independent providers of clinical treatment services, generally without referral from or supervision by psychologists or physicians.

Clinical social workers increasingly make the diagnoses, provide the treatment, authenticate clients' claim forms, and authorize third-party reimbursements, not only by private insurance carriers but also by TRICARE (formerly CHAMPUS) and Medicare. Today, social workers serve as expert witnesses in courts of law, as mental health managed care experts for major health insurance carriers, and as framers of clinical service regulations in the departments of both state and federal governments.

As lawyers have noted, "Professionals are held to a higher standard of behavior in their professional capacities than that of the general population" (Watkins & Watkins, 1989, p. 36). Hence, the recent recognition of social work's autonomous professional stature by the government, insurance companies, courts of law, and the public has helped create new forms of exposure and greater risk in practice. Some service settings, of course, involve inherently higher levels of potential peril than do others. Nonprofit organizations with foster care, adoption, day care, debt management, family planning, protective services, group home, camping, residential treatment, and sexual dysfunction programs, for example, place practitioners and managers at particularly high levels of risk. Even the public sector of social work practice is no longer protected. As Besharov (1985) has noted,

> Courts have all but abolished the doctrines of sovereign, governmental, and public officials' immunity, so that it has become easier to bring tort suits against public social service agencies and their employees. Similarly, the abolition of the doctrine of charitable immunity has exposed private agencies and their employees to greater liability. (p. 13)

Today, nonprofit managers must also look within to manage their risks as employers in a competitive and heterogeneous world (Strom-Gottfried, 2016). For example, do women have access to senior positions in the same way that men traditionally have? Are people of color well represented on staff, not just at the clerical or custodial level but in professional, supervisory, and managerial positions? Are appropriate accommodations made for people with disabilities, both as staff and as clients, in a barrier-free environment? Are ageist and homophobic biases toward colleagues and clients handled promptly, honestly, and openly? Many of these issues are dealt with, in part, when a union represents staff or when strong organizations are present in the broader community to ensure nondiscrimination and the ongoing accountability of organizations to their consumers of service, but increasingly such intermediaries are not at hand.

The foregoing realities would be cause enough for concern if professionals were well prepared for risk management issues in their graduate education; however, many are not (Besharov, 1985; Madden, 2003; Reamer, 2003; Stein, 2004). Professional codes of ethics are generally lightly covered in the curriculum; moreover, the legal dimension of ethical issues in practice receives scant attention in higher education curricula, despite the guidelines of accrediting bodies.

Hence, managers may have little preparation for this critical dimension of their professional responsibility. This situation is certainly no better with respect to members of other disciplines who are involved in nonprofit organizations. Indeed, managers may be skilled supervisors, wise administrators, and even creative fundraisers, but managing the institution's legal obligations and vulnerability is an area for which they are often apt to be unprepared and unqualified. Moreover, because staff members are likely to perceive themselves as good-doers and do-gooders, risk management may seem to be an oxymoron (Albert, 2000; Dickson, 1995).

Competing Values

As Quinn, Faerman, Thompson, McGrath, and Bright (2016) have suggested, competing values underpin any assessment of an organization's effectiveness. Organizations that follow an open-systems model, for example, may value behaviors and outcomes that would be perceived as less important to leaders who pursue a rational goal model. Simply put, "the Competing Values Approach suggests that the selection of various criteria of effectiveness reflects competing value choices" (Edwards, 1987, p. 5). As a manager, should one emphasize chance taking, creativity, and innovation or rules and regulations that may reduce risk, exposure, and potential organizational jeopardy, from without and within? Does promoting innovation and decision making at the level closest to the client enhance the organization's posture, or place its stability (in an unstable world) at too great a risk (Kurzman, 1977)?

To many observers, the term "risk management" connotes caution, collaboration, and consultation. Professionals who are trained to have expertise in autonomous practice may perceive such an agenda as a series of illegitimate boundaries circumscribing their judgment, discretion, and freedom to maintain service-centered interventions. Too much management of risk may indeed inhibit the freedom one wants to promote to keep the organization at the cutting edge—competitive and therefore stable in an ever-changing external world.

As Lewin (1997) noted, a dynamic field of forces conditions and constrains managers' decisions. In fact, recognition of and a healthy respect for the inevitable competing values just noted can lead managers to a different use of self that may strike a proper balance among several forces over time. A competing values approach gives recognition to this reality and provides a useful framework for analysis and conceptualization. The approach both highlights elements and values that are often overlooked (for example, risk management activity) and encourages managers to place the need for action in this arena in a broader perspective that may condition implementation. Quinn et al.'s (2016) perspectives can prod nonprofit managers to initiate instrumental activities toward the legitimate protection of the organization, its staff, and those whom it serves without placing an inappropriate or exclusionary value on this activity over others. In Simon's (1997) terms, an acknowledgment of competing values can lead to the development of a "satisficing" model of management that recognizes legitimate contending interests among the field of forces, without or within.

Areas of Risk

As the references to this chapter indicate, many books have addressed the vulnerabilities and liabilities inherent in professional practice. However, less emphasis has been placed on the nonprofit agency per se and on the role of the executive or manager in establishing and leading risk management activities (Carroll, 2011). In this section, I examine the major risks that require management and explore the complexity of the competing values that must be squarely addressed (Bullis, 1995; Reamer, 2015a).

Six risks in prototypical human services practice are most frequently noted. If these risks are not understood and approached from a preventive posture, they will most likely result in litigation or claims of unethical practice. (Note: Although the following discussion is addressed primarily to the human services, with social workers as one example, it is also applicable to other professionals in similar voluntary, charitable, nonprofit organizations.)

First, and perhaps best known, may be the employee's and organization's duty to warn and protect if the client discloses an intent to harm themselves or others. Codified in what has become known as the *Tarasoff* decision, a ruling by the California Supreme Court in 1976 imposed on therapists the duty to exercise reasonable care in the protection of potential victims from the violent acts of clients (Barker, 1984; *Tarasoff v. Board of Regents of the University of California,* 1976). The court concluded that therapists have "an affirmative duty to warn and protect" (*Tarasoff v. Board of Regents of the University of California,* 1976) when they determine, through appropriate standards of their profession, that their client presents a serious danger of violence to a particular person or persons. Although the *Tarasoff* case was decided by a state court, and thus technically may be of limited jurisdictional value, few cases have had as far reaching an effect (Hull & Holmes, 1989). Several landmark decisions in subsequent years affirmed the *Tarasoff* principle and extended its intent to cover nonlicensed mental health counselors and licensed mental health providers (*Hedlund v. Superior Court of Orange County,* 1983; *Jablonski v. United States,* 1983; *Peck v. Counseling Service of Addison County,* 1985). In the *Tarasoff* decision, the court said, in part,

> When a therapist determines, or pursuant to the standards of his or her profession should determine, that his or her patient presents a serious danger of violence to another, he [or she] incurs an obligation to use reasonable care to protect the intended victim against such danger. The discharge of this duty may require the therapist to take one or more of various steps, depending on the nature of the case. Thus it

may call for him [or her] to warn the intended victim or others likely to apprise the victim of the danger, to notify the police, or to take whatever other steps are reasonably necessary under the circumstances.

A second area of risk to human services organizations comes, ironically, from the duty to keep confidential all material that is shared with them and their practitioners in the course of a professional relationship. Section 1.07(c) of the National Association of Social Workers (NASW) (2017) *Code of Ethics,* for example, states that "social workers should protect the confidentiality of all information obtained in the course of professional service" (p. 11). However, confidentiality is not absolute, which is why the sentence continues, "except for compelling professional reasons" (see also Davidson & Davidson, 1998; Polowy, Morgan, Bailey, and Gorenberg, 2008). What the *Tarasoff* decision did was to delineate one such compelling professional reason and to clarify that the word "should" may imply an obligation to act and disclose. In the words of the *Tarasoff* decision, "The protective privilege ends where the public peril begins" (p. 242). Indeed, the concept of client confidentiality is governed for social workers by law in most states and federal courts today as privileged communication. The state statutes provide protection for service recipients similar to the protection they enjoy in the context of their relationships with attorneys, members of the clergy, and physicians (Dickson, 1998; Knapp & Van de Creek, 1987). However, almost all such statutes make exceptions to privilege when such disclosure is necessary to avert serious, foreseeable, and imminent harm to self or other identifiable persons or to prevent the abuse or neglect of children. In fact, all states today have a specific law that mandates professionals to report known or suspected cases of child abuse and define nonreporting as a prima facie case of unprofessional conduct.

A third professional obligation involves the duty to ensure continuity of service to people under care. The expectation is that the institution does not abandon or neglect a client who needs immediate care or who is currently under its care without making reasonable arrangements for the continuity of service. Such a duty obligates the organization to uncooperative and "undesirable" clients, whose hostility and initial unresponsiveness may indeed be a symptom of their need and their disorder. Being able to demonstrate outreach, empathy, flexibility, and appropriate referral to an alternate provider may be essential (Salzman, Furman, & Ohman, 2016).

Fourth, the duty to adequately record the services provided is incumbent on all providers and practitioners (Kagle & Kopels, 2008). As social workers and other human services providers achieve the status of and recognition as vendors, accurate and timely recording becomes essential to ensure that both institutions and clients are properly protected for the receipt of third-party payments. The failure to support a diagnosis included in the current *Diagnostic and Statistical Manual of Mental Disorders,* fifth edition (American Psychiatric Association, 2013), commonly known as the *DSM–5*, in recording services that have been provided to an insurance carrier to justify a fee payment, may be defined as an act of fraud in state statutes. In addition, many states that license professional practitioners define the failure to provide adequate recording of services and to retain such records for a specific number of years as grounds for charges of professional misconduct (Sidell, 2015).

Fifth, practitioners have a duty to diagnose and treat their clients properly. This is a major issue for organizations that have weak procedures for supervisory review and few standards to support interprofessional consultation and referrals (Corey, Corey, & Callanan, 2014; Houston-Vega, Nuehring, & Daguio, 1997; Reamer, 1989). The failure to refer a client to a physician to rule out biological, organic, or genetic conditions that may trigger psychological symptoms is perhaps the largest arena of risk. Alexander (1983) noted that half the claims for erroneous diagnoses made under an insurance trust's professional liability insurance program were based on a charge that the clients' problems were actually medical, not psychological. In addition, organizations need to provide for consultation in psychosocial areas for which individual providers may be poorly trained, such as learning disabilities, eating disorders, and substance abuse.

The expectation that practitioners reach an appropriate *DSM–5* diagnosis also implies that this correct assessment is recorded on insurance forms submitted to Medicaid, Medicare, and private insurance carriers. Because social workers and other human services providers are often recognized as eligible vendors of psychotherapeutic treatment, care must be taken to avoid errors and discrepancies in recording diagnoses, whether intentional or inadvertent. Research (Kutchins & Kirk, 2003) has shown that service recipients may place pressure on providers to report a less severe diagnosis than is indicated because of their fear of the potential adverse effects of labeling. Staff may conversely feel pressure to falsely increase the severity of the diagnosis or to exaggerate symptoms so the consumer can qualify for third-party payments (Holtfreter, 2008).

The sixth and final risk to practice is inherent in the duty to avoid sexual impropriety. Sexual acts performed under the guise of therapy are not permitted between clients and staff (Gabbard, 1989). Virtually all the codes governing the professional conduct of social workers in the 50 states (and five jurisdictions) that regulate their practice make this prohibition explicit.

Moreover, Section 1.09(a) of the NASW (2017) *Code of Ethics* makes no exceptions to its unequivocal statement that "social workers should under no circumstances engage in sexual activities . . . or sexual contact with current clients, whether such contact is consensual or forced" (p. 15). The codes of ethics of other mental health professions have similar prohibitions against sexual activities between therapists and their clients. Such activity cannot be defended under the guise of "supporting the transference" or helping to "overcome sexual inhibition or dysfunction."

Given the position of trust that the employing organization shares with its practitioners, courts may view employers as having culpability as well. The potential perils here are even greater than those of the risks previously described, because most insurance policies exclude coverage for intentional wrongdoing, such as sexual involvement with clients. Managers and supervisors, moreover, are generally viewed in the role of *respondeat superior*, a legal doctrine in which they share vicarious liability for tortuous acts committed by those under their supervision or in their employ (Israel, 2016; Jenkins, 2007; Rome, 2013).

I have highlighted these most serious risks and duties to demonstrate that those who lead nonprofit service organizations today need to demonstrate great caution and sound judgment. The litigious environment in which professionals currently practice makes it imperative that managers reduce their organization's exposures while preserving a spirit of flexibility and innovation. As Golensky and Hager (2020) stated,

> Nonprofit leaders should be more proactive in their communications with employees by putting in place site-specific internal procedures that provide clear guidance to staff (especially recent hires) regarding lines of accountability and performance expectations without circumscribing individual decision-making to the degree that workers are reduced to mere automatons. (p. 281)

Risk management procedures have to be put in place because good intentions provide insufficient protection. In addition to the possibility of government-sponsored criminal actions against nonprofit employers and their practitioners, civil actions by consumers are becoming more common and more successful. The defense against torts, such as the negligence of employers and the malpractice of individuals, requires as much careful thought as do preparation of the budget and composition of the board of directors. These exposures are shared by all nonprofit organizations, including churches, libraries, schools, civic associations, hospitals, museums, and cultural organizations (Edwards, 2020).

Recommended Responses

Four major recommendations flow from this discussion. They reflect a focus on the competing values that are intrinsic to the issues at hand and therefore deal with process and goals; maintenance of and competition among systems, planning, and training; and internal and external foci of organizational concern.

Insurance Protection

Today, no nonprofit organization can afford to be without adequate forms of insurance. Such coverage should include

- premises liability, covering all sites at which services may be delivered
- professional liability, including the activities of all paid staff, volunteers, and consultants
- coverage of officers and directors, to shield executives and members of the board of directors from individual and collective personal liability in the performance of their fiduciary duties
- vehicular insurance, generally at a level higher than the mandated state minimum
- bonding for all officers and staff who have the authority to sign contracts or manage the institution's income and assets
- cyberliability, with a first-party breach endorsement, to protect against a third-party information breach, for which the practitioner will be held accountable under the Health Insurance Portability and Accountability Act (P.L. 104-191; Reamer, 2013, 2021).

Such casualty policies should cover the organization and key participants for most losses and damages, including negligence, provided that one cannot prove nonfeasance or malfeasance (Angell & Pfaffle, 1988; Grobman, 2011; Reamer, 1995). In addition, insurance generally provides for funding of the potentially expensive legal defense against charges that may be brought, regardless of the outcome. Without adequate insurance, winning a case in court may actually be a Pyrrhic victory (Jones & Alcabes, 1989). Out-of-pocket legal fees and court costs may be so high that, in effect, one loses even when one wins. In summary, it is essential for the organization to obtain insurance coverage that is commensurate with the organizational scope and program complexity of its services (Tremper, 1989).

Legal Counsel

Every nonprofit organization should establish legal counsel in the same way it sets up an ongoing relationship with an accountant or program consultant. One should not wait until a crisis occurs and then select an attorney under pressure. Most organizational leaders try to ensure that one or more attorneys serve on their advisory board or board of directors so that they can get the frequent informal advice they may need on such issues as reviewing a lease, framing an amendment to the bylaws, or signing a governmental contract—frequently on a pro bono basis. However, an independent counsel is often warranted. First, some legal opinions may involve a potential conflict of interest for a board member because the questions involve actions by the board itself or one of its members. Second, the legal issues may be outside the board member's legal specialization and expertise. Third, the individual (or organization) that is taking legal action may be a client of the board member's firm.

Whether done by a board member or an external counsel, new legal agreements and contracts should be fully reviewed before they are signed. Given the principle of *respondeat superior* noted earlier, it is also important for an attorney to ensure that insurance covers those people, for example, who are agents of the facility's service (under the supervision of organizational employees), such as student interns, AmeriCorps workers, community volunteers, and trainees. As Frederic Reamer (2015b), a preeminent social work authority on risk management, observed,

> Volunteers enjoy individual protection under the federal Volunteer Protection Act of 1997. Generally speaking, this act provides immunity from tort [wrongful act] claims that might be filed against the volunteers of nonprofit organizations where the claim alleges that the volunteer carelessly injured another party in the course of helping the agency. . . . It is important to emphasize that the act does not provide immunity to the nonprofit agency itself; agency supervisors and administrators can be sued under the doctrine of *respondeat superior*. (p. 206)

On a proactive basis, an attorney should regularly explore the major federal, state, and local statutes (and evolving case law) that govern the organization, its funding, and its services and look at any need to amend or update the organization's bylaws.

Staff Training

The best way to avoid trouble is to prevent it from occurring. Professionals know the value of education and prevention, often deploying these skills on behalf of customers and clients with remarkable creativity and success. As managers, however, they often forget to apply what works in their own practice to the organizations for which they now are responsible.

In addition to ongoing service-centered training activities that may accompany monthly administrative meetings or periodic case conferences, it may be wise to institute quarterly half-day sessions for formal administrative training. Not only do such sessions provide line staff with the information they need for advancement into managerial positions, but they also send the message that organizational issues are everyone's concern (Besharov & Besharov, 1987; Kurzman, 2012). Experts can be invited to speak, or staff with special expertise can lead the sessions. From a risk management perspective, important items to cover may include

- state laws governing the requirements and procedures for reporting known or suspected cases of child or elder abuse or neglect
- principles that are embodied in the *Tarasoff* decision with regard to the duty to protect when there is serious potential danger posed by a client to self or to others
- current federal and state regulations on record keeping and retention (Kagle & Kopels, 2008; Sidell, 2015)
- statutes on privileged communication governing the several mental health professions and the specific principles of confidentiality embodied in those professions' ethical codes
- proper completion of insurance forms for third-party reimbursement, including the appropriate use of the *DSM–5*
- additional training for proper differential diagnoses in areas in which many professionals may be poorly trained, such as learning disabilities, organic pathology, psychopharmacology, and chemical dependence
- relevant state rules and standards of professional conduct for the licensed professions, as appropriate, such as nursing, social work, marriage and family counseling, psychology, nutrition, audiology, architecture, and accounting

Special emphasis must be given to the need to train staff to avoid even the appearance of sexual impropriety. Occasionally, it may be appropriate, for example, for a therapist to hug clients momentarily to console them; to stroke their wrists briefly during a moment of stress; or to compliment them on their dress or appearance if this is a new sign of strength and self-esteem. It would be naïve, however, not to understand that there is a thin line that would be easy for staff to cross. Moreover, one must remember the clinical dictum, especially working in the context of a helping relationship with troubled clients, that "perception is reality." The alarming rise in charges of professional misconduct that have been brought before disciplinary committees of licensing boards and committees of inquiry in various professional associations in recent years (charging service providers with both opposite-sex and same-sex misconduct) must be understood and underscored. As I have noted, such charges against social workers have become sufficiently prevalent that a cap has been placed on professional liability insurance coverage when a sexual impropriety by a practitioner has been documented (Besharov, 1985).

Moreover, leaders should note that this issue is not profession specific. An American Psychological Association study showed that, during a 10-year period, 45 percent of all malpractice awards through its professional liability coverage dealt with therapist–patient intimacy ("Therapist-Patient Sexual Intimacy," 1988). Bringing in members of appropriate professional societies' committees on inquiry to discuss the respective provisions of the various professional associations' codes of ethics in this area is warranted. In addition, it may be wise to invite a member of the disciplinary panel of relevant state licensing boards to speak about standards of conduct and case law experience regarding sexual impropriety. Training staff members to avoid giving even the possible suggestion of improper behavior in their speech, conduct, electronic communications, and presentation of self is crucial to limiting a facility's exposure (Lopez, 2014). If such a transgression occurs, the staff person should be quickly identified as "an impaired professional" and referred for appropriate help, and the consumer's needs and rights must be served and protected (Reamer, 2015b).

Internal Audit

All nonprofit organizations conduct a fiscal audit each year, if only because it is required by funding bodies and the Internal Revenue Service as a condition for maintaining their tax-exempt status. However, most managers do not retain outside experts to conduct a periodic program and management audit to ensure that risks are being properly managed (Reamer, 2001). An external auditor, a board member, and a senior member of the managerial staff should address the following questions:

- Are the organization's governmental licenses and accreditations in order?
- Are all eligible professional staff currently licensed and registered for practice?
- Are provisions for emergency actions (for example, fire drills, reporting of theft, involuntary hospitalization of clients, safety of staff, responding to accidents) well known and regularly updated?
- Have premiums for all forms of property and casualty insurance coverage been paid?
- Are procedures for the management of records being properly followed?
- Are governmental vouchers and records of insurance reimbursements being maintained in keeping with legal and contractual requirements? (Archambeault & Webber, 2018)
- Are supervisory evaluations being conducted and reviewed in a timely fashion?

A biennial internal management ethics audit of the appropriateness of such standard operating procedures and the staff's adherence to their provisions is a wise prophylactic risk management activity that may pay big dividends for the organization, the staff, and those they serve.

Conclusion

New opportunities have brought new risks. As professionals who are often managing regulated organizations in the context of a litigious society, nonprofit leaders can no longer consider risk management a luxury. The demands of clients, funding sources, and professional standards suggest that managing risks is part of the prudent manager's responsibility in implementing a strategy of primary and secondary prevention (Golensky & Hager, 2020). That is, risk management is better conceptualized as a proactive strategy of affirmation than as a reactive response to a crisis. Managers who organically build in this function should not find this activity any more burdensome than hiring staff and balancing the budget. Although managers have to respond to many competing values and demands as they control and adapt to their environment, the growth and stability of organizations are dependent on managers' competent performance of risk management functions. Nonprofit service organizations have legitimate survival needs because they must coexist with internal and external forces that constantly impinge on them. In a sense, they are social organisms that reflect the legitimate competing values to which they must respond. In this context, they must manage risks to thrive and survive, often in turbulent times, because consumers—often with few options in life—depend on them.

Skills Application Exercises

1. You are the manager of a hospital-based employee assistance program (EAP) that provides free and confidential professional mental health and substance abuse services to all hospital employees and their families. An emergency room nurse voluntarily comes to the EAP to see a counselor on your staff about her cocaine and alcohol addiction, which she says seems to be getting worse. Because she is exceedingly good at what she does and generally careful about when she snorts and drinks, her addiction has not been detected by supervisors or peers. She wants help with her problem, but only if she can stay on her job and only if the EAP promises her confidentiality. Provided that the EAP staff make these two promises, she indicates that she will do whatever they recommend, including coming in for daily EAP sessions, gradually eliminating her use of alcohol and cocaine, and joining Alcoholics Anonymous and Cocaine Anonymous in the community. She reminds your staff person that she is a voluntary self-referral and of the EAP's long-standing and well-known promise of confidentiality (Kurzman, 1988). Without revealing the client's identity, your EAP counselor wants to know whether you will permit him to honor the client's requests. What do you do, and why?

2. Your private community college has received a letter from a prominent negligence attorney alleging that a male faculty member at the college made explicit verbal and physical advances to a female student after evening classes and during advising sessions held in his office. It says that the student, in the context of a relationship of unequal power, was told that her course grade and letter of recommendation for senior college depended on her willingness to become sexually intimate with the faculty member. The attorney says that these advances made the student physically ill and unable to function at her well-paid job as an executive secretary because she could no longer concentrate at work. She further claims, through her attorney, that your faculty member's actions alienated the affection of her husband, a prominent physician, who wants a divorce. The client's attorney wants to meet with you to explore a $1 million settlement, in lieu of a protracted,

public, and potentially more costly outcome of litigation against you, the faculty member, and the college. As the college's vice president for academic affairs, would you meet with the client's attorney? What are your short- and long-range plans of action?

3. You are the new executive vice president of a center for the performing arts that has a symphony orchestra, theater repertory, opera company, music conservatory, experimental drama workshop, modern dance ensemble, and a ballet. You have several state-of-the-art facilities, many prominent performers, and a large number of performance support personnel. Your center receives income not only through ticket sales and subscriptions but also from government arts and humanities grants, rental agreements, teaching and training contracts, corporate sponsorships, foundation grants, and an endowment. You have a diverse professional, paraprofessional, and support staff and the immediate aid of three experienced deputies (for program, development, and administration). What is your plan of action, during your first year, to assess the adequacy and sufficiency of your organization's risk management policies and procedures?

References

Albert, R. (2000). *Law and social work practice* (2nd ed.). New York: Springer.

Alexander, C. A. (1983, November). *Professional liability insurance: Jeopardy and ethics*. Paper presented at the Professional Symposium of the National Association of Social Workers, Washington, DC.

American Psychiatric Association. (2013). *Diagnostic and statistical manual of mental disorders* (5th ed.). Washington, DC: American Psychiatric Publishing.

Angell, F. J., & Pfaffle, A. E. (1988). *The whole field of insurance and risk management* (3rd ed.). Mt. Vernon, NY: Chase Communications.

Archambeault, D. S., & Webber, S. (2018). Fraud survival in nonprofit organizations: Empirical evidence. *Nonprofit Management & Leadership, 29*, 29–46.

Association of Social Work Boards. (2020). *Social work laws and regulations: A comparison database.* Retrieved from http://members.aswb.org/services/social-work-regulations.

Barker, R. L. (1984). The *Tarasoff* paradox: Confidentiality and the duty to warn. *Social Thought, 10*(4), 3–12.

Besharov, D. (1985). *The vulnerable social worker.* Silver Spring, MD: National Association of Social Workers.

Besharov, D., & Besharov, S. H. (1987). Teaching about liability. *Social Work, 32*, 517–522.

Bullis, R. K. (1995). *Clinical social worker misconduct.* Chicago: Nelson-Hall.

Carroll, R. (Ed.) (2011). *Risk management handbook for healthcare organizations.* Hoboken, NJ: Wiley.

Corey, G., Corey, M., & Callanan, P. (2014). *Issues and ethics in the helping professions* (9th ed.). Belmont, CA: Wadsworth.

Davidson, J. R., & Davidson, T. (1998). Confidentiality and managed care: Ethical and legal concerns. In G. Shaimess & A. Lightburn (Eds.), *Humane managed care?* (pp. 281–292). Washington DC: NASW Press.

Dickson, D. T. (1995). *Law in the health and human services.* New York: Free Press.

Dickson, D. T. (1998). *Confidentiality and privacy in social work.* New York: Free Press.

Edwards, R. L. (1987). The competing values approach as an integrating framework for the management curriculum. *Administration in Social Work, 11*(1), 1–13.

Edwards, R. L. (2020). *Building a strong foundation: Fundraising for nonprofits* (2nd ed.). Washington, DC: NASW Press.

Gabbard, G. O. (Ed.). (1989). *Sexual exploitation in professional relationships.* Washington, DC: American Psychiatric Association.

Golensky, M., & Hager, M. A. (2020). Leadership by example. In M Golensky & M. Hager (Eds.), *Strategic leadership and management in nonprofit organizations: Theory and practice* (2nd ed., pp. 269–288). New York: Oxford University Press.

Grobman, G. M. (2011). *The nonprofit handbook* (6th ed.). Harrisburg, PA: White Hat Communications.

Health Insurance Portability and Accountability Act of 1996 (HIPAA), P.L. 104-191, 42 U.S.C. § 300gg, 29 U.S.C. §§ 1181–1183, and 42 U.S.C. §§ 1320d–1320d9.

Hedlund v. Superior Court of Orange County, 34 Cal.3d 695 (1983).

Herman, M. L. (2005). Risk management. In R. D. Herman (Ed.), *The Jossey-Bass handbook of nonprofit leadership and management* (2nd ed., pp. 560–585). San Francisco: Jossey-Bass.

Holtfreter, K. (2008). Determinants of fraud losses in nonprofit organizations. *Nonprofit Management and Leadership, 19*, 45–63.

Houston-Vega, M. K., Nuehring, E. M., & Daguio, E. R. (1997). *Prudent practice: A guide for managing malpractice risk.* Washington, DC: NASW Press.

Hull, L., & Holmes, G. (1989). Legal analysis and public agencies: The therapist's duty to warn. *New England Journal of Human Services, 9*(2), 31–34.

Israel, A. B. (2016). *Using the law: Practical decision making in mental health.* New York: Oxford University Press.

Jablonski v. United States, 712 F.2d 391 (1983).

Jenkins, P. (2007). *Counseling, psychotherapy and the law* (2nd ed.) Thousand Oaks, CA: SAGE.

Jones, J. A., & Alcabes, A. (1989). Clients don't sue: The invulnerable social worker. *Social Casework, 70,* 414–420.

Kagle, J., & Kopels, S. (2008). *Social work records* (3rd ed.) Longrove, IL: Waveland Press.

Knapp, S., & Van de Creek, L. (1987). *Privileged communication for mental health professionals.* New York: Van Nostrand Reinhold.

Kurzman, P. A. (1977). Rules and regulations in large-scale organizations: A theoretical approach to the problem. *Administration in Social Work, 1,* 421–431.

Kurzman, P. A. (1988). The ethical base for social work in the workplace. In G. M. Gould & M. L. Smith (Eds.), *Social work in the workplace* (pp. 16–27). New York: Springer.

Kurzman, P. A. (1995). Professional liability and malpractice. In R. L. Edwards (Ed.-in-Chief), *Encyclopedia of social work* (19th ed., Vol. 3, pp. 1921–1927). Washington, DC: NASW Press.

Kurzman, P. A. (2012). Workplace ethics: Issues for human service professionals in the new millennium. In R. Chadwick (Ed.), *Encyclopedia of applied ethics* (2nd ed., Vol. 4, pp. 555–560). Oxford, England: Elsevier.

Kutchins, H., & Kirk, S. A. (2003). *Making us crazy: DSM: The psychiatric bible and the creation of mental disorders.* New York: Free Press.

Lewin, K. (1997). *Field theory in social science.* Washington, DC: American Psychological Association.

Lopez, A. (2014). Social work, technology and ethical practices: A review and evaluation of the NASW Technology Standards. *Social Work in Health Care, 53,* 815–833.

Madden, R. G. (2003). *Essential law for social workers.* New York: Columbia University Press.

National Association of Social Workers. (2017). *Code of ethics.* Washington, DC: Author.

Peck v. Counseling Service of Addison County, 499 A.2d 422 (1985).

Polowy, C. I., Morgan, S., Bailey, W. D., & Gorenberg, C. (2008). Confidentiality and privileged communication. In T. Mizrahi & L. E. Davis (Eds.), *Encyclopedia of social work* (20th ed., Vol. 1, pp. 408–415). Washington, DC: NASW Press.

Quinn, R. E., Faerman, S. R., Thompson, M. P., McGrath, M. R., & Bright, D. S. (2016). *Becoming a master manager: A competing values approach.* Hoboken, NJ: Wiley.

Reamer, F. G. (1989). Liability issues in social work supervision. *Social Work, 34,* 445–448.

Reamer, F. G. (1995). Malpractice claims against social workers. *Social Work, 40,* 595–601.

Reamer, F. G. (2001). *The social work ethics audit: A risk management tool.* Washington, DC: NASW Press.

Reamer, F. G. (2003). *Social work malpractice and liability* (2nd ed.). New York: Columbia University Press.

Reamer, F. G. (2013). Social work in a digital age: Ethical and risk management challenges. *Social Work, 58,* 163–172.

Reamer, F. G. (2015a). Risk management in social work. In K. Corcoran & A. R. Roberts (Eds.), *Social workers' desk reference* (3rd ed., pp. 149–155). New York: Oxford University Press.

Reamer, F. G. (2015b). *Risk management in social work: Preventing professional malpractice, liability and disciplinary action.* New York: Columbia University Press.

Reamer, F. G. (2021). *Ethics and risk management in online and distance behavioral health.* San Diego, CA: Cognella Academic.

Rome, S. H. (2013). *Social work and the law: Judicial policy and forensic practice.* Boston: Pearson.

Salzman, A., Furman, D. M., & Ohman, K. (2016). *Law in social work practice* (3rd ed.). Boston: Cengage Learning.

Sidell, N. L. (2015). *Social work documentation: A guide to strengthening your case recording* (2nd ed.). Washington, DC: NASW Press.

Simon, H. A. (1997). *Administrative behavior* (4th ed.). New York: Simon & Schuster.

Slater, L., & Finck, K. (2012). *Social work practice and the law.* New York: Springer.

Stein, T. J. (2004). *The role of law in social work practice and administration.* New York: Columbia University Press.

Strom-Gottfried, K. (2016). *Straight talk about professional ethics* (2nd ed.). New York: Oxford University Press.

Tarasoff v. Board of Regents of the University of California, 17 Cal.3d 425, 131 Cal. Rptr. 14, 551 P.2d 344 (1976).

"Therapist-patient sexual intimacy." (1988, September–October). *EAP Digest,* p. 13.

Tremper, C. R. (1989). *Reconsidering legal liability and insurance for nonprofit organizations.* Lincoln, NE: Law College Education Services.

Watkins, S. A., & Watkins, J.C. (1989). Negligent endangerment: Malpractice in the clinical context. *Journal of Independent Social Work, 3*(3), 35–50.

11

Information and Communications Technology in Nonprofit Management and Leadership

Frederic G. Reamer

Information and communications technology (ICT) in nonprofit management and leadership has come of age. Today's time-starved agency executives and organizational leaders spend what may feel like endless hours during their congested days and evenings, scrolling through cascading email messages that seem to multiply exponentially, responding to text messages, logging into web conferencing sessions, learning about strategies to ensure that their organizations comply with strict federal and state technology regulations, analyzing data displayed on computerized spreadsheets, and managing electronic records software that enables both staffers and consumers to log in remotely. These dramatic developments have sown a wide range of unprecedented challenges for today's managers and leaders, many of which involve potentially competing values related to organizational effectiveness, expedience, informed consent, confidentiality and privacy, boundary issues, and conflicts of interest, among others.

None of this technology existed when most managers and leaders began their professional career, when administering agencies required taking pen to paper (Zimmerman & Broughton, 2006). In fact, ballpoint pens were invented by Massachusetts attorney John Loud during the very era when what are now known as nonprofit organizations were inaugurated (Casey, 2009). Over time, managers and leaders incorporated various forms of technology to assist their efforts, beginning with landline telephones, answering machines with cassettes, mimeograph machines, photocopiers, facsimile machines, overhead projectors that use cellulose acetate transparencies, and primitive calculators. Today's managers and leaders rely on smartphones, digital tablets, video conferencing software, electronic records, cloud storage, and online portals, among the many technology options. Their conversations are sprinkled with terms such as "encryption," "telehealth," "online social networking," "electronically stored information," "avatars," "blogs," "metadata," "short message service," "expert systems programmed with artificial intelligence," "voice over IP," "remote access," and "wireless networks."

Evolution of Information and Communications Technology in Nonprofit Organizations

What is known today as ICT first made its appearance in the 1940s, when solid-state devices, vacuum tubes, transistors, integrated circuits, and computer processors emerged (Harlow & Webb, 2003; Kowal, Kuzio, & Wawrzak-Chodaczek, 2015). Personal computers, which revolutionized office-based work in nonprofit organizations, emerged in the 1970s. In addition to word processing, these computers enabled staffers to access the World Wide Web, which became available in the 1980s and widely used by the public in the 1990s. Smartphones, which are now a staple in the lives of agency managers, staff, clients, and consumers, became available shortly thereafter. As a result of these developments, today's professionals can communicate and meet with each other remotely, store records and other information electronically, search online for information, prepare reports and other documents, deliver services to clients remotely, manage budgets, conduct online meetings, provide staff training, and analyze program evaluation data, among other tasks. Hardware includes mainframe computers, desktop computers, laptop computers, tablets, smartphones, noise-cancelling headphones, pan–tilt–zoom cameras, and smartwatches. Software includes word processing programs, electronic client and patient records, smartphone apps, spreadsheets, databases, instant messaging, online social networking, video applications, telephone applications, virtual training sites and simulations, and avatars (Zimmerman & Broughton, 2006).

In the human services, in particular, many resources and services emerged on the Internet as early as 1982 in the form of online self-help support groups (Kanani & Regehr, 2003; Reamer, 2013b). The first known fee-based Internet mental health service was established in the 1990s; by the late 1990s, groups of mental health clinicians were forming companies and e-clinics that offered online counseling services to the public using secure Web sites (Skinner & Zack, 2004).

The earliest discussions of electronic tools in the human services focused on practitioners' use of information technology (Schoech, 1999) and the ways in which they could use Internet resources, such as online chat rooms and collegial email distribution lists, professional networking sites, news groups, and email (Finn & Barak, 2010; Grant & Grobman, 1998; Martinez & Clark, 2000). Today's services include a much wider range of digital and electronic options to serve people who struggle with life's challenges. For example, a large number of human service professionals currently use video counseling, email chat, social networking Web sites, text messaging, avatar-based platforms, self-guided web-based interventions, smartphone apps, and other technology to provide services to clients, some of whom they have never met in person (Chan & Holosko, 2016; Chester & Glass, 2006; Kanani & Regehr, 2003; Lamendola, 2010; Menon & Miller-Cribbs, 2002; Reamer, 2012b, 2013b, 2017, 2018e; Rummell & Joyce, 2010; Zur, 2012). Social services agencies now typically rely on electronic client records that contain sensitive information that is stored in the cloud.

ICT innovations have also had a profound impact in other nonprofit settings, such as universities and museums. The COVID-19 pandemic, in particular, required managers and leaders in these organizations to pivot suddenly to ensure that professors could teach students remotely and museums could provide their patrons with remote access to their rich and vast collections. ICT has become essential, both for organizations' financial survival and to enable the delivery of services and resources that enhance the public's quality of life.

Some staffers in nonprofit organizations are using digital technology informally as a supplement to traditional face-to-face service delivery. Other practitioners and agencies have created formal distance service protocols that depend entirely on digital technology. In addition, some professionals' routine use of digital technology—especially social media and text messaging—in their daily lives has created new ways to interact and communicate with the people they serve. In fact, many organizations now communicate with clients and the general public via online social networking sites, such as Facebook.

These now-common forms of modern communication and data storage raise a number of compelling ethical quandaries that nonprofit managers and leaders must anticipate as they consider whether and how they will adopt various forms of ICT (Reamer, 2018b, 2021b). Key issues involve informed consent, confidentiality and privacy, boundary issues and conflicts of interest, documentation and records, collegial relationships, and practitioner competence. Ideally, nonprofit managers and leaders develop and monitor compliance with agency-based policies and protocols that address all of these phenomena.

ICT Functions in Nonprofit Organizations

Managers and leaders adopt ICT to perform four major functions: (1) deliver services to clients, consumers, patrons, and other constituents; (2) communicate with clients, consumers, patrons, and other constituents; (3) store information electronically; and (4) locate information online about clients, consumers, patrons, and constituents. They have access to a wide range of technology options that span across and intersect with these various functions.

Many nonprofit organizations now use ICT to deliver services remotely, a trend that was accelerated in response to the COVID-19 pandemic. For instance, in social service and mental health organizations, online counseling services are now available to clients (Anderson & Guyton, 2013; Barak & Grohol, 2011; Chang, 2005; McCarty & Clancy, 2002; Midkiff & Wyatt, 2008; Richards & Vigano, 2013; Santhiveeran, 2009). People who struggle with depression, borderline and bipolar issues, addiction, marital and relationship conflict, anxiety, eating disorders, grief, and other mental health and behavioral challenges can use electronic search engines to locate practitioners who offer counseling services using live online chat functions (Haberstroh, 2009). Clients can purchase these online therapeutic chat services in various time increments and pay by credit card.

Behavioral health professionals also provide local and long-distance counseling services by telephone, sometimes to clients they never meet in person. After providing a counselor with a username and credit card information, clients receive telephone counseling. Some practitioners provide such telephone counseling as a formal service. Others supplement traditional face-to-face counseling with occasional telephone counseling, email messages, and text messages—for example, when clients or clinicians are traveling away from home or when clients are in crisis situations.

In addition, many nonprofit behavioral health organizations offer live distance counseling using webcams, pan–tilt–zoom cameras, and monitors. Some practitioners use video counseling software that is compliant with the Health Insurance Portability and Accountability Act (HIPAA) of 1996 (P.L. 104-191), and others do not (Lindeman, 2011; Reamer, 2017). Another option for some organizations includes avatar-based services, where staffers and clients create a three-dimensional virtual world where they interact with each other visually via avatars rather than live images.

Other ICT options include a wide variety of online interventions designed to help people who struggle with diverse life challenges. Users first complete online questionnaires concerning their challenges and then receive electronic or automated feedback and resources generated by artificial intelligence software that can help them decide whether to address their issues. Those who indicate a wish for help are then provided links to professionals who offer distance services.

Also, many organizations now incorporate smartphone apps that clients and consumers can use. An increasing number of programs encourage (or require) clients and consumers to download apps to their smartphones to record information about themselves. For example, some behavioral health agencies invite clients to record on their smartphone app their clinical symptoms, behaviors, and moods; receive automated messages from treatment providers, including positive and supportive messages; obtain psychoeducation information; and get links to local resources, including locations of 12-step meetings. Clients who want to avoid high-risk locations (for example, a client in recovery who wants to avoid certain high-risk neighborhoods) can insert addresses into the app, which is programmed to send the client an electronic text warning if the client is in or near the high-risk location.

Some practitioners have the ability to enter information about clients into a smartphone app that can then be accessed remotely by colleagues who may have subsequent encounters with the same client. For example, practitioners employed by a program that provides street outreach services to people who struggle with homelessness can summarize their encounters in the smartphone app immediately after an encounter, including information about the homeless individual's unique housing challenges, health and behavioral health concerns, and eligibility for public benefits and services. This shared digital access (any time of the day or night) helps to facilitate practitioners' coordination of services without relying on office-based records.

Developing a Strategic Plan for ICT Implementation

Ideally, agency leaders and managers develop a sound plan for implementation of ICT. Key steps in a strategic plan would include developing a vision statement, performing an assessment and gap analysis, conducting a feasibility study, creating a planning document, implementing appropriate hardware and software, and monitoring implementation (Allison & Kaye, 2015; Bryson, 2018). The vision statement provides a broad overview of the ways in which ICT is relevant to the organization's mission. It describes how various forms of technology can enhance the agency's ability to communicate with clients and the general public, best serve clients and consumers, and store and manage their information.

The assessment identifies existing resources, including hardware and software as well as noteworthy gaps and logistical challenges. The assessment can also include discussion of the specific ways in which existing gaps limit the organization's ability to perform its key functions and fulfill its overarching mission.

The findings included in the assessment are linked directly to the feasibility study that identifies needed resources, such as personnel responsible for implementation of ICT, available products, funds to purchase and install hardware and software, and staff training. This information can be incorporated into a comprehensive planning document, which includes a detailed timetable.

It is important for agency managers to develop a plan to monitor efforts to implement the strategic plan and evaluate outcomes. Outcomes may include agency personnel's utilization of ICT, satisfaction with ICT, any limitations or obstacles that interfere with the optimal use of ICT, and costs.

Ethical Issues and Challenges

Managers and leaders of nonprofit organizations should address a number of core ethical issues as they make decisions about adopting ICT. These issues concern informed consent, confidentiality and privacy, legal issues, boundaries and conflicts of interest, documentation and records, collegial relationships, and practitioner competence (Barsky, 2017; Reamer, 2015a, 2015b). Careful attention to these questions can help protect clients, consumers, and nonprofit organizations.

Informed Consent

Informed consent has always been a key element of service delivery sponsored by nonprofit organizations (Berg, Appelbaum, Lidz, & Parker, 2001; Reamer, 2013a, 2015b). The advent of ICT, along with service organizations' provision of distance or remote services, has enhanced professionals' ethical duty to ensure that clients and consumers fully understand the nature of these services and the potential benefits and risks. This became especially relevant when COVID-19 emerged and forced many nonprofit organizations to obtain clients' and consumers' consent remotely.

Obtaining clients' and consumers' truly informed consent can be especially difficult when organization staffers never meet clients and consumers in person or never have the opportunity to speak with them directly about informed consent. Special challenges arise when minors contact organizations and request distance or remote services, particularly when professionals offer services funded by contracts or grants and do not require payment from either minor clients' parents or insurance companies. Indeed, laws around the world vary considerably regarding minors' right to obtain services from professionals without parental knowledge or consent (Reamer, 2015b).

Managers in nonprofit settings must ensure that the organizations they lead comply with emerging standards concerning informed consent and remote delivery of services. State and federal laws and regulations vary in interpretation and application of informed consent standards. In general, however, professionals agree that several conditions must be met for consent to be considered valid, and these long-standing standards are especially relevant to an organization's provision of online and distance services:

1. *Coercion and undue influence must not have played a role in the client's decision.* Professionals who use ICT often maintain some degree of control over clients' and consumers' lives (for example, by approving benefits, admission into programs, and the termination of services). Practitioners must ensure that clients and consumers do not feel pressured to grant consent for services provided remotely.

2. *Clients and consumers must be mentally capable of providing consent.* Clearly, some service recipients (for example, young children and individuals with serious mental illness, brain injury, or dementia) may be unable to comprehend the consent procedure. Others, however, may be only temporarily unable to consent, such as individuals who are under the short-term influence of alcohol or other drugs at the time consent is sought or who may experience transient psychotic symptoms. In general, agency staffers should assess clients' and consumers' ability to reason and make informed choices, comprehend relevant facts and retain this information, appreciate current circumstances, and communicate wishes. Service recipients who are unable to consent to online and distance services at a given moment may be able to consent in the future if the incapacity is temporary.

3. *Consent forms and procedures must be valid.* Agency professionals sometimes present clients and consumers with general, broadly worded consent forms that may violate clients' rights to be informed and may be considered invalid if challenged in a court of law. Staffers should include details that refer to specific activities involving the use of technology, information to be released, or technology-based

interventions. Typical elements include details of the nature and purpose of a service or disclosure of information; advantages and disadvantages of an intervention; substantial or possible risks to clients and consumers, if any are present (including risks uniquely associated with online and distance services and storage of sensitive information in electronic records); potential effects on clients' and consumers' families, jobs, social activities, and other important aspects of their lives; alternatives to the proposed intervention or disclosure; and anticipated costs for clients and consumers, if any. All of this information should be presented in clear, understandable language and in a manner that encourages them to ask questions for clarification. Consent forms should always be dated and include a reasonable expiration date.

4. *Nonprofit staff should be especially sensitive to clients' and consumers' cultural and ethnic differences related to the use of technology and the meaning of concepts such as self-determination and consent.* When necessary, forms should be translated into clients' and consumers' primary language, and competent interpreter services should be provided. Staff should never ask clients and consumers to sign blank consent forms, even when they believe they have the client's permission to insert details at a later time.

5. *Clients and consumers must have the right to refuse or withdraw consent.* Agency staffers should be prepared for the possibility that clients will exercise these rights, particularly with respect to the delivery of online and distance services. Staffers should inform clients and consumers of their rights and help them make thoughtful and informed decisions on the basis of all available facts and information about potential benefits and risks (Reamer, 2013a, 2015a; Recupero & Rainey, 2005).

When agency staff provide behavioral health services to clients and consumers remotely, the informed consent form should include statements such as the following:*

- This informed consent form contains important information focusing on providing services remotely using the phone or the Internet. Please read this carefully and let me know if you have any questions. When you sign this document, it will represent an agreement between us.

---

*This list is adapted from information provided to the public by the TrustPARMA (2021). Also see Reamer (2021b).

- One of the benefits of remote service delivery is that you and I can engage in services without being in the same physical location. This can be helpful in ensuring continuity of care if you and I are not in the same location, move to a different location, take an extended vacation, or are otherwise unable to continue to meet in person. It is also more convenient and takes less time. Using technology to provide assistance, however, requires technical competence on both our parts. Although there are benefits to remote service delivery, there are some differences between services provided in person and remotely, as well as some risks.

- Because our meetings will take place outside of my office, there is potential for other people to overhear our conversations if you are not in a private place during the session. On my end, I will take reasonable steps to ensure your privacy. But it is important for you to make sure you find a private location for our conversation where you will not be interrupted. It is also important for you to protect the privacy of our conversation on your cellphone or other device. You should communicate with me only while in a room or area where other people are not present and cannot overhear the conversation.

- Please be aware that technology may stop working during our conversation, other people might be able to get access to our private conversation, or stored data could be accessed by unauthorized people or companies.

- Usually, I will not provide remote services to people who are currently in a crisis situation requiring high levels of support and intervention. Before we begin our work together, we will develop an emergency response plan to address potential crisis situations that may arise during the course of our work.

- For communication between our online or remote sessions, I only use email communication and text messaging, with your permission, and only for administrative purposes, unless we have made another agreement. This means that email exchanges and text messages with my office should be limited to administrative matters. This includes things such as setting and changing appointments, billing matters, and other related issues. You should be aware that I cannot guarantee the confidentiality of any information communicated by email or text. Therefore, I will not discuss any sensitive or private information by email or text and prefer that you do not either. Also, I do not always regularly check my email or texts, so these methods should not be used if there is an emergency.

- If an urgent issue arises, you should feel free to attempt to reach me by phone. I will try to return your call within 24 hours, except on weekends and holidays. If you are unable to reach me and feel that you cannot wait for me to return your call, contact your family physician or the nearest hospital emergency department. If I will be unavailable for an extended time, I will provide you with the name of a colleague to contact in my absence, if necessary.

- I have a legal and ethical responsibility to make my best efforts to protect all communications that are a part of our work together. However, the nature of electronic communication technologies is such that I cannot guarantee that our communications will be kept confidential or that other people may not gain access to our communications. I will try to use updated encryption methods, firewalls, and back-up systems to help keep your information private, but there is a risk that our electronic communications may be compromised, unsecured, or accessed by others. You should also take reasonable steps to ensure the security of our communications (for example, only using secure networks for our sessions and having passwords to protect the device you use). Please let me know if you have any questions about the exceptions to confidentiality that I have explained to you.

- I will let you know if I decide that providing services to you remotely is no longer appropriate. We will discuss your possible use of in-person services or referrals to another professional who can provide appropriate services.

- Assessing and evaluating threats and other emergencies can be more difficult when providing and receiving services remotely. To address some of these difficulties, we will create an emergency plan before beginning our work together. I will ask you to identify an emergency contact person who is near your location and who I will contact in the event of a crisis or emergency. I will ask that you sign a separate authorization form allowing me to contact your emergency contact person if needed during such a crisis or emergency.

- If one of our sessions is interrupted for any reason (such as the technological connection fails) and you are having an emergency, do not call me back; instead, call 911 or go to your nearest hospital emergency department. Call me back after you have called or obtained emergency services. If the session is interrupted and you are not having an emergency, disconnect from the session and I will wait two minutes and then recontact you via the platform on which we agreed to conduct our work together. If you do not receive a call back within two minutes, then call me on the phone number I provided you (XXX-XXX-XXXX).

- Please do not record our sessions in any way unless agreed to in writing by mutual consent. I will maintain a record of our session in accordance with my policies in the same way I maintain records of in-person sessions.

Agency managers, of course, may want to modify these statements to suit their unique clientele and practice setting.

Confidentiality and Privacy

Professionals in nonprofit organizations have always understood their obligation to protect client and consumer privacy and confidentiality and to be familiar with widely recognized exceptions; for example; when mandatory reporting laws concerning abuse and neglect require disclosure of information without client or consumer consent or when laws or court orders require such disclosure during legal proceedings. The rapid emergence of ICT in nonprofit organizations to deliver services and communicate with clients and consumers has added a new layer of challenging privacy and confidentiality issues that agency managers should address. Fortunately, sophisticated encryption technology can protect privacy and confidentiality very effectively, although it is not foolproof. Nonetheless, many professionals believe that encryption offers significantly more protection than do traditional paper documents (Hu, Chen, & Hou, 2010).

For example, nonprofit social service agencies that offer video counseling services must recognize that staffers have much less control over confidentiality than when they provide traditional office-based services. For instance, a client receiving video counseling services may invite a family member or acquaintance to sit in on a session—outside of camera range—without the counselor's knowledge or consent.

Encryption of online communications is more challenging with some forms of technology than with others. Agency staff cannot presume that the Internet sites and electronic tools they use are necessarily encrypted. Indeed, managers are wise not to assume that Internet sites and electronic tools they use are truly encrypted, and ultimately the ethical burden is on nonprofit managers to ensure trustworthy encryption by carefully examining statements and guarantees made by software vendors.

To practice ethically, agency managers who authorize use of ICT must develop privacy and confidentiality protocols that include several key elements. The staff must review and always adhere to relevant laws and regulations. For example, managers who oversee distance and remote behavioral health services should consult federal and state laws pertaining to the confidentiality of health and mental health records (and the exceptions to clients' right to confidentiality) to protect clients and third parties from harm.

Moreover, managers must develop sound policies concerning staffers conducting online searches to gather information about clients and consumers (deploying widely used online search engines) without their knowledge or consent; some clients and consumers may feel overexposed and violated by staff's attempts to conduct online searches for information about them (Clinton, Silverman, & Brendel, 2010). In the human services, the presumption is that staff members will generally respect client privacy and avoid searching online for information about clients without their knowledge or consent (National Association of Social Workers [NASW], 2021; NASW, Association of Social Work Boards, Council on Social Work Education, & Clinical Social Work Association, 2017). Emerging standards in the human services acknowledge that there are exceptional instances in which it may be ethical for professionals to conduct such online searches for information about clients. Examples might include situations in which a high-risk, vulnerable client who has been receiving mental health services has disappeared and not been in contact with the provider, or when a staff member who provides home-based services searches publicly available judicial databases to determine whether there may be a safety risk during home visits. Nonprofit managers would do well to establish written policies and protocols that spell out when such online searches would be appropriate and the criteria and procedures staff should use to make such determinations.

Legal Dimensions

In addition, nonprofit managers must ensure that staff know how to respond to subpoenas and court orders to release what lawyers refer to as electronically stored information (ESI); legal and ethical standards are evolving regarding third parties' right to ESI during legal proceedings and the clinician's ability to protect this information (Grimm, Ziccardi, & Major, 2009).

Likely, most contemporary managers did not learn how to protect ESI when they completed their professional education; until recently, this content was not even included in educational curricula for students of management and administration. ESI is generally defined as all information stored in computers and other electronic or digital devices. This includes e-mail, voicemail, instant and text messages, databases, metadata, and any other digital images and files. During legal proceedings (for example, when agency clients are involved in termination of parental rights proceedings, child custody disputes, divorce transactions, malpractice litigation, workers' compensation proceedings, and criminal court matters), attorneys may seek to access staff's ESI, usually through subpoenas and court orders. In fact, there is now a subspecialty (known in legal circles as e-discovery) that refers to any process in which electronic data are sought, located, secured, and searched with the intent of using such data as evidence in a civil or criminal legal case.

Attorneys now learn about how to access ESI and about pertinent legal guidelines concerning what can and cannot be discovered. For example, the Federal Rules of Civil Procedure (U.S. Government Printing Office, 2020) that have, since 1938, governed court procedure for civil cases in federal courts have been amended to include guidelines pertaining to discovery of ESI. The rules now state that a party in a civil matter may formally request that another party

> produce and permit the requesting party or its representative to inspect, copy, test, or sample the following items in the responding party's possession, custody, or control . . . any designated documents or electronically stored information—including writings, drawings, graphs, charts, photographs, sound recordings, images, and other data or data compilations—stored in any medium from which information can be obtained either directly or, if necessary, after translation by the responding party into a reasonably usable form. (Federal Rules of Civil Procedure, 2020, Rule 34, p. 56)

Also, managers should ensure that staff's means of electronic data gathering adhere to the privacy and security standards of applicable laws. These laws may address electronic transactions, client rights, and allowable disclosure (Association of Social Work Boards, 2015). An increasing number of nonprofit organizations and individual practitioners are conducting what are known as privacy audits to ensure compliance with current standards. Many of the current privacy audit standards were developed with two prominent sets of federal standards in mind: HIPAA and the Health Information Technology for Economic and Clinical Health (HITECH) Act (P.L. 111-5) of 2009. HIPAA, which has become the gold standard related to privacy, is very well known. As managers know, HIPAA was enacted in 1996 by the U.S. Congress and signed by President Bill Clinton, setting the standard for protecting sensitive client data. Any health care provider that deals with protected health information (PHI) must ensure that all of the required physical, network, and process security measures are in place and followed.

Less well known is the HITECH Act, part of the larger American Recovery and Reinvestment Act of 2009 (P.L. 111-5), which includes provisions requiring organizations to conduct privacy audits. Subtitle D of the HITECH Act addresses the privacy and security concerns associated with the electronic transmission of health information, in part through several provisions that strengthen the civil and criminal enforcement of the HIPAA rules. Organizations and third-party payers are expected to monitor for breaches of PHI from both internal and external sources.

In 2012, the U.S. Office for Civil Rights released criteria that its auditors use to validate compliance with federal regulations. They provide a useful guide for nonprofit organizations that conduct their own privacy audits. Key audit activities include the following:

- Determine the activities that will be tracked or audited: Obtain and review documentation to determine whether audit controls have been implemented over information systems that contain or use PHI.
- Select the tools that will be deployed for auditing activity reviews: Inquire of management as to whether systems and applications have been evaluated to determine whether upgrades are necessary. Obtain and review documentation of tools or applications that management has identified to capture the appropriate audit information.
- Develop and deploy the information review and audit policy: Obtain and review formal or informal policies and procedures and evaluate the content to understand whether a formal audit policy is in place to communicate the details of the entity's audits and reviews to the workforce. Obtain and review an email, or some form of communication, showing that the audit policy has been successfully communicated to the workforce.
- Develop appropriate standard operating protocols: Obtain and review the procedures management has put in place to determine the systems and applications to be audited and how they will be audited.

The American Health Information Management Association (AHIMA) —a prominent organization dedicated to improving the management of health-related information—has developed comprehensive protocols for professionals who want to conduct privacy audits. Their guidelines are especially valuable for nonprofit managers. According to AHIMA, privacy audits should produce detailed audit logs that are useful for the following:

- detecting unauthorized access to client information
- establishing a culture of responsibility and accountability
- reducing the risk associated with inappropriate access
- providing forensic evidence during investigations of suspected and known security incidents and breaches to client privacy, especially if sanctions against a workforce member, business associate, or other contracted agent will be applied
- tracking disclosures of PHI
- responding to client privacy concerns regarding unauthorized access by family members, friends, or others
- evaluating the overall effectiveness of the organization's policy and user education regarding appropriate access and use of client information (this includes comparing actual workforce activity with expected activity and discovering where additional training or education may be necessary to reduce errors)
- detecting new threats and intrusion attempts
- identifying potential problems
- addressing compliance with regulatory and accreditation requirements

Boundary Issues and Conflicts of Interest

Seasoned agency managers understand their duty to avoid conflicts of interest that may harm their organizations and those whom they serve (Brownlee, 1996; Campbell & Gordon, 2003; Daley & Doughty, 2006; Reamer, 2012a, 2018f, 2021a; Zur, 2007). Nonprofit organizations' use of ICT has introduced new and complicated boundary issues that require sound policies and protocols. In the human services, for example, agency staffers sometimes receive requests from current and former clients asking to be social networking friends. Electronic contact with current and former clients on social networking sites can lead to boundary confusion (Gabbard, Kassaw, & Perez-Garcia, 2011; MacDonald, Sohn, & Ellis, 2010; Recupero & Reamer, 2018). Electronic message exchanges between staffers and clients that occur outside of normal business hours, especially if the staffer uses a personal social networking site or email address, may blur practitioner–client boundaries. Professionals who choose not to accept a client's friend request on a social networking site (to maintain clear boundaries) may inadvertently cause the client to feel a sense of rejection. Staff should anticipate this possibility and explain to clients how they handle clients' Facebook requests.

In addition, clients and consumers who are able to access staffers' publicly available social networking sites may learn a great deal of personal information about them (with respect to their personal and family relationships, social and religious activities, and political views); this reality may introduce complex boundary conundrums with the practitioner–client relationship. Some leaders have managed this risk by limiting employees' Facebook communications to sites expressly designed for agency communications with the public—as opposed to staff members' personal Facebook communications. Managers should ensure that staff understand that they must maintain strict privacy settings on their online social networking sites to minimize this risk.

Moreover, newer forms of distance service delivery may introduce conflicts of interest previously unknown to managers in nonprofit organizations. For example, some video counseling software used by staffers in nonprofit mental health agencies is offered free to the agencies that employ them; the Web sites' sponsors pay for their development and maintenance. In return, sponsors post electronic links to the online screen that take users to Web sites that include information about their products and services. Agency clients may believe that the professionals who are serving them (and their employers) are endorsing these products and services or benefit from sales.

Documentation and Records

Maintaining high-quality records is essential in nonprofit organizations, especially when staff provide clinical services. Records are necessary for thorough client assessment; planning and delivery of services; accountability to clients, insurers, agencies, courts, and utilization review organizations; ensuring continuity and coordination of services; providing quality supervision; and evaluating services (Sidell, 2015). Managers must develop strict protocols to ensure that staffers' professionally relevant email, text, and social networking (for example, Facebook) exchanges are documented properly in case records. These are relatively new expectations that are not reflected in long-standing training and literature on professional documentation (Sidell, 2015).

To practice ethically, nonprofit managers who authorize staffers to use digital and other technology to provide distance services must develop records and documentation protocols that include several key elements. Guidelines should ensure proper encryption; reasonable and appropriate access by colleagues to electronic records and documents (for example, when a staff member is incapacitated and a colleague provides coverage); documentation of remote sessions, e-mail, text messages, and cybertherapy communications; compliance with laws, regulations, and agency policies concerning record and document retention; and proper disposal and destruction of records. Insurance companies now cover remote counseling, requiring agencies and practitioners to comply with strict documentation guidelines. Hence, many agencies wisely subscribe to HIPAA-compliant online software packages to ensure proper protection.

Nonprofit managers who maintain electronic records in their organizations for clinical services should be familiar with HIPAA's specific protection of what the law refers to as "psychotherapy notes." The federal law, known as the Privacy Rule, defines psychotherapy notes as those recorded by a mental health professional who is documenting or analyzing the contents of a conversation during a private, group, joint, or family counseling session. They are *separate* from the rest of the client's health record (for example, they may constitute a separate tab in the electronic record labeled "psychotherapy notes"). Psychotherapy notes usually include clinical observations; the counselor's impressions or hypotheses regarding diagnosis; questions to ask supervisors; and any thoughts or feelings they have about a client's unique situation. Unlike traditional progress notes, psychotherapy notes are private and do not include medication details or records, test results, summaries of diagnoses or treatment plans, symptoms or prognoses, or summaries of client progress. After clinical encounters, clinicians can refer to their notes when determining an effective treatment plan. To be considered psychotherapy notes under the law, these notes must be kept separate from clients' general records and billing information. Clinicians and their employing agencies are not permitted to share psychotherapy notes with third parties without a client's authorization; even the client does not have the right to access these notes.

Staff members who enter progress notes, psychotherapy notes, and other important information in electronic records should be aware of the possible risks. In addition to the possibility of security breaches, managers should ensure that staff avoid what has become known as "copy and paste bloat," which occurs when, to save time, practitioners copy previous entries into a new note (Siegler & Adelman, 2009; Sulmasy, Lopez, Horwitch, & American College of Physicians Ethics, Professionalism, and Human Rights Committee, 2017). Hasty copying and pasting, especially without careful proofreading, can lead to significant errors. The pasted note may include details that are not accurate and that can lead to misinterpretation when reviewed by agency colleagues. In addition to perpetuating inaccuracies, such copying and pasting can constitute fraud. There is also a related risk of note bloat in electronic records that occurs when copied and pasted notes include excessive extraneous details (Sulmasy et al., 2017).

Another risk associated with electronic records is the problem of autopopulation. Some practitioners' and agencies' electronic records automatically populate, or fill in, different data fields when a user logs into a record. This can lead to inaccuracies when the data that are filled in are not current (Sukel, 2019).

Managers and supervisors should also advise staff who use electronic records to log off once they have completed their entries. If they do not do so, another staff member's subsequent entries could mistakenly be attributed to the employee who neglected to log off. This, too, could expose the staff member who did not log off to significant malpractice exposure if the notes that are wrongly attributed contain errors or are substandard.

Many nonprofits now permit staffers to access clients' electronic records remotely, which is convenient when a professional is on call after hours and needs to access up-to-date client information during a consultation. However, such remote access also comes with risks. For example, staff that access clients' records from their homes or public computers must ensure that family members or strangers do not view the online information inappropriately if they share a computer. Managers should acquaint staff with this risk; agency policies should address this issue to ensure protection of clients' privacy.

To protect clients and reduce risk, staffers who use electronic records should develop guidelines and protocols that include these key elements:

- Avoid cutting and pasting.
- Understand the software's automatic populating features and their implications. Moreover, where appropriate, remove the automatic population function.
- Periodically print out a representative sample of client records and review them for accuracy and clarity.
- Understand the ways in which the software creates a digital footprint and permanent record of each keystroke and entry. In this context, identify which parties may be able to access the electronic record and the potential implications for both clients and service providers.
- Create security protections on hardware and software. In addition to encryption, the software should include an automatic lock-out after a specified period of inactivity.
- Ensure compliance with federal and state confidentiality laws. Enter into appropriate confidentiality agreements with third parties that may have access to clients' electronic health records.

Another potential danger is associated with what have become known as client portals. An increasing number of nonprofit agencies, especially those linked to hospitals and other integrated care settings, permit clients to access all or a portion of their electronic records by logging in with a unique username and password. On the one hand, allowing clients to access their records can enhance their knowledge about their condition and active involvement in their care. On the other hand, such access can lead to a privacy breach and client misunderstanding of the electronic record's content (for example, misinterpreting the language of a clinical diagnosis or narrative). To reduce risk, managers who permit clients to access their electronic record should develop guidelines that include a number of key elements:

1. To protect client privacy and prevent security breaches:

    - Require each client to register with a unique username and password.
    - Screen any sensitive client information that might be posted.
    - Discuss portal access guidelines in all privacy and security policies and procedures that are provided to clients.
    - Review policies related to clients' use of portals in the organization's annual information technology security risk assessment.

2. To reduce the risk of inappropriate client use of portals:

    - Describe appropriate and inappropriate use.
    - Specify how clients may communicate through the portal and what they should expect for a response turnaround time.
    - Outline the extent to which clients are permitted to upload information to their electronic record, as well as the content of information that is acceptable.
    - Have the client sign a portal user agreement and provide them with a signed copy.
    - Include information at the portal entry about guidelines for use, including that it should not be used for emergencies; also include instructions for what to do in the event of an emergency.
    - Follow relevant federal and state laws related to privacy, confidentiality, privileged communication, and informed consent. Legal consultation may be appropriate in this regard.
    - Comply with federal and state confidentiality laws and enter into appropriate confidentiality agreements with third parties who may access clients' electronic health records.
    - Create policies governing use of the portal by minors, including access to information in the portal by minors' parents and guardians.

Collegial Relationships

In their organizations, nonprofit managers must also set standards governing employees' treatment of one another on online and other electronic platforms. More specifically, managers should develop policies that address employees' online treatment of colleagues, including cyberbullying, online harassment, and making derogatory or defamatory comments; disclosing private, confidential, or sensitive information about the work or personal life of any colleague without consent, including messages, photographs, videos, or any other material that could invade or compromise a colleague's privacy; taking reasonable steps to correct or remove any inaccurate or offensive information they have posted online or transmitted about a colleague using technology; acknowledging the work of and contributions made by others and avoiding the use of technology to present the work of others as their own; taking appropriate action should they believe that a colleague who provides electronic services is behaving unethically, is not using appropriate safeguards, or is allowing unauthorized access to electronically stored information; and using professional judgment in taking steps to discourage, prevent, expose, and correct any efforts by colleagues who knowingly produce, possess, download, or transmit illicit or illegal content or images in electronic format. A single online post, email message, or text message can go viral; once they click "send," staffers lose all control over that message's digital destinations.

Defamation occurs when individuals make false statements that injure the reputation of another party and expose them to public contempt, hatred, ridicule, or condemnation. Defamation can take two forms: libel and slander. Libel occurs when the communication is in written form—for example, in a Facebook posting, email message, text message, or tweet about a colleague. Slander occurs when the communication is in oral form—for example, when a staff member makes demeaning and derogatory comments about a colleague. This might occur during an agency-sponsored Skype or Zoom call online.

In the digital age, agency staff members can be legally liable for defamation of character if they post online comments or send electronic messages about a colleague that have the following three elements: (1) the allegations about the colleague were untrue; (2) the staffer knew or should have known that the comments were untrue; and (3) the comments caused some injury to the colleague.

Managers' and employees' defamatory statements about colleagues—for example, about their alleged incompetence, unethical conduct, or mental status—can cause the colleague emotional distress, damage the colleague's reputation, or cause financial harm by jeopardizing the colleague's career in some way. Ideally, of course, employees and staff should address workplace and colleague disputes constructively, thoughtfully, and face to face instead of airing their grievances electronically.

Practitioner Competence

Nonprofit managers and supervisors certainly understand their obligation to hire qualified and competent employees. Nevertheless, the emergence of digital tools and other technology-driven options has added a new set of essential competencies. Use of this technology requires a great deal of technical mastery, in addition to awareness of, and compliance with, rapidly developing standards and ethical guidelines. Managers are responsible for designing and implementing protocols to ensure that their staff have the necessary competencies. This is especially so when staff who have relatively little experience using ICT to provide services remotely must do so suddenly, for example, in the midst of a pandemic such as COVID-19.

To practice ethically, staff members in nonprofit organizations who use ICT must obtain training and continuing education focused explicitly on the use of distance service-delivery technology. Such training should include developing protocols for screening potential clients, obtaining clients' informed consent, assessing clinical needs, maintaining confidentiality, implementing distance interventions, maintaining clear boundaries, managing documentation and client records, and terminating services (Reamer, 2018c, 2018d, 2019, 2021b). Such knowledge and skills include knowing how to communicate effectively while using ICT, including how to handle emergency situations from a remote location and how to apply the laws of both the staff's and client's jurisdiction; sensitivity to the client's culture; attending to clients' unique needs and challenges; and ensuring that the technology is in working order to provide effective services and avoid disruption.

One should also note that an increasing number of nonprofit organizations are using technology to serve clients who live in other states. Hence, nonprofit managers must keep current with evolving licensing laws and regulations regarding use of technology to provide services across jurisdictional lines. Many states' laws prohibit professionals from providing distance services that are received in states in which the practitioners do not hold a license, except in emergency circumstances recognized by law.

Conclusion

Nonprofit organization management and leadership have been transformed by the emergence of ICT. Most contemporary organizational leaders completed their formal education before currently available technology was invented and therefore at a time when relationships with clients and consumers were limited to ongoing face-to-face meetings and services. In contrast, today's agencies have the capacity to serve clients and consumers they may never meet in person.

Practitioners now use ICT to communicate using video, text messaging, and email, often for clinical and case management purposes. Moreover, staff are now navigating boundary issues related to clients', consumers', and staffers' use of online social networking sites and electronic search engines. In fact, staff in integrated care settings today are often managing complex confidentiality issues pertaining to colleagues' access to sensitive information about clients and consumers stored in electronic records (Reamer, 2018a).

Today's nonprofit leaders and managers must therefore make thoughtful decisions about the ways in which they will incorporate ICT into their organizations' repertoires to provide services and manage information. They must reflect anew on the meaning and nature of the professional/client–consumer relationship and the ways in which use of ICT enhances or detracts from it. They must also keep in mind that this is a rapidly developing component of professional practice, one in which ethical and risk management standards will continue to evolve.

Skills Application Exercises

1. You are the executive director of a community mental health center in a large metropolitan area. Recently, your agency received a large federal grant to design and deliver distance behavioral health services to rural, underserved communities in your state. The client population includes people who live far from your mental health center and who struggle with a wide range of mental health challenges. Services will include remote video counseling and text-based communications between agency staff and clients. Prepare a comprehensive list of issues you would need to address as part of a strategic plan to introduce this technology and remote service delivery to your agency. What specific steps would you take to implement this plan (including hiring of relevant personnel)?

2. You are the clinical director of an outpatient substance use disorders treatment program. Your staff includes licensed social workers, mental health counselors, and addictions professionals. Your agency is in the process of seeking national accreditation. Your agency provides clients with remote counseling and case management services using smartphone apps, video, email, and text messaging. Agency staff document services in an electronic record. Clients are invited to create an online portal that enables them to access their service providers' case notes and exchange messages. In anticipation of a visit by funders and an accreditation site visit team, the agency's executive director asked you to chair a task force that would identify (1) relevant ethical issues associated with the agency's use of technology to serve clients and (2) specific steps the agency has taken to protect clients who use this technology (Edwards, 2020). What ethical issues would be on your list? What specific steps would you take to ensure that the agency adequately addresses them?

3. You are the director of risk management in a large urban hospital. Your board of directors approved implementation of state-of-the-art electronic health record software that can be accessed by hospital employees. The software will also provide patients with the opportunity to access their health records remotely. What policies and protocols would you put in place to determine which hospital staff should be permitted to access PHI that is included in patients' records? What criteria would you establish to determine which specific information in the records practitioners would be permitted to access? What policies and protocols would you establish governing patients' access to their own electronic health records (to protect patient privacy and ensure patient safety)?

4. You are the executive director of a large program that provides residential and outpatient services to children and adolescents who have been abused and neglected. Recently, your agency began using ICT to provide remote services to clients who have been discharged from the residential program to provide comprehensive follow-up care. Your agency documents services to clients in electronic records and uses video, texting, and email messaging to serve clients living in the community. You want to conduct a privacy audit using guidelines developed by the Office for Civil Rights to ensure compliance with federal regulations that were summarized in this chapter. In addition, you want to draw on relevant recommendations made by the

American Health Information Management Association (also summarized herein). What specific steps would you take to conduct the privacy audit? What information would you need to conduct it?

References

Allison, M., & Kaye, J. (2015). *Strategic planning for nonprofit organizations: A practical guide for dynamic times* (3rd ed.). Hoboken, NJ: Wiley.

American Recovery and Reinvestment Act of 2009, P.L. 111-5, 123 Stat. 115.

Anderson, S. C., & Guyton, M. R. (2013). Ethics in an age of information seekers: A survey of licensed healthcare providers about online social networking. *Journal of Technology in Human Services, 31*, 112–128.

Association of Social Work Boards. (2015). *Model regulatory standards for technology and social work practice.* Culpeper, VA: Author.

Barak, A., & Grohol, J. M. (2011). Current and future trends in Internet-supported mental health interventions. *Journal of Technology in Human Services, 29*, 155–196.

Barsky, A. (2017). Social work practice and technology: Ethical issues and policy responses. *Journal of Technology in Human Services, 35,* 8–19.

Berg, J. W., Appelbaum, P. S., Lidz, C. W., & Parker, L. S. (2001). *Informed consent: Legal theory and clinical practice* (2nd ed.). Oxford, England: Oxford University Press.

Brownlee, K. (1996). The ethics of nonsexual dual relationships: A dilemma for the rural mental health professional. *Community Mental Health Journal, 32*, 497–503.

Bryson, J. (2018). *Strategic planning for public and nonprofit organizations* (5th ed.). Hoboken, NJ: Wiley.

Campbell, C. D., & Gordon, M. C. (2003). Acknowledging the inevitable: Understanding multiple relationships in rural practice. *Professional Psychology: Research and Practice, 34*, 430–434.

Casey, W. (2009). *Firsts: Origins of everyday things that changed the world.* New York: Alpha Press.

Chan, C., & Holosko, M. (2016). A review of information and communication technology enhanced social work interventions. *Research on Social Work Practice, 26*, 88–100.

Chang, T. (2005). Online counseling: Prioritizing psychoeducation, self-help, and mutual help for counseling psychology research and practice. *Counseling Psychologist, 33*, 881–890.

Chester, A., & Glass, C. A. (2006). Online counseling: A descriptive analysis of therapy services on the internet. *British Journal of Guidance and Counseling, 34,* 145–160.

Clinton, B. K., Silverman, B., & Brendel, D. (2010). Patient-targeted Googling: The ethics of searching online for patient information. *Harvard Review of Psychiatry, 18,* 103–112.

Daley, M. R., & Doughty, M. O. (2006). Ethics complaints in social work practice: A rural–urban comparison. *Journal of Social Work Values and Ethics, 3*(1), 44–60. Retrieved from http://jswve.org/download/2006-1/JSWVE-Spring-2006-Complete.pdf

Edwards, R. L. (2020). *Building a strong foundation: Fundraising for nonprofits* (2nd ed.). Washington, DC: NASW Press.

Finn, J., & Barak, A. (2010). A descriptive study of e-counsellor attitudes, ethics, and practice. *Counselling and Psychotherapy Review, 24,* 268–277.

Gabbard, G., Kassaw, G., & Perez-Garcia, G. (2011). Professional boundaries in the era of the Internet. *Academic Psychiatry, 35,* 168–174.

Grant, G. B., & Grobman, L. M. (1998). *The social worker's Internet handbook.* Harrisburg, PA: White Hat Communications.

Grimm, P. W., Ziccardi, M. V., & Major, A. W. (2009). Back to the future: Lorraine v. Markel American Insurance Co. and new findings on the admissibility of electronically stored information. *Akron Law Review, 42,* 357–418.

Haberstroh, S. (2009). Strategies and resources for conducting online counseling. *Journal of Professional Counseling: Practice, Theory and Research, 37,* 1–20.

Harlow, E., & Webb, S. (Eds.). (2003). *Information and communication technologies in the welfare services.* London: Jessica Kingsley.

Health Insurance Portability and Accountability Act of 1996 (HIPAA), P.L. 104-191, 42 U.S.C. § 300gg, 29 U.S.C. §§ 1181–1183, and 42 U.S.C. §§ 1320d–1320d9.

Health Information Technology for Economic and Clinical Health Act of 2009, P.L. 111-5, 42 U.S.C. 300jj (*et seq.*; 17901 *et seq.*).

Hu, J., Chen, H., & Hou, T. (2010). A hybrid public key infrastructure solution (HPKI) for HIPAA privacy/security regulations. *Computer Standards and Interfaces, 32,* 274–280.

Kanani, K., & Regehr, C. (2003). Clinical, ethical, and legal issues in e-therapy. *Families in Society, 84,* 155–162.

Kowal, J., Kuzio, A., & Wawrzak-Chodaczek, M. (2015). *Communication and information technology in society.* Newcastle upon Tyne, England: Cambridge Scholars Publishing.

Lamendola, W. (2010). Social work and social presence in an online world. *Journal of Technology in the Human Services, 28,* 108–119.

Lindeman, D. (2011). Interview: Lessons from a leader in telehealth diffusion: A conversation with Adam Darkins of the Veterans Health Administration. *Ageing International, 36,* 146–154.

MacDonald, J., Sohn, S., & Ellis, P. (2010). Privacy, professionalism and Facebook: A dilemma for young doctors. *Medical Education, 44,* 805–813.

Martinez, R. C., & Clark, C. L. (2000). *The social worker's guide to the Internet.* Boston: Allyn & Bacon.

McCarty, D., & Clancy, C. (2002). Telehealth: Implications for social work practice. *Social Work, 47,* 153–161.

Menon, G. M., & Miller-Cribbs, J. (2002). Online social work practice: Issues and guidelines for the profession. *Advances in Social Work, 3,* 104–116.

Midkiff, D., & Wyatt, W. J. (2008). Ethical issues in the provision of online mental health services (etherapy). *Technology in Human Services, 26,* 310–332.

National Association of Social Workers. (2021). *National Association of Social Workers code of ethics.* Retrieved from https://www.socialworkers.org/About/Ethics/Code-of-Ethics/Code-of-Ethics-English

National Association of Social Workers, Association of Social Work Boards, Council on Social Work Education, & Clinical Social Work Association. (2017). *Standards for technology in social work practice.* Washington, DC: National Association of Social Workers.

Reamer, F. G. (2012a). *Boundary issues and dual relationships in the human services.* New York: Columbia University Press.

Reamer, F. G. (2012b). The digital and electronic revolution in social work: Rethinking the meaning of ethical practice. *Ethics and Social Welfare, 7,* 2–19.

Reamer, F. G. (2013a). Distance and online social work education: Novel ethical challenges. *Journal of Teaching in Social Work, 33,* 369–384.

Reamer, F. G. (2013b). Social work in a digital age: Ethical and risk management challenges. *Social Work, 58,* 163–172.

Reamer, F. G. (2015a). Clinical social work in a digital environment: Ethical and risk-management challenges. *Clinical Social Work Journal, 43,* 120–132.

Reamer, F. G. (2015b). *Risk management in social work: Preventing professional malpractice, liability, and disciplinary action.* New York: Columbia University Press.

Reamer, F. G. (2017). Evolving ethical standards in the digital age. *Australian Social Work, 70,* 148–159.

Reamer, F. G. (2018a). Ethical issues in integrated health care: Implications for social workers. *Health & Social Work, 43*, 118–124.

Reamer, F. G. (2018b). Ethical standards for social workers' use of technology: Emerging consensus. *Journal of Social Work Values and Ethics, 15*, 71–80.

Reamer, F. G. (2018c). *Ethical standards in social work: A review of the NASW code of ethics* (3rd ed.). Washington, DC: NASW Press.

Reamer, F. G. (2018d). Evolving standards of care in the age of cybertechnology. *Behavioral Sciences and the Law, 36*, 257–269.

Reamer, F. G. (2018e). *The social work ethics casebook: Cases and commentary* (2nd ed.). Washington, DC: NASW Press.

Reamer, F. G. (2018f). *Social work values and ethics* (5th ed.). New York: Columbia University Press.

Reamer, F. G. (2019). Social work education in a digital world: Technology standards for education and practice. *Journal of Social Work Education, 55*, 420–432.

Reamer, F. G. (2021a). *Boundary issues and dual relationships in the human services* (3rd ed.). New York: Columbia University Press.

Reamer, F. G. (2021b). *Ethics and risk management in online and distance social work*. San Diego: Cognella.

Recupero, P., & Rainey, S. E. (2005). Forensic aspects of e-therapy. *Journal of Psychiatric Practice, 11*, 405–410.

Recupero, P., & Reamer, F. (2018). The Internet and forensic ethics. In E. Griffith (Ed.), *Ethics challenges in forensic psychiatry and psychology practice* (pp. 208–222). New York: Columbia University Press.

Richards, D., & Vigano, N. (2013). Online counseling: A narrative and critical review of the literature. *Journal of Clinical Psychology, 69*, 994–1011.

Rummell, C. M., & Joyce, N. R. (2010). "So wat do u want to wrk on 2 day?": The ethical implications of online counselling. *Ethics and Behavior, 20*, 482–496.

Santhiveeran, J. (2009). Compliance of social work e-therapy websites to the NASW code of ethics. *Social Work in Health Care, 48*, 1–13.

Schoech, D. (1999). *Human services technology: Understanding, designing, and implementing computer and Internet applications in social services*. Philadelphia: Haworth Press.

Sidell, N. L. (2015). *Social work documentation: A guide to strengthening your case recording* (2nd ed.). Washington, DC: NASW Press.

Siegler, E., & Adelman, R. (2009). Copy and paste: A remediable hazard of electronic health records. *American Journal of Medicine, 122*, 495–496.

Skinner, A., & Zack, J. S. (2004). Counseling and the Internet. *American Behavioral Scientist, 48*, 434–446.

Sukel, K. (2019, May 23). Is your EHR a malpractice risk? *Medical Economics, 96*(11). Retrieved from https://www.medicaleconomics.com/news/your-ehr-malpractice-risk

Sulmasy, L., Lopez, A., Horwitch, C., & American College of Physicians Ethics, Professionalism, and Human Rights Committee. (2017). Ethical implications of the electronic health record: In the service of the patient. *Journal of General Internal Medicine, 32*, 935–939.

TrustPARMA. (2021). *Resources for practitioners for telepsychology and COVID-19.* Retrieved from https://parma.trustinsurance.com/Workshops-Webinars/Telepsychology

U.S. Government Publishing Office. (2020). *Federal rules of civil procedure.* Washington, DC: Author.

Zimmerman, L., & Broughton, A. (2006). Assessing, planning, and managing information technology. In R. L. Edwards & J. A. Yankey (Eds.), *Effectively managing nonprofit organizations* (pp. 327–344). Washington, DC: NASW Press.

Zur, O. (2007). *Boundaries in psychotherapy: Ethical and clinical explorations.* Washington, DC: American Psychological Association.

Zur, O. (2012). Telepsychology or telementalhealth in the digital age: The future is here. *California Psychologist, 45*(1), 13–15.

PART FIVE
Directing Skills

DIRECTING SKILLS ENCOMPASS THOSE REQUISITE FOR EXCELLENCE IN MACRO management. Expertise in this area emphasizes a leader's ability to see the big picture and to have the conceptual foresight and wisdom to think both inside and outside the box at the same time. Thinking strategically (as well as tactically), appreciating the manifest (as well as latent) strengths inherent in one's board, and being open to both inter- and intrapreneurial innovation are all part of the equation.

In chapter 12, Thomas P. Holland and Myra Blackmon introduce us to the importance of building a strong board of directors. Starting with a review of the core functions of a board, proper criteria for selection of its members, and a board's key functions, they demonstrate how effective boards can add value when properly deployed. Yet Holland and Blackmon are not shy about discussing the building, supporting, and nurturing functions that executives must perform on a systematic basis if they want to reap the rewards that a high-performing board has the capacity to provide.

In chapter 13, Allison Zippay offers a view of strategic management and planning that explicitly underscores the need to make this often-neglected element of leadership more prominent and defined on the always crowded executive agenda. If one accepts the premise that leaders always face choices that represent competing values, then what managerial vision will support long-term planning and strategic management? In this context, Zippay puts forward a conceptual framework to guide a response, in tandem with clear criteria for the selection of a superordinate organizational strategy to address these strategic issues.

In chapter 14, Stephanie Cosner entices readers with the notion of promoting social innovation as a core responsibility of the nonprofit leader. Although many organizational scholars may view entrepreneurship as the primary province of the for-profit corporate arena, Cosner asks us to consider and to embrace its relevance for the nonprofit sector as well. She speaks persuasively about the need for nonprofit leaders to gradually modify their institutional culture in this regard and to consciously increase staff interest and competency in this area while they pursue the fiscal resources, in-house technology, and human capital to ensure they will have the capacity to engage in social innovation. She concludes with the conviction that such imaginative activity is both an emerging opportunity and a responsibility of nonprofit leaders if they are to provide comprehensive creative solutions.

12

Achieving an Effective, High-Performing Board

Thomas P. Holland and Myra Blackmon

The competing values framework suggests that managers must be adept at performing many roles simultaneously (see chapter 1). Some of these roles involve attending to the organization's external environment and providing appropriate structure. Given that nonprofit organizations are established to accomplish societal objectives, managers must be aware of environmental trends that affect the organization and its users, supporters, clients, or patrons. Managers must be concerned about the process of establishing organizational goals, ensuring organizational continuity and goodwill, and stimulating the individual and collective achievement of staff and volunteers.

The governing board, often called the board of directors or board of trustees, is a nonprofit organization's most important volunteer entity. Having an effective, supportive, and involved governing board is essential for an organization's long-term success. The governing board carries out a range of vital functions for any nonprofit organization. Its members—sometimes called trustees, overseers, or directors—are people whom the community entrusts the power to act as fiduciaries and to guide their organizations with care, skill, and integrity. They represent the voice of society and are expected to act on behalf of the interests of the community, constituents, and sponsors. Creating, nurturing, and renewing this core group of leaders are basic requisites for an organization's survival and effectiveness.

Basic Functions of the Board

The board has a wide range of functions and responsibilities. As summarized by Houle (1989) and others (Klein, 2016; Scott, 2000; Widmer & Houchin, 2000), these functions and responsibilities include

- formulating and sustaining the mission of the organization, then ensuring that each service and activity of the organization is consistent with the mission and focused on accomplishing the collective goals

- representing the interests of those sponsors whose resources allow the organization to pursue its mission while balancing those interests with the needs of the intended beneficiaries of the services

- translating values into policies that guide the operations of the organization, which provides the top-level manager (hereinafter referred to as the chief executive officer, or CEO) and staff with rules to govern operations and clarifies the allowable parameters for action

- selecting, guiding, overseeing, and evaluating the organization's CEO while allowing that person sufficient latitude to accomplish operating goals and objectives without board interference in day-to-day operations

- obtaining, allocating, and monitoring the use of the organization's resources, which includes fiduciary responsibility and accountability for all financial resources, as well as helping to "make fundraising an organizational priority and participate in it personally" (Bray, 2019, p. 11).

- working with the CEO to develop long-range plans and to revise them periodically; such plans also provide the basis for evaluation of the CEO and the organization's overall performance

- ensuring that all legal and ethical responsibilities of the organization are being fulfilled, especially in a rapidly changing, technology-driven environment

- ensuring that the organization's goals and objectives are being achieved as efficiently and effectively as possible, including setting aside time at regular intervals to assess the board's own performance and composition

In summary, the board is the focus of power and legitimacy of the organization. It brings together representatives of the major stakeholders in the organization and seeks to synthesize their values and concerns into guiding principles for mobilizing and using resources. The board is the arena within which all the competing values, interests, and perspectives are articulated, examined, and resolved into a single direction for the future of the organization. The responsibility of implementing the policy directives of the board falls on the CEO (Carver, 2002b).

Committees and Advisory Groups

Boards have multiple responsibilities—so many, in fact, that they usually delegate specific tasks to a variety of committees the board creates (for example, financial planning, nominating, evaluating the executive, fundraising, personnel, services). These work groups develop specific plans and recommendations for consideration by the full board at its regular meetings, and they may be charged with the responsibility for overseeing the CEO's implementation of recommendations approved by the board.

In addition to regular committees, some boards also create special ancillary structures or advisory groups to provide the board and CEO with particular resources or forms of assistance. For example, a need for specialized expertise in some program or service areas (for example, accessibility by people with special needs, analysis of legislative bills) may prompt the board to establish an advisory group of leading experts in the relevant area that may also include some of the organization's senior staff. Such groups may work closely with the board's own committees and assist their efforts to provide recommendations to the full board, or they may link with the CEO or other management staff, who in turn present the group's recommendations to the board. It is the board's job to determine how best to use ancillary groups to meet the organization's overall goals. To be most effective, a board should have standing committees that directly correspond to the types of decisions and judgments that make up most of its governing work.

Criteria for Selecting Members

The board is composed of leaders who are committed to carrying out their responsibilities so that the organization thrives. For most nonprofit organizations, selecting these members is the responsibility of the board itself, carried out by its committee on nominations. The goal is to have a cohesive group of hard-working, resourceful, creative, and dedicated trustees who work together effectively to mobilize concerted action across the community or region on behalf of the constituencies that the organization intends to serve. The board should be large enough to allow it to carry out its duties yet small enough to be a cohesive working group. It should encompass that blend of diverse characteristics and skills required to carry out the organization's mission (Brown, 2007; Preston & Brown, 2004).

Numerous criteria should be considered in identifying potential board candidates. The following are some of the most important attributes of a good board candidate:

- The candidate should have an interest in learning about and working on the issues of primary concern to the organization and should be interested in and committed to the organization's specific programs or services. As their operating environment grows more complex, boards find it helpful to include members with related areas of interest, such as public policy, legislative processes, financial management, law, fundraising, and community relations.
- The candidate should have a reputation as an opinion leader and be esteemed in the broader community or region. This reputation should include the ability and willingness to open doors to various resources the organization needs.
- The candidate should have the ability to contribute money to the organization or to bring access to others who can provide funds, including key individuals, corporations, and foundations.
- The candidate should have the ability to identify the major issues facing the organization, to focus clearly on the tasks facing the board, and to work effectively with the group to achieve its goals.
- The candidate should have the interpersonal skills and sensitivities necessary to develop, nurture, and sustain communications within the board and among the board members and various outside groups.
- The candidate should play a leadership role with a specific constituency that is important to the organization. This constituency may be defined in terms of age, geographic area, gender, race, profession, or other relevant characteristics.
- The candidate should have a confirmed willingness to make their skills, talents, and time available to the organization. Without this commitment, any other characteristics are of limited value to the organization.

Characteristics of Effective Boards

In addition to being composed of individuals with desirable characteristics, strong boards also have several distinguishing features that relate to the whole group. Researchers (Chait, Holland, & Taylor, 1993; Holland, Chait,

& Taylor, 1989) have found that effective boards differ from ineffective ones on several dimensions: contextual, educational, interpersonal, analytical, political, and strategic.

Contextual Dimension

Effective boards understand and take into account the culture and norms of the organizations they govern. They adapt to the distinctive characteristics and culture of the organization and its staff. Relying on the organization's mission statement, values, and traditions to guide their decisions, they act so as to exemplify and reinforce its core values and commitments. They cultivate this competence in various ways:

- orienting new members to the organization's values, norms, and traditions
- conveying history by inviting former members, administrators, and "living legends" to share background information
- discussing the concepts of shared governance, collegiality, and consensus with guidance of current leaders
- reviewing the organization's hallmark characteristics and basic values with an emphasis on what sets it apart from competitors
- using readings, stories, pledges, and other practices to resocialize members to the board's role and the organization's values
- maintaining explicit consciousness that their actions and decisions are statements of values

Educational Dimension

Effective boards take the necessary steps to ensure that their members are knowledgeable about the organization; the profession; and the board's own roles, responsibilities, and performance. They consciously create opportunities for board education and development. They regularly seek information and feedback on the board's performance. They pause periodically to self-reflect, assess strengths and limitations, and examine and learn from the board's experiences, including its mistakes.

Board members learn how to improve their performance through educational programs and retreats where matters of substance and process are examined. They use introspection on the board's internal operations and the ways that it carries out business. They reflect on the lessons they can learn from their own experiences and mistakes. Other ways that effective boards strengthen this educational competency include the following:

- setting aside some time at each meeting for a seminar or workshop to learn about an important matter of substance or process or to discuss a common reading
- conducting extended retreats every year or two for similar purposes, analyzing the board's operations and its mistakes, or both
- asking members and senior staff to report briefly on the best ideas they heard at a recent conference or meeting
- meeting periodically with role counterparts from comparable organizations
- rotating committee assignments so that members come to know many aspects of the organization
- establishing internal feedback mechanisms such as evaluative comments from members at the end of each meeting, seeking feedback from senior staff and outside observers, and conducting annual surveys of members on individual and collective performance
- using technology, such as board portals, webinars, and online discussions, to provide ready access to in-depth information or updates on recent developments

Interpersonal Dimension

Effective boards nurture the development of their members as a working group, attend to the board's collective welfare, and foster a sense of cohesiveness. They create a sense of inclusiveness among all members, with equal access to information and equal opportunity to participate and influence decisions. They develop goals for the group, and they recognize group achievements (Nicholson, Newton, & McGregor-Lowndes, 2012; Puyvelde, Brown, Walker, & Tenuta, 2018). They identify and cultivate leadership within the board. Board members develop this competence in many ways, including

- creating a sense of inclusiveness through events that enable members to become better acquainted with one another, distributing or posting online annual notebooks with up-to-date biographical sketches of each member, building some slack time into the schedule for informal interaction, and sharing information widely and communicating regularly
- communicating group norms and standards by pairing newcomers with a mentor or coach and by being sure that everyone understands the informal rules of the game

- cultivating the notion of the board as a group by establishing and publicizing group goals for the board itself
- ensuring that the board has strong leadership by systematically grooming its future leaders and encouraging individual growth in skills and contributions to the group.

Analytical Dimension

Effective boards recognize the complexities and subtleties of issues and accept ambiguity and uncertainty as healthy preconditions for critical discussions. They approach matters from a broad institutional outlook, and they critically dissect and examine all aspects of multifaceted issues. They raise doubts, explore trade-offs, and encourage expressions of differences of opinion. This competence is cultivated by

- fostering cognitive complexity by using multiple frames of reference to analyze issues and events
- seeking concrete and even contradictory information on ambiguous matters
- asking a few members to be critical evaluators or devil's advocates, exploring the downside of recommendations and worst-case scenarios
- developing contingency and crisis plans
- having members role-play perspectives of key constituencies
- brainstorming alternative views of issues
- consulting outsiders and seeking different viewpoints
- reinforcing and rewarding constructive criticism

Political Dimension

Effective boards accept as a primary responsibility the need to develop and maintain healthy relationships among major constituencies. They respect the integrity of the governance process and the legitimate roles and responsibilities of other stakeholders. They consult often and communicate directly with key constituencies, and they attempt to minimize conflict and win–lose situations. (Dee & Hendrick, 2006). Board members nurture this competence by

- broadening channels of communication by distributing profiles of board members and annual board reports, inviting staff and consumers

to serve on board committees, periodically inviting outside leaders to address the board, visiting with staff, and establishing multiconstituency task forces
- working closely with the CEO to develop and maintain processes that enable board members to communicate directly with stakeholders
- monitoring the health of relationships and morale in the organization
- avoiding win–lose polarizations and keeping options open
- being sensitive to the legitimate roles and responsibilities of all stakeholders
- using technology and social media to nurture relationships and keep a finger on the pulse of major constituencies
- protecting the integrity of the governance process

Strategic Dimension

Effective boards help the organization envision a direction and shape a strategy for the future. They cultivate and concentrate on processes that sharpen organizational priorities. They organize themselves and conduct their business in light of the organization's strategic priorities. They anticipate potential problems and act before issues become crises. They cultivate this competence in the following ways:

- focusing attention on strategic issues by asking the CEO to present an annual update on organizational priorities and strategy, establishing board priorities and work plans, and developing an annual agenda for the board and its committees
- structuring meetings to concentrate on strategic priorities by prioritizing items on the agenda, providing overviews of the major topics and linkages among committee agendas, and providing a preface to each major policy issue to place it in a larger context
- reinforcing attention on priorities by providing key questions for discussion in advance of meetings, prominently displaying the annual or continuous agenda, reserving time at each meeting for the CEO to discuss future issues, and making use of a consent agenda
- developing a board information system that is strategic, normative, selective, and graphic
- monitoring the use of board time and attention

Such behaviors enable a board to add value to the organization by taking actions and reaching decisions that enhance the organization's long-term vitality and quality. Effective boards intentionally cultivate these skills and apply them in several ways.

How Boards Add Value to Organizations

The skills and practices of high-performing boards serve as examples for other boards to consider. Although not every practice may be transferable, boards that want to improve their effectiveness can selectively draw on the lessons offered by their high-performing counterparts and adapt them locally (Carver, 2002a; Holland, Ritvo, & Kovner, 1997; Taylor, Chait, & Holland, 1996).

Setting Priorities

One basic way that effective nonprofit boards add value to their organizations is by helping the CEO determine what matters most. Working closely with the CEO, the board identifies and examines the most significant issues facing the organization and influencing its future. Not every matter is equally important, and not all issues can be addressed, so the work becomes setting relative priorities. The board concentrates its attention on identifying and addressing such matters.

Boards also add value by creating opportunities for CEOs to think aloud about questions and concerns well before it is necessary to come to conclusions or make recommendations. However, boards do not add much value by listening passively to voluminous reports. If they are to help as sounding boards for executives, they must make time for candid discussion of embryonic ideas, ambiguous issues, and unclear challenges in the road ahead. Through such unstructured discussions, boards can help CEOs frame the issues and reflect on the values, alternative directions, and trade-offs that may eventually lead to a recommendation. Such exploratory discussions allow members' wisdom and counsel to contribute to the definition of issues the organization must face in the future.

Effective boards encourage experimentation, trying out new approaches and alternative ways of dealing with issues. The seeds of change can come from insightful questions that help others think outside the box of old assumptions and patterns. Raising critical questions and challenging assumptions can stimulate new ideas and creative alternatives for the future of the organization (Pound, 1993; Schein, 1993).

Monitoring Progress

Another way that effective boards apply their skills and add value to organizations is by actively monitoring their own progress and assessing their own performance. Most boards are given reams of data on inputs, number of clients or patrons served, and costs of various programs. Less attention is given to the effects or results of those activities. Part of the problem is lack of agreement on what would serve as appropriate indicators of effectiveness. Many board members are unsure how to go about measuring performance or results of the organization's activities (Harrison & Murray, 2014; Tacon, Walters & Cornforth, 2017).

Strong boards have developed sets of specific performance indicators that enable them to monitor performance. These "dashboards" of indicators of key aspects of performance include periodic information on such areas as the number of clients completing recommended services, costs per contact and per program, staff assessments of outcomes, and client or patron satisfaction.

These indicators are especially important as a component of the organization's strategic management plan. Each goal in that plan should have accompanying indicators that allow the board to monitor progress toward its accomplishment. For example, if the plan calls for improvements in the quality of services or staff morale, the board and staff should work together to identify appropriate ways to measure the results of efforts intended to achieve those goals. These indicators should provide the board with means to assess progress, to see whether midcourse corrections are needed, and to draw conclusions about the effects of changes.

Modeling Behavior

Most important, effective boards model the behaviors they desire in others (Holland, 1997a, 2002). Boards are appropriately seen as the leaders of the organization, and their decisions are subjected to critical scrutiny by all constituencies. Boards are appropriately concerned about the quality, costs, productivity, and innovation of staff; however, many boards are hesitant to apply the same expectations to themselves. Boards that call for accountability of staff have far greater credibility if they walk the talk and show by example how quality improvements are made.

Board members cannot be both leaders of change for the organization and followers of the status quo. If they want staff to identify and implement changes that reduce costs and increase productivity, then they should demonstrate that they have defined their own productivity, measured it carefully, and made changes that increase the value they add to the organization. Such efforts put the boards' own actions in line with its policies for the whole organization and demonstrate commitment to them for others to observe and follow.

Conditions for Successful Board Development

In considering efforts to improve board performance, boards encounter many obstacles, some of which they can anticipate. These obstacles include ambiguous expectations, weak accountability, unclear returns on the investments of time for development, and members' discomfort with giving up familiar patterns and practicing new ones. Overcoming these barriers requires the board's concerted and sustained attention. For these efforts to be successful, several conditions must be met:

- A board must be ready for change and accept the importance of attending to and improving its own performance. Board development cannot be imposed on members or top-level management. The CEO, the chairperson, and a substantial number of board leaders must have concerns about the board's performance and want to work on improving it. These leaders must initiate the process with enthusiasm and a clear commitment to working with the board to bring about changes. Many of the members must come to share these concerns in the context of loyalty to the organization and its mission.

- The board must integrate development of improved performance and its business items, rather than doing the business and then doing development. Distinguishing board development from the "real" work of the board is a false dichotomy. The processes of learning how to work together more effectively should be embedded within the efforts to carry out the instrumental expectations of the board. Learning involves looking at the board's tasks and identifying ways that enable the group to work better and produce more useful results.

- The focus of development efforts should be on changing a board's behavior rather than changing attitudes or personalities. Exhortations and prescriptions do not work nearly as well as changes in routines, procedures, or structures for doing work together. With such practical steps as bringing thoughtful questions, providing relevant information on the issue, dividing into small groups to brainstorm alternatives, members will begin to think and act differently. Behaviors are more likely to change when board members make recommendations and encourage critical and analytical thinking about issues before the group.

Leading and Managing Nonprofit Organizations

- Development activities should be individually tailored to the specific needs and concerns of the board. Although a retreat approach is often useful in getting started, the board should build development activities into its ongoing agenda and ways of doing business rather than being treated as a separate activity. This responds to the expectations of many members who tend to see the board's effectiveness primarily as a means to advance the organization's performance rather than see board development as an end in itself.
- The best approaches link process and substance. For example, asking the board to set goals for itself or to formulate indicators to monitor its performance sets in motion a process that builds cohesion and educates participants while also generating substantive products.

Board development is an extensive, long-term process, not a quick fix. To sustain the process, some members must be "product champions" for the board and its performance, just as some advocate balanced budgets or client satisfaction. The pressures of business as usual are strong, and without continuing attention to how well the board is performing, it will settle back into comfortable ways of working that may not match the needs of a changing organization or environment.

Initiating Attention to the Board's Performance

Boards can productively use recent successes or problems as occasions to reflect on what happened and how the board contributed to the results. Both positive and negative situations provide opportunities for the board to consider how it has performed during the time leading up to this point. The board can think together about how it wants to perform in dealing with similar situations in the future. Such reflection invites members to look beyond mere reaction to external events and to consider ways in which the board might carry out its business more intentionally and provide more effective leadership. Whatever the issue, the board can ask itself how it has contributed to the successes and problems in the area and what lessons it should take from these experiences to become more effective in the future.

Even when it is not facing critical turning points, the board can periodically ask its CEO to talk about some of the major challenges on the horizon or to describe the organizational issues that keep the CEO awake at night. The group can then discuss how it has contributed to the organization's readiness to deal with these matters and how it could prepare itself to provide stronger leadership in the future.

The board should include in its agenda some time at each meeting for candid, off-the-record talk with the CEO about the most complex or troublesome issues coming in the months or years ahead. Then it should explore ways that the board could become a stronger partner with the CEO in working on those issues. Thus, the board uses work on substantive challenges to the organization as an opportunity to learn how to improve its own performance.

Another opportunity for the board to examine its own performance is in discussions of how the organization deals with accountability for its use of resources. Most boards expect the CEO to report on how staff are being held accountable, and many boards specify expectations of the executive and criteria for assessing that person's performance. Fewer boards, however, apply the same principles to themselves and have clear evidence of how the board itself accounts for its use of time and resources.

Developing ways to demonstrate the board's own accountability is crucial to modeling the behaviors it expects of others in the organization. Initiating such a process begins by recognizing that the board has a duty of accountability for its responsibilities and then engaging in candid discussions of how well it is carrying out this obligation (Holland, 2002). Useful questions for group discussion include the following:

- How is this board adding value to the organization beyond the contributions of staff and administration?
- What steps should the board take to improve its performance and increase the value it adds to the organization?
- What criteria or indicators are appropriate for monitoring and demonstrating the board's improving performance?

Rather than approaching this matter in terms of forced compliance with external rules or avoidance of public embarrassment, it is more productive to approach accountability as a matter of mutual expectations and shared commitments among members. Conversations about goals and promises to one another about steps the board will take together serve to build a climate of responsibility and mutual commitment to one another. Such commitments guide behavior more powerfully than external rules or threats (Fry, 1995). Intentional examination of the board's commitments and the ways in which it ensures that they are carried out sets the stage for further steps to strengthen individual and group performance.

Boards can take advantage of a wide variety of opportunities to look at their own performance and the value that they add to the organization. Efforts to look at this area are prompted by participants' desires to increase the value the board adds to the organization and to maximize its contributions to the accomplishment of its mission. However they are expressed, members' concerns provide vital signals that it is time to begin involving others in reflections on the group's work together. As one experienced board leader advised, "Don't hesitate to ask yourself and others, 'Is this board truly adding as much value to this organization as it could? Could we do better?'" Raising these questions may seem like a small beginning, but numerous boards have found that they are vital first steps toward important changes.

Although every member of the board should be concerned about how well the group is doing its job, it is important that these concerns move away from individuals and toward shared ownership by the full group. The board's leaders are vital to this step, and it usually falls to them to initiate open attention to the board's performance. Anyone can propose a discussion of how the board is working, but the positive response and commitment of the CEO and board chair are essential to the success of efforts to bring issues before the whole group.

The best orchestra or sports team steps back from each performance and reviews how well it did and where changes could be made to improve future work. High-performing groups take time for practice and for reviewing their performance, thus learning and growing together as a team (Senge, 1994). Boards can learn from these examples. As the leader of one strong board noted, "After we've finished working on a particularly difficult problem, we try to take some time to reflect together on what we can learn from what we've just come through." Boards that take time together to examine and reflect on their own performance learn new ways that will guide them to increased effectiveness as leaders.

Using Assessments to Identify Targets for Change

Initial discussions about board performance can be carried to an important next step by getting more extensive information from all participants regarding their views of the board's work, areas warranting attention, and suggestions for change. It is useful to broaden the inquiry so that participants can find out whether their concerns are things that more than just a few want to work on. An assessment of the full board supports this step. As one experienced member emphasized,

> Any board interested in improving should get going with an evaluation of its strengths and weaknesses. It should ask a whole series of tough questions about what's working well and what isn't. You can't

just depend on a few insiders to run things. You're ALL the owners of the institution and all responsible for finding ways that enable you to help it work better.

In addition to gathering information for everyone to examine, a crucial function of board assessment is that it serves to spread responsibility for findings and conclusions across the whole group, thus building shared ownership of conclusions and consensus for undertaking steps of change. In the words of one board chairperson,

> The most important result of starting to evaluate our work as a board was that the group began to think about itself purposively and to ask questions about how we could do our work better in the future. It got all of us going with taking responsibility for improving the quality of our own work.

Approaches to board assessment may be divided into two areas of focus: (1) group performance and (2) individual performance. A few approaches link these domains. Many boards have used one or more assessment methods to identify aspects of board performance that members see as needing improvement. They can choose from numerous resources and approaches, and many national associations have developed board assessment tools. The various approaches include self-evaluations, constituency surveys, third-party reviews, internal reviews by an ad hoc or standing committee on trusteeship, reflective discussion of critical incidents, and feedback at the conclusion of meetings.

One comprehensive board self-assessment package is offered by BoardSource (https://boardsource.org/), with versions tailored to several different types of nonprofit; another approach is based on the six competencies of effective boards (Jackson & Holland, 1998). The National Council of Nonprofits (https://www.councilofnonprofits.org) offers links to a number of free or low-cost self-assessment tools. Other approaches range from brief evaluations at the end of meetings to bringing in outside evaluators to interview and summarize the views of board members, staff, consumers, and sponsors.

Each approach to board assessment has strengths and limitations. They vary in time and resources required and in vulnerability to bias. A board should begin by experimenting with whatever approach to assessment seems comfortable and appropriate and then evaluating the usefulness of the results. It should revise and expand the steps in ways that the group finds helpful and comprehensible. At some point, the group should invite in some outsiders who bring objectivity and experience with other boards for comparisons and for innovative ideas.

Retreats as a Means to Work on Board Performance

Many boards have found that retreats are powerful tools for stimulating and extending board growth. A retreat is typically a one- or two-day special meeting, held off site and away from wherever the group usually meets. Retreats allow the group to devote extended time to working on a major issue, such as developing or updating its strategic plan, gaining a better understanding of the external environment, clarifying its mission, evaluating a possible new market, or solving some problem. In this section, we consider their use specifically for working on improvements in the board's own performance.

A board development retreat is an investment in the future of the board and the organization it governs. It provides an opportunity to step back from routine business agendas for an in-depth look at the future and the board's role in it. A retreat can be a major boost to the board's efforts to make more effective and efficient use of the time it gives to the organization (Holland, 1997b; Savage, 1995; Scott, 2000). Boards have found that their retreats served several important purposes, such as

- strengthening performance through a review of governance process and the board's roles and responsibilities
- assessing the board's contributions to the organization and identifying ways that it can add greater value
- establishing priorities for the board and identifying strategies and actions to achieve them
- enhancing collegiality and working relationships among board members and between board and staff
- determining the next steps in board development and in the implementation of overall action plans

A board may use numerous resources in planning and conducting its retreat. BoardSource publishes useful resource materials on board development and maintains lists of consultants and facilitators in many regions of the country. Similar resources are available through the national associations of many other organizations.

A retreat can generate a great deal of enthusiasm among participants. However, a board can lose momentum when it returns to its regular meeting schedule and reverts to familiar old patterns. Likewise, turnover in membership introduces newcomers who are unacquainted with the board's efforts to change behavior and improve performance. Agenda items that are scheduled almost automatically demand attention, and promises made at a retreat may well be forgotten like New Year's resolutions. Therefore, it is essential to have explicit methods to remind everyone of the agreements and changes identified at the retreat. The board should require as part of its agendas regular evidence of how those resolutions are being implemented. The underlying goal is to build habits of reflection and learning into the group's culture, so that both newcomers and old-timers are socialized into effective patterns of behavior.

Ongoing Board Education

Incorporating educational activities into board meetings is a vital practice for making ongoing improvements in the board's performance. Boards should be models of learning organizations (Senge, 1994). The assembled intellectual abilities of members are extended by acquiring new knowledge and skills as a group and by identifying and developing improved ways to carry out their work.

Rather than simply relying only on past knowledge and skill, effective boards acknowledge their need to learn and take responsibility for continuing to expand their competencies. They identify topics and issues to examine, develop appropriate programs and resources, and encourage all members to participate in ongoing educational sessions. Effective boards encourage ongoing education among their members by bringing in special speakers, holding mini-seminars and study groups, visiting other boards, attending conferences on governance, and rotating committee assignments (Scott, 2000; Taylor et al., 1996).

It is especially important to have thorough orientation programs for incoming members. New members get off to a good start when they receive clear expectations for board membership, extensive orientation to the board's roles and responsibilities, and information about the organization. Assigning an experienced member as a mentor for a newcomer is another useful practice that provides both with a greater awareness of board performance.

Outside speakers and mentors from other boards are also useful resources to help a board learn. Many national and regional associations can recommend knowledgeable leaders to serve in such educational or consultative roles, and some boards also recruit resource people from similar organizations in their region. Any board can occasionally use outside consultants, mentors, or evaluators to help the group gain independent perspectives on its performance, identify issues needing its attention, and learn about best practices of other boards.

Better boards enlarge their educational process by helping every member develop learning plans that enable them to make greater contributions to the group in the following year. This practice may be as simple as rotating committee assignments or as extensive as sending members to conferences on governance and bringing in speakers on topics of interest to members. Some boards establish procedures for all their members to set individual performance goals and to obtain feedback on their progress. They use feedback to coach members on improving their contributions to the group's overall effectiveness. They use coaching sessions and mentors for underperformers and term limits to ease out chronic poor performers. In these ways, boards can use individual and group goals as well as monitoring and feedback to sustain attention to improved performance.

Restructuring Meeting Time and Committee Work

An important approach to improving performance is to restructure the board's use of committees and meeting time to emphasize its strategic priorities (Carver, 1990). Careful use of the scarce resource of meeting time is a concern of many members, and many sense that agendas pack too many issues into limited meeting time. Meeting agendas should be designed so that they sustain focus on the few, most important issues of strategy and policy. Preparation for making changes in the agenda may begin with having a member simply monitor the amount of time that the board spends on each issue in a meeting and rate its relevance to the board's priorities. The board can discuss the feedback and consider the relationship between its priorities and its actual use of time.

Better use of meeting time can result from setting clear priorities for the board's attention and leaving nonessential items for individual review. Strong boards limit meeting agendas to a few, top-priority matters, avoiding attempts to cover the waterfront. They cluster routine reports and unexceptional motions that require board approval into a consent agenda to be voted on in one action rather than separately. Any member can request that an item be separated out for discussion, thus protecting the board's ultimate right to examine any issue. However, the practice allows the board to concentrate most of its attention on the organization's highest priorities and avoid getting bogged down in operational details.

As Eadie (2012, pp. 75–76) suggested, a well-designed committee structure for a nonprofit board will, at a minimum, consist of

- a governance or board operations committee accountable for coordinating the board's governing work, developing the board agenda, setting board performance targets and monitoring performance, and maintaining the board–CEO working relationship, including evaluating CEO performance

- a planning committee accountable for working with the CEO in mapping out processes to involve board members in the planning cycle (ranging from values and vision to the annual operating plan and budget), coordinating board member involvement in planning, and recommending key planning products to the full board
- a performance monitoring committee accountable for working with the CEO in designing financial and programmatic performance reports that the board should regularly see, monitoring organizational performance, and reporting performance results to the full board
- an external relations committee accountable for overseeing communication with key external stakeholders, coordinating board member involvement in external relations, and recommending board action on such governing products as an updated image statement, a set of external relations goals, and positions on key pieces of legislation in the hopper

Restructuring how the board organizes and charges its committees is another way to improve performance. Instead of committees that mirror management divisions (for example, personnel, programs, finances), boards should let form follow function. The strategic priorities provide the point of departure from which work group assignments and meeting agendas are derived. In addition to a limited number of standing committees, such as those just identified, other committees or task forces may from time to time need to be established. These committees or task forces should be constructed to focus members' efforts on each of the board's goals, and each committee or task force should be dissolved when a goal is attained.

Rather than using board meeting time to hear routine committee reports, the board can structure its meetings to focus on one or two goals or priorities at each meeting. Then those committees or task groups who have done the background preparation can lead meaningful discussions on matters that require the board's input or decision making. Leaders should make sure that every agenda item begins with a clear statement of the question being presented to the board and how the issue is linked with a goal or priority of the board.

For changes to outlast individuals and become embedded in the board's culture, there must be some champions for the group's performance, in the same manner that a finance committee or buildings and grounds committee carries its portfolio. The board can, to build in advocacy for itself, create a task group charged with reminding the board of its commitments, monitoring its performance, and periodically recommending actions that will strengthen meeting processes. Strong boards have their committee on nominations or some other permanent group take the responsibility for developing and implementing steps for monitoring board meetings, soliciting participants' assessments and recommendations for improvement, and arranging for periodic board education sessions and retreats on issues of interest.

Many of these boards expand the duties of the nominating committee to include periodic assessments of individual and group performance. This group uses findings to coach members in expanding their leadership contributions to the board, to identify people to nominate for additional terms, to identify skills needed in new members, and to plan regular educational sessions in areas in which the board needs improvement.

The committee's experience in carrying out these tasks is applicable in its nominations of future members. It broadens the scope of characteristics sought in new members to include skills in working with groups, linkages to key constituencies, ability to contribute new perspectives to examining issues, and a track record of making positive contributions to group communication and learning.

Boards that restructure their meeting agendas and committees can then monitor the usefulness of those changes by evaluating their meetings, including plenary sessions and committee meetings, and getting feedback and suggestions to improve future meetings. Brief assessment forms, followed by discussion of participants' concerns and recommendations, can lead to more productive and satisfying meetings.

Fundraising is a key responsibility of the board in which it may selectively involve others. Some boards create an honorary trusteeship status for people whose major role is limited to making financial contributions or providing access to others who can make such contributions. Through its capital campaign committee or its fundraising committee, the board can link with these individuals and draw on their specialized resources to advance its overall plans (see chapter 4 for a more complete discussion of fundraising). As Klein (2016) pointed out,

> The reason that board members must take a leadership role in fundraising is simple: they have the most legal responsibility for the organization and are chosen because they are willing to take this responsibility seriously. Their behavior sets an example. When they give, other people will give and when they don't, other people don't. (p. 37)

Building Group Cohesion and Teamwork

The thoughtfully constructed orientation of many members makes structural changes more attractive than efforts explicitly directed at relationships, processes, or communications. However, the most effective boards take careful steps to transform an assembly of talented individuals into a well-integrated group.

Many board members are comfortable providing individual expertise or advice to the CEO, whereas others see their service taking place on a committee related to their area of interest. The most effective boards go beyond these efforts and also emphasize the whole group as the decision-making unit. A cohesive board makes better decisions than do individuals, yet it draws on members' multiple perspectives to avoid the traps of groupthink.

Transforming an assembly of skilled individuals into a well-integrated team is a long and difficult process. It requires taking critical issues to the group for deliberation and taking the time to hear the views of each participant rather than relying on a few leaders to predigest issues and present foregone conclusions. It is essential that issues taken to the board be vital to the future of the organization and not merely window dressing. It requires making sure that everyone has equal access to information about the issues and the organization. Dedicated board Web site portals can provide an easy and secure way for board members to stay up to date and prepare for important discussions. It requires taking time for members to get to know one another beyond the formal setting of the boardroom. Strong boards pay careful attention to communications among members, to nurturing and sustaining inclusive relationships, and to developing a sense of mutual responsibility for the board's success. They are aware that silent members may have some important concerns that the board needs to hear. Social events and informal time for conversations are important means to build trusting relationships.

The most effective steps for building group cohesion are the ones that closely link instrumental and relational components and allow members to deal with the latter by means of overt attention to the former. For example, working to formulate goals for the board itself is a good means to build group cohesion while also serving to focus the board's use of time and energy. Goals for the board should be distinct from—but lead to—the overall goals it has for the organization. They specifically identify what the board will do to maximize its contributions to the attainment of the organization's strategic goals.

The board identifies its goals, which should be kept in everyone's awareness by being posted in conspicuous places and by being repeated in meetings and at the beginning of reports. Keeping the board's own goals paramount in meetings, using the agenda plan, and maintaining the focus of each report or discussion keeps everyone clear about the purpose and direction of each step. It also allows the board to monitor and evaluate its own progress toward its goals.

Formulating specific goals for the board also helps the process of clarifying expectations of the board as a group and of individual members, officers, committees, and senior staff. It is important to make sure that each participant understands what is expected of them and how those expectations contribute to achieving the overall goals. Setting goals for the board as a whole and periodically reviewing progress toward them serves to maintain the board's attention to its own performance and how it adds value to the organization. The board should regularly monitor indicators of its performance and make sure that each member has this information. Sharing this information with outsiders and inviting their assessments of progress further sharpens accountability for performance.

Throughout these steps, the underlying concern is to develop a stronger sense of inclusiveness and cohesiveness among board members as a group. This requires paying careful attention to communications among members and intentionally nurturing and sustaining inclusive relationships. These processes should begin at recruitment and orientation, be carried forward by all leaders, and be reinforced at social times and retreats. Strong boards are careful to schedule social time and informal interaction for their members. They celebrate members' accomplishments, have meals together before or after meetings, take breaks for refreshments, regularly use name tags, and participate as a group in social events sponsored by the organization.

Role of the CEO

CEOs play a central role in creating and sustaining an effective board. They most often initiate attention to the board's performance and advocate for improvements. No longer content with the cynical advice to "keep them in the dark so they'll leave you alone," good executives realize that their boards can be their best partners in creating a strong organization. They invest time in examining the group's performance and educating members in leadership skills.

If boards are to improve, CEOs must be committed to leading efforts to learn better ways of working together and take the initiative in raising members' sights and expectations of themselves. Working closely with the chairperson of the board, the CEO raises performance questions with the group and helps members consider new approaches to the board's work. The CEO describes approaches to governance that raise aspirations and prepare the group to make changes in its own patterns and helps the group to focus its attention on those aspects that warrant attention and then identify specific steps for change. The CEO raises group expectations and aspirations by initiating questions about group performance, suggesting alternative approaches to dealing with issues and offering new possibilities for improving group effectiveness.

By opening up discussion about the board's performance, the CEO demonstrates that it is appropriate to direct attention to the board's own work and to explore ways of improving it. Rather than avoiding discontents or treating problems as occasions to blame someone, effective CEOs turn problems into occasions for the group to learn more effective ways of carrying out its work. They help move discontents from back channels to the forefront of everyone's attention, and they invite the group to take on responsibility for identifying solutions to problems and better ways to deal with issues. Good CEOs model respectful listening and constructive feedback to improve the quality of work, inviting others to join in similar steps. In so doing, they confirm that everyone in the leadership group is committed to doing their jobs more effectively, not just avoiding criticism, blaming others, or settling for business as usual.

Effective CEOs expect and tolerate the anxiety that can come with questioning old assumptions and relinquishing familiar practices for the unknown. Their persistence in seeking improvements, even when solutions may not yet be apparent, encourages experimentation with new approaches to dealing with tasks. They invite others to try out alternatives without fear of being blamed for mistakes along the way. Reflecting on experiences together, identifying areas to change, and trying out new ways are difficult but crucial steps in learning for anyone in the organization, including the board. CEOs recognize and celebrate incremental steps toward goals of improved board performance, thus establishing it as a model for others in the organization.

Conclusion

By working intentionally on its own performance, a board makes some fundamental changes in the ways it uses its time and energy and moves beyond the temporary quick fix that solves immediate problems. It makes how it is carrying out its work part of its agenda, not something separate from and independent of ongoing tasks and responsibilities (Holland, Leslie,

& Holzhalb, 1993). The board makes fundamental changes in its culture, reinventing and rejuvenating itself. It incorporates into its basic sense of responsibility a continuing concern with improving the quality of its performance rather than seeing it as something separate or occasional. Leaders can reinforce this understanding by pausing occasionally at key points in the agenda to invite reflection on how the group dealt with the issue and what could be done to improve the process next time. Such reflective practices become part of the group's culture.

Time and intentional work are essential for changes to become integrated into the board's culture. To ensure that lessons are learned and used, boards have found that they must allow enough time to fully address their concerns and explore alternatives. This cannot be accomplished at one meeting; rather, some attention should be devoted to regular reflection on the group's work performance.

The group should insist on allocating time to discuss how it dealt with key agenda items as well as working on the tasks themselves. Reflecting this way for even a few minutes per meeting can lead to greater board efficiency and effectiveness. It can also ensure that minor irritants do not mushroom into major problems.

Taking time to reflect on how the board has used its time and attention, particularly after dealing with a difficult issue, enhances the group's ownership of its own processes and performance. These discussions should take place at the conclusion of each meeting and allow members to share perceptions of performance and consider ways to improve future meetings.

Effective boards attend to how they work together as well as to what they do. Members take responsibility for initiating discussions of ways the group does its work and seek ways to improve performance. They take advantage of breaks or turning points in the organization's experience to draw attention to the board's role in leadership and change. They test their perceptions with others and identify shared group concerns. They move ahead through assessments of group performance to identify specific issues and goals for change. They lay the foundation for ongoing work using retreats and mindful follow-up. They reinforce and institutionalize changes via in-meeting discussions of feedback on performance and educational sessions that contribute to strengthening the board's effectiveness. These efforts bridge the gap between learning and doing, integrating reflection with work. They help the group develop a culture of active responsibility for making ongoing, self-directed improvements in its own performance.

By taking consistent initiatives to improve their work together, boards set the example for others and show how to add greater value to their organizations. However, boards are rarely able to initiate such activities by themselves; they generally require strong leadership and direction from their CEO. The payoff can be substantial. As one senior chairperson summarized his group's experience,

> Our board members' sense of the importance of working on our own performance went from zero to extremely high. I've had a lot of experience as a member of several national corporate boards and initially was impatient with more time spent on this area. But now it has become a basic part of the way this board works. . . . To come through all the changes this organization faced, you really have to become a team with many skilled players. . . . We started off with some retreats and had some speakers who really opened my eyes. . . . Now board development is fully owned by this board, and one of our members arranges for us to work together on some topic for about an hour at every meeting. We're all committed to moving ahead with our own education as a board so we will be more effective leaders of this organization in the future.

Skills Application Exercises

Example 1: Metropolitan Family Services Board

Beth Jefferson, CEO of the Metropolitan Family Services Center, and Frank Watson, chair of its board, were talking over lunch about how the board was performing and possible ways in which it might be improved. "I think we will continue to feel pressure from managed care and from other service providers coming into our area," Beth reflected. "I think we should get the board to work on doing a better job so we can survive the rapid changes of the coming years."

"But we already have a fine board," Frank responded. "Our members have their hands full with overseeing all we do now. All the committees are working hard, and most of our members have many years of experience in their roles. They've all done good work, so I don't see why you think we need to change."

"Perhaps we're victims of our own past success," said Beth. "There's no doubt that our committee structure and our membership have served us well in the past, and I don't mean to be critical, it's just that things are changing from how they were even a few years ago. The population we serve is getting younger, poorer, and more troubled. Their problems are very different from those we faced when we started. I doubt that many on our board know much about our current clients. If we're going to understand our community and the people we're supposed to be serving, we need some new blood."

"But we'd be losing a lot of wisdom and experience by changing membership just for the sake of change," replied Frank. "After all, these folks have come through many years with the center and know it inside and out. They trust you and each other, and they work together well. I just don't see how changing the people will accomplish what you seem to want. It certainly will cause a lot of disruption. There's lots to lose and little to gain, as I see it."

"It's certainly true that our board members have been helpful," Beth acknowledged. "But they seldom dig in and help improve recommendations that I bring to the table. They're willing to listen and raise a few questions, but the weight is all on me to come up with the ideas and the plans. They're passive reactors, not real leaders. I don't think most of them are actively in touch with much of the community. As a matter of fact, I fear this group really has no clear goals or criteria for evaluating the quality of anything, other than how comfortable they feel about where I'm taking them. That may have been acceptable in the past, but I want some bright and capable partners who can really contribute to our understanding of trends and political issues, people who can actively chart a course into the future. Maybe we could start by suggesting term limits and then talk about what characteristics we'd like to see in new nominees. Perhaps we could plan some new education sessions for the board on changes in the community."

"I'm afraid many of our members would view your efforts to change the board as a power grab," Frank replied. "A few may be willing to retire, but most are just pleased with the way things are going and would resist change. I doubt they'd understand what you're trying to do. You know the old saying, 'If it ain't broke, don't fix it.' Why not just leave well enough alone?"

Discussion Questions

1. What are some of this board's strengths, and what are some of its weaknesses? How would you rate it on each of the characteristics of effective boards presented in this chapter?

2. What opportunities and constraints confront Beth in moving forward on her goals for the board? How could she take advantage of the opportunities, build on strengths, and overcome weaknesses?
3. What should be Beth's short-range and long-range objectives? What resources could she draw on for each?
4. How would you describe Beth and Frank's relationship? What important steps should each take to work together more effectively?
5. Develop an action plan for Beth, identifying important steps and resources.
6. What criteria should she use to monitor progress toward her objectives?

Example 2: Westside Community Center

The slow-moving traffic drew little attention from Wilma Johnson this afternoon. She was headed for Westside's quarterly board meeting and was decidedly uncomfortable about what lay ahead. "Why do I keep on doing this when it's so frustrating?" Wilma grumbled to herself.

Four years earlier, Wilma had been a bit rattled by Executive Director Don Carlisle's call asking her to serve on the board. She was sure that the request had been linked to her family's ownership of one of the largest manufacturing corporations in the city, but the prospect of helping improve the quality of what was already a top-notch community center had caught her interest.

She'd like to feel that she was a part of such an effort to "ratchet up Westside," as Don had put it, so she had agreed to this venture onto a nonprofit board. Over her first year on the Westside board, Wilma had kept a low profile as she watched how the group conducted its business. The organization's budget had been balanced every year, and membership and participation were growing, largely because of good-quality programs.

Everyone on the board and the management team seemed quite content with how things were going for the organization. Although fund accounting still struck her as a curious way of financial management, Wilma really enjoyed the occasional talks by senior members of the staff at board meetings.

The four meetings a year were efficient, usually starting with committee meetings in the afternoon, followed by a social dinner, sometimes including a staff "show and tell," after which the board met as a whole from 7:00 p.m. until about 10:00 p.m. to hear and discuss committee reports. Some of the committee reports were thorough; others seemed vague and pointless. Neither evoked much response from anyone in the meetings, and Wilma wondered whether others found these sessions as tedious and boring as she did. Only occasionally were there recommended actions that were not routine and, for all intents and purposes, predetermined. "Surely," Wilma mused to herself, "there's more to being a board member than approving contracts with suppliers, building renovation projects, and joint activities with other organizations in the city." The only real discussion each year was about setting membership fees and staff salaries.

When Wilma joined the board, she had acquiesced to the request that she serve on the fundraising campaign committee. Soon, however, she became dismayed at the confusion in signals from the CEO and the committee chairman. She made several calls to friends and opened some doors that led to other contributions. However, the campaign ended far short of its goal, and it seemed to have concluded with a whimper, not a bang. Even more curious, from Wilma's perspective, the board had never addressed the lingering dissatisfactions from that experience. Two years later, Don was pushing hard for the board to start yet another campaign, this time with an even higher goal.

One evening after the end of the last campaign, Wilma and several other members of the board had talked in the parking lot after a board meeting about what might have gone wrong. Part of the problem seemed to be that the organization had no clear strategic plan, a point another member had brought up at the next board meeting. Don had really gone to work on that challenge and had done a fine job with it. Over the next nine months, a series of planning meetings included many of the board members and several staff and community leaders. The plan that emerged was saluted by everyone—staff and board—as excellent, distinctive, and comprehensive. There was a sense that the document, although ambitious and a bit ambiguous in places, had instilled in Westside a new sense of purpose and overall direction.

Why, then, Wilma wondered, was she still uncomfortable? The strategic plan was unquestionably good, just what the organization needed. However, the subsequent board meetings seemed to have continued with business as usual, with only occasional references to the plan. It did not appear to have had any evident effect on either the substance or the processes of meetings. At the most recent meeting, Don had pushed hard for the board to authorize the new campaign. Backed by the board chair, Don called for volunteers to form a campaign committee. Even so, few members had responded. The usual suspects had raised their hands but with little evident enthusiasm. The spark just did not seem to be there for anyone in the room.

During a break in the meeting, Arnold Moore, the chair of the committee on programs and services, had commented to Wilma and a few others gathered around the coffee urn that there seemed to be a lethargy in the room. Everyone, including Wilma, had nodded in agreement, but no one raised the issue once the meeting resumed. Apparently, nobody wanted to seem like a troublemaker, Wilma surmised, especially without some specific reason or recommendation about how to improve things.

After that meeting, Wilma had tried to engage Don in some conversation about her unease, but his response somehow seemed to miss the point. "I'm not sure that our board members see how we fit into the plan," she said to him. "Isn't the board itself one of the organization's strategic assets that should be included in our thinking somehow? Shouldn't life on the board be different now that we actually have a strategic plan?"

"Certainly, the board is central to the plan," insisted Don. "Its job now is just to roll up its sleeves and get to work raising the money so Westside can achieve the goals detailed in the plan. We're all counting on the board this time, Wilma, to make sure that we reach our target. And frankly, I see you as a key player."

"Get on board or get out of the way," Wilma thought as she drove to the next board meeting. That was a motto that Wilma had often heard among her own company's senior staff when a new venture was getting started, and now she was hearing it at Westside. Why did it seem so irritating now? "Maybe it's just me," Wilma mused as she pulled into the parking lot. "Am I simply getting too old for all this? Should I just get out of the way, resign this volunteer position, and take that long overdue vacation?"

The meeting was just getting under way when Wilma walked into the conference room. "Welcome, ladies and gentlemen," boomed the chair. "We have a full agenda this evening, so I hope you are prepared to work a little later than usual. In addition to all our usual committee reports, we have two bids for renovations to review, a proposal for some changes in programs and in membership regulations, plus several budgetary adjustments. Then I'd like for us to get back to preparations for the campaign and see what we need to do to get that project launched. Any questions before we dig in?"

By the time the meeting ended, Wilma was exasperated by what she regarded as an endless stream of trivia and minutiae. On her way out to the parking lot, she walked with Freddie Ackerman, assistant director of Westside, and said, "Freddie, you know this organization and this board better than I do. Am I crazy to think that the board should be dealing regularly with crucial issues like strengthening our competitive advantage, monitoring the quality of our programs, improving our market share, and controlling costs? It seems like our leaders steer clear of issues like that in favor of discussions of program regulations and rehabbing the physical plant. Those things may be important to somebody, but frankly, they just sap my energy. Furthermore, I just don't think the board's heart will be in another campaign now. So, I have two questions for you: First, am I correct in my perceptions about what a board should be and what this one is? And second, if I am correct, what can we do to change things? I really hope you can help me out, because I've about had it."

Discussion Questions

1. Why do board members sometimes raise questions and offer comments outside the board room that they would not inside the board room? What, if anything, should a CEO or a board chairperson do about this?
2. If you were Freddie, how would you answer Wilma's two questions?
3. Why do some boards have difficulty focusing on strategy instead of operations?
4. What, if anything, should this board do differently? What should the executive director do? What should Freddie do? What should the board chair do? What should Wilma do?
5. What goals should this board set for itself (as distinct from goals it has for the organization)? How should it go about that process?
6. How could this board know whether and when it was improving its performance? What indicators should it monitor?
7. What are the implications for these issues for the development of effective trustees and volunteers for a nonprofit organization?

Group Discussion

Executive Director Don Carlisle has called together the executive committee of the Westside board and made the following request: "Please help me come up with a plan that will significantly improve how our board adds value added to Westside. I am particularly concerned that we make effective use of these folks in our upcoming campaign. Our plan should include specific objectives, a credible approach, assignable tasks, observable outcomes, and minimal expenses." Your assignment is to develop and present the key features of the plan, including your recommendations and the reasoning that supports each of them.

References

Bray, I. (2019). *Effective fundraising for nonprofits: Real-world strategies that work* (6th ed.). Berkeley, CA: Nolo.

Brown, W. (2007). Board development practices and competent board members. *Nonprofit Management and Leadership, 17*, 301–307.

Carver, J. (1990). *Boards that make a difference.* San Francisco: Jossey-Bass.

Carver, J. (2002a). *Corporate boards that add value.* San Francisco: Jossey-Bass.

Carver, J. (2002b). *John Carver on board leadership.* San Francisco: Jossey-Bass.

Chait, R. P., Holland, T. P., & Taylor, B. E. (1993). *The effective board of trustees.* Phoenix, AZ: Oryx Press.

Dee, J., & Hendrick, A. (2006). Communication and donor relations. *Nonprofit Management and Leadership, 18*, 107–119.

Eadie, D. (2012). *Leading out-of-the-box change—The chief executive's essential guide to achieving nonprofit innovation and growth.* Oldsmar, FL: Governance Edge.

Fry, R. E. (1995). Accountability in organizational life: Problem or opportunity for nonprofits? *Nonprofit Management and Leadership, 6*, 181–195.

Harrison, Y., & Murray, V. (2014). The effect of an on-line self-assessment tool on nonprofit board performance. *Nonprofit and Voluntary Sector Quarterly, 44*, 1129–1151.

Holland, T. P. (1997a). Board self-assessment: A model of accountability. *Not-for-Profit CEO Monthly Letter, 4*(1), 5–9.

Holland, T. P. (1997b). Setting the stage: Planning board retreats. *Board Member, 6*(4), 10–11.

Holland, T. P. (2002). Board accountability: Some lessons from the field. *Nonprofit Management and Leadership, 12*, 409–428.

Holland, T. P., Chait, R. P., & Taylor, B. E. (1989). Board effectiveness: Identifying and measuring trustee competencies. *Journal of Research in Higher Education, 30*, 451–469.

Holland, T. P., Leslie, D., & Holzhalb, C. (1993). Culture and change in nonprofit boards. *Nonprofit Management and Leadership, 4*, 141–155.

Holland, T. P., Ritvo, R. A., & Kovner, A. R. (1997). *Improving board effectiveness: Practical lessons for nonprofit healthcare organizations.* Chicago: American Hospital Association.

Houle, C. O. (1989). *Governing boards: Their nature and nurture.* San Francisco: Jossey-Bass.

Jackson, D. K., & Holland, T. P. (1998). Measuring the effectiveness of nonprofit boards. *Nonprofit and Voluntary Sector Quarterly, 27*, 159–182.

Klein, K. (2016). *Fundraising for social change.* Hoboken, NJ: Wiley.

Nicholson, G., Newton, C., & McGregor-Lowndes, M. (2012). The nonprofit board as a team: Pilot results and initial insights. *Nonprofit Management and Leadership, 22*, 461–481.

Pound, J. (1993). The promise of the governed corporation. *Harvard Business Review, 73*(2), 89–98.

Preston, J. B., & Brown, W. A. (2004). Commitment and performance of nonprofit board members. *Nonprofit Management & Leadership, 15*, 221–238.

Puyvelde, S., Brown, W., Walker, V., & Tenuta, R. (2018). Board effectiveness in nonprofit organizations. *Nonprofit and Voluntary Sector Quarterly, 47*, 1290–1310.

Savage, T. J. (1995). *Seven steps to a more effective board.* Rockville, MD: Cheswick Center.

Schein, E. H. (1993). How can organizations learn faster? The challenge of entering the green room. *Sloan Management Review, 34*, 85–92.

Scott, K. T. (2000). *Creating caring and capable boards.* San Francisco: Jossey-Bass.

Senge, P. (1994). *The fifth discipline: The art and practice of the learning organization.* New York: Doubleday.

Tacon, R., Walters, G., & Cornforth, C. (2017). Accountability in nonprofit governance: A process-based study. *Nonprofit and Voluntary Sector Quarterly, 46*, 685–704.

Taylor, B. E., Chait, R. P., & Holland, T. P. (1996). The new work of the nonprofit board. *Harvard Business Review, 74*(5), 36–46.

Widmer, C., & Houchin, S. (2000). *The art of trusteeship.* San Francisco: Jossey-Bass.

Additional Reading

Association for Governing Boards of Universities and Colleges. (1986). *Self-study criteria for governing boards of independent colleges and universities.* Washington, DC: Author.

Bowen, W. G. (1994). *Inside the boardroom.* New York: Wiley.

Brudney, J., & Nobbie, P. D. (2002). Training policy governance in nonprofit boards of directors. *Nonprofit Management & Leadership, 12*, 387–408.

Chait, R. P. (1994). *The new activism of corporate boards and the implications for campus governance.* Washington, DC: Association of Governing Boards of Universities and Colleges.

Chait, R. P., Holland, T. P., & Taylor, B. E. (1996). *Improving the performance of governing boards.* Phoenix, AZ: Oryx Press.

Drucker, P. F. (1990). Lessons for successful nonprofit governance. *Nonprofit Management and Leadership, 1,* 7–14.

Eadie, D. C. (1994). *Boards that work: A practical guide for building effective association boards.* Washington, DC: American Society of Association Executives.

Eadie, D. C. (1997). *Changing by design: A practical approach to leading innovation in nonprofit organizations.* San Francisco: Jossey-Bass.

Eadie, D. C., & Edwards, R. L. (1993). Board leadership by design. *Nonprofit World, 11*(2), 12–15.

Herman, R. D., & Van Til, J. (1989). *Nonprofit boards of directors: Analyses and applications.* New Brunswick, NJ: Transaction.

Holland, T. P. (1991). Self-assessment by nonprofit boards. *Nonprofit Management and Leadership, 2,* 25–36.

Holland, T. P. (1996). *How to build a more effective board.* Washington, DC: National Center for Nonprofit Boards.

Iecovich, E. (2004). Responsibilities and roles of boards: The Israeli case. *Nonprofit Management and Leadership, 15,* 5–24.

Smith, D. H. (1995). *Entrusted: The moral responsibilities of trusteeship.* Bloomington: Indiana University Press.

Zander, A. (1993). *Making boards effective: The dynamics of governing boards.* San Francisco: Jossey-Bass.

13

Managing and Planning Strategically

Allison Zippay

Strategic management is foundational to the work of nonprofit leaders and managers. Its practices sit squarely in the competing values framework introduced in chapter 1 as managers juggle multiple roles, perspectives, and skill sets to implement mission-focused strategies. Within this process, they scan ever-changing internal and external environments; identify key actions to advance organizational goals; engage community and internal constituents; and assess strategic objectives to inform decision making and monitor organizational health and aims (Bryce, 2017; Golensky & Hager, 2020; Laurett & Ferreira, 2018). With its activities aligned with the directing skills outlined in the competing values framework, strategic management is goal and task oriented and provides structure and direction. As leaders, strategic managers inspire the development of strategic and creative initiatives with diverse stakeholder teams to realize organizational social missions. This chapter describes (1) what strategic management is, (2) how it works, and (3) how it promotes organizational innovation, quality, and performance.

Strategic Management Defined

A strategy is a plan of action designed to accomplish an overall aim. The core elements of strategic management have been defined as information gathering and assessment; strategy formulation and design; strategy implementation; and monitoring and evaluation (Laurett & Ferreira, 2018; Steiss, 2005; Stone, Bigelow, & Crittendon, 1999). Planning—systematically developing a blueprint for action—is infused throughout the process of strategic management.

Strategic management is an intentional, ongoing practice. In its ideal, managers mindfully incorporate planning, design, and evaluation to implement courses of action with the organizational mission as the guiding star. In reality, this process is often messy, complicated, nonlinear, and reactive. However, the strategic management framework—information gathering, strategy formulation, strategy implementation, and assessment—provides a grounding for organizing and directing goal-focused agency policy and practice in ever-shifting environments. Strategic management applies to all aspects of organizational functions. In nonprofits, strategy formulation and management have historically centered on program and services design. Increasingly, strategic management is applied across a range of operational areas such as digital communications, marketing, differentiation or branding, technology and information systems, human resources models, policies and practices to enhance diversity and inclusion, and innovation and entrepreneurship (Akingbola, 2013; Bryce, 2017; Bucher, Jager, & Cardoza, 2016; Golensky & Hager, 2020; Powers, 2016; Rhine, 2015; Weerawardena & Mort, 2012). The core elements of a strategic management framework are further defined in the following sections.

Information Gathering and Assessment

Within strategic management, decisions are information based. A key starting point for data collection involves an environmental assessment. The external and internal environments—or surrounding conditions—of organizations have implications for all aspects of functioning. Strategic management includes an ongoing scanning and assessment of these environments, and that information is critical to the design of strategy (Allison & Kay, 2015; Hafsi & Thomas, 2005; Laurett & Ferreira, 2018).

The external environments of nonprofit organizations include the economy; private and public funders and donors; the socioeconomic demographics of the communities being served; local or regional nonprofit and for-profit partners and competitors; local, state, and federal regulations; tax codes that affect charitable giving; politics, elections, and changes in political administrations; trends in national or regional models of programs or practice; emerging technology; and many other factors. The internal environments of nonprofit organizations include physical space, organizational structure and leadership, staff, boards and community constituents, consumers and clients, financial resources, technology and information systems, organizational culture and climate, and policies and procedures (Bryson, 2018; Golensky & Hager, 2020).

Before formulating strategies, managers gather data and document and assess current and trending external and internal environments. Such external and internal factors are ever-changing, and tracking these dynamic conditions is critically important to the relevancy and currency of organizational goals and activities (Hafsi & Thomas, 2005). That evidence informs decision making regarding strategy design.

Strategy Formulation and Design

As noted, a strategy is a plan of action intended to accomplish an overall aim. Strategy formulation is the process of choosing and designing courses of action—selected from among alternatives—to achieve defined organizational goals and objectives (Mishra & Mohanty, 2020). Incorporating information from the assessment of external and internal environments, managers variously work with their staff, leadership teams, and constituents to choose key organizational issues to be addressed and delineate the program or organizational goals and objectives that operationalize those issues. Strategy formulation is a creative process; it involves specifying issues and problems to address and designing solutions in the form of programs or policies or practices. Some nonprofits incorporate design thinking into strategy formulation. Originally used for product design in business, design thinking is increasingly applied to the issues and problems that confront nonprofit organizations. The process may challenge long-held assumptions to generate novel and innovative solutions, and it prioritizes the development of a deeper understanding of the diverse contexts and experiences of those using the organization's products or services (Dunne, 2018a, 2018b).

Such strategy formulation can range from the relatively small and routine to the significant and novel. As an example of a routine response, an assessment by a community preschool of local census data revealed a large increase in new families with very young children, prompting a projected change in staffing to accommodate the shift. On a larger and more innovative scale, with documented rates of opioid overdoses skyrocketing, a statewide network of substance abuse treatment centers drew up plans for funding and launching a pilot peer navigator program to link those in treatment with recovery resources via peers who had been successful in their own recovery. The common ground in these two examples is that decisions about courses of action are information based. Leaders and managers conduct ongoing environmental scans to gauge—through the collection of data and information—the ways in which dynamic, shifting external and internal conditions affect operations, initiatives, and organizational goals and then plan and strategize accordingly.

Strategy Implementation

Implementation represents the execution of the formulated strategies and their goals and objectives. In a written document, action steps are delineated, staff roles are specified, products and timelines are prescribed, and a strategic budget is designed to align with the formulated strategies. These action plans are written as blueprints for achieving particular program or strategic goals and objectives, with clear measures for their accomplishment.

Monitoring and Evaluation

The strategy implementation or action plans are monitored and assessed according to whether written objectives, timelines, and deliverables are achieved. The assessment uses stated measures to include analysis of both process (how an initiative was implemented) and outcomes. The results of the assessment are then fed back to leadership, managers, and staff to be incorporated into an ongoing reevaluation of the initiatives. What worked? What did not work? Why? The aim is to have a continuous feedback loop in which this evidence informs ongoing decisions regarding program operations.

Strategic Management Process

The formality of the process of strategic management can vary widely across organizations, as well as within organizations across different projects or managers. Strategic management can be initiated as a structured, systematic process with a focus on in-depth, comprehensive procedures of information gathering and strategy formulation, or it can be a more nimble operation that embodies an approach to managerial thinking and acting—quickly scanning information that is incorporated into ongoing strategy formulation and implementation. A more in-depth approach might be used for large-scale initiatives or as part of a major strategic planning effort. Less intensive approaches might be applied to smaller, more routine decisions and incorporated into ongoing management practice. As such, strategic management is in its essence a model for strategic thinking as a manager and leader (Bryson, 2018; Golensky & Hager, 2020; Laurett & Ferreira, 2018).

As noted, planning—systematically developing a blueprint for action—is infused throughout the strategic management process. As with approaches to the strategic management framework, such planning can be highly structured, in depth, and long term (that is, strategic planning) or more focused and short term (business plans, action plans, work plans, and others). The more formal approaches to planning are captured in highly defined strategic planning frameworks, such as the classic multistep models that typically span three to five years and include the steps of initiating the planning process, clarifying mission and mandates, conducting a stakeholder analysis, assessing the environment, identifying strategic issues, formulating strategies, establishing organizational visions, implementing strategies, and evaluation and monitoring (Bryson, 2018). Other models of planning lift elements from this detailed multistep approach to provide guidelines for shorter-term and more task-specific plans (Kettner, Moroney, & Martin, 2017).

As an ongoing process, strategic management may be conducted in alignment with an organization's extant or newly developed strategic plan, or it may follow its own shorter-term, task-specific, and less comprehensive planning process. Many larger nonprofits routinely conduct strategic planning, and some organizations do not, or do so only occasionally. The value of strategic planning is in its deep and extensive examination of organizational environments, structures, and issues; its constituent participatory processes; and the development of a multiyear vision, direction, and priorities for action. It anchors organizational leadership, staff, and constituents in a common purpose that is mission driven and future oriented. Research has indicated that among nonprofit organizations, strategic planning is associated with stronger fiscal performance, goal accomplishment, and board effectiveness (Bryson, 2018; Laurett & Ferreira, 2018; Siciliano, 1996). In organizations with a strategic plan, strategic management processes are aligned with the issues and directives identified via that formal planning process. However, strategic planning is also very time, labor, and resource intensive and may be infrequently updated or absent in some organizations. As an ongoing and, ideally, adaptive and agile practice, strategic management may also follow a systematic, yet less comprehensive, planning framework that incorporates a more abbreviated environmental scan and issue identification, with more highly specific delineations of strategic initiatives, implementation, and evaluation plans.

Although planning models present a systematic framework for strategic management practice, the realities of nonprofit organizational life with regard to politics, staff dynamics, resources, work overloads, and a range of other issues and uncertainties mean that these processes are implemented in unpredictable, imperfect, and seldom-linear environments. As such, implementation must be approached with an acknowledgment of the need for flexibility and adaptation as well as a keen awareness of ever-changing external and internal politics, power dynamics, economics, and other factors that may shape decisions and actions, all while underscoring the importance of acute strategic thinking and response. As leaders in this process, managers model strategic thinking, commitment, and a collaborative spirit as they build and motivate creative, productive teams of staff and stakeholders. The following sections provide descriptions of how the core elements of strategic management are executed, within a range of situations, expectations, and organizational needs.

Evidence to Inform Decisions: Information Gathering and Assessment

All strategic management processes are anchored by the organization's mission, and a first step is a reading and review of its mission statement. In some instances, the mission may be tweaked or revised to better fit shifts in organizational environments or direction, a process that is folded into the assessment and strategy development phases. Another initial step involves reviewing, updating, or conducting a stakeholder analysis. Stakeholders are unique to each organization and to each strategic planning or management initiative. Stakeholders are any individuals, groups, or organizations that are directly or indirectly involved in the organization, both internally and externally. These stakeholders are key to the organization's life and future and will participate in or be affected by strategic initiatives. Identifying the members of this network is an essential element of information gathering and crucial to an analysis of strategy choice and implementation. Examples of internal stakeholders are staff, volunteers, board members, clients or consumers, donors, funders, and others. External stakeholders may include local community officials, vendors, nonprofit partners, media, and competitors. Many resources and exercises are available with examples of how to identify, map, and analyze stakeholder interests and roles (Bryson, 2018; Bryson & Alston, 2011). To various degrees, stakeholders are participants in the strategic management process because they contribute to assessments, strategic thinking, design, and decision making and are directly or indirectly affected by the choice and implementation of strategic initiatives.

Environmental scans are the next critical component of strategic management processes. Again, strategic management is information based, and evidence informs strategy formulation. Managers determine what data are essential to decision making and strategy formulation and how and to what degree that information will be scanned, collected, and tracked. This information gathering varies according to goals, initiatives, and tasks. External and internal environmental scans or assessments can be broad and comprehensive, with a wide scope, or they can be highly focused and targeted. Strategic management initiatives that include a formal strategic planning process often have expansive environmental assessments that cover political, economic, social, and technological forces (Bryson, 2018; Yankey & Vogelsang-Coombs, 2013). In his seminal definition of a mixed scanning approach, Etizoni (1967) noted that comprehensive assessments are not often practical or needed and that managers can continuously scan their environments by using a wide-angle lens to assess the big picture external to the organization and a zoom lens to track the internal. All strategic management, regardless of the scope of the initiative, infuses various levels of ongoing data and information collection to inform strategy development and implementation.

Data that inform strategic management are drawn from both secondary and primary sources. Secondary sources contain existing data or information that has already been collected; for example, U.S. Census data; state and local demographics; reports issued by foundations, think tanks, or federal agencies; and national or local program evaluations. Primary sources include information that the organization collects directly, such as staff satisfaction surveys, focus groups with service users, internal program evaluations, and data collected via management information systems. Critical information also includes political trends and forces and how these affect organizational life. How these data are gathered and analyzed depends on the extent of the data-gathering task and organizational resources and structure, and the data typically include both quantitative and qualitative information. Managers build ongoing information collection into their management information systems, agency and program evaluations, staff performance reviews, and other ongoing practices. Some larger organizations have an evaluation or research staff or may contract or hire consultants for more extensive data analysis or collection. Others delegate data collection across a range of staff or assemble committees of volunteers from community constituents to participate in the process (Albright, 2004; Bryson, 2018).

Once data on external and internal environments have been collected, a critical next step is to identify from this information emergent challenges and opportunities for the organization. In classic strategic planning models, this is called "SWOT" (strengths, weaknesses, opportunities, and threats) analysis, with internal factors typically analyzed in terms of strengths and weaknesses and external factors in terms of opportunities and threats (Bryson, 2018). In recent years, the term "SWOC"—with the word "challenges" replacing "threats"—has sometimes been used. In addition, the acronym "SOAR" (strengths, opportunities, aspirations, results) has been applied as a more strengths-based and appreciative framework in some organizations (Ortega, 2020).

Formal strategic planning typically involves very focused and extensive SWOT–SWOC or SOAR exercises, and many resources are available on a range of methods and techniques that can be applied to conduct them (Bryson, 2018; Bryson & Alston, 2011). With regard to external data, the analytic focus is on currency, trends, and projections. How are environmental conditions (politics, economic forces, demographics, and so on) affecting organizational functioning, outlook, and goals? What are current and future challenges and opportunities for the organization? With regard to internal factors (staffing, fiscal procedures, physical space, programming, service orientation, and so on), assessment is focused on strengths and limitations. How are internal organizational operations supporting goal attainment and organizational health? What works well? What are the organization's strengths? What hinders growth and accomplishment?

Such SWOT–SWOC processes are conducted using various types of assessment and prioritization techniques. Exactly how these assessments and prioritizations are organized and administered, however, depends on the ways in which strategic management is being approached and applied. After data are collected, analyzed, and summarized, some constellation of leaders, managers, staff, or constituents—or all of these—identify and rank key issues. All strategic management efforts—those that follow a formal and expansive strategic planning process as well as those that are more informal, targeted efforts—incorporate some set of techniques meant to gauge views regarding prioritization. Those methods could include surveys, checklists and Likert scales, Delphi techniques (surveying experts), focus groups, and a wide range of ranking methods with quirky names (for example, Snow Card Technique, Five Whys, Bubble Sort, MoSCoW) (Altexsoft, 2019; Bryson & Alston, 2011). For example, participants may be given a list of five identified organizational challenges and asked to rank them from one to five in order of their importance of being addressed. The MoSCoW technique asks participants to rate a set of statements as must haves, should haves, could haves, or will not haves. Many organizations use web-based polls or surveys, and focus groups are commonly used. Numerous Web sites provide examples of ranking techniques, and prioritization software is available as well.

When strategic management is an ongoing practice—and not primarily a component of a strategic planning process conducted once every five years—various levels of environmental scans should be a routine and abiding element of organizational life. Systems of ongoing environmental assessments are in place, with additional, targeted efforts implemented as specific initiatives, issues, or problems arise. These efforts can take many forms. For example, for external scans, leaders and managers are typically members or followers of national and local networks, action organizations, think tanks, research organizations, and others with email distribution lists and Web sites that provide ongoing topic-specific information and policy briefs. External scans also involve keeping up with news cycles, social media, and the press. In nonprofit organizations, integrated internal scans may include various management information systems, dashboards, annual reports, program evaluations, performance reviews, and staff surveys.

A hallmark of nonprofit planning and management is that these assessment processes, including SWOT–SWOC exercises, are also participatory, and they draw on input—at various times and at varying levels—from a range of constituents and stakeholders across staff, consumers, and board and community members (Arnstein, 1969; Balaswamy & Dabelko, 2002; Forester, 1980; Jaskyte, 2013; Mosley, 2016). Participatory processes provide an essential democratic voice and critical input from a range of constituents, with attention to diversity, inclusion, and power dynamics at all levels. Such participatory practices are vital to the social mission, values, and planning and management processes within nonprofit organizations (Russ, 2008; Saxton, 2005).

Attending to the strategic management element of information gathering, leaders and managers keenly and actively work to stay current with external and internal economic, social, and political trends and projections as they relate to organizational mission, goals, and emerging issues. This knowledge then feeds strategy formulation and design.

Creative Process: Strategy Formulation and Design

As noted earlier, strategy formulation involves designing and choosing courses of action. It is a creative process that is mission and goal directed and informed by evidence from the environmental scans. This evidence and the prioritization of organizational opportunities, challenges, strengths, and limitations anchor the identification of key issues and problems. Managers work with their leadership teams, staff, and constituents to choose key organizational issues to be addressed. Brainstorming sessions parse alternative designs by weighing pros and cons and evaluating alternatives according to criteria such as political feasibility, financing, costs and benefits, effectiveness (what is the evidence that a particular approach can resolve the issue?), staff resources, operational feasibility, and alignment with the organizational mission (Golensky & Hager, 2020; Mishra & Mohanty, 2020). As with environmental assessments, this process is participatory, with leaders and managers variously drawing input from differing levels of staff, boards, community, consumer, and other stakeholder groups. Again, participatory practices aim for diverse and inclusive voices and input. Sometimes, formal prioritization techniques, such as ranking exercises and focus groups, are used to facilitate the choice of courses of action (Bryson, 2018). Most often, managers and leadership teams review the summaries of pros and cons for the various design paths to guide and make decisions.

As mentioned, some nonprofits have begun to incorporate design thinking in the process of strategy formulation. With origins in business and technology industries, design thinking has been described as a human-centered approach that draws on the experiences of product customers and clients to inform designs (T. Brown & Wyatt, 2010; Dunne, 2018b). With a focus on cutting-edge thinking, teams work together to identify a problem and brainstorm resolutions. The process encourages teams to build on each other's ideas with a "yes, and" ideation, and there is a focus on agile processes and short time frames for idea generation. An experiential component is typically an element as well, as team members draw plans, construct models, and apply hands-on methods for modeling and testing ideas (Dunne, 2018a, 2018b).

Once a course of action has been selected, its goal and objectives must be articulated. The goal represents an overall statement of purpose, and the objectives lay out measurable steps for achieving that goal. There are many examples of how to write measurable objectives, including both outcome objectives (intended effects) and process objectives (how the outcome objective will be accomplished; most outcome objectives have several aligned process objectives). Measurable objectives should follow the SMART objectives outline: specific, measurable, achievable, realistic, and time based (Ortega, 2020). Some begin the process with the specification of a logic model, delineating inputs, processes, outputs, outcomes, and impact as a way to think through the results to be achieved (outputs, outcomes, impact) and how to accomplish them (inputs, processes; Golensky & Hager, 2020; McLaughlin & Jordan, 1999). One of the most specific sets of instructions for writing objectives was delineated by Kettner et al. (2017) in their text *Designing and Managing Programs: An Effectiveness-Based Approach*. They recommended that all objectives include a specified time frame, target of change, product or outcome to be achieved, criteria for measurement, and designation of responsibility for monitoring and measuring the objective (Kettner et al., 2017, p. 115). An example of an outcome and process objective using this format is as follows:

- Outcome objective: To decrease homelessness in Norwood County [target of change] by 10 percent [outcome to be achieved] by January xx [time frame] as measured by the "point in time count" conducted annually by a Housing and Urban Development–sponsored team [criteria for measurement] and administered by the director of the Norwood Coalition for Homeless [responsibility for monitoring].

- Process objective: To hire five outreach caseworkers to work with homeless individuals in Norwood County [target of change and outcome] by August xx [time frame] as measured by the personnel records of the Norwood County Coalition for the Homeless [criteria for measurement] and administered by the director of the Coalition [responsibility for monitoring].

These highly specific objectives then provide very clear directions for writing an action plan for the implementation of the strategy and for its monitoring and evaluation.

Blueprint for Action: Strategy Implementation

Strategy implementation represents the execution of the chosen strategies, according to a specific and detailed plan of action. In a formal strategic planning process, implementation plans are often general outlines, with the details to be determined in the future (although in some efforts, they are much more specific) (Allison & Kay, 2015). Strategic management, however, is meant to be guided by detailed action plans, as defined by the stated goals and objectives of a particular initiative. The action plans—which might also be called task plans, work plans, or program plans—are a to-do list with a breakdown of what needs to be done, by whom, and in what time frame (McNamara, 2007). Time frames are typically specified in a Gantt chart or time line. Web sites provide many resources on how to write action plans, and software for project management, including writing action plans, proliferates.

Budgets are an integral component of an organization's planning system; they are themselves a blueprint for action because they specify operations in fiscal terms. Strategic budgets reflect the strategies and actions delineated in the goals and objectives of a strategic plan or strategic management process. As such, a strategic budget is a key element of a strategy implementation plan. Strategic budgets are often developed as a component of a formal strategic planning process and are typically—but not always—integrated into ongoing strategic management processes

(Bryce, 2017; Bryson, 2018; Steiss, 2005). Strategic budgets that are developed in concert with a formal strategic planning process align allocations to the resource and personnel requirements of defined strategic initiatives. They are long-range forecasts that cover more than one year, as aligned with multiyear strategic organizational initiatives. Different from standard incremental line-item budgets that detail annual revenues and expenses, strategic budgets may be organized around fewer categories and line items to mark strategic direction (Dropkin, Halpin, & La Touche, 2007; Steiss, 2005). The budgeting is driven by the goals and objectives articulated in strategic planning or management processes.

Without a close alliance among planning, strategic management, and budgeting, strategies are not viable with regard to implementation. If resources are not strategically designated, an action plan cannot be realized because funds are not appropriately quantified or directed (Bryson, 2018). Among the variations in strategic budgeting are models such as performance budgeting, which uses performance measures to operationalize the goals and outcome objectives of strategic planning and strategic management initiatives, and activity-based budgeting, which prioritizes and allocates resources according to planning goals and related projects (Poister, 2003; Poister, Aristigueta, & Hall, 2015; Szatmary, 2011).

With regard to strategy implementation, management is ultimately responsible for monitoring and ensuring its execution, no matter who is designated on the strategic implementation and action plans for task completion. Highly specific plans expedite managers' supervisory function because the operations are easier to track. These plans also provide a frame for discussing and assessing program strengths and limitations and for catching problems as they emerge. As such, both the specification of measurable objectives and detailed action plans guide the next element of monitoring and assessment in strategic management.

Feedback Loop: Monitoring and Evaluation

Strategic management infuses evidence and information on effectiveness throughout its proceedings. The information obtained from the measures of process and outcome objectives is fed back to leaders, managers, and staff for ongoing program corrections, improvements, adaptations, or reversals. Key to strategic management is that information exchanges are regular and continuous rather than infrequent or static. These feedback channels should be specified by leaders and managers so that they are incorporated into ongoing practice, not forgotten or neglected in the midst of hectic schedules, work overloads, and unexpected events. These channels could include scheduled discussions at staff or leadership meetings regarding the progress on and outcomes of initiatives; discussions of progress toward objectives in one-on-one staff meetings and performance reviews; reports via Web site dashboard information or in program briefs; or updates to boards, community partners and service users, and others.

The actual assessment of objectives follows standard program evaluation procedures (M. Brown & Hale, 2014; Klay, 1991; Poister et al., 2015), using the measures identified (ideally) in the written objectives or in a program or evaluation plan. Depending on the scope of evaluation and assessment efforts, and the organization's size and resources, outcome and process evaluations may be the responsibility of research or evaluation staff, or they may be outsourced to evaluation teams or consultants. In nonprofit organizations, these assessment responsibilities are more commonly incorporated into the job descriptions of managers, program coordinators, program assistants, interns, or others. Data collection occurs across the range of methods used in assessment according to what is appropriate to the initiative: individual surveys, focus groups, interviews with key informants, program attendance records, pre- and posttests, validated scales, and others. The sources of information should provide a range of perspectives relevant to the initiative with potential surveys or input from service users, providers, management and leadership staff, and community members and partners, with a focus on encompassing diversity and inclusivity with regard to voices and input.

From data collected for environmental scans through evidence gathered for monitoring and assessment, the infusion of information and evaluation throughout the strategic management process has implications for organizational creativity, quality, and effectiveness.

Promoting Organizational Innovation, Quality, and Performance

Originating in the business sector with a focus on competitive advantage and profits, models of strategic management were adapted for nonprofit organizations by focusing on the advancement of social mission, including enhanced organizational performance and outcomes and information-driven management of programs, operations, and resources (Al-Tabbaa, Leach, & March, 2014; Laurett & Ferreira, 2018). Strategic management practices within nonprofit organizations over the past decades were spurred, in part, by funders and donors who increasingly required recipient organizations to adopt professional management practices and to use strategic planning or other planning methods (Patti, 2013; Siciliano, 1997; United Way of America, 1986).

Research has indicated that the utilization of planning and strategic management practices by nonprofit organizations is positively associated with goal attainment, internal capacity building, financial performance, strong governance structures, and program effectiveness (Helmig, Ingerfurth, & Pinz, 2014; LeRoux & Wright, 2010; Ogliastri, Jager, & Prado, 2016; Ollila, 2013; Watson-Thompson, Fawcett, & Schultz, 2008). Although formal strategic planning models continue to be widely used, particularly in larger nonprofit organizations, emphasis within strategic management practice has increasingly embraced an approach that—at its core—underscores nimble and informed strategic thinking and decision making (Weerawardena & Mort, 2012). Again, key tenets of the practice are that leaders and managers continuously and intentionally incorporate information on ever-shifting internal and external organizational factors and trends to develop and adapt mission- and goal-directed strategies that advance effective programs and operations. Politics, unpredicted events, budget shortfalls, staff turnover, and a host of complex factors routinely interrupt and may threaten to derail management plans and systems—hence the focus on flexibility, agility, and solution-focused strategic thinking and decision making.

Recent trends promoting design thinking encourage out-of-the-box ideas and innovation, with a focus on drawing on consumer and constituent insights to inform the process and outcomes (Dunne, 2018b; Schaffer & Ashkenas, 2005). Strategic management requires the integration of a complex set of conceptual, technical, and relational skills and tasks. Managers must lead the process by embracing and modeling its mission-focused, creative, participatory, information-based structure across a range of diverse, project-specific stakeholders and objectives. There are many actors, interests, and initiatives to coordinate, consult, and inspire.

Within the competing values framework, strategic management—with its focus on the directing skills of goal-oriented actions and tasks—draws from across the leadership roles of boundary spanning, coordination, and human relations. Throughout the process of strategic management, leaders serve in capacities that are variously innovative, technical, structured, unpredictable, team based, inclusive, facilitative, evaluative, and directive. The strategic management framework provides a scaffolding for navigating complex environments and decisions toward a goal of organizational health and effectiveness and, perhaps, provides an opportunity for innovative and transformational leadership.

Skills Application Exercise

The Elliott Street Community Center is a private nonprofit organization located in a mid-sized city in the Midwest. Its history goes back over a century when it was founded as the Elliott Street Settlement in 1910. The community center still owns and occupies the same building in which it was founded; several adjacent buildings were purchased as well over the course of decades. In 1910, the neighborhood was made up primarily of poor, low-income, and working-class residents, many of whom were recent immigrants from Eastern Europe, and the settlement house programs included a reading room and lecture series open to all in the community, English-language lessons, and training in various occupational trades.

Today, the community center operates an after-school program (kindergarten through sixth grade), music and arts programs for children and adults, general equivalency degree programs, and classes in English as a second language. They also rent space to a Head Start program and a local theater company and lease a parking lot to a neighborhood restaurant. The center focuses on serving low-income groups, although some programs are available on a sliding scale basis to all, regardless of income. Today, the neighborhood consists of residents with a wide mix of income levels, including professionals, recent college graduates, and blue-collar and lower-income families, and it is a racially diverse community, including Black, Latinx, Asian, and White residents. Real estate values have skyrocketed, and rents are rising as well. The original settlement house building has fallen into disrepair over many years and is in need of major renovations that can no longer be delayed. It is expected that costs will be high, and a major capital campaign would be one option to pursue.

The president of the board of directors has called for a meeting with the executive director to begin a process of discernment about how to proceed. Assume the role of the executive director and apply a strategic management framework as you discuss the following questions:

1. What data and information should be collected and assessed to inform decision making?
2. What would be a goal of the discernment process?
3. What groups or individuals might participate in the strategy formulation process?
4. Brainstorm some of the alternative courses of action (strategies) that might be proposed. How might various constituents of the organization react to these proposals? What are the pros and cons of various courses of action?

5. In what ways could the management of this process be described as strategic?
6. Which directing skills from the competing values framework (see chapter 1) would be used?

References

Akingbola, K. (2013). A model of strategic nonprofit human resource management. *Voluntas, 24*, 214–240.

Albright, K. S. (2004). Environmental scanning: Radar for success. *Information Management Journal, 38*(3), 38–44.

Allison, M., & Kay, J. (2015). *Strategic planning for nonprofit organizations.* New York: Wiley.

Al-Tabbaa, O., Leach, D., & March, J. (2014). Collaboration between nonprofit and business sectors: A framework to guide strategy development for nonprofit organizations. *Voluntas, 25*, 657–678.

Altexsoft. (2019). *The most popular prioritization techniques and methods: MoSCoW, RICE, KANO model, walking skeleton, and others.* Retrieved from https://www.altexsoft.com/blog/business/most-popular-prioritization-techniques-and-methods-moscow-rice-kano-model-walking-skeleton-and-others/

Arnstein, S. (1969). A ladder of citizen participation. *Journal of the American Institute of Planners, 35*, 216–224.

Balaswamy, S., & Dabelko, H. I. (2002). Using a stakeholder participatory model in a community-wide service needs assessment of elderly residents: A case study. *Journal of Community Practice, 10*(1), 55–70.

Brown, M., & Hale, K. (2014). *Applied research methods in public and nonprofit organizations.* San Francisco: Jossey-Bass.

Brown, T., & Wyatt, J. (2010, Winter). Design thinking for social innovation. *Stanford Social Innovation Review.* Retrieved from https://ssir.org/articles/entry/design_thinking_for_social_innovation#

Bryce, H. J. (2017). *Financial and strategic management for nonprofit organizations: A comprehensive reference to legal, financial, management, and operations rules and guidelines for nonprofits* (4th ed.). Berlin: Walter DeGruyter.

Bryson, J. M. (2018). *Strategic planning for public and nonprofit organizations* (5th ed.). New York: Wiley.

Bryson, J. M., & Alston, F. K. (2011). *Creating your strategic plan: A workbook for public and nonprofit organizations* (3rd ed.). San Francisco: Jossey-Bass.

Bucher, S., Jager, U. P., & Cardoza, G. (2016). FUNDES: Becoming a strategically mindful nonprofit. *Journal of Business Research, 69*, 4489–4498.

Dropkin, M., Halpin, J., & La Touche, B. (2007). *The budget-building book for nonprofits: A step-by-step guide for managers and boards* (2nd ed.). San Francisco: Jossey-Bass.

Dunne, D. (2018a). *Design thinking at work: How innovative organizations are embracing design*. Toronto: University of Toronto Press.

Dunne, D. (2018b). Implementing design thinking in organizations: An exploratory study. *Journal of Organization Design, 7*, Article 16.

Etzioni, A. (1967). Mixed-scanning: A "third" approach to decision-making. *Public Administration Reviews, 27*, 385–392.

Forester, J. (1980). Critical theory and planning practice. *Journal of the American Planning Association, 46*, 275–286.

Golensky, M., & Hager, M. (2020). *Strategic leadership and management in nonprofit organizations: Theory and practice* (2nd ed.). New York: Oxford University Press.

Hafsi, T., & Thomas, H. (2005). Strategic management and change in high dependency environments: The case of a philanthropic organization. *Voluntas, 16*, 329–351.

Helmig, B., Ingerfurth, S., & Pinz, A. (2014). Success and failure of nonprofit organizations: Theoretical foundations, empirical evidence, and future research. *Voluntas, 25*, 1509–1538.

Jaskyte, K. (2013). Management: Practice interventions. In C. Franklin (Ed.-in-Chief), *Encyclopedia of social work*. Washington, DC, and New York: NASW Press and Oxford University Press. doi:10.1093/acrefore/9780199975839.013.590

Kettner, P., Moroney, R., & Martin, L. (2017). *Designing and managing programs: An effectiveness-based approach* (5th ed.). Los Angeles: SAGE.

Klay, W. E. (1991). Strategic management and evaluation: Rivals, partners, or just fellow travellers? *Evaluation and Program Planning, 14*, 281–289.

Laurett, R., & Ferreira, J. J. (2018). Strategy in nonprofit organizations: A systematic literature review and agenda for future research. *Voluntas, 29*, 881–897.

LeRoux, K., & Wright, N. S. (2010). Does performance measurement improve strategic decision making? Findings from a national survey of nonprofit social services agencies. *Nonprofit and Voluntary Sector Quarterly, 39*, 571–587.

McLaughlin, J., & Jordan, G. (1999). A tool for telling your program's performance story. *Evaluation and Program Planning, 22*(1), 65–72.

McNamara, C. (2007). *The field guide to nonprofit planning and facilitation*. Minneapolis: Authenticity Consulting.

Mishra, S., & Mohanty, B. (2020). Approaches to strategy formulations: A content analysis of definitions of strategy. *Journal of Management & Organization*. Advance online publication. doi:10.1017/jmo.2019.86

Mosley, J. (2016). Nonprofit organizations' involvement in participatory processes: The need for Democratic accountability. *Nonprofit Policy Forum, 7*, 77–83.

Ogliastri, E., Jager, U. P., & Prado, A. (2016). Strategy and structure in high-performing nonprofits: Insights from Iberoamerican cases. *Voluntas, 27*, 222–234.

Ollila, S. (2013). Productivity in public welfare services is changing: The standpoint of strategic competence-based management. *Social Work in Public Health, 28*, 566–574.

Ortega, D. (2020). *Strategic planning using SMART, SWOT, and SOAR analysis*. Retrieved from https://toughnickel.com/business/Strategic-Planning-Using-SOAR-and-SWOT-and-SMART-Objectives

Patti, R. J. (2013). Management: Overview. In C. Franklin (Ed.-in-Chief), *Encyclopedia of social work*. Washington, DC, and New York: NASW Press and Oxford University Press. doi:10.1093/acrefore/9780199975839.013.589

Poister, T. H. (2003). *Measuring performance in public and nonprofit organizations*. San Francisco: Jossey-Bass.

Poister, T., Aristigueta, M., & Hall, J. (2015). *Managing and measuring performance in public and nonprofit organizations: An integrated approach*. San Francisco: Jossey-Bass.

Powers, M. (2016). NGO publicity and reinforcing path dependencies explaining the persistence of media-centered publicity strategies. *International Journal of Press/Politics, 21*, 490–507.

Rhine, A. S. (2015). An examination of the perceptions of stakeholders on authentic leadership in strategic planning in nonprofit arts organizations. *Journal of Arts Management, Law, and Society, 45*, 3–21.

Russ, T. (2008) Communicating change: A review and critical analysis of programmatic and participatory implementation approaches. *Journal of Change Management, 8*, 199–211.

Saxton, G. (2005). The participatory revolution in nonprofit management: The emerging participatory society and its implications for nonprofit organization, governance, and management. *Public Manager, 34*, 34–39.

Schaffer, R., & Ashkenas, R. (2005). *Rapid results: How 100-day projects build the capacity for large-scale change*. San Francisco: Jossey-Bass.

Siciliano, J. (1996). The relationship between formal planning and performance in nonprofit organizations. *Nonprofit Management and Leadership, 74*, 387–403.

Steiss, A. W. (Ed.). (2005). *Strategic management for public and nonprofit organizations.* New York: Marcel Dekker.

Stone, M., Bigelow, B., & Crittendon, N. (1999). Research on strategic management in nonprofit organizations, synthesis, analysis, and future directions. *Administration and Society, 31*, 378–423.

Szatmary, D. (2011). Activity-based budgeting in higher education. *Continuing Higher Education Review, 75*(Fall), 69–85.

United Way of America. (1986). *Strategic management and the United Way.* Alexandria, VA: J. A. Yankey.

Watson-Thompson, J., Fawcett, S., & Schultz, J. (2008). Differential effects of strategic planning on community change in two urban neighborhood coalitions. *American Journal of Community Psychology, 42*, 25–38.

Weerawardena, J., & Mort, G. S. (2012). Competitive strategy in socially entrepreneurial nonprofit organizations: Innovation and differentiation. *Journal of Public Policy and Marketing, 31*, 91–101.

Yankey, J. A., & Vogelsang-Coombs, V. (2013). Strategic planning. In C. Franklin (Ed.-in-Chief), *Encyclopedia of social work.* New York: Oxford University Press. doi:10.1093/acrefore/9780199975839.013.380

14

Social Innovation: Entrepreneurship, Intrapreneurship, and Enterprise

Stephanie Cosner

Current economic, demographic, and social trends have created more challenges for nonprofits to respond to social issues. With significant competition for scarce resources, retraction of the welfare state, changes in longevity and health, globalization, emergent social problems, and extant problems for which solutions are inadequate, nonprofits are often faced with trying to do more with less. In this context, solving for and responding to social problems feels even more challenging.

Although this confluence of factors presents hardships for nonprofits trying to respond, recent times have also brought many innovations into the world of solving social problems. For-profit, nonprofit, and public entities have come together to address problems by using business, technology, and other innovative solutions. Examples include technology innovations, such as smartphone apps, robotics, and gaming; new business models, including social enterprises and social business; new funding models, including crowdfunding and social impact bonds; and programmatic or product-based solutions, such as participant-directed services, urban farming, and low-cost solar-powered cooking products. Many examples of social innovation stem from social work and social service organizations (Nandan, Bent-Goodley, & Mandayam, 2019).

This work in innovation to solve social problems provides new opportunities for nonprofits. Many nonprofits are expanding their footprint with the addition of market-based activities in their organizations. Nonprofits may establish social enterprises, apply for social impact bonds, or use new fundraising strategies, such as crowdfunding and cause marketing. They may make greater use of social networking and social media or integrate apps into service delivery.

To do this work requires new thinking and strategies of nonprofit leaders. Within their organizations, leaders need to build the context for innovation and create support structures to facilitate this work (Shier & Handy, 2016; Shier, Handy, & Jennings, 2019). As a directing skill, becoming prepared for innovation is about helping an organization to set goals, improve efficiency, and become more effective. This framing of innovation as an active skill is distinct from other work that focuses on innovation as an outcome (Rüedel & Lurtz, 2012). In this context, social innovation becomes a legitimate path for nonprofit organizations to pursue, in contrast to the reliance on the emergent hero model of innovation (Dacin, Dacin, & Tracey, 2011), in which a sole inventor emerges. Nandan et al. (2019) challenged the field of social work to purposefully embed social entrepreneurship, intrapreneurship, and innovation into its work. For nonprofit managers to engage in this pursuit requires that they understand innovation concepts and strengthen related skills.

Defining Social Innovation for Nonprofit Organizations

Many definitions of *social innovation* have been proposed, with common themes related to social transformation or significant progress on a social issue (Rüedel & Lurtz, 2012). Distinct from other innovations that may focus on operational effectiveness or incremental change, social innovation relates to innovations that distinctly seek to advance a social mission. Expanding on the outcome focus of many definitions, Berzin and Camarena (2018) added the concept of social innovation as pathway and process. Specifically, they defined *social innovation* as

> an umbrella term that encompasses multiple pathways and processes that address the root causes of social injustices. The solutions are more effective, efficient, and/or sustainable—socially, economically and environmentally—than previous solutions and are a result of collaboration with diverse stakeholders. (p. 5)

Although social innovation represents this expanded concept or umbrella term, other conceptualizations have focused exclusively on the pathway to change.

Social entrepreneurship was defined more than 20 years ago with a focus on the creation of new organizations or change in the social sector. Bornstein's (2003; Bornstein & Davis, 2010) seminal work demonstrated how one person with innovative ideas can bring about positive change. Such transformations were led by individuals acting boldly without limitation from resource constraints and with attention to constituencies served to achieve social value (Dees, 1998). Entrepreneurship has more recently been recognized in the nonprofit human service context, with a focus on social purpose (Mthembu & Barnard, 2019; Saebi, Foss, & Linder, 2018). In these conceptualizations, entrepreneurs share a common propensity for innovation, risk taking, seeking opportunities, and resourcefulness. Social entrepreneurs do this work with social mission as the central tenet. Using an entrepreneurial pathway toward change requires the engagement of an individual or small group inspired to create change by taking direct action to develop a solution, often persevering in the face of failure and driving solutions to completion (Martin & Osberg, 2007). Common to this approach is individually driven change without attention to existing organizations.

Although entrepreneurship has produced promising social innovations, it would be a mistake to ignore the assets, capacity, and knowledge that existing organizations bring to solving social problems. Intrapreneurship stands as an alternative path to social innovation, characterized by entrepreneurial activities within an existing organizational structure for social aims (Berzin & Pitt-Catsouphes, 2015a; Berzin, Pitt-Catsouphes, & Gaitan, 2016; Nandan, London, & Bent-Goodley, 2015). Pinchot and Pellman (1999) originally conceptualized intrapreneurship as work done by individuals within an organization with respect to developing new ideas, projects, or products. Innovation through intrapreneurial approaches avoids the entrepreneurial challenges of building organizational capacity, reliance on individual leadership, difficulty in moving to scale, and developing sustainable structures. Moreover, existing nonprofit organizations bring capacity and skills to social problem solving and community relationships and a deep understanding of the social needs that are exploited with this approach.

Building the Context for Nonprofit Engagement in Social Innovation

Although paths to innovation may include both entrepreneurial and intrapreneurial approaches, an important element for nonprofit managers is the ability to build the conditions for innovation to emerge. It is a fallacy of innovation that the best approach is to wait for the sole inventor to emerge. Companies purposefully build the conditions for innovation and put time, energy, and resources into creating the conditions for experimentation. Much of the innovations and major inventions of the past 100 years have occurred not through the work of individual genius but as a result of team approaches and organizational investment. Viewing social innovation as a directing skill confirms the ability to purposefully learn and develop this area. Nonprofit managers looking to spawn social innovation need to create conditions that

- develop their leadership competency for innovation
- create a culture that rewards risk taking and sparks creativity
- develop human capital with diverse ideas and opportunities for collaboration
- provide space and resources for experimentation

Develop Leadership Competency for Innovation

As nonprofit organizations consider innovation strategies, there is deliberate work in which managers can engage. The organizational change literature is replete with studies of characteristics that suggest that strong leadership is critical for innovation. Leaders with a commitment to innovation focus on a future orientation, with the willingness to take risks. They develop bold vision and communicate widely across the organization. In chapter 1, Edwards defines the difference between managers and leaders, with the leader's role being to set organizational tone and influence people to meet these objectives. Innovation requires managers to be leaders for influence. They must create an environment that supports others in their pursuit of new ideas, encourages their ability to take risks, and tolerates failure. Kouzes and Postner's (2003) exemplary leadership practices can be extended to innovation by modeling risk taking and experimentation, using a vision of the future to inspire change, challenging the status quo, creating the environment for innovation to emerge, and celebrating innovation successes and failures. Leaders for innovation have the ability to deal with change and navigate stakeholders, both internally and externally. In addition, they practice shared leadership that gives attention to distributive power, supporting leadership across the organization and developing staff. Nonprofit managers looking to support innovation in their organization can work toward developing these skills.

Support Innovation Culture

Building on the attributes of the leader, organizational climate and culture facilitate innovation (Glisson, 2015; Shier & Handy, 2016). Organizations need to create a common vision and mindset that supports experimentation, tolerance for risk, empathy, openness to ideation, and orientation toward incremental progress and continual improvement. These common facets of innovation culture create a landscape in which trying things out is welcome. It is a culture in which risk is rewarded and failure is accepted as part of the process of improvement. In this context, encouraging broad ideas lends itself to finding the right solution. As Nobel Prize–winning scientist Linus Pauling has often been cited as saying, "The best way to have a good idea is to have a lot of ideas." Once good ideas have been surfaced, continual improvement and refinement are part of the innovation process. Organizations that want to foster innovation build an environment with room for ideation and improvement until the right idea emerges.

Socially innovative organizations also create a culture that promotes collaboration and connection (Nilsson & Paddock, 2014). They draw heavily on the experiences of people within the organization and reinforce this culture continually. As Nilsson and Paddock (2014) remarked, in bringing in these experiences, "They do so not just in special retreats or workshops, but in the routine meetings and conversations that make up most of organizational life. . . . We call this practice 'inscaping.'" It is a powerful perspective that fundamentally includes voice, emotion, aspiration, and ideas from across the organization. Empathy is often considered a critical part of innovation work because it puts the user's perspective at the forefront. Drawing on the strength of many members of an organization allows this perspective to emerge. This type of inclusive practice coupled with a culture that embodies an openness to experimentation creates the conditions for innovation.

Develop Diverse Human Capital

Nilsson and Paddock (2014) asserted that socially innovative organizations are distinct in their reliance on the inclusion of perspectives, collaboration, and connection. In their words, the answer to what enables organizations to be innovative is "how they connect with each other." This reliance on human connection positions nonprofits to be able to nurture innovation among staff. Staff engagement is particularly relevant to innovation work (Shier et al., 2019), and it can be nurtured through transparency, trust, clearly articulated vision, clear communication, opportunities for advancement, employee empowerment, and reward structures. Diversity in the organization also fosters broad ideas and inclusion. Diversity can be looked at through broad categorical lenses, such as gender, age, race, ethnicity, disability, and veteran status, or as staff-level characteristics, such as organizational tenure, functional area, or years of experience. In social innovation work, engaging people with a wide set of skills and various backgrounds strengthens the likelihood for diverse thought.

Beyond building diverse staff and using strategies of engagement, innovation requires a significant investment in teams. Nonprofit organizations that want to support innovation work nurture diverse teams with the resources and power to move work forward. Diverse teams take on different structures because they are distinct from typical hierarchical or functional organized team structures. Diverse teams function with potential beyond the individual inventor, allowing them to foster creativity and support the emergence of truly unique ideas (Boynton & Fisher, 2005). They support the inclusion of ideas from all team members and welcome the challenge of coming together with diverse perspectives. Nonprofit managers who want to foster innovation take the time to build diverse teams, provide them with resources, and give them the autonomy that allows innovation to emerge.

Provide Resources for Innovation

As nonprofit leaders commit to building for innovation, specific investment in this work is required. People ascertain an organization's values in part by observing how the organization allocates resources. Therefore, building innovation culture, human capital, and mindset only works in conjunction with financial resources, time, and space for this work. This approach can take many different forms, but real investment in each of them is needed. Varying in scale and scope, resource investment might be obtained through dedicated time, space, or financial investment.

Nonprofit staff often work in resource-constrained environments, with limited time dedicated to developing new projects. It is not that piloting and program development are uncommon, but that traditional planning processes and program implementation take up the bulk of time. There is less room for creativity and experimentation. When new ideas are developed, the expectation is often a create-and-implement approach rather than a focus on continual creation through incremental change and continuous improvement. In an innovation approach, iteration becomes the constant work of the organization rather than the means to a final product. Building for innovation requires staff resources and attention to these activities. Dedicated staff who work on innovation mimic large-scale research and development efforts at for-profit companies. Specific innovation teams create the resources for this work to emerge. When creating dedicated teams is not possible, investing in a limited way, by putting aside specific time, holding an innovation meeting, or creating a specific innovation project, can spur this type of creative work.

Space for innovation can be conceptualized in varying ways in a nonprofit context. In some communities, public–private–nonprofit partnerships have yielded major development of physical spaces, design centers, or innovation hubs as the catalyst for innovation to flourish (Morel, Dupont, & Boudarel, 2018). In other settings, smaller investment in internal spaces can support these efforts. Physical space that encourages collaboration, open conversation, and spontaneous interaction lends itself to this work. The use of raw materials, color, light, quotes, and slogans that spur creativity can be small investments toward this aim. Using different materials in the physical space creates a message of ingenuity and openness to varying perspectives. The availability of materials often associated with innovation such as white boards, markers, sticky notes, and art materials may shape conversations or meetings differently. Having a variety of resources on hand is connected to creativity and inspiration. Although some nonprofits might invest in true maker spaces dedicated to innovation work and some may be part of larger collaborative efforts that have distinct innovation space, others can work with limited resources to create contexts that support innovation.

Financial investment for innovation may come through specific resources for experimentation, piloting, or development. Specific allocations for idea generation and development can support innovation work. Structures that include ideation sessions, competitions, hackathons, innovation labs, and retreats provide structure and resources to support innovation in organizations. Berzin and Camarena (2018) described low-investment activities that can be integrated into particular meetings; for example, root cause analysis, ideation activities, and prototyping approaches. Deeper investment might involve providing internal grants for innovation work or seed money for competitions or running innovation labs with teams given the resources, time, and space for ideation, development, and implementation. In each of these cases, the financial investment not only provides the resource for the work but also signals the organization's support for innovation.

Specific Strategies for Social Innovation

In addition to building the right environment, nonprofit managers can actively pursue certain strategies for innovation. Some strategies support innovation work, and others become the solutions. Certain strategies have more commonly been used to pursue innovation in the nonprofit context.

Although innovation does not follow one path, examples of specific innovative strategies commonly used by nonprofits include

- human-centered design as an approach to fostering innovation
- social enterprise
- innovations in resource development
- technology-driven solutions

Human-Centered Design

Human-centered design (also called design thinking) is a promising approach that nonprofit managers can use to foster innovation in their organizations (Nandan, Jaskyte, & Mandayam, 2020). Human-centered design has been developed over the past 25 years to produce solutions using an expanded approach to assessment and solution generation (Brown & Wyatt, 2010). The approach has more recently been applied to solving social problems, and it has shown utility in the nonprofit context. At its core, human-centered design uses inspiration, ideation, and implementation as critical stages to move from understanding a problem to developing multiple solutions, to moving potential solutions, to real-world applications (Brown, 2009). Unique to this approach is its focus on placing the experiences of end users at the forefront of the design process. In addition, the methodology relies on an interactive approach to developing, generating, and testing ideas to narrow in on a solution (see Nandan et al., 2020). This approach, known as rapid prototyping, allows the exploration of multiple potential solutions and the use of continuous iteration to develop the best solution.

Design thinking strategies have been applied in nonprofit organizations, both to stimulate innovative ideas and to create a leadership development opportunity for staff (Berzin & Pitt-Catsouphes, 2015b). Specific examples of design thinking projects in human service organizations include a reform project for Georgia's child welfare system and one county's effort to address the mental and emotional health of teenagers (Nandan et al., 2020). Common to these projects was the ability to create novel solutions to entrenched problems by generating numerous potential solutions.

Social Enterprise

Considering pathways to innovation, social enterprise may be particularly alluring to nonprofit managers. Many nonprofits are examining different ways to diversify revenue and make use of business principles to support their work. "Social enterprise" refers to the use of business practices, models, or market-driven approaches to advance social, environmental, and human rights agendas. Different from other businesses, social enterprises address social need and serve the common good as the primary purpose of their efforts. Although revenue and commercial activity are also drivers, social mission remains the primary focus. Social enterprises serve three main purposes:

1. Provide an additional income source and provide unrestricted funds.
2. Employ hard-to-employ populations and provide skills development opportunities.
3. Create a market or business with the primary goal of social impact.

Revenue from social enterprise can be considered a potential option to support financial sustainability, add additional unrestricted income, or fill gaps in program costs. Social enterprise can also be used to train and employ populations that would otherwise have difficulty entering the traditional market. This approach provides the potential to expand to new customers or clients, create new products or services for existing customers, or develop completely new products or services. Nonprofits may be drawn to specific earned income strategies, including fee for service, revenue from product sales, payment for services purchased, subscriptions, paid training or train-the-trainer models, or rent or leases of equipment or buildings. For nonprofits, social enterprise may less often be used for the creation of a market or business with social impact and may instead be used in conjunction with existing nonmarket strategies.

As a training platform, social enterprise can be a powerful tool to support populations who struggle to find employment in traditional markets. One example of this approach is a nonprofit book-selling business, More Than Words (https://mtwyouth.org), that trains and employs youth who are involved in the foster care or court systems, homeless, or out of school. Another example, UTEC (https://utecinc.org/), an agency that serves disconnected youth, has developed multiple social enterprises, including mattress recycling, food services, and woodworking, and created employment and development opportunities for youth with a history of incarceration or serious criminal involvement. These powerful models support populations in need using market-based strategies.

Although social enterprises offer potential innovation, they are in no way a panacea. Social enterprises tend to not be highly profitable and often have costs associated with developing and implementing them. To be successful, social enterprises must address a true market need and build on the organization's assets. Nonprofit organizations need to commit only to enterprises that connect clearly to mission and are feasible for the organization's capacity.

Innovations in Resource Development

Although social enterprise provides one strategy for innovation, nonprofit managers should consider other innovations in resource development in this time of scarcity. New mechanisms to support nonprofit work have proliferated and created opportunities, but they have also increased competition for resources. New approaches to individual charitable giving and institutional philanthropy should be explored.

Driven in part by information and communications technology, nonprofits now have easier access to a wide group of people to support their work. For example, crowdfunding is the approach of raising small amounts of money from several individuals, often through the Internet or a social media platform. It opens the possibility of engaging individuals beyond the traditional donor base for specific projects or work. Web sites that allow individuals to raise money with this approach have proliferated. Nonprofit managers can consider how they could use similar campaigns in their work.

Venture philanthropy, another philanthropic approach, uses specific investment in a cause or organization to achieve social aims. This approach borrows from the traditional venture capital approach of investing in companies with support and extends the relationship between the giver and receiver. In venture philanthropy, foundations or individuals who provide philanthropic support also engage in capacity building and more direct engagement. Different from grants, which tend to limit the relationship between grantee and grantor to reports about how grant money is used, venture philanthropy creates more intensive engagement, monitoring, and support.

Another innovation in resource development comes from the public sector and engages nonprofits and investors. This approach, social impact bonds (also called pay-for-success), creates a contract among the public sector, an investor, and the organization delivering services or responsible for achieving a particular social outcome. The governing authority agrees to pay for better social outcomes and, if achieved, passes the savings on to the investor who supported the endeavor. This performance-based approach creates a three-way relationship, with all parties having a stake in achieving clearly defined outcomes. Each of these mechanisms creates new opportunities for nonprofit managers to support their mission.

Technology-Driven Solutions

As nonprofits consider embracing innovation, many solutions are driven by or supported by technology. "Information and communications technology" refers to the collective set of technologies used to communicate, including those for the storage, transmission, and manipulation of information (see chapter 11). Compared with for-profit organizations, nonprofit organizations have been slow to adopt technologies (Zorn, Flanagin, & Shoham, 2011). Yet many opportunities exist for nonprofits to use technology in ways that extend far beyond traditional operational functions. Technology infusion has often been considered a hallmark of innovation.

Technology can provide a platform for innovation through strategies such as crowdsourcing for idea generation or development. Technology-driven competitions through social media may engage larger sets of the population in responding to social issues, or they may allow nonprofits to test prototype solutions. Data mining and data analytics may drive an understanding of complex problems and broaden the ability to look across issues. Technology also provides the potential for innovative solutions to social problems. Many mobile applications are being used in communication, treatment, and tracking. Apps are being designed to support people with health and mental health problems and for issues as wide ranging as homelessness, suicide, and domestic violence. Interactive web- and app-based platforms create opportunities for services that are flexible and highly personalized and can reach broad populations. Virtual communities provide new opportunities to connect clients, engage end users, and provide support. Gaming environments have been used for innovative solutions to youth violence and for treatment of posttraumatic stress disorder and depression. Robotics have become increasingly common in health settings. As nonprofits consider strategies for innovation, part of this work involves developing technology competence and considering technology-based solutions. As Berzin and Camarena (2018, p. 48) stated, "It is the paradigm shift in which nonprofits approach technology as an imperative that will drive innovation and further [their] mission."

Conclusion

Innovation can provide a broad set of tools and strategies for nonprofit managers to respond to social issues in an ever-shifting environment. Social innovation provides pathways and approaches to support problem solving, as well as skills that nonprofit managers need to operate differently in the present context. Social entrepreneurship defines a set of principles that can be extended into the nonprofit environment through intrapreneurship. Social enterprise provides one of a set of solutions to resource development.

For nonprofit managers, emerging social issues often compete with existing problems, and there are seemingly fewer resources to do the same or even more work. At their core, nonprofit organizations exist to respond to social problems. It is the shared mission of the sector to do everything possible to support clients and use every possible strategy to address social needs. Social innovation offers an additional path to respond to social needs. Advances in technology, emergent business models, practice advances, and new approaches to problem solving create complementary paths to traditional research and program development.

To be ready for this context, nonprofit managers can explicitly work to develop skills that foster social innovation. They can create a workforce that has the time and resources to engage in experimentation and exploration. Managers can advance innovation by building diverse human capital, creating diverse teams, and amplifying shared voices. They can design physical spaces that encourage creativity and use human-centered design practices as part of everyday work. Nonprofit organizations can realign culture and resources to clarify shared ownership, openness to risk taking, and support for innovation. Real investment is needed in the sector to support these efforts.

Extending beyond their organization, nonprofit managers need to advocate more broadly for innovation in the sector. In working with funders, they need to create stronger pathways to social innovation. Current support for innovation has often been through competitions and foundation work that rewards the sole inventor, the establishment of new organizations, or the scaling of entrepreneurial ideas. A realignment of these priorities would put resources for innovation into existing organizations. Venture philanthropy and social impact bonds are two approaches that provide resources for innovation in nonprofits. Moving nonprofits into innovation takes concerted work, but as with any skill, the capacity for innovation can be developed.

Skill Application Exercises

1. Understanding innovative solutions: Innovation takes on different forms, depending on your field or the issues your organization tackles. Take note of innovation in your social problem area. Consider innovative solutions.

- What social problem is your field trying to address? What do you see as the most innovative solutions to this problem? Are there leaders from outside the nonprofit sector?
- What about innovative solutions your organization has engaged in? What are the most innovative approaches you have taken in the past five years to change services, delivery, or process?

2. Innovation in organization and culture: Culture and climate foster experimentation and creativity. Developing resources and staff can support the emergence of innovation. Re-examine your organization's culture and climate.

   - What parts of your organization's culture support risk taking and creativity? Are there cultural barriers that discourage failure or trial?
   - How does the human capital in your organization foster innovation? Is there an openness to diversity of ideas or perspectives? How could this be strengthened?
   - Name your organization's resources for innovation. If a robust set of financial incentives, resources, space, or time allocation for innovation do not exist, develop a suggested list. Include some that are low, medium, and high investment.

3. Building an innovation strategy:

   - Challenge your organization to use the human-centered design process for one meeting or one project (see Berzin & Camerena, 2018; Brown, 2009; or https://www.ideou.com/pages/design-thinking, for ideas to get started).
   - Solve a problem in a new way. Bring a particular issue or problem to a group discussion. Challenge yourselves to generate solutions using technology, social enterprise, or new funding approaches. Consider product-based or process-oriented solutions. How do these solutions compare with the current services, products, and programs you offer? Could any of these new ideas be incorporated into existing approaches?
   - Your organization has a new solution for your target issue. Consider new approaches to support funding and development. Do you have strategic funding partners who might be interested? Do you need to develop new resources? Is it connected to your central mission?

References

Berzin, S. C., & Camarena, H. (2018). *Innovation from within: Redefining how nonprofits solve problems.* New York: Oxford University Press.

Berzin, S. C., & Pitt-Catsouphes, M. (2015a). Social innovation from the inside: Considering the intrapreneurship path. *Social Work, 60,* 360–362.

Berzin, S. C., & Pitt-Catsouphes, M. (2015b). Stimulating innovation within social sector organizations: The application of design thinking. *Journal of Entrepreneurship & Organization Management, 4*(3), 1–7.

Berzin, S. C., Pitt-Catsouphes, M., & Gaitan, P. (2016). Innovation and sustainability: An exploratory study of intrapreneurship among human service organizations. *Human Service Organizations: Management, Leadership, & Governance, 40,* 540–552.

Bornstein, D. (2003). *How to change the world: Social entrepreneurs and the power of new ideas.* New York: Oxford University Press.

Bornstein, D., & Davis, S. (2010). *Social entrepreneurship: What everyone needs to know.* New York: Oxford University Press.

Boynton, A., & Fisher, B. (2005). *Virtuoso teams: Lessons from team that changed their worlds.* Boston: Prentice Hall/Financial Times.

Brown, T. (2009). *Change by design: How design thinking transforms organizations and inspires innovation.* New York: HarperCollins.

Brown, T., & Wyatt, J. (2010). Design thinking for social innovation. *Development Outreach, 12*(1), 29–43. doi:10.1596/1020-797X_12_1_29

Dacin, M. T., Dacin, P. A., & Tracey, P. (2011). Social entrepreneurship: A critique and future directions. *Organization Science, 22,* 1203–1213. doi:10.1287/orsc.1100.0620

Dees, J. G. (1998). *The meaning of social entrepreneurship.* Durham, NC: Center for the Advancement of Social Entrepreneurship. Retrieved from https://centers.fuqua.duke.edu/case/wp-content/uploads/sites/7/2015/03/Article_Dees_MeaningofSocialEntrepreneurship_2001.pdf

Glisson, C. (2015). The role of organizational culture and climate in innovation and effectiveness. *Human Service Organizations: Management, Leadership & Governance, 39,* 245–250.

Kouzes, J. M., & Posner, B. Z. (2003). *The leadership challenge workbook.* San Francisco: Jossey-Bass.

Martin, R. L., & Osberg, S. (2007). Social entrepreneurship: The case for definition. *Stanford Social Innovation Review, 5*(2). Retrieved from https://ssir.org/articles/entry/social_entrepreneurship_the_case_for_definition

Morel, L., Dupont, L., & Boudarel, M. R. (2018). Innovation spaces: New places for collective intelligence? In D. Uzunidis (Ed.), *Collective innovation processes* (pp. 87–107). London: ISTE/Wiley.

Mthembu, A., & Barnard, B. (2019). Social entrepreneurship: Objectives, innovation, implementation and impact on entrepreneurship. *Expert Journal of Business and Management, 7*, 147–177.

Nandan, M., Bent-Goodley, T. B., & Mandayam, G. (2019). *Social entrepreneurship, intrapreneurship, and social value creation: Relevance for contemporary social work practice.* Washington, DC: NASW Press.

Nandan, M., Jaskyte, K., & Mandayam, G. (2020). Human centered design as a new approach to creative problem solving: Its usefulness and applicability for social work practice. *Human Service Organizations: Management, Leadership & Governance, 44*, 310–316. doi:10.1080/23303131.2020.1737294

Nandan, M., London, M., & Bent-Goodley, T. (2015). Social workers as social change agents: Social innovation, social intrapreneurship, and social entrepreneurship. *Human Service Organizations: Management, Leadership & Governance, 39*, 38–56. doi:10.1080/23303131.2014.955236

Nilsson, W., & Paddock, T. (2014, Winter). Social innovation from the inside out. *Stanford Social Innovation Review.* Retrieved from https://ssir.org/articles/entry/social_innovation_from_the_inside_out

Pinchot, G., & Pellman, R. (1999). *Intrapreneuring in action: A handbook for business innovation.* San Francisco: Barrett-Koehler.

Rüedel, D., & Lurtz, K. (2012). *Mapping the various meanings of social innovation: Towards a differentiated understanding of an emerging concept.* Oestrich-Winkel, Germany: EBS Business.

Saebi, T., Foss, N. J., & Linder, S. (2018). Social entrepreneurship research: Past achievements and future promises. *Journal of Management, 45*, 70–95. doi:10.1177/0149206318793196

Shier, M. L., & Handy, F. (2016). Cross-sector partnerships: Factors supporting social innovation by nonprofits. *Human Service Organizations: Management, Leadership & Governance, 40*, 253–266. doi:10.1080/23303131.2015.1117556

Shier, M. L., Handy, F., & Jennings, C. (2019). Interorganizational conditions supporting social innovations by human service nonprofits. *Nonprofit and Voluntary Sector Quarterly, 48*, 173–193. doi:10.1177/0899764018797477

Zorn, T. E., Flanagin, A. J., & Shoham, M. D. (2011). Institutional and noninstitutional influences on information and communication technology adoption and use among nonprofit organizations. *Human Communication Research, 37*(1), 1–33. doi:10.1111/j.1468-2958.2010.01387.x

PART SIX

Leading Nonprofits in Uncertain Times

As pointed out in chapter 1 and throughout this book, those who have the responsibility of leading and managing nonprofit organizations function in an environment of competing values. In the nonprofit world, change is virtually constant, and those leading nonprofits find they must play multiple roles and draw on a variety of different skills, often more or less simultaneously. In the day-to-day world of nonprofit management, it is easy to get bogged down with the work at hand and lose sight of the reason for it all. It is important for nonprofit leaders and managers to periodically pause and ask themselves such questions as "Why?" "So what?" and "What difference does it make?" and to engage other members of their organizations in discussions on these questions. The answers should have a great deal to do with the organization's mission and with the people and communities the organization serves.

In chapter 15, Melinda Manning and Kimberly Strom address a range of ethical issues confronting nonprofit leaders and managers, stressing the particular importance of ethical behavior for nonprofit organizations. They point out that many nonprofits serve as public charities and work with some of the most vulnerable parts of their communities. Manning and Strom discuss various definitions of ethical leadership, ethical dilemmas confronting nonprofit managers, and a range of ethical challenges arising from conflicts of interest, conflicts of commitment, governance, finance, fundraising, and accountability. Manning and Strom suggest that ethical leaders need to create cultures that reinforce ethical practices.

In chapter 16, Daniel A. Lebold and Richard L. Edwards discuss the impact on nonprofit organizations of rapid and unexpected shifts in funding. They consider the critical impact on the nonprofit sector of the COVID-19 pandemic, which led to massive unemployment across the nation and caused unprecedented stresses on nonprofits and those whom they serve. Lebold and Edwards consider what nonprofit organizations need to do to weather extreme conditions that may lead to major decreases in funding and increases in demands for their services. They compare how nonprofits were affected by and how they responded to both the COVID-19 pandemic of 2020 and the Great Recession of 2008–2009, considering their impacts on nonprofit managers and staff. They also suggest specific steps that nonprofit leaders and managers can implement to more effectively manage when confronted with financial uncertainty and organizational decline. Finally, Lebold and Edwards include an example of guiding principles that nonprofit leaders and managers can follow to prepare their organizations to deal with severe economic challenges.

15

Ethical Issues in Nonprofit Leadership

Melinda Manning and Kimberly Strom

There is no check-box for ethical leadership. It is an ongoing individual and organizational journey.

—Linda Fisher Thornton

Ethics must begin at the top of an organization. It is a leadership issue and the chief executive must set the example.

—Edward Hennessy

Scandals involving business leaders have dominated the news in the past decade, from serial sexual harassers Harvey Weinstein and Roger Ailes to "pharma bro" Martin Shkreli, who arbitrarily raised the price of a lifesaving drug by 5,000 percent, to Elizabeth Holmes, who essentially created imaginary medical technology (Mohan, 2019). Notable instances of wrongdoing have, unfortunately, not been limited to the for-profit world. Highly respected charities such as Oxfam, UNICEF, Red Cross, and Wounded Warriors have been accused of offenses ranging from covering up sex abuse claims to misusing donations for personal use (Missionbox, 2019). These ethical lapses have led to public distrust and created widespread cynicism about those in leadership positions. A new focus on ethical leadership in all types of organizations is necessary to rebuild trust in institutions, ensure accountability, and protect against some of the enormous financial losses that have resulted from these ethical failures.

Ethical behavior is particularly important in the nonprofit sector. For starters, many nonprofit organizations serve as public charities and work with the most vulnerable members of their communities, from abandoned animals to people living with mental and physical disabilities to people experiencing poverty, violence, and abuse. Vulnerable groups require careful handling and safeguards to protect them and to ensure effective service delivery (O'Neill, 2001). Ethical shortcuts by staff could lead to dangerous conditions and irreparable harm to clients. Ethical behaviors are modeled from the top down. Frontline workers are more likely to engage in ethical behaviors when they see their managers, supervisors, and those in higher-level leadership positions acting ethically.

Ethical behavior is also important because many nonprofits' sole or major source of funding is donations. U.S. charities raised nearly $428 billion in 2018, a slight increase over 2017 (Giving USA, 2019). In 2019, about 73 percent of Americans donated to some type of nonprofit (Jones, 2020). Charitable giving encompasses about 2 percent of the U.S. gross domestic product (Charity Watch, 2020). These donations vary from million-dollar bequests from wealthy families or corporations to "penny drives" by schoolchildren. Donors have reasonable and often lofty expectations that their donations of every size will be used wisely to further the cause or causes that inspired them to donate in the first place. Fundraisers often makes promises, either directly or indirectly, about how the funds or items are to be used by the charity. When nonprofits do not maintain good stewardship practices, vulnerable clients may not receive the services that they need, and funders will choose to donate elsewhere. After the United Way of the National Capital scandal that involved financial fraud by top staff, donations dropped from $45 to $18 million (Whorishky & Salmon, 2003). Unethical behavior by one nonprofit can even hurt donations to others. A 2018 survey found that 60 percent of participants reported that they would give less that year after learning about various nonprofit scandals (Missionbox, 2019).

Last, many nonprofits intend to promote positive community values. Charitable organizations can create ways for different groups to work together toward common goals; solve a range of societal problems; and help communities grow stronger, healthier, and more inclusive. The approximately 1.3 million charitable nonprofits in the United States touch the lives of almost every American and provide direct and indirect benefits to millions (National Council of Nonprofits, 2020e). As a result of this potentially wide sphere of influence, nonprofits that display ethical leadership practices could serve as role models for both other organizations and individuals (Brown, Treviño, & Harrison, 2005).

Ethical Leadership

One widely used definition of *ethical leadership* is "the demonstration of normatively appropriate conduct through personal actions and interpersonal relationships, and the promotion of such conduct to followers through two-way communication, reinforcement, and decision-making" (Brown et al., 2005, p. 120). This definition characterizes ethical leadership as an entirely different form of leadership than leadership with an ethical aspect (Mayer, Kuenzi, Greenbaum, Bardes, & Salvador, 2009). This type of leadership has two main aspects: the moral person and the moral manager. In the moral person aspect, as with virtue ethics, personal attributes such as integrity and concern for others form ethical leaders. The moral manager aspect focuses on the ways in which leaders influence their subordinates' ethical behaviors (Trevino, Brown, & Hartman, 2003).

Other researchers have described ethical leadership as leadership that values the rights and dignity of other individuals (Ciulla, 2004). It is more than keeping staff from doing the wrong thing; it is empowering employees to do the right thing (Freeman & Stewart, 2006). Some leaders may have the ethically correct intentions but because of their incompetence are unable to put their values into practice and thus make unethical decisions (Ciulla, 2005).

In a study of cross-cultural aspects of ethical leadership, key attributes included ethical awareness, character and integrity, community and people orientation, motivating, encouraging and empowering, and managing ethical responsibility (Resick, Hanges, Dickson, & Mitchelson, 2006). Regarding that final attribute, managing ethical responsibility, ethical leaders are viewed as those who do not tolerate misconduct within the organization and who will educate as well as discipline employees and volunteers for ethical lapses as needed (Trevino et al., 2003).

Nonprofit leaders have powerful capacity to create ethical organizations by valuing and communicating integrity. Everyone takes their cues from the tone at the top. What behaviors are condoned? Do words and deeds align with stated values? Who is held accountable? Is anyone allowed to bend the rules or cut corners? Ethics are influenced by organizational culture and climate (Malloy & Agarwal, 2001). Organizational culture is shaped by the nonprofit's values and behaviors and maintained by an array of communications and interactions. Climate refers to the ways that culture is manifested in the realities of the workplace. The ethical culture and climate establish the boundaries of acceptable and unacceptable behaviors. The 2007 National Nonprofit Ethics Survey found that nonprofits with strong ethical cultures have supervisors who reward ethical conduct, leaders who display integrity, a strong commitment to ethics among all employees, and a culture in which even routine decisions are made in accordance with the organization's stated values (Ethics Resource Center, 2007). Ethical principles need to be considered in all organizational functions, including strategic planning, personnel management, compensation and benefits, audits, communications, and public relations (Rhode & Packel, 2009), as well as inclusive, transparent decision making (Malloy & Agarwal, 2001). Nonprofit leaders should be willing to ask the tough ethical questions, such as "Is this fair?" and "Is this the right thing to do?" Leaders not only need to ask these types of questions, they also need to be able to hear critical feedback from stakeholders (Rhode & Packel, 2009).

The Markkula Center of Applied Ethics describes six ways in which leaders can reinforce their organization's ethical climate: (1) modeling and revealing their character and values to others, (2) creating community through shared values, (3) encouraging ethical behavior in all aspects of work, (4) definitively and publicly clarifying their role, (5) reexamining and clarifying the organization's culture, and (6) designing ethical systems within the organization (Skeet, 2017).

Ultimately, ethical culture may hinge on the behaviors of the top leadership. "No organizational mission statement or ceremonial platitudes can counter the impact of seeing leaders withhold crucial information, play favorites with promotion, stifle dissent, or pursue their own self-interest at the organization's expense" (Rhode & Packel, 2009, p. 12).

Ethics and Ethical Dilemmas

The field of ethics concerns itself with the understanding of right and wrong. Building on roots in philosophy and religion, the questions of what is right and how right behavior should be determined infuse daily life in ways big and small. How can scarce resources such as food or medicine be distributed? What are universal human rights? Is it unethical to surveil employees on social media? Should medical professionals or government leaders withhold information about risks of an epidemic from the public? Is it ethical to confront friends, colleagues, or family members who make racist or sexist comments?

In nonprofit leadership, matters of ethics can include malfeasance (intentional wrongdoing) and nonfeasance (the failure to do the right thing) (Thomas & Strom-Gottfried, 2018). Decisions about right and wrong are influenced by an array of laws and regulations, governing board decisions, accrediting bodies, professional standards, organizational mission, values, policies and bylaws, and personal integrity. Principled, ethical leadership requires the commitment to these various conventions. It also demands having adequate processes for ethical decision making and support in maintaining personal and organizational integrity.

Some ethical choices are not clear-cut. Ethical dilemmas arise as a result of competing goods or rights. For example, clients rely on a social work organization for in-home care, but coronavirus disease 2019 (COVID-19) has made protective equipment scarce, and state orders require nonessential workers to stay at home. Should an administrator advocate for staff to be considered essential and thus require them to visit clients, potentially exposing the clients, workers, and their respective families to risk of virus transmission? In situations such as this, it is easy to see that there are reasonable arguments to be made on both sides, and thus effective leaders must have the will and capacity to make sound decisions among competing priorities or values.

The Institute of Global Ethics classifies ethical dilemmas as arising from at least one of the following competing goods (Kidder, 1995): justice versus mercy, truth versus loyalty, individual versus community or other individuals, and short term versus long term.

Justice versus Mercy

In this ethical dilemma, justice speaks to the importance of following established rules, guidelines, or eligibility criteria, whereas mercy involves grace, contextual factors, teachable moments, and second chances. For example, a dilemma of this type might arise when hiring criteria require certain educational credentials, but those qualifications disadvantage candidates of color or persons whose lived experience would prepare them well for the particular job.

Truth versus Loyalty

In social work and other health and human services positions, professionals make commitments (loyalty) to protect private personnel, organizational, or client information. Nevertheless, situations may arise in which the right course of action would be to break the promise of confidentiality and share the truth. Administrators and supervisors may be aware of strategic organizational changes or budget cuts that would be unethical to share prematurely, yet they may also feel obligated to notify staff about the possible changes lest employees make decisions based on a false sense of security.

Individual versus Community or Other Individuals

Many situations can give rise to conflicts of interest when the needs of one individual or group are incompatible with those of another. Nonprofit leaders often work at the crossroads of competing demands, amid the interests of clients, staff, board members, funders, and the public. Each of these stakeholders has meritorious needs, expectations, and interests, but fulfilling the obligations to one group can sometimes clash with fulfilling those of another. In a climate of anti-immigrant suspicion and backlash, for example, an agency serving Latinx or refugee populations may create policies and procedures to protect the safety of clients even though this stance puts the staff and management at odds with governmental authorities such as local police or Immigration and Customs Enforcement. It is worth noting that this situation is also an example of the other three categories of dilemmas. As is often the case, complex ethical challenges can involve more than one pair of goods or rights.

Short Term versus Long Term

Many decisions in nonprofit organizations weigh short-term against long-term benefits. Is the effort of applying for a grant to start a new program worth the opportunity and sunk costs? Will ongoing funding be available to sustain the program? Will it fit with other services to further the agency's mission? These and other dilemmas involve ethical as well as financial and practical considerations. When communities come together to protest injustice, it makes sense that organizations whose missions focus on civil rights and social justice turn out to support the shared cause. However, what if backlash from government funders, donors, or influential board members jeopardizes the organization's funding? Social workers are expected to work for social justice, and, in ethics terms, being congruent with one's professional values and organizational mission is good in both the short term and the long term. So is keeping the agency financially viable and protecting activist workers from retaliation. Certain political actions can jeopardize the organization's nonprofit status (Thomas & Strom-Gottfried, 2018). Clearly, leaders' decisions must take an array of interests into account. Their personal convictions are important, but the results of their decisions will redound to clients, staff, and the organization as a whole. Examples such as this speak to the importance of leaders possessing both sound ethical decision-making ability and the moral courage to act on the decisions they have made.

Ethical Decision Making

Many models exist for reflecting on and resolving ethical dilemmas. Although the form and priorities vary, most frameworks involve the consideration of values, ethical principles, laws, and circumstances in weighing alternative choices. Rarely is the result a commonly accepted and clearly defined path: The process and result of decision making is contextual, involving rational and emotional reactions, external pressures and priorities, and professional obligations. The ethical dilemmas that emerge in nonprofit organizations may not allow for protracted deliberations; therefore, leaders must be well prepared to respond appropriately in demanding and emergent situations. Ethical decision-making processes can be used in response to crisis situations or in post hoc reflection on decisions made without benefit of prior deliberation. Decision making is a nonlinear process that often includes the following elements in various configurations:

1. Generating and weighing options: Although ethical dilemmas can often feel like no-win situations, a key to resolution is avoiding false dichotomies, finding alternative or incremental possibilities, and considering the pros and cons of various choices. For instance, how do the options fit with prevailing laws, regulations, and policies? With personal and organizational values and principles? With fiduciary responsibilities of leadership? With ethical standards?

2. Seeking consultation—"It's lonely at the top": Administrative roles can be isolated, both by the singular nature of the positions and by the burden of the related responsibilities. Isolation can also be self-imposed when leaders' pride, ego, or fear prohibit reaching out for assistance. Effective leadership requires humility, integrity, and self-discipline (George, 2003). These resources are vital in the face of ethical dilemmas, and ethical decision making is further enhanced by experts who can help the leader process and weigh options. The expertise may be in house (board of directors, human resources, diversity and equity, clinical) or external, via consultants, networking, or professional associations and coalitions. Beyond generating and weighing options, consultation can help leaders think through difficult conversations and other process considerations, and they can help evaluate ethical decisions and outcomes after the fact.

3. Planning how to carry out the decision: How a decision is enacted often affects the outcome. Imagine, for example, a nonprofit that decides it cannot accept a philanthropic gift because the donor's reputation is

antithetical to the organization's mission and values. Under any circumstance, this is a fraught decision that will have short-term and long-term implications for the nonprofit, its leadership, its clientele, and its donor base. How the decision is communicated to various stakeholders will be key in yielding the best possible outcome from a challenging situation.

4. Evaluating: Some ethical dilemmas are unique, but over time, most will be variations within the categories of competing goods described earlier. Reflecting on dilemmas, how the outcomes were chosen and enacted, and how well or poorly they turned out is important for two reasons. First, if the decision had negative effects, evaluation can indicate whether anything can be done to mitigate those harms, to make amends, or rescind the action. Second, regardless of how well the decision worked out, evaluation helps leaders build their ethical fitness (Kidder, 2005) so that future dilemmas may be seen as variants on past experiences and adroitly addressed.

Moral Courage

Although it is vital to make wise decisions, leadership still requires having the will to act ethically. Moral courage describes action on behalf of principles, in the face of possible harms (Kidder, 2005). In nonprofit settings, these harms can take the form of retaliation, exclusion from decision making, shunning by peers, or job termination. Leaders can develop their capacity for courage by understanding the personal and organizational barriers to action, studying role models, seeking support, and developing skills for engaging in difficult conversations (Strom, 2020).

Common impediments to acting with courage include deference to authority, lack of confidence, burnout, conflict avoidance, fear of reprisal, or feeling that action is futile (Strom-Gottfried, 2019a; Weinberg, 2009). Group dynamics can also repress candid discussions and ethical action. Groupthink occurs when teams value apparent consensus and nondissent. As such, troubling decisions or plans are not examined or questioned because each member of the group assumes that others are in agreement with the decision and there is therefore no merit in speaking up. The bystander effect is a form of collective irresponsibility that occurs when a problem is really an elephant in the room, but because many people are aware of it, none feel the personal impetus to speak out or take action.

All members of nonprofit organizations can strive to understand and overcome the barriers to ethical action and foster courageous followership

(Chaleff, 2009; Strom-Gottfried, 2019b). This involves an express commitment to integrity and accountability, openness to dissenting voices and perspectives, transparent processes, humility, and a willingness to own mistakes and make amends. People develop and sustain the capacity for courage from their faith traditions and from mentors, coaches, and inspirational figures. Understanding the dynamics of difficult conversations helps to put courage into action. It requires the ability to broach delicate topics, listen thoroughly, and articulate sensitive positions. An employee concerned about a colleague's or supervisor's actions might preface the comment with a defusing statement, such as "You know how I respect your work and value our relationship, and I'm sure you'd want me to be honest with you. . . ." Inappropriate jokes or actions might be met with a self-involving statement, such as "I'm not comfortable when staff discuss patients in that way." An ill-considered decision or pressure for groupthink may be countered with questions: "What questions might we face by those who are affected by this decision?" or "How does this fit with our mission and standards?" Statements such as "I'm not sure I heard you correctly. Did you mean to say . . . ?" or "I'm uncomfortable with what I just heard [saw]" can set the stage for conversations about an array of problematic organizational behaviors ranging from bullying to bigotry to proposals for fraudulent or illegal activity. Organizational culture and moral courage contribute to the will and readiness of individuals to act with integrity.

Common Ethical Challenges in Nonprofit Leadership

It is hard to imagine almost any management or administrative decision that is unencumbered by ethical considerations. Ethical nonprofits must have the structures, policies, personnel, and commitment to operate legally and ethically. Still, as noted earlier, dilemmas will arise when the distinction between right and wrong is not well defined, and the leader must chart a course amid competing goods or rights. Common challenges in nonprofits involve conflicts of interest, conflicts of commitment, governance, finance, fundraising, and accountability.

Conflicts of Interest

The Internal Revenue Service (2019) defined *conflicts of interest* as occurring when an individual's "obligation to further the organization's charitable purposes is at odds with their own financial interests." Private inurements are defined by tax law and occur when insiders (for example, board members, employees) receive a private benefit from the organization, such as when a board member of a museum is given free admission to all museum exhibits. These, like other types of conflicts of interest, are not by themselves illegal, but they must be carefully managed through established policies and procedures (Legal Center for Nonprofits, 2020).

Conflicts show up in myriad ways: children of former board members gaining admission to colleges and universities despite not meeting the same requirements as other applicants, relatives of donors hired by the organization without transparent search processes, and board members' companies selling products or services to the organization. All of these can pose ethical challenges for the organization's leaders. However, conflicts of interest can result in positive results for the organization, such as when a board member rents space to the nonprofit at a reduced rate. This situation is still a conflict of interest and, although allowable under the law, should be recognized by the board and leadership as such (Renz, 2019).

Conflicts of Commitment

Another common type of conflict of interest is the conflict of loyalty or commitment, also known as duality of interest. In this type of conflict, an individual member owes loyalty to more than one interest. For example, a board member serving on several boards in a related field could inadvertently share proprietary information between the organizations or engage in fundraising activities for one organization that affect the fundraising prospects of the other (Renz, 2019). Another example is a board member who sits on several boards having to decide to which organization to recruit a friend for open board positions. Nonprofit leaders should also be aware of conflicts that involve nonfinancial benefits to members. These conflicts could involve something as simple as allowing a board member to use a nonprofit facility for a private function or allowing a member to store items in the organization's offices (Renz, 2019). More problematic examples could include board members ordering supplies via the nonprofit to get out of paying sales tax.

Governance

A nonprofit's structure, policies, and processes have a significant effect on integrity and can also give rise to ethical dilemmas (Thomas & Strom-Gottfried, 2018). Prominent features of governance rest with the board of directors and its willingness and ability to execute its fiduciary responsibilities.

Does the nonprofit have sufficient risk assessment and internal controls? Does the board exercise proper oversight of the executive management? Can board members understand financial statements? Does the board culture support incisive questions about matters of concern?

The competing goods notion of ethical dilemmas can apply to governance issues. Many nonprofit board members choose to serve because they endorse the mission or issues addressed by the nonprofit or they want to give back to the community; however, these interests may not be compatible with the time, acumen, and courage to delve deeply into the organization's finances, fundraising, leadership, and the related laws and regulations. Do they understand the differentiation of roles between staff and the governing board or the implications of various forms of grants and contracts vis-à-vis services and staffing? Do they struggle with relations with prominent community members or influential founders? This loyalty can blind them to inappropriate activities and conflicts of interest (Chui, 2011). Executive leaders may view the board as a group of supporters to be managed and thus discourage robust oversight.

Finance

Beyond the obvious issues around using donations and grant funds only for their intended purposes, nonprofit organizations may encounter ethical concerns in determining what funds to accept (Rhode & Packel, 2009). Examples include cancer charities refusing donations from tobacco companies or beer manufacturers donating to help fight against HIV (Gharib, 2018).

Donations from disgraced individuals such as Harvey Weinstein and Jeffrey Epstein caused controversy when organizations chose to keep the funds or did not condemn the actions of the problematic donors (Schaeffer, 2019). Leaders may have to examine the price of acceptance in determining whether to accept a particular gift. Problematic gifts risk alienating not only other donors but also employees, volunteers, and current and future clients. However, the most ethical choice may be to accept a problematic gift to keep the lights on, meet programmatic goals, or continue to serve clients (Breeze, 2017). Leaders should particularly examine potential gifts that are pledged as a part of campaigns to improve the image of problematic individuals or businesses such as grants from oil companies to environmental organizations (Rhode & Packel, 2009). The ultimate ethical question for leaders may be whether accepting funds from a questionable individual or organization fits with the nonprofit's values.

Fundraising

Nonprofit fundraising is sophisticated, complex, and vital (see chapter 4). The competition can be fierce as worthy charitable organizations vie for finite philanthropic support. New strategies, laws, and technological advances allow nonprofits to better target and pursue potential donors. Even legal, accepted practices can raise ethical concerns, especially in organizations that work with vulnerable or traditionally marginalized groups. For example, "grateful patient programs" in health care target well-to-do patients for exceptional attention during the course of care and prepare physicians and other members of the health care team to converse with satisfied patients about making charitable gifts to the organizations (Strom-Gottfried, 2019b). "Photolisting" pictures and information about youths available for adoption is considered an effective practice for securing adoptive families and for stimulating support for child-serving agencies (Strom-Gottfried, 2014). Accepted practices such as these raise ethical issues of dignity and fairness, as well as risks of coercion and conflicts of interest, even if their intent is positive.

Nonprofit leaders should be aware of the array of issues that can come up in modern fundraising and insist that all staff abide by the code of ethics set forth by the Association of Fundraising Professionals (AFP; 2019). Fundraising is regulated by most states, and certain documents must be made available to the public (National Council on Nonprofits, 2020c). There is general agreement that fundraisers should not receive commissions on the amount of funds raised and that undue pressure should not be used on individuals to encourage them to make gifts. There is some evidence that these high-pressure techniques actually depress giving rates to charities overall (National Council on Nonprofits, 2020c)

Restricted gifts are an area in which ethical concerns may arise. A restricted gift is any donation that the donor mandates be used only for a particular purpose (National Council on Nonprofits, 2020c). Even when gift agreements are carefully drafted, circumstances may change for nonprofits, and carrying out the restrictions may no longer be feasible. Numerous high-profile cases involving restricted gifts have ended up in the courts, causing damage to nonprofits in terms of both finances and reputation. In one case, the Brooklyn Museum had to ask a judge to change the terms of the bequest of Colonel Michael Friedsam, who had asked that his collection remain intact. This action was necessary after museum staff discovered that many of the artifacts he donated were fake, mislabeled, or not museum quality. In another case, Fisk University filed suit to sell part of its donated art collection to raise the funds to keep the university from closing (Cohen, 2013).

Legally, nonprofits have an obligation to abide by donor restrictions, unless the courts allow for *cy pres* (changing the donor's intent) or deviation (changing how the nonprofit carries out the intention) or if the donor accepts revisions to gift agreement (Gary, 2010). Sometimes the question is how an organization should stick to a gift agreement when it may no longer be in the best interest of the nonprofit as a whole (Cohen, 2013). To avoid these types of conflicts, some nonprofits choose not to accept any restricted gifts (National Council of Nonprofits, 2020c). This strategy may mean that the organization misses some large bequests because potential donors are often more motivated to give if they get to set the terms (Gary, 2010).

Accountability

Accountability in nonprofits can be both a source of ethical dilemmas and the foundation for ethical leadership. Accountability refers to

- transparency: making information about the organization and its programs available and accessible to the general public
- justification: making available to the various stakeholders the reasoning behind the nonprofit's actions and decisions
- compliance: ongoing monitoring of all programs to ensure that they meet all standards, including those required by state and federal law
- enforcement: holding staff and volunteers accountable for deficiencies in transparency, justification, or compliance (Ebrahaim & Weisband, 2007)

Nonprofit organizations must answer to a wide variety of stakeholders, including clients, donors, community partners, volunteers, foundations, and government agencies. It can be challenging for leaders to decide which stakeholders to prioritize (Winberry, 2017) and how candid to be with them about challenges the organization is facing. Leaders may focus on upward accountability to powerful interests such as funding agencies or big donors (Twersky, Buchanan, & Threlfall, 2013), whereas the nonprofit's mission, vision, and values might instead prioritize the organization's clientele or beneficiaries (downward accountability) (M. Edwards & Hulme, 1996). Because they lack power and a ready constituency, it can be difficult to involve service users in governance, advisory, or evaluative functions. Too often, they are co-opted or given token roles, and vocal complaints about the organization may be minimized or marginalized (Twersky et al., 2013).

Evaluation can be extremely difficult in nonprofits because some charitable programs may have nonquantifiable outcomes. How does one evaluate lofty goals such as "creating a just society" or "improving education"? However, every nonprofit can have a strategic plan with some specific measures and goals that helps ensure that resources are used responsibly. Leaders should share these benchmarks openly so that stakeholders can help hold the organization accountable. This plan should include sharing information about both good and bad outcomes of programmatic efforts (Rhode & Packel, 2009).

Despite these challenges, a commitment to accountability is fundamental to ethical operations. Leaders can work to adopt or create codes of ethics, conflict of interest, and confidentiality policies for their organizations (National Council of Nonprofits, 2020a), with many examples of best practices of nonprofit policies readily available online. Integrating codified rules and procedures into an organizational structure can help to create consistent standards, define and refine expectations, and convey a trustworthy public image. However, to be effective, such rules must be fully integrated into every layer of the organization. In addition, there must be procedures for employees to report any ethical concerns, mechanisms to act on unethical behavior, and highly visible and effective protections from retaliation (Rhode & Packel, 2009).

Nonprofit leaders also need to ensure that all resources are being used responsibly. Watchdog groups such as Charity Navigator and Charity Watch grade nonprofits on the percentage of donations that are used for administrative costs and on the percentage actually spent on programs. Scores given by these organizations may influence where prospective donors give funds (Rhode & Packel, 2009). Leaders should promote the use of self-assessment tools focused on financial management practices to help ensure that the right policies are in place and that all board members, employees, and volunteers are appropriately educated on correct financial practices. Board members particularly need to understand their role in overseeing finances and managing restricted funds (National Council of Nonprofits, 2020d).

In addition to abiding by the AFP's Code of Ethical Standards, organizations should consider adopting the AFP's "Donor's Bill of Rights." These standards help nonprofits improve transparency in fundraising endeavors and ensure that all donors are treated with respect (National Council of Nonprofits, 2020b). Donors should also always be informed of what their gift is being used for, receive acknowledgment of their gift, have their personal information handled as confidentially as allowed by law, and have their names deleted from future mailing lists if they wish (R. L. Edwards, 2020; Pettey, 2013).

Managing conflicts of interest is ongoing work. Board members and other leaders should complete conflict of interest questionnaires every year and encourage a culture of candor that will encourage everyone to disclose all potential conflicts. Another suggestion is to spend time at board meetings discussing hypothetical conflicts to practice handling potential conflicts (National Council of Nonprofits, 2020a).

Transparency is vital for establishing trust and a key factor in maintaining an ethical culture. All nonprofits should strive to make critical information about the organization's efforts widely available (Charity Navigator, 2020). The easiest way to do this is to publish this information on the organization's Web site and continue to update it as new information becomes available.

Conclusion

Jurkiewicz and Massey (1998) stated that nonprofit leaders

> must project high levels of ethical reasoning as a prerequisite to being entrusted with scarce resources and toward the end of not only achieving public good but also reflecting back favorably on both the organization and the individuals who provided the funding. (p. 175)

In light of various scandals across the range of nonprofit organizations, the future of the charitable sphere may depend on leaders sustaining societal expectations of honest conduct. The public holds nonprofits to higher ethical standards than most for-profit and governmental organizations (Smith & Richmond, 2007). It is up to nonprofit leaders to ensure that their organizations can meet these high expectations and are worthy to receive tax-exempt status and other benefits.

Ethical nonprofit leadership encompasses both being and doing. These leaders must not only practice what they preach; they must also intentionally create a culture that reinforces ethical practices. When needed, these leaders stop to reexamine the culture and work to identify gaps between the organization's values and the stated policy and procedure (Skeet, 2017). To lead a values-driven organization, a nonprofit leader must actually practice those values espoused by their employer. When nonprofit leaders do not live up to the organization's ideals, the stakeholders may feel betrayed, and the work of the organization may suffer (O'Neill, 2001). Nonprofit leaders do not have to be saints, but they should be willing to always strive for the most ethical practices available.

Skills Application Exercise

Review the following case vignette and address the discussion questions in writing or in conversation with classmates or colleagues.

The global COVID-19 pandemic hit the United States in March 2020, leading to widespread stay-at-home orders and shuttering most businesses, schools, government offices, recreational facilities, and nonprofit organizations. Accompanying the virus itself, the need for health, mental health, and basic social services escalated. Imagine that you operate a home health agency serving frail older adults and persons with disabilities. Personal protective equipment is in short supply, and your staff are occupied with caring for their own family members and educating their children from home, yet calls keep coming in from desperate clients and caregivers who need your services. Hospitals are trying to discharge patients to create safe beds for virus admissions; they are also calling with referrals for your agency's services.

1. What are the competing goods in this scenario?
2. What options do you envision for ethical outcomes?
3. List the pros and cons of your options.
4. What resources, people, and organizations would you consult to make your decisions?
5. Are you aware of any laws, regulations, policies, values, or standards that would influence your choices?
6. Although the pandemic is unprecedented, have you ever faced similar ethical dilemmas?
7. How can you carry out this decision in such a way as to mitigate harms?
8. What would be the signs of a poor outcome? A successful choice?

References

Association of Fundraising Professionals. (2019). *Code of ethical standards*. Retrieved from https://afpglobal.org/ethicsmain/code-ethical-standards

Breeze, B. (2017, November 24). Should charities accept contrition cash from dubious donors? *The Guardian*. Retrieved from https://www.theguardian.com/voluntary-sector-network/2017/nov/24/charities-contrition-cash-rich-dubious-donors-harvey-weinstein

Brown, M. E., Treviño, L. K., & Harrison, D. (2005). Ethical leadership: A social learning perspective for construct development and testing. *Organizational Behavior and Human Decision Processes, 97*, 117–134. doi:10.1016/j.obhdp.2005.03.002

Challeff, I. (2009). *The courageous follower: Standing up to and for our leaders* (3rd ed.). San Francisco: Berrett-Koehler.

Charity Navigator. (2020). *How do we rate charities' accountability and transparency?* Retrieved from https://www.charitynavigator.org/index.cfm?bay=content.view&cpid=1093

Charity Watch. (2020). *High assets charities.* Retrieved from https://www.charitywatch.org/high-asset-charities

Chui, L. (2011). *Lessons from the Second Mile scandal for nonprofits and their boards.* Retrieved from https://www.philanthropy.com/article/lessons-from-the-second-mile-scandal-for-nonprofits-and-their-boards/

Ciulla, J. B. (2004). The ethical challenges of nonprofit leaders. In R. E. Riggio & S. S. Orr (Eds.), *Improving leadership in nonprofit organizations* (pp. 63–75). San Francisco: Jossey-Bass.

Ciulla, J. B. (2005). Integrating leadership with ethics: Is good leadership contrary to human nature? In P. J. Doh & S. A. Stumpf (Eds.), *Handbook on responsible leadership and governance in global business* (pp. 159–179). Cheltenham, England: Edward Elgar.

Cohen, P. (2013, February 3). Museums grapple with the strings attached to gifts. *New York Times.* Retrieved from https://www.nytimes.com/2013/02/05/arts/design/museums-grapple-with-onerous-restrictions-on-donations.html

Ebrahim, A., & Weisband, E. (Eds.). (2007). *Global accountabilities: Participation, pluralism, and public ethics.* Cambridge, England: Cambridge University Press.

Edwards, M., & Hulme, D. (1996). *Beyond the magic bullet: NGO performance and accountability in the post-cold war world.* West Hartford, CT: Kumarian Press.

Edwards, R. L. (2020). *Building a strong foundation: Fundraising for nonprofits* (2nd ed.). Washington, DC: NASW Press.

Ethics Resource Center. (2007). *National nonprofit ethics survey: An inside view of nonprofit sector ethics.* Retrieved from https://community.corporatecompliance.org/HigherLogic/System/DownloadDocumentFile.ashx?DocumenFileKey=8625367f-2c62-4c82-ae5f-293bc6eded03&forceDialog=0

Freeman, R. E., & Stewart, L. (2006). *Developing ethical leadership.* Charlottesville, VA: Business Roundtable Institute for Corporate Ethics. Retrieved from http://www.corporate-ethics.org/pdf/ethical_leadership.pdf

Gary, S. N. (2010). The problems with donor intent: Interpretation, enforcement, and doing the right thing. *Chicago-Kent Law Review, 85*, Article 5. Retrieved from https://scholarship.kentlaw.iit.edu/cgi/viewcontent.cgi?article=3766&context=cklawreview

George, B. (2003). *Authentic leadership: Rediscovering the secrets to creating lasting value.* San Francisco: Jossey-Bass.

Gharib, M. (2018, March 23). *Your thoughts: When do charitable partnerships cross an ethical line?* Retrieved from https://www.npr.org/sections/goatsandsoda/2018/03/23/595696499/your-thoughts-when-do-charitable-partnerships-cross-an-ethical-line

Giving USA. (2019). *Giving USA 2019: Americans gave $427.71 billion to charity in 2018 amid complex year for charitable giving.* Retrieved from https://givingusa.org/giving-usa-2019-americans-gave-427-71-billion-to-charity-in-2018-amid-complex-year-for-charitable-giving/

Internal Revenue Service. (2019). *Form 1023: Purpose of conflict of interest policy.* Retrieved from https://www.irs.gov/charities-non-profits/form-1023-purpose-of-conflict-of-interest-policy

Jones, J. (2020). *Percentage of Americans donating to charity at new low.* Retrieved from https://news.gallup.com/poll/310880/percentage-americans-donating-charity-new-low.aspx

Jurkiewicz, C. L. & Massey, T. K., Jr. (1998). The influence of ethical reasoning on leader effectiveness. *Nonprofit Management & Leadership, 9,* 173–186. doi:10.1002/nml.9204

Kidder, R. M. (1995). *How good people make tough choices: Resolving the dilemmas of ethical living.* New York: Simon & Schuster

Kidder, R. M. (2005). *Moral courage: Taking action when your values are put to the test.* New York: William Morrow.

Legal Center for Nonprofits. (2020). *Conflicts of interest—An introduction.* Retrieved from http://www.legalcenterfornonprofits.org/2020/03/27/conflicts-of-interest-an-introduction/

Malloy, D. C., & Agarwal, J. (2001). Ethical climate in nonprofit organizations: Propositions and implications. *Nonprofit Management & Leadership, 12,* 39–54.

Mayer, D. M., Kuenzi, M., Greenbaum, R., Bardes, M., & Salvador, R. B. (2009). How low does ethical leadership flow? Test of a trickle-down model. *Organizational Behavior and Human Decision Processes, 108,* 1–13.

Missionbox. (2019). *Will nonprofit scandals significantly lessen your 2018 charitable donations?* Retrieved from https://www.missionbox.com/article/732/will-nonprofit-scandals-significantly-lessen-your-2018-charitable-donations

Mohan, P. (2019). *These are the worst scandals of the past decade.* Retrieved from https://www.fastcompany.com/90444328/these-are-the-worst-scandals-of-the-last-decade

National Council of Nonprofits. (2020a). *Conflicts of interest.* Retrieved from https://www.councilofnonprofits.org/tools-resources/conflicts-of-interest

National Council of Nonprofits. (2020b). *Ethical leadership for nonprofits.* Retrieved from https://www.councilofnonprofits.org/tools-resources/ethical-leadership-nonprofits

National Council of Nonprofits. (2020c). *Ethical fundraising.* Retrieved from https://www.councilofnonprofits.org/tools-resources/ethical-fundraising

National Council of Nonprofits. (2020d). *Financial management.* Retrieved from https://www.councilofnonprofits.org/tools-resources/financial-management

National Council of Nonprofits. (2020e). *Nonprofit impact in communities.* Retrieved from https://www.councilofnonprofits.org/nonprofit-impact-communities

O'Neill, M. (2001). Administrative ethics in nonprofit organizations. In T. L. Cooper (Ed.), *Handbook of administrative ethics* (pp. 623–628). New York: Marcel Dekker.

Pettey, J. G. (Ed.). (2013). *Nonprofit fundraising strategy: A guide to ethical decision making and regulation for nonprofit organizations.* New York: Wiley.

Renz, D. (2019, October 31). *Nonprofit Quarterly charity conflicts of interest: A guide.* Retrieved from https://nonprofitquarterly.org/charity-conflicts-of-interest-a-guide/

Resick, C. J., Hanges, P. J., Dickson, M. W., & Mitchelson, J. K. (2006). A cross-cultural examination of the endorsement of ethical leadership. *Journal of Business Ethics, 63*, 345–359.

Rhode, D. L., & Packel, A. K. (2009). Ethics and nonprofits. *Stanford Social Innovation Review, Summer.* Retrieved from https://www.leadingage.org/sites/default/files/Ethics_and_Nonprofits_0.pdf

Schaeffer, S. (2019, July 12). Harvard's Jeffrey Epstein hypocrisy: Harvard drops #MeToo image when donations are at risk. *USA Today.* Retrieved from https://www.usatoday.com/story/opinion/2019/07/12/jeffrey-epstein-harvard-me-too-donations-sex-abuse-column/1702579001/

Skeet, A. (2017). *A model for exploring an ethical leadership practice.* Retrieved from https://www.scu.edu/ethics/leadership-ethics-blog/practice-of-ethical-leadership/

Smith, P. C., & Richmond, K. A. (2007). Call for greater accountability within the US nonprofit sector. *Academy of Accounting and Financial Studies*

Journal, 11(2), 75–123. Retrieved from https://www.abacademies.org/articles/aafsjvol1122007.pdf#page=83

Strom, K. J. (2020). Moral courage. In A. Viera & R. Kramer (Eds.), *Management and leadership skills for medical faculty: A practical handbook* (pp. 209–217). New York: Springer Science + Business.

Strom-Gottfried, K. J. (2014). *Straight talk about professional ethics* (2nd ed.). Chicago: Lyceum Books.

Strom-Gottfried, K. J. (2019a). Ethical action in challenging times. In S. Marson & R. McKinney (Eds.), *The Routledge handbook of social work ethics and values* (pp. 65–72). New York: Routledge.

Strom-Gottfried, K. J. (2019b). Ethics in health care. In S. Gehlert & T. Browne (Eds.), *Handbook of health social work* (pp. 39–70). Hoboken, NJ: Wiley.

Thomas, M., & Strom-Gottfried, K. (2018). *Best of boards: Sound governance and leadership for nonprofit organizations* (2nd ed.). New York: Wiley.

Trevino, L. K., Brown, M. E., & Hartman, L. P. (2003). A qualitative investigation of perceived executive ethical leadership: Perceptions from inside and outside the executive suite. *Human Relations, 56,* 5–38.

Twersky, F., Buchanan, P., & Threlfall, V. (2013, *Spring*). Listening to those who matter most, the beneficiaries. *Stanford Social Innovation Review.* Retrieved from https://ssir.org/articles/entry/listening_to_those_who_matter_most_the_beneficiaries

Weinberg, M. (2009). Moral distress: A missing but relevant concept for ethics in social work. *Canadian Social Work Review, 26,* 139–169.

Whorishkey, P., & Salmon, J. (2003, August 17). Charity concealed pilfering: Auditors had flagged United Way ex-chief. *Fort Wayne Journal Gazette,* p. 7

Winberry, N. (2017, August 28). *How can nonprofit organizations improve accountability to the populations they serve?* [Arizona State University Lodestar Center for Philanthropy and Nonprofit Innovation Blog]. Retrieved from https://lodestar.asu.edu/blog/2017/08/how-can-nonprofit-organizations-improve-accountability-populations-they-serve

16

Managing Financial Uncertainty

Daniel A. Lebold and Richard L. Edwards

Rapid and unexpected shifts in funding—up or down—frequently have strong negative effects on the delivery of services provided by nonprofit organizations and on the clients or patrons they serve. Sizable increases or decreases in annual revenues can also affect an organization's mission and the types and frequency of services offered or cause significant shifts in staffing. Less obvious is the impact of budget changes on the lives of the people who work in nonprofit organizations. Few situations create more stress for nonprofit leaders and managers, or force them to navigate in an environment of competing values, than conditions of financial uncertainty.

This chapter addresses the potential causes of organizational decline, the impact of budgetary reductions (or increases) on managers and staff in nonprofit organizations, and strategies that nonprofit managers can use when facing budgetary crises. The chapter reviews the literature on downsizing, rightsizing, cutback management, and retrenchment and draws on the personal experiences of upper-level managers in organizations that have experienced major funding cuts necessitating a significant reduction or shift in programs or workforce.

Perhaps never have these issues been more critical for nonprofits than in the fiscal environment resulting from the 2020 coronavirus disease 2019 (COVID-19) pandemic. The subsequent wave of massive unemployment, and related social and economic havoc that followed, caused unprecedented stresses on nonprofits and their consumers, in many cases in terms of both sharp reductions in funding and increased need for services. Weathering such extreme conditions, or even thriving, depends on

- a clear and compelling organizational mission
- the ability to evaluate potential threats, opportunities, and possible responses
- adaptability in choosing the right strategy
- resolve when executing necessary but difficult decisions
- maintaining a motivated and productive workforce

In addition, understanding how past world events and crises have affected different types of nonprofit organizations, positively or negatively, can help to clarify which strategies may best align with an organization's core mission and operational structures.

A New Era of Fiscal Austerity

For most of the 20th century, government policies regarding funding for social welfare, community development, and the arts and humanities evolved from an "activist ideology" (Firstenberg, 1996). From President Franklin D. Roosevelt's Works Progress Administration initiatives in the 1930s to President Lyndon B. Johnson's War on Poverty in the mid-1960s, it was popularly accepted that government had both a role in and a responsibility for providing solutions to chronic social and economic problems (Firstenberg, 1996; Newland, 1996). This period, which peaked in the 1960s and early 1970s, represented nearly 50 years of almost uninterrupted growth in government support of social programs (Cooke, Reid, & Edwards, 1997).

During that era of federal expansion, many nonprofit organizations came to depend heavily on the widely available federal funds for their services, leading some nonprofit managers and board members to assume, falsely, that those dollars would always be available. Public sentiment toward the federal government began to sour in the 1970s as a result of American involvement in the Vietnam War, the Watergate scandals during President Richard M. Nixon's administration, and the economic recession triggered by an international oil embargo. By the time Ronald Reagan assumed the presidency in 1980, antigovernment rhetoric was at a then all-time high. Government was no longer viewed as a problem solver but as the cause of many economic and social problems (Firstenberg, 1996; Newland, 1996).

In the mid-1990s and through the early 2000s, the rapid growth of the U.S. stock market—powered by low oil prices, new home construction, the broad-base commercialization of the Internet, and a surge in health and technology sector profits—created new wealth that fueled an unprecedented expansion in the nonprofit sector. Thousands of new nonprofit organizations were established in the United States during this period, more foundations were created, and the value of their endowments increased.

However, by the beginning of the new millennium, this rapid expansion began to level off as a new economic recession set in, and public attention and funding priorities shifted to national and global crises. These included the September 11, 2001, terrorist attacks on the World Trade Center and the Pentagon; the ensuing war on terror; the AIDS crisis; rising concerns about climate change; and worldwide reaction to scores of natural disasters. The post-9/11 era was characterized by a sluggish economy, federal tax cuts, flat wages, and relatively low-asset growth for many of the nation's largest foundations. These conditions led to significant decreases in available funding for nonprofits from nearly all sources, including government, corporations, foundations, and, to a lesser degree, individuals.

During this period, nonprofits faced additional challenges. The avalanche of corporate accounting frauds, beginning in 2001 with Enron and WorldCom, added to a growing public mistrust of nonprofits. The antecedents of this mistrust began nearly a decade earlier with the 1992 firing of William Aramony, president of the United Way of America, who was ultimately convicted of 25 counts of embezzlement (Kellerman, 2004; Stanford GSB Staff, 2003). United Way donations declined 42 percent after Aramony resigned in disgrace, and many community nonprofits suffered after the scandal. In 2002, the U.S. Congress passed the American Competitiveness and Corporate Accountability Act, also referred to as the Sarbanes–Oxley of 2002 Act (P.L. 107-204). The purpose of this law was to ensure financial accountability and rebuild public trust in the corporate community. As more states began to enact specific legislation aimed at for-profit organizations, this climate of increased fiscal oversight had implications for nonprofit organizations as well.

The nonprofit sector was hit hard again by the Great Recession of 2008–2009 that affected the U.S. and global economies. This recession resulted in financial disaster for millions of Americans.

> Ten million foreclosures were filed against homeowners in 2008 and 2009 . . . 23 percent of private homes slid into negative equity by the third quarter of 2009, and the U.S. unemployment rate jumped from 4.7 percent to over 10 percent. . . . Bank failures, a shrinking economy, and shaken consumer confidence convinced Congress and a newly elected President Obama to pass a nearly $840 billion stimulus package to jump-start the economy: the American Recovery and Reinvestment Act. (Pratt & Aanestad, 2020, p. 28)

In addition to the financial impact of the Great Recession, the economy was rocked by a major financial scandal resulting in the arrest in 2008 and subsequent conviction and imprisonment of Bernie Madoff for his Ponzi scheme that bilked investors of nearly $65 billion (Hayes, 2020). Included among these investors were a number of nonprofit foundations and organizations, some of which went out of business as a result of the losses associated with the Madoff scheme.

After the Great Recession, many nonprofits not only survived but thrived in its aftermath. The sector grew significantly as a whole as more nonprofit organizations were created, the workforce expanded, and giving to nonprofits increased on an annual basis (Pratt & Aanestad, 2020). However, although many nonprofits thrived and new organizations were created, this growth obscures the fact that many smaller nonprofits lost ground, never fully recovered, or closed, which negatively affected many of the most vulnerable populations (McCambridge & Dietz, 2020).

Several important trends emerged during this time with broad implications for the sector as a whole. Between the end of the Great Recession in 2009 and the end of 2018, inflation-adjusted total giving to nonprofits increased 33 percent (Giving USA, 2019, p. 49). However, it is important to note that although giving to nonprofits declined during the Great Recession, and although there was a rebound in the postrecession years, the comeback represented a change in who was giving. After the recession, a smaller proportion of American households were donating to nonprofits. At the same time, those who continued to contribute were giving larger gifts, so overall philanthropy increased during this period.

The Great Recession also affected the mix of revenue sources for many nonprofits; that is, the percentage of their revenues coming from contributions, gifts and grants, program service revenues and membership fees, special events, and other sources such as investment income. Many of the largest nonprofits, such as health and educational organizations, "were heavily reliant on revenue from commercial sources before the recession, and (if anything) even more reliant on those program service revenues during and after the recovery period" (McCambridge & Dietz, 2020, p. 9).

Another factor at play related to donor giving behavior is the Tax Cuts and Jobs Act of 2017 (TCJA) (P.L. 105-277), which the U.S. Congress passed and President Trump signed in December 2017. This legislation significantly altered federal tax policy in many ways. A change in the amount of the standard deduction available to taxpayers had an impact on the tax deductibility of charitable donations and appeared to be having a negative impact on giving to nonprofits before the COVID-19 pandemic.

> The Tax Policy Center (TPC) released an analysis in January 2018, estimating that the new law would lead to approximately a 5 percent decline in charitable giving, and that future contributions will come from fewer and wealthier donors. . . . In June of 2018, a report from the American Enterprise Institute (AEI) predicted that the TCJA will reduce charitable giving by $17.2 billion, or 4 percent, on a static basis (assuming fixed GDP) and $16.3 billion, or a 3.8 percent on a dynamic basis (assuming modest economic growth). . . . The report projects that 83 percent of the decline in charitable giving will derive from an increase in the number of taxpayers who claim the standard deduction in 2018. . . . The remainder of the decline in charitable giving will primarily stem from lower marginal tax rates for high-income Americans. (Giving USA, 2019, p. 85)

The net effect of the TCJA has caused many economists to predict a continuing downward trend in the number of people who will be donating to charity because the higher standard deduction reduces their overall tax benefit (Dickler & Epperson, 2019).

Even before the 2020 COVID-19 pandemic, it was recognized that nonprofits are affected differently by external events and crises, depending on to their specific mission or business model. Although many fared well postrecession, a closer look reveals that some fared better than others across the nonprofit sector. For example, although most nonprofit revenues declined by 1.6 percent on average during the Great Recession, health and human services nonprofits were the exception with increases of more than 6 percent (McCambridge & Dietz, 2020, p. 8). In fact, during the years leading up to the Great Recession, health and human services agencies (excluding hospitals) experienced increases of more than 15 percent on average. Yet during the postrecession period, these same organizations fared less well. Unlike the majority of nonprofits across the sector, "contributions to health and human services organizations increased at a lower rate than other public charities during the post-recession years, increasing by only 1.0 percent between 2010 and 2015" (McCambridge & Dietz, 2020, p. 8), compared with the 6 percent experienced on average by other organizations.

Many nonprofits closed between 2008 and 2009, with closure rates being highest for international, public, societal benefit, religious, and mutual or membership benefit organizations. The lowest closure rates were for organizations categorized as human services and environmental public charities (McCambridge & Dietz, 2020).

Heading into the COVID-19 recession that began in early 2020, many nonprofits were already financially vulnerable. As the numbers of infections skyrocketed—resulting in hundreds of thousands of deaths—extraordinary measures were taken to contain the virus. Schools were closed, businesses were shut, travel was severely curtailed, and in many parts of the nation health care systems were overloaded. Unemployment rates reached a Great Depression level (Krugman, 2020). To reduce transmission of the COVID-19 virus through social distancing, public spaces and all types of businesses in which employees and people gather were forced to shut down—including public parks, sporting events, hotels, retail stores, schools, universities, and restaurants, as well as many nonprofit organizations ranging from human services organizations to theaters, museums, zoos, and botanical gardens. The need to impose work-from-home policies or shut down major sectors of the economy—and the widespread unemployment that ensued—created enormous challenges and a series of conditions affecting nearly every nonprofit's operations, service delivery, and sources of funding.

Never before have nonprofit leaders had to respond to so many internal and external crises at once. The immediate priority was creating a safe working environment for both staff and patrons by implementing mitigation strategies to reduce the threat of infection. When in-person meetings were restricted or shut down entirely, services had to be redesigned and delivered through new virtual technologies or other means of social distancing. Many human services organizations experienced increased demand for services while simultaneously experiencing rapid declines in both funding and capacity. In contrast, a host of other nonprofits, such as museums, daycare centers, and performing arts organizations, experienced the opposite: a significant decrease in or no demand for services that negatively affected both patronage and funding. These extreme conditions led to shuttered work environments, staff layoffs or furloughs, severe cuts in revenues from program fees, loss of charitable donations, cancelled fundraising events such as galas or golf outings, or sudden increases in overhead costs associated with office renovations or technology upgrades needed to comply with social distancing and to transform and innovate new ways of delivering programs and services.

In response to the COVID-19 pandemic, MacIntosh (2020) identified three types of nonprofit organizations that were being affected differently during the crisis:

- *Hibernators: organizations that are completely unable to operate during the crisis.* These types of organizations—museums, after-school programs, theaters, zoos, botanical gardens, concert halls, and other venues—had to shut their doors completely, thus eliminating their major sources of revenues.

- *Responders: organizations that may see an increased demand for their services while also facing significant revenue shortfalls.* Many hospitals, for example, had to ramp up to provide services to patients with COVID-19 but at the same time had to cancel elective surgeries that ordinarily generate significant revenues. These organizations may include health clinics, homeless shelters, food pantries, operators of residential facilities for people with developmental disabilities, and broad-spectrum human services agencies.
- *Hybrids: organizations that offer programs that can still be provided, to some degree, despite the crisis, but that are not directly related to reducing the spread of the virus or mitigating its short-term impacts.* Hybrid organizations might include programs that provide workforce training and development, advocacy, re-entry programs for formerly incarcerated persons, and others.

Defining which business model an organization fits into, and how it is affected by external threats, is important when evaluating which response strategies may be most effective in mitigating a crisis. Although the specific longer term impacts of the COVID-19 pandemic remain to be seen, the economic repercussions on the nonprofit sector will likely be felt for many years to come.

Whether one looks at financial crises or the impact of major disasters, nonprofit leaders in the 21st century are facing a period of rapid change and disruption in an increasingly interconnected world. It is essential that nonprofit managers develop new skills to deal with this environment where funding streams are increasingly complex and difficult to predict, competition for scarce resources has reached an all-time high, and nonprofits are closing. Organizations that are most likely to survive, or even to thrive, will be those with leaders who understand the many competing values they will need to confront and who have acquired the necessary skills to effectively navigate these turbulent times.

Overview of Organizational Decline

All nonprofit organizations will eventually face financial uncertainty or decline in a major source of revenue. When this happens, hard choices are required, sometimes involving cutting services or staff. It is important that nonprofit managers also recognize the organizational and individual responses that accompany shifting financial resources. Regrettably, many nonprofit managers, as with their counterparts in other fields, tend to be inadequately prepared to manage effectively under conditions of rapid change or decline. This tendency is not surprising, given that most managers have more experience in—and receive more training for—responding to conditions of growth.

Growth has been viewed as consistent with the ideology and values of American culture, and most organizations assume they must increase their budgets annually just to keep up with inflation (Otten, 2017). The idea that "bigger" or "more" is better has long been an internalized assumption held by many nonprofit managers and their staffs. In fact, a 2017 study of 300 nonprofit professionals reported that "forty-five percent [of respondents] rated growth as extremely important for their organizations, and another 36% said it was very important" (Otten, 2017). The enhancement of economies of scale, the ability to absorb shocks that accompany environmental changes, and increased productive capacity are among the presumed benefits of largeness. Managers tend to be regarded as successful if they produce more, obtain larger budgets, and expand their organizations, and they too are often regarded as ineffective if they do the reverse. The question is, how big is too big? Most experts agree that modest growth is desirable, but there are often unintended or even undesirable consequences that can come with unmitigated expansion.

Sudden windfalls in funding can have potentially destabilizing effects on nonprofit organizations and their missions. According to Young (2000), sudden windfalls and shortfalls are, in many ways, conceptual twins; they can either disrupt an organization's ability to plan effectively or lead to significant adjustments in the organization's activities and priorities. For example, if an unanticipated large gift is received that significantly increases the relative size or scope of what had previously been considered a peripheral or low-priority activity, incorporating the windfall into the budget may divert critical resources away from higher priorities that could yield bigger results, financially, in terms of mission, or both. Making long-term adjustments to the organization's mission or core programs in response to a one-time funding windfall could lead to a dramatic fluctuation in activities and staffing or create a situation in which the organization cannot sustain the new initiative once the windfall has run out. It is always important to carefully consider how a new and sizable influx of funding may, in the long run, alter the organization's focus on its overall mission.

Much has been written about organizational decline in both the nonprofit and the corporate sectors (Cameron, Sutton, & Whetten, 1988; Edwards, Cooke, & Reid, 1996; Edwards, Lebold, & Yankey, 1998; La Piana & MacIntosh, 2020; MacIntosh, 2020). Fashionable topics in the literature regarding cutback management include downsizing, deregulation, and devolution. The literature in the 1990s focused on retrenchment, rightsizing, reinvention, and re-engineering (DuBran, 1996; Lebold & Edwards, 2006;

Newland, 1996). Even so, management training programs rarely focus on developing skills related to managing under conditions of decline. Most current organizational theory is based on assumptions of growth; decline tends to be either ignored or treated as an aberration.

As a nonprofit leader, it is important to understand that when financial crises occur, the potential for stagnation—or revitalization—will depend on the key decisions that you and your leadership team make when responding to the underlying conditions that are causing the downturn. What follows is a discussion of the causes and stages of decline, as well as potential responses.

Causes of Organizational Decline

The most common causes of organizational decline include economic shifts in the external environment, competition, resistance to change or innovation, crisis inaction, mismanagement or overexpansion of program activities or staff, obsolete technology, overreliance on a single funding source that ends, loss of a competitive edge in a particular niche service, or organizational atrophy (Banning, 1990; Cameron et al., 1988; Gupta, 2010). In some cases, shortfalls may be the result of a single event, such as a factory closing that displaces hundreds or thousands of workers who were the primary supporters of a local United Way campaign or massive unemployment such as that resulting from the COVID-19 pandemic. Scandals can also inflict enormous damage on an organization's credibility and cause substantial losses of financial support. Mismanagement or uncontrolled growth in services beyond available resources can lead to instability and budget shortfalls.

Gupta (2010) suggested that "an organization undergoes changes in its conceptual and structural dimensions over a period of time, analogous to biological organisms, it is born, and it attains growth, gets matured and eventually dies." The time horizon on this final stage is perhaps the most important and difficult to ascertain.

Although biological models are frequently used to describe organizational behavior, they generally fail to include research about the later stages of decline and death. This reluctance to concentrate on the stages of decline and death ignores important findings in the life cycle literature.

> An organization enters the decline phases when it experiences continuous reduction in resources and revenue over a substantial period of time. Ironically, the decline can be recognized with certainty only when it is too late to recover from it, early signs are often mistaken to be temporary. (Gupta, 2010)

He described the following stages of decline:

- Blinded stage: "In this stage, the organization fails to recognize any of the internal or external changes that may threaten its survival. Usually, causes for the decline are present but are not evident; the leadership tends to be insensitive and simply fails to make a connection between the observed changes and a possible decline."
- Inaction stage: "Unlike in the blinded stage, the signs of deteriorating performance are clearly evident in this stage, but the leadership still fails to take any action. Leaders often view them as temporary changes and instead of interpreting them as a threat, they choose to take 'wait and see' approach, perhaps because this approach has worked in the past."
- Faulty action stage: "In this stage, the organization is clearly on its downfall and pressure to take corrective action is very high. The vertical and horizontal information from within the organization and the external environment increases manifolds along with its complexity. The overload of conflicting information & suggestive actions, combined with time pressure, compels the leadership to centralize decision making . . . the decision makers tend to make quick, risky and often fault decisions that further accelerates the decline."
- Crisis stage: "The organization reaches a crisis stage when all prior actions have failed and it becomes obvious that without any major change, its survival is questionable."
- Dissolution stage: "This is the last stage of its demise and is irreversible."

Of course, conditions of decline do not necessarily result in an organization's closure, and with effective leadership and strategic choices, declines can often be reversed. Typically, a combination of factors ultimately leads to retrenchment requiring cutbacks in programs or staff. Whatever the situation, as a manager, it is imperative that you carefully identify and fully understand the specific cause or causes of the crisis to develop strategies that will ensure the organization's ultimate survival.

Responding to Budget Shortfalls

In an ideal world, the best response to dealing with a budget shortfall is to have contingency plans in place before a crisis occurs. For this reason, and for the financial health of the organization, all nonprofits should build into their strategic planning a series of countermeasures to fall back on in the event of an unexpected loss in funding or serious economic downturn. These plans should include a set of values and principles to guide decision making during a crisis and policies to direct a portion of the agency's annual discretionary income, or "profit," into an operational reserve.

Often referred to as a "rainy day fund," operational reserves provide an alternate source of liquidity to cover such things as unforeseen building repairs or technology upgrades or to provide temporary bridge funding when confronting a temporary (not structural) funding shortfall or economic decline. In a worst-case scenario, the operational reserve should allow the organization to continue essential operations while it reduces services, transitions staff and clients, or closes programs. An operational reserve should be considered part of a nonprofit board's fiduciary responsibility, and policies should be developed to ensure financial resiliency, preparedness when dealing with unexpected shortfalls, and readiness in response to new growth opportunities (Propel Nonprofits, 2020).

The actual size of an operational reserve may differ depending on both an organization's size and its mission. The National Council of Nonprofits has a number of resources designed to help nonprofit managers and their boards determine the optimal size of discretionary funding recommended for a specific organization's size and structure, but most experts recommend having at least three to six months in cash reserves. This is especially important for human services organizations that have an ethical and professional obligation to transition clients to new service providers should they need to discontinue services. It is a cautionary note that fewer than 25 percent of nonprofits today responded that they have six months in cash reserves, and nearly 10 percent reported that they had less than 30 days in cash reserves on hand (Nonprofit Finance Fund, 2018).

Another component of managing financial uncertainty is reducing internal financial risk. The Alliance for Nonprofit Management (2008) listed the most common financial and management risks facing nonprofits as fraud, bad investments, misuse of funds, failure to pay taxes, loss of tax-exempt status as a result of inappropriate political activities, unethical fundraising practices, and theft of physical property. It recommended a series of internal measures to mitigate financial risks, including general management and accounting controls with appropriate checks and balances to safeguard against theft or loss of assets.

Under conditions of growth, the availability of slack resources makes it easier for nonprofit managers to work through most problems. That is, when sufficient resources are available, people are more likely to be able to get what they want from the organization, and staff tend to feel more valued and secure. Slack resources produce conditions that are favorable to experimentation and innovation and create buffers for management and staff within the organization.

However, when resources are tight—when there are no slack resources or the budget begins to head into a deficit situation—personal management skills become more critical for the effective management of the organization. In organizations that are experiencing cutbacks, there is often a mood of anger and hostility. Employees feel insecure or threatened. Scapegoating is common, managers are blamed, and employees believe that management should have foreseen the problem and acted earlier to lessen the impact. Because slack resources are no longer available, managers are less able to neutralize conflicting interest groups or "buy" internal consensus. Adaptation by addition is no longer possible. During a financial crisis, managers must also contend with their own high levels of stress that, as a consequence, may cause them to become overly formal in their interactions with staff. Decision making often becomes more centralized as managers begin to feel a need to maintain control.

These common mistakes often contribute to high levels of manager and staff stress, low trust, secretiveness, decreased morale, and high staff turnover. Unfortunately, too many nonprofit managers find that their knowledge and skills may be inadequate for the challenges presented by decline, even when steps were taken to prepare for, or anticipate, a potential downturn. This was especially true during the COVID-19 pandemic, where the sheer scale of staff layoffs, business closures, and financial shortfalls were both catastrophic and unprecedented.

Navigating a financial crisis is never easy, but there are lessons that can be taken from nonprofit leaders and organizations that have experienced financial setbacks and emerged with even greater resolve and capacity to carry out their missions.

Impact on Managers

Studies on cutback management suggest that managers often tend to deal with conditions of decline by focusing on internal organizational concerns to the relative exclusion of external concerns, often with a wait-and-see attitude. Although the tendency to focus on internal issues is natural, it can be dysfunctional. To be effective, managers must be able to concurrently demonstrate multiple dimensions of leadership (see chapter 1), particularly when confronting significant organizational crises. Analyzing the nonprofit's internal processes is critical—that is, revenue trends, expenses, monthly utilization reviews, service productivity—but it is just as important to understand the current crisis in the context of the broader external environment.

During periods of retrenchment, there is a tendency for middle managers to distance themselves from upper management, choosing instead to align with their team to avoid being the target of anger and hostility should layoffs become necessary. Middle managers may suggest to their direct staff that upper management or the board is to blame for the funding shortfalls. They may also deal with their stress by diverting their attention away from bigger, more looming problems, focusing instead on day-to-day operations that feel safer and more familiar. This avoidance of the crisis, however, tends to diminish the amount of creativity and expertise that is available from within the ranks, and it severely limits the number of ideas that may lead to practical solutions.

Organizations with multiple program units often experience fierce lines of division between programs driven by competing managers and staff who are struggling to protect their turf. If, however, a fiscal crisis threatens the entire organization (as opposed to a single program unit), middle managers across programs may join forces in opposition to upper-level managers. Similarly, executive-level managers may attempt to defer blame by telling middle managers that individual program units are responsible for independently maintaining the financial viability. Unfortunately, because middle managers have only limited control over their total budgets—particularly the indirect portion that supports the nonprofit's overhead—program managers often feel frustrated and trapped by deficit-reducing measures that they alone cannot control.

As time wears on and problems multiply, friction between ranks and resistance to change can weaken the nonprofit's ability to weather severe economic storms. These conditions can cloud a manager's judgment and cause the decision-making process to become muddled. At worst, existing problems become exacerbated, and new problems are created, causing the crisis to be prolonged indefinitely.

Often, one of the first actions nonprofit managers take when confronted with declining resources is to institute a hiring freeze and order that positions that become vacant be left unfilled. They then develop revised budget projections that take into account the savings that are expected by not filling positions that became vacant through attrition (that is, retirements or resignations). However, when attrition and hiring freezes are instituted, staff may have to assume a greater workload. This change may be regarded as a move to make staff more productive and the organization more efficient. Over time, however, such a strategy may have an adverse effect on the cohesion and morale of the staff, whose higher levels of stress may lead to greater absenteeism, decreased individual efficiency, and increased turnover.

At best, attrition represents personnel decision by default and, as with across-the-board reductions, does not require nonprofit managers, staff, and board members to undertake the arduous task of defining and setting priorities for specific goals for each service program. Both approaches ignore the possibility that the value of maintaining established staffing patterns in key areas may more than justify making disproportionate cuts in other areas.

Another deficit-reducing strategy is to trim the frills from the budget by reducing or eliminating various support services, including janitorial, equipment, building maintenance, secretarial, or contract services. Benefits such as reimbursement for continuing education or professional development activities are curtailed or eliminated. Managers do so to protect or shield their professional staff members as long as possible and out of a desire to maintain direct services to clients or patrons.

Over time, though, these actions can also lead to increased stress on staff and may contribute to high turnover. The organization may find itself with a predominantly younger, less experienced staff that is not able to provide the same quality of services that more experienced staff might have been able to provide. The net result is that the organization may experience gaps in knowledge or expertise, the flow of information may be impeded by not having sufficient support staff, and operations may be increasingly less stable. These conditions may curtail productivity and the delivery of services, which may have a further adverse effect on funding, services, or both.

Another common strategy is to institute across-the-board cuts. The rationale behind this strategy is that the organization will continue to do all it has been doing, albeit on a reduced level. Managers may find the across-the-board approach to be the fairest and least painful, and it may be effective when the reductions in resources are relatively small and likely to be short term. However, when reductions in resources are major and likely to persist for a long time, the across-the-board strategy will lessen the effectiveness of all aspects of the nonprofit's programming. Reducing staff in revenue-producing programs, no matter how fair it may appear, is unwise. In the long run, it is far better for an organization to right size and do fewer things strategically well than to adopt a one-size-fits-all approach. Nonprofit consultants at the Bridgespan Group have warned that "across the board cuts to an already lean budget . . . can make a terrible situation fatal if those cuts fail to preserve the capabilities critical to the organization's longer-term survival" (Waldron & Nayak, 2020).

Impact on Staff

Studies on cutback management, or managing under conditions of decline, tend to focus more on the impact of cutbacks on managers and strategies for dealing with declining resources rather than on staff in lower ranks. However, all employees are affected by funding cuts, even when their jobs are not lost. Despite the best professional efforts of staff to avoid letting their concerns interfere with their relationships with volunteers, clients, or patrons, it is a mistake to assume that these stakeholders are not adversely affected. Consequently, it is essential that, when a nonprofit is confronted with declining resources, manager concern themselves with the range of reactions of employees at all levels. Aamodt (2010) suggested that when the worst does happen and layoffs are required, the consequences for employees and their families can be devastating:

> From a health perspective, [downsized employees] report increases in headaches, stomach upsets, sleeping problems, cholesterol levels, physical illness, hospitalization rates, heart trouble, hypertension, ulcers, vision problems, and shortness of breath. Emotionally, [downsized workers] report high levels of stress, increased drug and alcohol abuse, more marital problems, and feelings of depression, unhappiness, anger. . . . Socially, [they] are reluctant to share their feelings with friends, avoid family and friends due to feelings of embarrassment and shame. (p. 540)

As employees become more aware of the reality of funding cuts, they will often react with anger, frequently focused at the organization's managers, who are blamed for the situation. As their initial anger subsides, staff may begin to acknowledge the reality of the situation and attempt to bargain for the survival of their particular unit, program, or job. When such bargaining fails, depression often sets in. At this point, employees may feel helpless and hopeless, believing that the situation is beyond their control. If they can work through their depression, they are more likely to settle into a state of acceptance. Unfortunately, not all staff members who are affected by cutbacks will be able to work through these stages to the point of acceptance. Many will leave the organization still angry or depressed.

When confronted with the specter of declining resources, nonprofit managers can take several actions that will help staff deal more effectively with the situation. They must first recognize that their own level of stress will likely increase and thus take steps to identify and handle their responses to this stress. There are a variety of effective ways to reduce stress, from doing more physical exercise to creating and participating in support groups with other managers who are in a similar situation. In some cases, it may be helpful and entirely appropriate to consult with an executive coach who has expertise in dealing with cutback management.

Identifying and dealing with stress involves grappling with a paradox. It is not uncommon for managers who are stressed to react by withdrawing, keeping information to themselves, and becoming more autocratic in making decisions. Managers must resist these tendencies and make the effort to be more open about sharing information and decision making. Herman and McCambridge (2009) described open communication and transparency as "the soul of fairness. Enlightened nonprofit leaders keep employees informed of what the organization's financial situation is on a continual basis and, therefore, when circumstances start to decline, employees are well aware of the stress facing the organization . . . ." It is also important to pay particular attention to those in the organization who will have the responsibility and burden of telling others that they are being laid off or that their jobs have been eliminated. This is an extremely difficult task emotionally that usually falls on middle managers, and its emotional impact should not be overlooked or minimized.

Managing rumors is an important component of managerial activity in dealing with declining resources. Decisions must be made about what and when to tell the staff. Rumors serve the purpose of helping staff structure and reduce their anxiety and offer a way to make sense of the situation. In other words, rumors often enable staff to gain a sense of control. Members of the management team can counteract rumors by recognizing the purposes that rumors serve and by providing alternative mechanisms for staff to meet their needs for greater control. These mechanisms include helping staff members at all levels of the organization structure their anxiety by engaging them in planning activities as well as by providing them with opportunities to express their negative feelings.

Managers should engage staff in scenario-planning exercises to reaffirm their organization's mission and identify the goals and core activities that are most critical. "Scenario planning helps organization leaders navigate uncertainty while providing structure around making key strategic decisions" (Waldron, Searle, & Jaskula-Ranga, 2020). A review of the nonprofit's core mission can also help to identify those individuals within the organization who have the most knowledge, skills, and necessary training to deliver critical programs. With this assessment, managers and their teams can be encouraged to generate a series of best-case–worst-case scenarios with various alternatives for each scenario. Analysis of different scenario models can then be used to structure plans for making decisions about retrenchment or layoffs. "Providing ongoing information and involving people in providing input on staff cuts can improve decision making and present an organization with options it otherwise might not have entertained" (Herman & McCambridge, 2009).

Of course, union contracts and civil service regulations may set limits on the ability to make staffing decisions under conditions of decline. When such contracts or regulations exist, it is incumbent on managers to be well informed about state and federal laws governing specific requirements and restrictions in the region. When no such contracts or regulations exist, managers may have more latitude in making decisions about retrenchment. In either case, decisions about who to keep and who to let go should be based on judgments about which staff members can contribute most to the nonprofit's core mission and which will best enable the organization to be positioned to take advantage of environmental opportunities that arise in the future.

When decisions are made to lay off particular staff members, these individuals should be informed as early as possible to afford them the maximum chance to find other jobs. Managers should provide them with a range of supports or outplacement services. These supports may include assistance in preparing résumés, ensuring that they will be able to get reference letters that indicate the circumstances under which their employment was terminated, and offering opportunities to vent their feelings about the situation. In addition, managers may find it helpful to arrange for a representative of the local unemployment compensation office to meet with staff to explain how to apply for unemployment compensation, how long it will take for them to receive their first check, how much money they can expect to receive, and how long they may be eligible to collect benefits. This kind of information is essential to staff members who must plan how they will manage their lives in the period immediately after being laid off. Moreover, treating employees who lose their jobs with fairness, compassion, and respect helps to maintain morale and confidence among those employees who are likely to remain.

Strategic Steps in Managing Organizational Decline

Determine the Scope of the Problem

When faced with severe shortfalls in funding, a range of strategies can be deployed, depending on the nature of the specific crisis. The first step is to determine the cause or causes of the decline. Behn (1988) argued that the understanding of a management problem is dependent on how severe it is perceived to be. Questions that must be carefully considered include the following:

- Is the problem likely to be short term or long term?
- Is the problem related to internal mismanagement or a lack of internal professional expertise?
- Is the problem related to inefficiencies caused by inadequate technology or a critical staffing position?
- Is the problem the result of a local or national trend in a particular industry?
- Is the crisis due to new competition from an alternative vendor or service provider?
- Is the problem the result of lost credibility resulting from scandal or fraud?
- Is the problem related to lack of visibility or marketing?
- How serious is the problem? That is, can the crisis be averted through short-term and limited cutbacks, or is the problem more serious, likely requiring a longer term retrenchment?

Selecting Strategies to Model

Deciding what or whom to cut is one of the most difficult decisions nonprofit managers will make, and the results of those decision will likely affect many people throughout the organization. However, the tools and framework outlined in this chapter are designed to help you identify the most critical services and activities within your organization's mission that are at greatest risk and provide a mission-based and values-driven approach to implementing necessary cutbacks intended to maximize the organization's chances of continued operation and long-term health.

The most common strategies nonprofit managers turn to when responding to decline or funding shortfall are cost reductions, mission realignment, political influence, cooperative strategies and mergers, refinancing, commercialization and fundraising, relocation, employee furloughs, and downsizing (Cascio, 2009; DuBran, 1996; MacIntosh, 2020; Palmer, 1997).

Cost Reductions
Cost reductions are most often used when the source of the cutback is temporary and when their impact will not likely affect the nonprofit's long-term performance. However, many nonprofit managers mistakenly use across-the-board cutbacks without fully addressing the real budget problems facing

their organization. Such overuse of cost reductions often leads to continued funding shortfalls and a further decline in the organization.

Mission Realignment

Mission realignment may be necessary if an organization begins to invest in programs or activities that extend beyond its primary purpose or mission. Often referred to as "mission drift," evaluating which core activities are critical to the organization's mission is especially important during times of decline or retrenchment.

Political Influence

Political influence is used as an attempt to reverse externally imposed funding cuts, often when funding is received from government sources. This strategy usually involves board members, clients, patrons, local citizens, or other stakeholders who may be in a position of power to influence decision makers in the community. Although political leverage tends to be a slower process and rarely leads to an immediate funding solution, in times of emergency—such as the COVID-19 pandemic—state and federal authorities may issue emergency grant funding to increase the capacity of local nonprofits to provide critical services to those in need.

Cooperative Strategies and Mergers

Cooperative strategies and mergers are frequently used when two or more organizations determine that cost savings can be made by combining elements of their programs or services. Also referred to as "survival sharing," these strategies move away from a stance of competition to one of cooperation. "Any organization concerned about whether it will be able to endure as a standalone entity may still have time to explore a merger or other similar transaction, but this possibility will quickly evaporate as time passes and cash depletes" (MacIntosh, 2020, p. 5). Cooperation strategies are often used among program units within organizations that are particularly large or complex. An extreme form of cooperation is a merger between two independent organizations. Although mergers may save money in the long term, they are costly and extremely disruptive in the short term and can cause significant staff turnover or a change in leadership. Also, because mergers typically take at least 6–18 months—or even longer—to explore or implement, they are not likely to be a viable option during times of emergency.

Refinancing

Refinancing is a strategy often used in the arts and humanities sectors. Many performing arts organizations will borrow money from a bank or lender against anticipated future growth in earned income through ticket sales (MacIntosh,

2020; Palmer, 1997). Shortfalls result when proceeds are insufficient to cover costs, forcing organizations to then refinance to avoid defaulting on their loan. These types of strategies are used for short-term crises when shortfalls are deemed temporary and future revenues are clearly identified.

Commercialization and Fundraising

Commercialization and fundraising involve a change in marketing strategy, usually through raising ticket prices, increasing fees for services, or expanding fundraising activities to raise additional funds for the organization. Fundraising activities, including special events, should be considered and may help attract attention to the needs of the organization, as well as increase the level of financial support from individuals, foundations, and corporations (see chapter 4). When in-person special events were severely curtailed or postponed during the COVID-19 pandemic, many organizations quickly shifted to virtual events, such as online auctions, to raise money for their organizations (Edwards, 2020).

Relocation

Relocations are used when the cost of overhead for an existing facility becomes too expensive. Relocation may help reduce property taxes; involve a merger with another similar organization; or simply be a move to a smaller, less expensive facility. In some cases, relocation parallels a reduction in the overall scope of the services provided. However, many costs are associated with moving an organization, both in terms of real dollars needed to carry out the move and in the loss in productivity and potential loss of customers or clients who may not know where the new facility is located. For organizations that have multiple sites, it may be necessary to close one or more satellite locations to consolidate overhead expenditures. Moreover, long-term lease obligations may make relocation difficult, if not impossible.

Although it is still too early to predict how the COVID-19 pandemic will affect nonprofits long term, many nonprofit leaders—after the experience of working at home, mandated to slow transmission of the virus—are already considering whether they will need the same amount of office space or whether some operations can continue to be managed from home after the pandemic subsides.

Employee Furloughs

According to Cascio (2009), "the use of mandatory furloughs rose sharply in 2009, largely as a strategy to control labor costs while retaining talent" (p. 9). Furloughs of workers were also used in response to the 2020 COVID-19 pandemic. Cascio warned that "several important legal risks accompany such programs, including concerns about disparate impact on protected groups" (p. 9) and issues related to exempt and non-exempt employees who are furloughed for less than full-week periods. Organizations that have unions may also have specific restrictions or limitations. "It is always important to check with state law to determine if an extended furlough might trigger an obligation to pay final wages" (Cascio, 2009, p. 10).

Downsizing

Downsizing has been a focus of much concern since the mid-1970s because of the many organizations, both for profit and nonprofit, that have experienced it. Downsizing is typically used either when organizations become too large or when substantial budget shortfalls necessitate immediate reductions in staff. According to Cascio (2009), downsizing is essentially the planned elimination of positions or jobs. However, for many organizations, downsizing has been shown not to be a long-term cost-saving strategy. Many organizations that have downsized discover that low employee morale, decreased productivity, and the high cost of rehiring and retraining led to even further decline and retrenchment (Cascio, 2009; Perry, 1988). Depending on the circumstances, you may have no choice but to downsize your workforce. When that is the case, it will probably be one of the most difficult and painful situations you will encounter during your career as a nonprofit manager.

When it is determined that staff reductions are necessary, DuBran (1996) suggested the following four steps:

1. Eliminate low-value and no-value activities.
2. Keep future work requirements in mind.
3. Identify the tasks that retained employees will perform.
4. Decide which workers will be let go.

DuBran (1996) further recommended that once it is determined who will be laid off, managers should make the cuts as quickly and completely as possible. In the long run, it will be far less disruptive to make a single round of cuts quickly than to make several rounds over a protracted time. Prolonging cutback decisions only increases staff insecurities and further demoralizes the workforce.

Determining the criteria to use when deciding whom to lay off is both complicated and controversial. Decisions are often based on seniority, employment status (part-time and temporary workers), voluntary resignations and early retirements, and performance. All of these options have advantages and disadvantages.

DuBran (1996) noted that basing layoff decisions on seniority may seem to be the most fair; however, managers lose control over which employees are maintained. Also, letting go of senior staff may have serious negative effects on the staff who are left behind and who now fear that loyalty to the firm no longer ensures job security. Similarly, dismissing workers according to function may appear to benefit overall operations but may be interpreted as political on the part of management to get rid of staff whom they do not like. Laying off temporary or part-time workers may have appeal because it protects job security for permanent employees. However, temporary employees are sometimes hired to carry out highly specialized tasks, and they are usually less expensive than permanent full-time employees. Hence, letting go of temporary workers may have a high negative impact on general operations but a relatively low impact on total budget.

Voluntary resignations and early retirement incentive strategies are often used by organizations that have a large workforce. Eligible employees are offered early retirement or severance packages that they can take now or risk being laid off later. The obvious disadvantage is that an organization may lose its most highly skilled workers because it is losing control of which employees it retains.

Basing layoff decisions on performance can be one of the most challenging, but more productive, methods of achieving a downsized workforce. Most experts agree that basing layoff decisions on performance both increases employee morale in the long run and minimizes productivity loss (Cascio, 2009; DuBran, 1996; Perry, 1988). Essentially, program managers are asked to assess their staff and make recommendations for termination or dismissal on the basis of individual performance measures. However, DuBran (1996) discouraged the practice of conducting performance appraisals strictly for the purpose of downsizing because they may appear too political.

Throughout the process of downsizing, it is essential that managers demonstrate compassion and understanding both for the workers who are laid off and for those who are retained but who may experience survivor's guilt. Outplacement services should be provided for displaced workers. It is also important to recognize that, although downsizing may be necessary, it will undoubtedly cause a loss in productivity and may prove to be more costly in the long term than other retrenchment strategies.

Scenario Modeling

Once retrenchment is determined to be necessary, managers are highly encouraged to first develop a clear set of principles and value statements to help guide the decision-making process before considering specific responses. Waldron et al. (2020) suggested creating an explicit list of principles to

- enable the leadership team and board to make faster and more consistent decisions
- ensure that equity-related considerations receive proper attention
- allow one to communicate the reasoning behind key decisions in a way that instills confidence and trust

Decision-making principles and value statements should be shared with members of the board and employees at all levels of the organization to increase transparency, reaffirm the organization's core mission and essential programs, and potentially stimulate new ideas and cost-saving measures to protect and maintain services essential to the community. Waldon et al. (2020) recommended starting with a list of principle categories and then work with the leadership team to generate a series of value statements for each principle. They suggest categories such as the following:

- Principles to protect the mission: evaluating the organization's capacity to continue, or ways to reprioritize services according to the greatest community need
- Principles to put people first: balancing issues of employee well-being, equity, seniority, talent, and mission-critical functions to maintain operations
- Principles to elevate equity: examination of income disparities across the organization when considering programmatic or operational shifts, pay cuts, furloughs, and layoffs
- Principles to focus on financial resilience: balancing pursuit of short-term revenue streams and utilization of operational reserves

With decision-making principles and potential responses in hand, the strategies managers choose will depend on the underlying scope and causes of the problem, the service sector and business model that drives operations, and the anticipated duration and subsequent residual impacts the crisis will have. Therefore, managers must carefully evaluate the problem in all its complexity—both internal and external forces affecting the organization—and develop a well-planned series of contingency plans to address it

Working with nonprofit executives during the 2020 global pandemic, one consulting firm noted a new foreboding reality:

> Nonprofit leaders have taken heroic steps to continue their organizations' important work as COVID-19 swept across the world. They've [struggled] to make sure their cash is under control, provide emergency relief, and keep staff and constituents safe—all while staying

on mission under extraordinary stress. Yet they still can't be sure how the pandemic will affect society, the economy, or their own field six months or a year from now. (Waldon et al., 2020)

This unprecedented level of uncertainty, affecting virtually all types and sizes of nonprofits, requires new ways of assessing and mitigating risk—at levels not seen in more than a generation.

The literature on risk management and scenario planning is rich with examples and tools to help nonprofit leaders navigate the difficult choices they may need to implement to protect the short- and long-term mission and health of their organizations. The model described next, developed by the Bridgespan Group (Waldron et al., 2020), illustrates how many nonprofit organizations used scenario planning during the COVID-19 pandemic.

The Bridgespan Group Model

The following text is from "Making Sense of Uncertainty: Nonprofit Scenario Planning During a Crisis," by L. Waldron, R. Searle, & A. Jankul-Ranga, 2020. Retrieved from https://www.bridgespan.org/insights/library/strategy-development/nonprofit-scenario-planning-during-a-crisis. Copyright 2020 by the Bridgespan Group. Reprinted with permission from the Bridgespan Group.

Decision making under uncertainty starts with clarity on **guiding principles** for your organization. ... The principles reflect your organization's unique mission, values, and circumstances, and articulate how you will approach tough tradeoffs balancing your mission, finances, staff, equity, and other considerations. They'll also help you communicate the rationale behind tough decisions to key stakeholders. If you haven't already aligned on guiding principles in your initial crisis response, you'll want do to so before embarking on the four-step scenario planning process outlined [see Figure 16.1].

Step 1. Identify Key Drivers at Risk

With guiding principles in hand, you'll start scenario planning by identifying the drivers of your organization's economics and impact. These are the elements or variables that animate your day, or keep you up at night, typically in three categories—programs, operations, and funding. Examples might include: program activities, number of clients or patrons served, and other mission deliverables; revenue from grants, program fees, earned income, and fundraising; and operational expenses such as personnel, occupancy, and administrative functions required to run the organization.

Figure 16.1 Scenario Planning Process

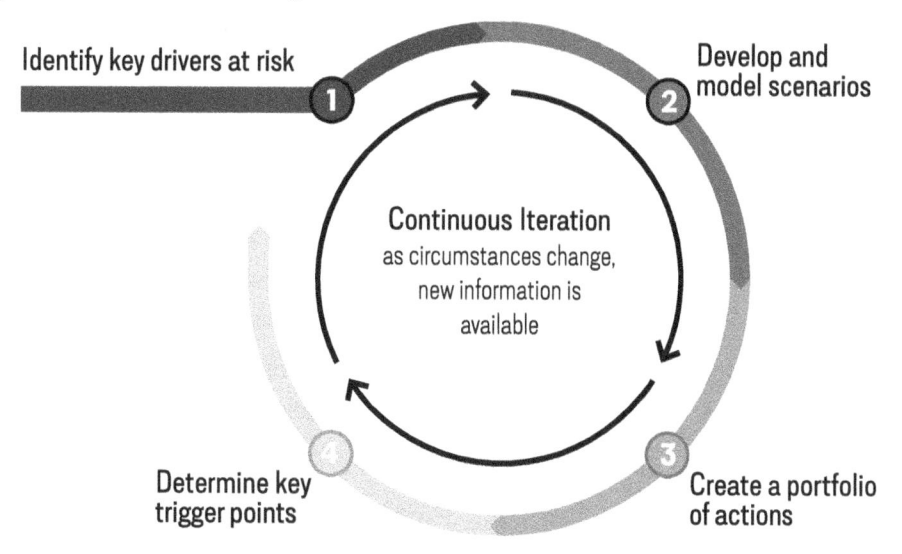

1. Identify key drivers at risk
2. Develop and model scenarios
3. Create a portfolio of actions
4. Determine key trigger points

Continuous Iteration as circumstances change, new information is available

You may have a long list of drivers, so you'll want to prioritize them by level of importance and level of risk. In evaluating levels of risk, consider three questions:

- What is the nature of the risk associated with the driver?
- What is the likelihood that the risk plays itself out?
- If the risk played out, how much of an impact would it have?

A risk with a high likelihood and high impact of course indicates a high level of risk. But so much is uncertain, so you'll have to rely on a combination of external sources (such as guidance from public health experts or economic data) and good judgement to make best guess assessments across all drivers and their risks.

Step 2. Develop and Model Scenarios

Develop best-, moderate-, and worst-case scenarios that reflect the full spectrum of possible outcomes for your organization. Your scenarios should anchor on the key drivers—the ones that are high importance and high risk—that you prioritized in Step 1. As you assessed the level of risk for each, you probably thought about external factors—for example, government social distancing rules, the pace of economic recovery, unemployment rates, school closures, and public attitudes about engaging in certain kinds of activities (like volunteering, seeking health services, or going to a cultural institution)—that are beyond your control. Now, it's time to build scenarios around those external factors, focusing on how the few that are most relevant to your organization play out in best, moderate, and worst cases.

Anchor your financial modeling in a time horizon that is relevant for your organization and budget cycle (e.g., six months). Some will find it helpful to consider multiple time horizons. But whatever your time horizon, remember two things:

- **Don't aim for precision.** The goal is to work with your management team to understand possible outcomes and plan accordingly.
- **Don't underestimate the worst case.** Your worst-case scenario should reflect possibilities that could have serious consequences for the organization.

Step 3. Create a Portfolio of Actions

Next, you want to develop a set of actions that would allow you to effectively manage against each scenario—or across all of them.

Actions typically fall into one of three main categories:

1. Appropriate for any scenario: These actions are likely to benefit the organization's ability to deliver impact and support its financial health under any future scenario.
2. Smaller-scale and more flexible: These actions can be executed quickly, and potentially reversed, if needed.
3. Larger and more permanent: These actions involve large-scale investments or cost reduction measures and may be harder to reverse.

The actions will likely have some economic cost or benefit. Quantify the potential costs incurred or savings achieved for each action individually, over whatever time horizon the action would be implemented. Then, calculate the total estimated costs incurred or savings achieved by each set of actions for your best-, moderate-, and worst-case scenarios. And keep your guiding principles top of mind; they will serve as an invaluable compass to ensure your actions balance these financial costs and benefits with your mission, your staff, equity, and the other considerations that your leadership team agreed upon.

Step 4. Determine Key Trigger Points

This last step involves identifying clear trigger points that will prompt decision making and action on the part of your leadership team. At what point would you have to let which staff go? When should you press pause on certain employee benefits? What will prompt you to shut down a program delivery site or open a new one where needs are increasing? These are tough questions requiring tough answers, but these trigger points—whether signaled by internal metrics or external events—can serve as guardrails for you and your leadership team through the crisis and its aftermath. They will also help speed up decision making down the road. You may want several trigger points, or one that is the best gauge for multiple actions.

See Waldron et al. (2020) for a more detailed presentation of this model and examples.

Lessons from the COVID-19 Pandemic's Effects on Nonprofits

Coming out of the economic recession resulting from the COVID-19 pandemic, a number of lessons have been learned, and the following strategies are recommended for nonprofits that are facing severe economic challenges (La Piana & MacIntosh, 2020; MacIntosh, 2020; Waldron et al., 2020):

- Refocus on your mission: The foundation for your decision making should be "What best advances the long-term mission of the nonprofit?" A clear understanding of your mission—with a set of carefully constructed guiding principles—provides a coherent foundation for decision making.

- Conserve cash: Carefully review every item in your expense budget, with an eye toward what expenses can be reduced, deferred, or eliminated. For many nonprofits, the largest portion of their expenses are personnel related, followed by rent, and then everything else. Staff reductions should be considered. Determine whether payments for mortgages, leases, equipment, supplies, and the like can be delayed.

- Accelerate revenue: Explore whether any funders with outstanding grant commitments can accelerate their payments and see whether any of your major donors will be willing to accelerate gift pledges.

- Explore new fundraising opportunities: Are any of your donors willing to step up and help? Are there local, state, or federal grants available as emergency funding to responder organizations providing direct support to the community?

- Shorten time horizons: Do not engage in magical thinking ("Everything will be ok"). Get ready to make hard decisions.

- Explore strategic restructuring: Consider whether there are opportunities for mergers and other forms of collaboration, or even whether it is time to consider dissolution of the nonprofit.
- Plan for the longer term: Do not weather the crisis—learn from it and formulate plans for how to better weather future crises. Develop scenario strategies for future potential downturns and commit resources to saving at least three to six months in operational reserves.

Many nonprofit managers who have had to steer their organizations through severe financial crises find during such turbulent times that they need to have more frequent and intense interaction with their board leadership. Some have found that weekly meetings with their board chairs, and monthly or even more frequent meetings of the entire board membership, are critical. As a manager, you need the support of your board for the hard decisions you will need to make. If your board is well constructed, with strong individuals who represent the community you serve and who genuinely care about your organization and what it does, you can gain from their wisdom and support. Moreover, some may be willing to help with the process of seeking alternative funding, as well as help buffer you and your management staff from some of the negative publicity that may be attendant to laying off personnel and reducing service programs.

Conclusion

Managers of nonprofit organizations are confronting a new era of fiscal austerity prompted by a profound philosophical shift in the perception of federal responsibility and a subsequent reduction in government funding for many community-based programs. Clearly, nonprofits will continue to experience increased demand for services in an environment of shrinking financial resources and increased competition for private dollars.

Effective nonprofit managers must be able to recognize their own reactions to stress and find ways to handle it effectively. Having done so, managers should involve staff in developing a set of decision-making values and principles based on the organization's core program and delineating the agency's mission, primary functions, and goals. At the same time, managers should pursue resource development strategies to increase revenues.

If layoffs are necessitated by dwindling resources, decisions should be guided by a predetermined set of decision-making principles and made in a straightforward, honest manner that respects the dignity of all employees across the organization. Outplacement assistance should be provided to staff who are losing their jobs. It is evident that these varied responses to organizational decline will require both technical and interactional skills.

Skills Application Exercise

Assume you are the director of large nonprofit shelter for runaway youths. Your programs include a 24-hour crisis hotline, a 24-hour runaway shelter (which provides meals, individual and group counseling, peer support, and crisis intervention), in-home family unification services, and services to prevent physical and sexual abuse (counseling and public education). Your funding sources include government grants (65 percent), small grants from foundations and corporations (20 percent), fees (10 percent), and individual donations (5 percent). You have been advised that your government funding will be reduced by 20 percent over the next two years. The board of county commissioners has requested that you submit your plan for dealing with these budgetary cuts. What managerial actions or approaches would you take? Include in your plan your responses to these questions:

1. What activities can your nonprofit stop performing?
2. What activities can your nonprofit get other organizations to do?
3. What activities can be performed more effectively?
4. How can you reduce the cost of labor?
5. How can you increase your nonprofit's revenues?

References

Aamodt, M. G. (2010). *Industrial/organizational psychology: An applied approach* (6th ed.). Belmont, CA: Wadsworth.

Alliance for Nonprofit Management. (2008). *The most common financial, management risks facing nonprofits.* Retrieved from https://eclkc.ohs.acf.hhs.gov/fiscal-management/article/most-common-financial-management-risks-facing-nonprofits

Banning, R. L. (1990, September). The dynamics of downsizing. *Personnel Journal*, pp. 68–75.

Behn, R. D. (1988). The fundamentals of cutback management. In K. S. Cameron, R. I. Sutton, & D. A. Whetton (Eds.), *Readings in organizational decline: Frameworks, research, and prescriptions* (pp. 247–356). Cambridge, MA: Ballinger.

Cameron, K. S., Sutton, R. I., & Whetten, D. A. (1988). *Readings in organizational decline: Frameworks, research, and prescriptions.* Cambridge, MA: Ballinger.

Cascio, W. F. (2009). *Employment downsizing and its alternatives: Strategies for long-term success.* Alexandria, VA: SHRM Foundation.

Cooke, P. W., Reid, P. N., & Edwards, R. L. (1997). Management: New developments and directions. In R. L. Edwards (Ed.-in-Chief), *Encyclopedia of social work* (19th ed., 1997 Suppl., pp. 229–242). Washington, DC: NASW Press.

Dickler, J., & Epperson, S. (2019). *What the new tax law means for your charitable giving.* Retrieved from https://www.cnbc.com/2018/05/11/what-the-new-tax-law-means-for-your-charitable-giving.html

DuBran, A. J. (1996). *Reengineering survival guide: Managing and succeeding in the changing workplace.* Cincinnati: Thomson Executive Press.

Edwards, R. L. (2020). *Building a strong foundation: Fundraising for nonprofit organizations* (2nd ed.). Washington, DC: NASW Press.

Edwards, R. L., Cooke, P. W., & Reid, P. N. (1996). Social work management in an era of diminishing federal responsibility. *Social Work, 41*, 46–79.

Edwards, R. L., Lebold, D. A., & Yankey, J. A. (1998). Managing organizational decline. In R. L. Edwards, J. A. Yankey, & M. A. Altpeter (Eds.), *Skills for effective management of nonprofit organizations* (pp. 279–300). Washington, DC: NASW Press.

Firstenberg, P. B. (1996). *The 21st century nonprofit: Remaking the organization in the post-government era.* New York: Foundation Center.

Giving USA. (2019). *Giving USA 2019: American gave $427.71 billion to charity in 2018 amid complex year for charitable giving.* Retrieved from https://givingusa.org/giving-usa-2019-americans-gave-427-71-billion-to-charity-in-2018-amid-complex-year-for-charitable-giving/

Gupta, A. (2010). *Organizational life-cycle & decline.* Retrieved from http://www.practical-management.com/Organization-Development/Organizational-lifecycle-and-decline.html

Hayes, A. (2020). *Who is Bernie Madoff?* Retrieved from https://www.investopedia.com/terms/b/bernard-madoff.asp

Herman, M., & McCambridge, R. (2009). *Compassionate layoffs: Proceed with care.* Retrieved from https://nonprofitquarterly.org/compassionate-layoffs-proceed-with-care/

Kellerman, B. (2004). *Bad leadership: What it is, how it happens, why it matters.* Cambridge, MA: Harvard Business Press Books.

Krugman, P. (2020, May 12). How to create a pandemic depression. *The New York Times,* p. A26.

La Piana, D., & MacIntosh, J. (2020, April 6). 8 steps nonprofits should take now to survive the pandemic fallout. *The Chronicle of Philanthropy.* Retrieved from https://www.philanthropy.com/article/8-Steps-Nonprofits-Should-take/248427?cid_home

Lebold, D. A., & Edwards, R. L. (2006). Managing financial uncertainty. In R. L. Edwards & J. A. Yankey (Eds.), *Effectively managing nonprofit organizations* (pp. 431–456). Washington, DC: NASW Pres.

MacIntosh, J. (2020). *Tough times call for tough action: A decision framework for nonprofit leaders & boards.* New York: SeaChange Partners. Retrieved from http://gd7xi2tioeh408c7o34706rc-wpengine.netdna-ssl.com/wp-content/uploads/2020/04/COVID-19-Nonprofit-Decision-Framework.pdf

McCambridge, R., & Dietz, N. (2020). Nonprofits in recession: Winners and losers. *Nonprofit Quarterly, 27*(3), 6–21.

Morris, G., Roberts, D., MacIntosh, J., & Bordone, A. (2018). *The financial health of the United States nonprofit sector: Facts and observations.* New York: Oliver Wyman. Retrieved from http://gd7xi2tioeh408c7o34706rc-wpengine.netdna-ssl.com/wp-content/uploads/2020/01/The-Financial-Health-of-the-US-Nonprofit-Sector.pdf

Newland, C. A. (1996). The national government in transition. In J. L. Perry (Ed.), *Handbook of public administration* (2nd ed., pp. 19–35). San Francisco: Jossey-Bass.

Nonprofit Finance Fund. (2018). *2018 state of the nonprofit sector survey (2018).* Retrieved from https://nff.org/packard

Otten, L. (2017). *Is bigger always better? Money vs. mission.* Retrieved from https://www.lasallenonprofitcenter.org/bigger-always-better-money-vs-mission/

Palmer, I. (1997). Arts management cutback strategies: A cross-sector analysis. *Nonprofit Management and Leadership, 7,* 271–290.

Perry, T. P. (1988). Least-cost alternatives to layoffs in declining industries. In K. S. Cameron, R. I. Sutton, & D. A. Whetton (Eds.), *Readings in organizational decline: Frameworks, research, and prescriptions* (pp. 357–368). Cambridge, MA: Ballinger.

Pratt, J., & Aanestad, K. (2020, Spring). Deconstructing the (not-so-great) nonprofit recession. *Nonprofit Quarterly.* Retrieved from https://nonprofitquarterly.org/deconstructing-the-not-so-great-nonprofit-recession/

Propel Nonprofits. (2020). *Operating reserves with nonprofit policy examples.* Retrieved from https://www.propelnonprofits.org/resources/nonprofit-operating-reserves-policy-examples/#:~:text=A%20commonly%20used%20reserve%20goal,one%20full%20payroll%20including%20taxes

Sarbanes–Oxley Act of 2002, P.L. 107-204, 116 Stat. 745.

Stanford GSB Staff. (2003). *What led to Enron, WorldCom and the like?* Retrieved from https://www.gsb.stanford.edu/insights/what-led-enron-worldcom

Tax Cuts and Jobs Act, P.L. 105-277, 131 Stat. 2054 (2017).

Waldron, L., & Nayak, P. (2020). *A compass for the crisis: Nonprofit decision making in the COVID-19 pandemic.* Retrieved from https://www.bridge span.org/insights/library/organizational-effectiveness/nonprofit-decision -making-in-covid-19-crisis

Waldron, L., Searle, R., & Jaskula-Ranga, A. (2020). *Making sense of uncertainty: Nonprofit scenario planning during a crisis.* Retrieved from https://www.bridgespan.org/insights/library/strategy-development/ nonprofit-scenario-planning-covid-19

Young, D. R. (2000, Nov. 2). Windfalls and sudden losses: How should nonprofits respond? *NonProfit Times*, p. 16.

Appendix

Sampling of Web Sites Related to Nonprofit Management

Renette Bayne Issaka

The following is a list of organizations and periodicals that nonprofit leaders and managers may find helpful.

Organizations

Alliance for Nonprofit Management
c/o TSNE Mission Works
89 South Street, Suite 700
Boston, MA 02111
(800) 732-2034
E-mail: info@allianceonline.org
https://allianceonline.org

This is a professional association of organizations and individuals devoted to improving the management and governance capacities of nonprofit organizations.

Association of Fundraising Professionals
4300 Wilson Boulevard, Suite 300
Arlington, VA 22203
(800) 666-3863/(703) 684-0410
E-mail: afp@afpglobal.org
https://www.afpglobal.org

Formerly called the American Association of Fundraising Executives, the Association of Fundraising Professionals (AFP) is a membership organization of fundraising professionals that helps nonprofits plan and manage fundraising programs, studies trends in American philanthropy, and publishes a quarterly membership magazine and a growing collection of online-only content to help members succeed. AFP also has a certification program for fundraising executives.

BBB Wise Giving Alliance
3033 Wilson Boulevard, Suite 710
Arlington, VA 22201
(703) 247-9321
https://www.give.org

The BBB Wise Giving Alliance helps donors make informed giving decisions and promotes high standards of conduct among organizations that solicit contributions from the public. It produces reports about national charities, evaluating them against comprehensive Standards for Charity Accountability, and publishes a magazine, the *Wise Giving Guide,* three times a year.

BoardSource
1828 L Street, NW, Suite 900
Washington, DC 20136-5104
(202) 349-2544
https://boardsource.org

This organization is dedicated to improving the effectiveness of nonprofit organizations by strengthening their boards.

Candid (created by a merger of the Foundation Center and GuideStar)
32 Old Slip, 24th Floor
New York, NY 10005
(646) 927-4892
https://candid.org

This organization, which is primarily supported by foundations, provides a range of valuable information about grants through its publications and online databases. Its publications include the *Foundation Directory* and *Foundation Grants Index.*

Center for Community Change
1536 U Street, NW
Washington, DC 20009
(202) 339-9300
https://www.communitychange.org

This organization provides resources for nonprofits assisting low-income populations and helps racial and ethnic groups with planning, organizing, and fundraising issues.

Center for Disaster Philanthropy
One Thomas Circle, NW, Suite 700
Washington, DC 20005
(202) 464-2018
https://disasterphilanthropy.org

The Center for Disaster Philanthropy (CDP) disseminates information to help funders learn, presents opportunities for collaboration, and helps leverage their collective strength through funds and other activities. The CDP offers grants to support medium- and long-term recovery efforts in communities affected by a variety of disasters, including hurricanes, flooding, wildfires, earthquakes, tornadoes, and manmade disasters. With a focus on vulnerable and at-risk populations, the CDP prioritizes investments in community-based organizations to support a range of programs critical for individuals and communities to recover.

Center on Nonprofits and Philanthropy
500 L'Enfant Plaza, SW
Washington, DC 20024
(202) 833-7200
https://www.urban.org/policy-centers/center-nonprofits-and-philanthropy

A unit of the Urban Institute, the Center on Nonprofits and Philanthropy (CNP) works across all sectors to increase the impact of actors on the front lines of social change. By partnering with change makers, sharing knowledge, and analyzing results, the CNP is amplifying these efforts to improve practice, inform policy, and advance public understanding.

Council for Advancement and Support of Education
1307 New York Avenue, NW, Suite 1000
Washington, DC 20005-4701
(202) 328-CASE (2273)
https://www.case.org

This is an organization of educational institutions that provides professional development opportunities for fundraising professionals in education.

Council on Foundations
1255 23rd Street, NW, Suite 200
Washington, DC 20037
(202) 466-6512
https://www.cof.org

The Council on Foundations is a membership organization of various types of foundations, corporate grant makers, and trust companies that seeks to promote responsible and effective grant making. It also encourages collaboration among grant makers and promotes the formation of new foundations. It publishes the bimonthly *Foundation News* and other useful publications.

Grantsmanship Center
350 South Bixel Street, Suite 110
Los Angeles, CA 90017
(800) 421-9512
https://www.tgci.com

The Grantmanship Center is a national training organization that conducts workshops across the country on grant writing, program management, fundraising, and other topics of relevance to nonprofits. It also produces several publications of value to nonprofit personnel.

Independent Sector
1602 L Street, NW, Suite 900
Washington, DC 20036
(202) 467-6100
https://independentsector.org

This organization is made up of national voluntary organizations, foundations, and corporations with major philanthropic programs. It works to enhance giving, volunteering, and nonprofit initiatives.

Indiana University Lilly Family School of Philanthropy
University Hall, Suite 3000
301 University Boulevard
Indianapolis, IN 46202-5146
(317) 274-4200
https://philanthropy.iupui.edu

This university-based center serves the nonprofit philanthropy sector through teaching, research, and service. It engages in and shares research on various aspects of philanthropy and nonprofit management and provides training to fundraising professionals.

National Committee on Planned Giving
200 South Meridian Street, Suite 510
Indianapolis, IN 46225
(317) 269-6274
https://charitablegiftplanners.org

This organization is concerned with gift planning. It publishes a range of resource materials on planned giving; sponsors training programs and conferences; and provides members with access to resources, opportunities for online learning, and connectivity with each other.

National Committee for Responsive Philanthropy
1900 L Street, NW, Suite 825
Washington, DC 20036
(202) 387-9177
https://www.ncrp.org

This organization of local and national nonprofits seeks to improve the accountability and accessibility of philanthropic organizations and to increase the responsiveness of philanthropic organizations (i.e., foundations) to organizations that are seeking to achieve social justice and fairer representation of those who are economically and politically disenfranchised. Its publications include a variety of bulletins, action alerts, and occasional publications on charitable giving trends.

National Council of Nonprofits
1001 G Street, NW, Suite 700
Washington, DC 20001
(202) 962-0322
https://www.councilofnonprofits.org

This organization serves as a resource and advocate for charitable nonprofits. It produces and curates tools, resources, and samples for nonprofits.

Periodicals

Chronicle of Philanthropy
https://philanthropy.com

This monthly publication covers virtually all aspects of philanthropy.

Human Service Organizations: Management, Leadership & Governance
https://www.tandfonline.com/toc/wasw21/current

Published quarterly by Taylor and Francis Publishers, this journal is dedicated to research and practice in nonprofit human services, including issues related to contemporary management, leadership, and governance.

Nonprofit Management & Leadership
https://onlinelibrary.wiley.com/journal/15427854

Published quarterly by John Wiley & Sons, this peer-reviewed journal includes scholarly articles on all aspects of management and leadership important to nonprofit organizations and leaders.

Nonprofit Quarterly
https://nonprofitquarterly.org

This quarterly magazine provides research-based articles and resources to educate the nonprofit sector by focusing on management, fundraising practices, philanthropy, and governance and board management.

Nonprofit and Voluntary Sector Quarterly
https://journals.sagepub.com/home/nvs

Published quarterly by Sage, this peer-reviewed academic journal covers research on the nonprofit and voluntary sector.

Nonprofit World
https://www.snpo.org/publications/nonprofitworld.php

This magazine, published quarterly by the Society for Nonprofit Organizations, covers everything from board governance and development to the issues affecting day-to-day operations of a nonprofit, including accounting, communications, fundraising, human resource issues and management, volunteer management, and branding and marketing.

Philanthropy News Digest
http://philanthropynewsdigest.org

Published by Candid, this online resource covers a wide range of topics of interest to nonprofit leaders, including matters related to philanthropy.

Index

Note: Figures and tables are indicated by *f* and *t*.

A

Abernathy, Penelope Muse, 33
accountability, 14, 50, 82, 171, 198–199, 224, 379–381
accounts payable, in financial statements, 201*f*, 205
accounts receivable, in financial statements, 201*f*, 202–203
acquisition mailings, 81
action plan, 61–64
ADA. *See* Americans with Disabilities Act (ADA) of 1990
adhocracy decision culture, 169–170, 169*t*, 171*t*, 172
advertising, 32, 33, 111. *See also* promotion
Age Discrimination in Employment Act of 1967, 107–108
aging, of population, 144
ambassador, board members as, 90
American Legislative Exchange Council, 65*t*
Americans with Disabilities Act (ADA) of 1990, 108
appreciative leadership, 145
apps, smartphone, 271, 359. *See also* client portals
assets
  in financial statements, 201*f*, 205
  in statement of activities, 206*f*
  Association of Fundraising Professionals, 79
assumptions, 59
audience, target, 39

audit
  diversity, 157–158
  financial, 212
  privacy, 280–281, 289
  risk, 260–261
austerity, fiscal, 388–393
autopopulation, in records, 283–284

B

Baby Boomers, 73
BARS. *See* behaviorally anchored rating scales (BARS)
Baskin, Jonathan Salem, 44
Begala, Paul, 53
behaviorally anchored rating scales (BARS), 128–129, 129*t*
behavior modeling, by board, 306–307
benchmarking, 45, 104, 105, 380
benefits, staff, 118–119
bias
  in performance appraisals, 129–131
  in recruitment, 147
Black Lives Matter, 150–151
board
  advisory groups in, 299
  analytical dimension and, 303
  assessments, 310–311
  behavior modeling by, 306–307
  in capital campaign, 90–91
  CEO and, 318–319
  change targets and, 310–311
  committees in, 299, 314–316
  contextual dimension and, 301
  development, 307–318

425

board—(cont'd)
 educational dimension and, 301–302
 education for, ongoing, 313–314
 effective. characteristics of, 300–305
 examples, 321–326
 functions of, 298–299
 fundraising and, 316
 group cohesion in, 317–318
 interpersonal dimension and, 302–303
 officer and director insurance for, 257
 performance of, attention to, 308–310
 political dimension and, 303–304
 priority setting by, 305
 progress monitoring by, 306
 retreats, 312–313
 selection criteria for, 299–300
 strategic dimension of, 304–305
 teamwork in, 317–318, 320
 value added by, 305–307
bonds, social impact, 358
boundary issues, with information and communication technology, 281–282
boundary-spanning skills, 12, 13f, 14–15
bridge building, 58
Bridgespan Group model, 410–413, 411f
Brookings Institution, 66t
budget cuts, 400
budget mechanisms, 212–214, 213f
budget shortfalls, 396–398
builder, board members as, 90
buildings, in financial statements, 201f
bureaucracy, 55

C
capability, of consent, 273
capital, human, 353–354
capital campaign, 89–96, 94t
Carville, James, 53
cash and cash equivalents, in financial statements, 200, 201f
cash flow statement, 210–211
cause-related marketing, 74–75
central tendency, in performance evaluation, 130
CEO. *See* chief executive officer (CEO)
Chamarro-Primuzik, Thomas, 191
change, organizational, 9–10

change targets, 310–311
character, 5
chief executive officer (CEO), 8–9, 13, 305, 308, 318–319. *See also* board
Civil Rights Act of 1964, 106–107
clan decision culture, 168–169, 169t, 170–171, 171t, 185
client portals, 284–285
climate assessment, 149–150
Clinton, Bill, 50
Clinton, Hillary, 56
coaching, 122t
coalition building, 57–58
coercion, consent and, 273
collegial relationships, and information and communication technology, 286–287
commercialization, 406
comparison group study, 236
compensation, staff, 118–119
competing values framework, 11–13, 12f, 13f, 21–22
 human resources in, 102–137, 110f, 113t–116t, 122t–123t, 124t, 125f–126f, 129t, 132t
 program evaluation in, 224–225
 strategic management and, 343
conceptual skills, 10, 11f
conferences, in staff development, 122t
confidence, 6
confidentiality
 ethics and, 259, 272
 information and communications technology and, 269
 with information and communication technology, 277–278, 289
 loyalty and, 371
 risk and, 254
conflict, human resources and, 108–109
conflicts of commitment, 376
conflicts of interest, 281–282, 375–376
consent, informed, 272–277
contacts, for major gifts, 85–86
content
 jargon in, 38
 in media, 35–38
 personal vs. abstract, 37

continuity of service, risk and, 254
contract services, in statement of activities, 206*f*
contrast effects, in performance evaluation, 131
contributions, in statement of activities, 206*f*, 208–209. *See also* fundraising
control group, 237
controls, internal, 214–217, 216*t*
coordinating skills, 12, 13*f*, 17–18
Council of State Governments, 65*t*
courage, moral, 374–375
COVID-19 pandemic, 398, 409, 410
   financial uncertainty and, 387, 391–392
   fundraising and, 69, 71, 72, 77, 406
   human resources and, 103, 105
   information and communications technology and, 269, 270, 272, 287
   lessons from, 413–414
   political influence and, 405
   unemployment and, 395
credibility, 59
crisis communications, 41–43
crowdsourcing, 359
culture. *See also* diversity; organizational culture
   decision, 166, 168–170, 169*t*
   of giving, 80–83
   innovation, 352–353, 361
   lock, 173–174, 173*f*
   organizational, 16
   subculture solidification, 170–172, 171*t*
   team, 149–150
cyberliability insurance, 257

D

decision crystallization, 188
decision culture, 166, 168–170, 169*t*
decision evaluation, 190
decision making
   choice in, as loss, 164–165
   concepts in, 164–168
   consultation in, 373
   decision building vs., 166
   decision constructing vs., 166
   "do-it, fix-it method" in, 186
   ethical, 373–374
   garbage can model in, 186
   groupthink in, 185
   managerial, 19–20
   organizational decline and, 409
   quality in, 165
   rules of, 165–166, 182–185
   "same as last year" in, 186
   subculture solidification and, 170–172, 171*t*
   values and, 165, 168, 182–189
   waste and, 191–192
decision management, 167
decision manager, 167
decision mosaic, 166–167
decision randomness, 186
decline. *See* organizational decline
defamation, 286–287
deferred revenue, in financial statements, 201*f*, 205
demographics
   diversity and, 141–144
   fundraising and, 73
demonization, 57
depreciation
   in financial statements, 201*f*
   in statement of activities, 207*f*
   derivatives, 202
design thinking, 343
development, staff, 120–123, 122*t*–123*t*, 147–149
developmental evaluation, 233
diagnosis, risk and, 255
directing skills, 12, 13*f*, 18–19
disabled persons, 143–144. *See also* Americans with Disabilities Act (ADA) of 1990
discharge, employee, 134–136
discipline, employee, 135–136
discrimination, human resources and, 106–109
disparate impact, discrimination and, 106–107
diversity. *See also* inclusion
   aging and, 144
   audit, 157–158
   communication of commitment to stakeholders, 152–153

diversity—(cont'd)
  defined, 140–141
  demographic change and, 141–144
  disabled persons and, 143–144
  economic impact of, 151–152
  as ethical and moral imperative,
    150–151
  ethnic, 142
  examples, 154–155
  hiring and, 146–147
  immigration and, 142–143
  inclusion vs., 141
  management and, 146–150
  mentorship and, 148
  racial, 142
  recruitment and, 146–147
  social innovation and, 353–354
  team culture and, 149–150
  vignettes, 155–157
documentation
  information and communication
    technology and, 282–285
  for major gifts, 86–87
"do-it, fix-it method," 186
Donor Bill of Rights, 79
dosage analysis, 237–238
doubtful accounts, in financial
  statements, 201f
downsizing, 136–137, 407–408
drug testing, in statement of
  activities, 207
duty segregation, 217, 218f, 218t–219t
duty to protect, 253–254
duty to warn, 253–254

E
education, in staff development, 122t
electronically stored information (ESI),
  278–279
employee discipline, 135–136
employee furloughs, 406–407
employee separations, 132–137
employment tests, 112
encryption, 277
enterprise, social, 356–358
entrepreneurship, social, 350–351
entry-level management, 10

environmental scanning, 104–105,
  335–336
e-philanthropy, 73–74
Equal Employment Opportunity Act of
  1972, 107, 113t–116t
equality, equity vs., 141
Equal Pay Act of 1963, 107
equipment
  in financial statements, 201f,
    204–205
  in statement of activities, 207
equity
  communication of commitment to
    stakeholders, 152–153
  economic impact of, 151–152
  equality vs., 141
  as ethical and moral imperative,
    150–151
  leadership and, 144–146
  management and, 146–150
equity stake rule, in decision
  making, 183
ESI. See electronically stored
  information (ESI)
ethical decision making, 373–374
ethical dilemmas, 370–372
ethics
  accountability and, 379–381
  common challenges of, 375–381
  conflicts of commitment and, 376
  conflicts of interest and, 375–376
  diversity and, 150–151
  financial, 377
  fundraising and, 368, 378–379
  governance and, 376–377
  importance of, 367–368
  individual vs. community in, 372
  with information and communication
    technology, 269, 272–287
  integrity and, 369
  justice vs. mercy in, 371
  leadership and, 367–382
  moral courage and, 374–375
  organizational culture and, 369–370
  short-term vs. long-term view in, 372
  truth vs. loyalty in, 371
  values and, 368

ethnic diversity, 142. *See also* diversity
evaluation. *See also* performance appraisals; program evaluation
  meetings, 189
  organizational, 190
  in strategic management, 333, 341–342
events, in statement of activities, 210
executive management, 8–9, 163
expenses
  in financial statements, 201*f*, 205
  in statement of activities, 206*f*–207*f*, 209–210
expert rule, in decision making, 183
exposure, legal environment and, 250–251. *See also* risk
extensive rule, in decision making, 183

F
Family and Medical Leave Act (FMLA) of 1993, 107, 108
Federal Election Commission, 65*t*
feedback
  in performance evaluation, 131–132, 132*t*
  in professional development, 148–149
  in strategic management, 341–342
finances. *See also* fundraising
  accountability and, 198–199
  audits of, 212
  budget shortfalls and, 396–398
  duty segregation and, 217, 218*f*, 218*t*–219*t*
  ethics and, 377
  fraud in, 214–217, 216*t*
  internal controls and, 214–217, 216*t*
  "rainy day fund" and, 397
  refinancing, 405–406
  social innovation and, 355
  tax benefits in, 197–198
financial statements, 199–211, 201*f*, 206*f*–207*f*, 220
fiscal austerity, 388–393
FMLA. *See* Family and Medical Leave Act (FMLA) of 1993
food, in statement of activities, 207
formative evaluation, 232, 233

fraud, financial, 214–217, 216*t*
fund appeals, 80–83
funding, human resources and, 104–106
fundraising. *See also* finances
  board and, 316
  capital campaigns in, 89–96, 94*t*
  cause-related marketing and, 74–75
  commercialization and, 406
  cultivation of major gifts in, 83–89
  culture of giving in, 80–83
  demographic shifts and, 73
  e-philanthropy and, 73–74
  ethics and, 368, 378–379
  fundamentals, 76–80
  leadership and, 91–92
  making the ask in, 87–89
  motivation to give, 82–83
  multilayered strategies in, 76–78
  professional standards in, 79
  scandals and, 77
  sources, 70
  staffing for, 78–79, 78*f*
  stewardship in, 96
  strategic giving and, 74–75
  success strategies, 80
  taxes and, 75–76
  trends in, 69–76
  trust and, 79
furloughs, 406–407

G
Gallo, Dean, 53
garbage can model, 186
Generation X, 73
Gergen, David, 55–56
gift pyramid, 94–95, 94*t*
gifts-in-kind, 208–209
giving. *See* fundraising
goal definition, 19
goal-oriented process, 18
goals, in promotion, 36
goal setting, in capital campaign, 93–95, 94*t*
Goleman, Daniel, 5
Gore, Al, 50
governance, ethics and, 376–377. *See also* board

Index

communication of commitment to stakeholders, 152–153
diversity vs., 141
economic impact of, 151–152
as ethical and moral imperative, 150–151
leadership and, 144–146
management and, 146–150
professional development and, 147–149
information and communications technology (ICT)
  boundary issues with, 281–282
  client portals and, 284–285
  collegial relationships and, 286–287
  competence with, 287
  confidentiality and, 277–278
  conflicts of interest and, 281–282
  documentation and, 282–285
  ethics and, 269, 272–287
  evolution of, 268–269
  functions, 270–271
  history of, 268–269
  implementation strategy, 271–272
  informed consent and, 272–277
  interventions via, 270–271
  legal dimensions of, 278–281
  privacy and, 277–278, 289
  records and, 282–285
  vision statement, 271–272
informed consent, 272–277
innovation, strategic management and, 342–343. *See also* social innovation(s)
insurance
  as expense, 204, 207
  liability, 255
  in risk management, 257
  in statement of activities, 207
intensive rule, in decision making, 183
interest, in statement of activities, 207
internal process model, 12*f*
Internal Revenue Service, 65*t*, 69
internal staffing, 117
interrupted time series, 237
interviews
  job, 112–113, 113*t*–116*t*, 137
  media, 40

inventories, in financial statements, 201*f*, 204
investment income, in statement of activities, 206*f*, 209
investments, in financial statements, 201*f*, 202
involvement rule, in decision making, 183

J

jargon, 38
job description, 109, 110*f*, 155–156
job design, 103
job interviews, 112–113, 113*t*–116*t*, 137
joint costs, in statement of activities, 210
justice, mercy vs., 371

K

key drivers, 410–411, 411*f*
knowledge skills, 8

L

labor conditions, 105
land, in financial statements, 201*f*
language, unnecessary, 38
layoffs, 136–137, 403, 407–408
leadership
  appreciative, 145
  in capital campaign, 91–92
  character in, 5
  characteristics, 4–5
  effective, characteristics of, 3–4
  equity and, 144–146
  ethics and, 367–382
  executive, 163
  fundamental principles of, 5–6
  inclusion and, 144–146
  integrity and, 369
  management vs., 4–5
  mentality, 7–8
  moral courage and, 374–375
  natural, 4
  organizational hierarchy and, 9–11, 11*f*
  organizational life cycle and, 9–11, 11*f*
  relational, 145
  roles, 13*f*

government grants, in statement of activities, 206f, 209
government partner, 52–54
government resources, 65, 65t–66t
Graeber, David, 191
grants, government, in statement of activities, 206f, 209
grants receivable, in financial statements, 201f, 203–204
graphics, 37
Great Recession, 389–390
groupthink, 185
growth, economic, 394

H
halo error, 130
Health Information Technology for Economic and Clinical Health (HITECH) Act, 279–280
Health Insurance Portability and Accountability Act (HIPAA), 270, 279, 280, 283
Heritage Foundation, 66t
hibernators, in COVID-19 pandemic, 392
hierarchy, organizational, 9–11, 11f
hierarchy decision culture, 169, 169t, 171, 171t
HIPAA. See Health Insurance Portability and Accountability Act (HIPAA)
hiring. See human resources (HR); recruitment
hiring freeze, 399–400
HITECH Act. See Health Information Technology for Economic and Clinical Health (HITECH) Act
Holmes, Oliver Wendell, Jr., 249
horn error, 130
HR. See human resources (HR)
human capital, 353–354
human-centered design, 356
human relations model, 12f
human relations skills, 6–7, 11f, 12, 13f, 15–16
human resources (HR)
  Age Discrimination in Employment Act of 1967 and, 107–108
  Americans with Disabilities Act (ADA) of 1990 and, 108
  compensation and, 118–119
  in competing-values perspective, 102–137, 110f, 113t–116t, 122t–123t, 124t, 125f–126f, 129t, 132t
  complexity of, 101
  conflict and, 108–109
  development in, 120–123, 122t–123t
  discrimination and, 106–109
  as domain, 102–137, 110f, 113t–116t, 122t–123t, 124t, 125f–126f, 129t, 132t
  employee separations in, 132–137
  Equal Employment Opportunity Act of 1972 and, 107
  Equal Pay Act of 1963 and, 107
  external factors in, 104–108
  Family and Medical Leave Act (FMLA) of 1993 and, 107, 108
  funding and, 104–106
  internal influences in, 102–104
  job design in, 103
  job interviews and, 112–113, 113t–116t, 137
  job references and, 116–117
  orientation in, 120–121
  performance appraisals in, 123–137, 124t, 125f–126f, 129t, 132t
  Pregnancy Discrimination Act of 1978 and, 107
  recruitment in, 109–117, 110f, 113f–116f
  screening in, 111–113, 113t–116f
  selection in, 109–117, 110f, 113f–116f
  Social Security Act of 1935 and, 108
  Title VII and, 106–107
hybrids, in COVID-19 pandemic, 393

I
ICT. See information and communications technology (ICT)
immigration, 142–143
impact evaluation, 233, 234
inclusion. See also diversity
  board and, 302

leadership—(cont'd)
  skills, 9–11, 11f
  social innovation and, 352
  strengths-based, 145–146
  system and, 55–56
leave-behinds, 59
legal counsel, in risk management, 258
legal dimensions, with information
  and communication technology,
  278–281
legal environment, 250–251
legislators, 52–53, 55
leniency, in performance evaluation,
  130–131
LGBTQ persons, fundraising and, 73
liabilities, in financial statements, 201f
liability, legal environment and,
  250–251. *See also* risk
Library of Congress, 65t
licenses, in statement of activities, 207
life cycle, organizational, 9–11, 11f, 395
lobbying, 50–54
loyalty, truth *vs.*, 371

M
MacGuffin, 43
Madoff, Bernie, 390
major gifts, cultivation of, 83–89
management. *See also* board; strategic
    management
  diversity and, 146–150
  entry-level, 10
  equity and, 146–150
  executive, 8–9
  inclusion and, 146–150
  leadership vs., 4–5
  of meetings, 174–182, 178f, 179t, 182t
  organizational decline and, 398–400
  skills, 9–11, 11f
  management-by-objective (MBO), 128
managerial decision making, 19–20
market decision culture, 169, 169t,
    171–172, 171t
marketing
  cause-related, 74–75
  speak, 38
  in statement of activities, 207

markets, media, 40
MBO. *See* management-by-
    objective (MBO)
McNamara, Robert, 44
McNamara fallacy, 44–45
media. *See also* promotion
  changing landscape of, 32–34
  consolidation in, 33
  content in, 35–38
  interviews, 40
  markets, 40
  pitches, 38–40
  social, 33–34
  target audience and, 39
  types, 39
meetings
  cost of, 190–191
  evaluations, 189
  high-quality, 167
  managing, 174–182, 178f,
      179t, 182t
  no-more-reports rule in, 181, 182t
  no-new-business rule in, 181, 182t
  rule of agenda bell with, 178–180,
      178f, 182t
  rule of halves with, 176–178, 182t
  rule of sixths in, 177, 182t
  rule of three-quarters with,
      177–178, 182t
  rules for, 167–168, 182t
  three-characters rule in, 176, 182t
  waste and, 191–192
mental health professionals, social
    workers as, 250–251
mentorship, 16, 122t, 148
mercy, justice vs., 371
Millennials, 73
mission realignment, 404–405
moral courage, 374–375
mortgages, in financial statements,
    201f, 205

N
Napoli, Philip, 34
National Conference of State
    Legislatures, 65t
National Performance Review, 50

net assets
　in financial statements, 201f
　in statement of activities, 206f, 207
no-more-reports rule, 181, 182t
no-new-business rule, 181, 182t
nongovernmental organizations, 65t–66t
notes payable, in financial statements, 201f, 205

O

Occam's razor rule, in decision making, 183
officer and director insurance, 257
older individuals, 144
on-the-job training, 122t
open-systems model, 12f
optics rule, 183
organizational change, 9–10
organizational culture. *See also* diversity
　climate assessments and, 149–150
　ethics and, 369–370
　human resources and, 104
　management and, 16
organizational decline
　blinded stage of, 396
　Bridgespan Group model and, 410–413, 411f
　budget cuts and, 400
　budget shortfalls and, 396–398
　commercialization and, 406
　cooperative strategies and, 405
　cost reductions in, 404–405
　crisis stage of, 396
　decision making and, 409
　dissolution stage of, 396
　downsizing and, 407–408
　faulty action stage of, 396
　furloughs and, 406–407
　hiring freeze and, 399–400
　inaction stage of, 396
　life cycle and, 395
　management and, 398–400
　mergers and, 405
　mission realignment and, 405
　overview of, 393–403
　political influence and, 405
　refinancing and, 405–406
　relocation and, 406
　retrenchment and, 394–395
　scenario modeling and, 408–410
　scenario planning and, 402–403
　scope of, 403–404
　staff impact, 400–403
　stages of, 396
　strategic management of, 403–410
organizational evaluation, 190
organizational life cycle, 9–11, 11f, 395
orientation, staff, 120–121
outcome evaluation, 232, 234, 236–243, 238f
outreach programs, 58–59
overpromising, 37
Oxley, Michael, 198

P

Palmer, Donald, 191
Pauling, Linus, 353
payroll taxes, in statement of activities, 206f
Perelman, Jonathan, 38
performance appraisals, 123–137, 124t, 125f–126f, 129t, 132t
performance criteria, 123–124, 124t
performance measurement, 223
personalization, 58
"Peter Principle," 10
PHI. *See* protected health information (PHI)
photography, 37
pitches, media, 38–40
planning, 61–64
pledges receivable, in financial statements, 201f, 202–203
policymaker, board members as, 90
policy priorities, 54
postage, in statement of activities, 207
power rule, in decision making, 183
Pregnancy Discrimination Act of 1978, 107
premises liability insurance, 257
prepaid expenses, in financial statements, 201f, 204
primacy effects, in performance evaluation, 130–131

printing, in statement of activities, 207
privacy, with information and communication technology, 277–278, 289
proactiveness, 6
process, challenging, 7
process evaluation, 232, 233–234, 235
producer role, 18–19
professional development, 120–123, 122t–123t, 147–149
professional standards, in fundraising, 79
program evaluation
  analysis in, 239–242
  audience for, 222
  challenges in, 225–226
  competing values framework and, 224–225
  defined, 222
  design, 227–231
  external, 222
  formative, 232, 233
  guidance for, 226–235
  impact evaluation in, 233, 234
  learning from, 242–243
  measurement in, 239–242
  outcome evaluation in, 232, 234, 236–243, 238f
  process evaluation in, 232, 233–234, 235
  reasons for, 222–223
  research questions in, 231–232
  SMART objectives in, 227, 231
  theory, 227–231
  types of, 232–235
program revenue, in statement of activities, 206f, 209
progress monitoring, by board, 306
promotion. *See also* media
  crisis communications and, 41–43
  goals in, 36
  media landscape and, 32–34
  personal vs. abstract content in, 37
  takeaway messages in, 36–37, 39
property, in financial statements, 201f, 204–205
protected health information (PHI), 279–280, 289

R

racial diversity, 142. *See also* diversity
"rainy day fund," 397
ratio analysis, 213
rational goal model, 12f
recency effects, in performance evaluation, 130–131
records, information and communication technology and, 282–285
recruitment, 109–117, 110f, 113f–116f, 146–147
references, of job candidates, 116–117
refinancing, 405–406
relational leadership, 145
relevance, of initiatives, 36
relocation
  organizational decline and, 406
  in statement of activities, 207
research questions, in program evaluation, 231–232
resource(s). *See also* finances; fundraising
  government, 65, 65t–66t
  yourself as, 56–57
responders, in COVID-19 pandemic, 393
restrictions, in statement of activities, 206f
retirement, 134
retreats, board, 312–313
retrenchment, 394–395
risk
  areas of, 253–256
  audit, 260–261
  budget shortfalls and, 397
  competing values and, 252
  confidentiality and, 254
  continuity of service and, 254
  diagnosis and, 255
  duty to warn/protect and, 253–254
  legal counsel and, 258
  legal environment and, 250–251
  management, 252, 256
  responses to, 257–261
  sexual impropriety and, 255–256, 262–263
  staff training and, 259–260

rule of agenda bell, 178–180, 178*f*, 182*t*
rule of halves, 176–178, 182*t*
rule of sixths, 177, 182*t*
rule of three-quarters, 177–178, 182*t*
Rush University Medical Center, 154–155

S

salaries, in statement of activities, 206*f*
Sarbanes, Paul, 198
Sarbanes–Oxley Act, 198, 389
scandals, 77, 367
scenario modeling, 408–410, 411–412, 411*f*
scenario planning, 402–403
screening, in recruitment, 111–113, 113*t*–116*f*
security, in statement of activities, 207
selection, 109–117, 110*f*, 113*f*–116*f*
self-confidence, 6
separations, employee, 132–137
services, contributed, 208–209
sexual impropriety, risk and, 255–256, 262–263
Shapiro, Michael, 34
shipping, in statement of activities, 207
showing up, 56
significance, of initiatives, 36
SMART objectives, 227, 231, 339–340
smartphone apps, 271, 359. *See also* client portals
SOAR analysis, 336–337
social architects, 14
social enterprise, 356–358
social entrepreneurship, 350–351
social impact bonds, 358
social innovation(s)
  culture and, 352–353, 361
  defining, 350–351
  diversity and, 353–354
  engagement context, 351–355
  entrepreneurship and, 350–351
  examples of, 349
  financial investment in, 355
  human capital and, 353–354
  human-centered design and, 356
  leadership competency and, 352
  resource development and, 358
  resources for, 354–355
  social enterprise and, 356–358
  space for, 355
  strategies, 355–359, 361
  technology and, 359
social media, 32, 33–34, 44, 153, 338, 358, 359
Social Security Act of 1935, 108
split-interest agreements, 202
staff
  development, 120–123, 122*t*–123*t*, 147–149
  of government partners, 59
  organizational decline and impact on, 400–403
  orientation, 120–121
  performance appraisals, 123–137, 124*t*, 125*f*–126*f*, 129*t*, 132*t*
  training, as risk management, 259–260
staffing. *See also* human resources (HR)
  in crisis, 42
  for fundraising, 78–79, 78*f*
  internal, 117
stakeholders-not-in-the-room rule, in decision making, 183
State Innovation Exchange, 66*t*
statement of activities, 206–210, 206*f*–207*f*
statement of cash flows, 210–211
statement of financial position, 200–206, 201*f*
steward, board members as, 90
stewardship, 96
strategic giving, 74–75
strategic management
  assessment in, 331–332, 335–338
  competing values framework and, 343
  creative process in, 338–340
  data sources in, 336
  defined, 330–333
  environmental scanning in, 335–336
  evaluation in, 333, 341–342
  feedback loop of, 341–342
  implementation in, 333, 340–341

strategic management—(cont'd)
  information gathering in, 331–332, 335–338
  innovation and, 342–343
  monitoring in, 333, 341–342
  performance and, 342–343
  process, 333–342
  quality and, 342–343
  SMART objectives in, 339–340
  strategy formulation and design in, 332–333
  SWOT analysis in, 336–337
strengths-based leadership, 145–146
strictness, in performance evaluation, 130–131
subculture culture lock, 173–174, 173f
subculture solidification, 170–172, 171t
supplies, in statement of activities, 207
SWOC analysis, 336–337
SWOT analysis, 336–337
synergy, 7
system, leadership and, 55–56

T

takeaway messages, 36–37, 39
TAPinto, 34
Tarasoff v. Board of Regents of the University of California, 253–254
target audience, 39
tax benefits, 197–198
Tax Cuts and Jobs Act of 2017 (TCJA), 390–391
taxes
  fundraising and, 75–76
  in statement of activities, 206f
  tax reform, 390–391
tax returns, 212
TCJA. *See* Tax Cuts and Jobs Act of 2017 (TCJA)
team, crisis, 41
team culture, 149–150
technical skills, 11f
telephone, in statement of activities, 207
termination, employee, 134–136
tests, employment, 112
three-characters rule, 176, 182t
"three-deeps," 41

Title VII, 106–107
training, in risk management, 259–260
transparency, 379, 381
travel, in statement of activities, 207
treatment-as-usual control group, 237
trigger points, 412–413
trust, 5, 79
truth, loyalty vs., 371

U

undue influence, consent and, 273
Uniform Prudent Management of Institutional Funds Act, 208
United Way of Greater Cincinnati (UWGC), 155
unrelated business income tax (UBIT), 75–76
unsubstantiated claims, 37
utilities, in statement of activities, 207

V

values
  competing, risk and, 252
  decision making and, 165, 168, 182–189
  ethics and, 368
  organizational, 16
vehicular insurance, 257
venture philanthropy, 358
video assets, 37

W

waitlist control group, 236–237
waste, 191–192
Welch, Jack, 5–6
windfalls, 394
win-win, 7
workshops, 122t

Y

Yankelovich, Daniel, 44

About the Editors

Richard L. Edwards, PhD, ACSW, is chancellor emeritus and distinguished university professor at Rutgers, the State University of New Jersey. At Rutgers, Edwards formerly served as executive vice president for academic affairs and as dean of the School of Social Work. Previously, he served as dean of the School of Social Work and as interim provost at the University of North Carolina at Chapel Hill, dean of the Mandel School of Applied Social Sciences at Case Western Reserve University, and acting dean and associate dean of the School of Social Welfare at the University at Albany, State University of New York. Over the course of his career, Edwards has worked in a variety of nonprofit and public organizations as a supervisor and manager and has served on the boards of several nonprofits. Edwards is a former treasurer and president of the National Association of Social Workers. A frequent contributor to the nonprofit management literature, he served as editor-in-chief of *Human Services Organizations: Management, Leadership and Governance* and is the author, coauthor, and editor of several nonprofit management books, the most recent of which is *Building a Strong Foundation: Fundraising for Nonprofits* (2nd ed.; NASW Press, 2020).

Paul A. Kurzman, PhD, ACSW, holds a dual appointment as professor of social work at Hunter College and as professor of social welfare at the Graduate Center of the City University of New York, where he teaches social policy and macro practice in the MSW and PhD programs. He has served as executive director of a nonprofit agency, senior administrator in New York City's Human Resources Administration, program director of a workplace study center at Columbia University, and acting dean of the Silberman School of Social Work at Hunter College. Kurzman is editor-in-chief of the *Journal of Teaching in Social Work* and an author or editor of 12 books, the most recent of which is *Online and Distance Social Work Education: Current Practice and Future Trends* (Routledge, 2020). Kurzman served for 26 years as a member of the New York State Social Work Licensing Board and as president of the 10,000-member New York City chapter of the National Association of Social Workers, and he is currently vice president of the board of trustees of Hamilton Madison Settlement House in New York.

About the Contributors

Amy J. Armstrong, PhD, CRC, is chair of the Department of Rehabilitation Counseling and associate dean of faculty in the College of Health Professions at Virginia Commonwealth University. Her interests include resilience, well-being, community integration of people with disabilities, and appreciative leadership. She also has experience working in community services and personnel development.

Myra Blackmon, ABJ, MEd, spent much of her career as an executive staff member of the Girl Scouts of the United States of America and the United Way. She has consulted internationally on nonprofit communications, fundraising, and management.

Stephanie Cosner, PhD, is dean of the College of Social Sciences, Policy, and Practice at Simmons University. Before her arrival at Simmons, she was a faculty member at the Boston College School of Social Work, where she served as assistant dean and director of the doctoral program, developed and led the Social Innovation and Leadership Program, and served as codirector of the Boston College Center for Social Innovation.

Mathieu Despard, PhD, is an associate professor in the Department of Social Work of the School of Health and Human Services at the University of North Carolina at Greensboro. He is an expert on public and nonprofit human service organizations and evidence-informed program evaluation.

Alena C. Hampton, PhD, is the associate dean of the College of Health Professions at Virginia Commonwealth University and an assistant professor in the Department of Rehabilitation Counseling. She is a licensed clinical psychologist. Her research interests include well-being, resilience, and leadership.

Thomas P. Holland, PhD, was professor emeritus in the School of Social Work at the University of Georgia, where he also served as director of the Institute for Nonprofit Organizations. He published and consulted extensively on nonprofit management and governance. In 2018, the University of Georgia created the Thomas P. Holland Distinguished Professorship in Nonprofit Leadership.

Renette Bayne Issaka, MBA, CPA, is controller, Greater New York Councils of the Boy Scouts of America, and a Toastmasters District 46 area director. She has extensive experience as a financial manager of a variety of nonprofit organizations.

Daniel A. Lebold, MSW, serves as director of development for the Office of the Vice Provost for Global Affairs at the University of North Carolina (UNC) at Chapel Hill. Previously, he spent five years as vice president of development for Triangle Family Services, Inc., in Raleigh, North Carolina, and 10 years at the UNC School of Social Work, where he served as assistant dean for administration and director and clinical instructor for the UNC Nonprofit Leadership Certificate Program.

Melinda Manning, JD, MSW, is the director of the University of North Carolina Health Beacon Program and president of the Board of the North Carolina Coalition Against Sexual Assault. An alumna of the Teach for America program, she has taught classes in education, public policy, and social work. She is a former college administrator and appeared in the campus sexual assault documentary "The Hunting Ground."

Peter J. McDonough, BA, is a public policy and public affairs professional with more than 40 years of experience designing and executing successful public affairs and communications efforts to promote policy initiatives and the interests of public and private clients. He currently serves as the senior vice president for external affairs at Rutgers, the State University of New Jersey, where he also teaches at the Eagleton Institute of Politics. He is a consultant to the U.S. Department of State, providing media training to foreign government officials in emerging democracies. He was formerly the director of communications for New Jersey Governor Christine Todd Whitman, chief of staff for a member of the U.S. House of Representatives, and executive director of the New Jersey General Assembly.

Susan L. Parish, PhD, MSW, is dean of the College of Health Professions at Virginia Commonwealth University. Her research examines the impact of health and poverty policy and racism on the lives of people with disabilities and their families. In addition to her academic leadership roles, she administered residential and family support programs for people with developmental disabilities and their families.

Frederic G. Reamer, PhD, is a professor of social work at Rhode Island College and an internationally preeminent scholar and prolific author on ethics, record keeping, and information sharing in the age of technology and electronic communication.

Kimberly Strom, PhD, LISW, is Smith P. Theimann Jr. distinguished professor of ethics and professional practice and director of the Office of Ethics and Policy at the University of North Carolina at Chapel Hill, where she also served as associate dean in the School of Social Work. She is an internationally recognized scholar on academic leadership, moral courage, and ethics.

Marci S. Thomas, MHA, CPA, is clinical assistant professor in the Department of Health Policy and Administration at the University of North Carolina at Chapel Hill. Ms. Thomas writes and teaches continuing education for certified public accountants nationally on physician practice management, managed care, and various nonprofit topics. She also consults with nonprofits and health care organizations in the areas of financial management, process improvement, and governance, with an emphasis on the Sarbanes–Oxley Act of 2002.

Gregory Trevor, BA, has been an award-winning journalist and media relations professional for more than 30 years. He worked as a reporter for the *Asbury Park Press* in Trenton, New Jersey, and the *Charlotte Observer* in Raleigh, North Carolina. He has volunteered for, served on the board of, and worked for multiple nonprofits and public institutions, including the Port Authority of New York and New Jersey; Rutgers, the State University of New Jersey; and the University of Georgia. While working as a media relations professional for the Port Authority, Trevor survived the September 11, 2001, attacks on the World Trade Center in New York City.

John E. Tropman, PhD, is the Henry J. Meyer collegiate professor of social work at the University of Michigan, where he also teaches in the Executive Education Program of the Ross School of Business. He currently serves on the boards of the Network for Social Work Management and the Academy of Social Work and Social Welfare. He has published extensively on a wide range of nonprofit leadership and management issues.

Allison Zippay, PhD, is a professor in the School of Social Work at Rutgers, the State University of New Jersey, where she is also the director of the Center for Leadership and Management and the PhD in Social Work program. She teaches in the management and policy concentration in the School of Social Work and chairs the Doctoral Scholars Institute at the Network for Social Work Management. Her research focuses on community planning, supportive housing, and employment and income supports for low-income groups.